GENGHIS KHAN

and the Making of the

MODERN WORLD

GENGHIS KHAN

and the Making of the
Modern World

JACK WEATHERFORD

CROWN PUBLISHERS • NEW YORK

Published by Crown Publishers, New York, New York.
Member of the Crown Publishing Group, a division of Random House, Inc.
www.crownpublishing.com

CROWN is a trademark and the Crown colophon is a registered trademark of
Random House, Inc.

Illustrations by S. Badral, copyright © 2003 by Jack Weatherford and
Chinggis Khaan College.

Printed in the United States of America

BOOK DESIGN BY LEONARD HENDERSON
MAPS BY DAVID LINDROTH INC.

Library of Congress Cataloging-in-Publication Data
Weatherford, J. McIver.
Genghis Khan and the making of the modern world / Jack Weatherford.
1. Genghis Khan, 1162–1227.   2. Mongols—Kings and rulers—Biography.
3. Mongols—History.   I. Title.
DS22.G45W43 2004
950'.21'092—dc22   2003020659

ISBN 0-609-61062-7

10   9   8   7   6   5   4   3   2

First Edition

To the Young Mongols:

Never forget the Mongolian scholars

who were willing to sacrifice their lives to preserve your history.

Contents

—⁍—

CONTENTS

Royal Family of the Great Mongol Empire, Yeke Mongol Ulus

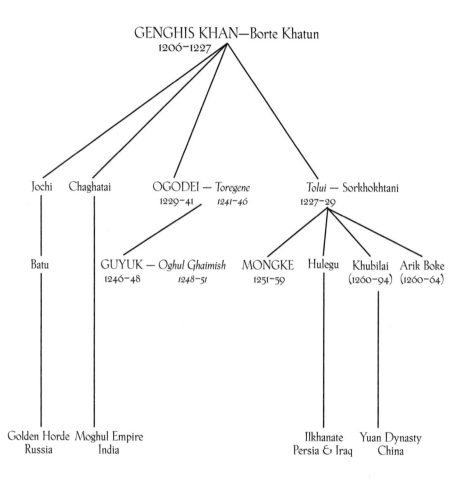

GENGHIS KHAN—Borte Khatun
1206–1227

Jochi   Chaghatai   OGODEI — *Toregene*
1229–41   *1241–46*

Tolui — Sorkhokhtani
1227–29

Batu   GUYUK — *Oghul Ghaimish*   MONGKE Hulegu Khubilai Arik Boke
1246–48   *1248–51*   1251–59   (1260–94) (1260–64)

Golden Horde Moghul Empire   Ilkhanate   Yuan Dynasty
Russia   India   Persia & Iraq   China

GREAT KHAN
Regent
Dates refer to reigns
(Dates in parentheses refer to contested reign)

This noble king was called Genghis Khan,
Who in his time was of so great renown
That there was nowhere in no region
So excellent a lord in all things.

GEOFFREY CHAUCER,
"The Squire's Tale,"
The Canterbury Tales (c. 1395)

GENGHIS KHAN
and the Making of the
MODERN WORLD

Introduction

The Missing Conqueror

Genghis Khan was a doer.
WASHINGTON POST, 1989

IN 1937, THE SOUL of Genghis Khan disappeared from the Buddhist monastery in central Mongolia along the River of the Moon below the black Shankh Mountains where the faithful lamas had protected and venerated it for centuries. During the 1930s, Stalin's henchmen executed some thirty thousand Mongols in a series of campaigns against their culture and religion. The troops ravaged one monastery after another, shot the monks, assaulted the nuns, broke the religious objects, looted the libraries, burned the scriptures, and demolished the temples. Reportedly, someone secretly rescued the embodiment of Genghis Khan's soul from the Shankh Monastery and whisked it away for safekeeping to the capital in Ulaanbaatar, where it ultimately disappeared.

Through the centuries on the rolling, grassy steppes of inner Asia, a warrior-herder carried a Spirit Banner, called a *sulde,* constructed by tying strands of hair from his best stallions to the shaft of a spear, just below its blade. Whenever he erected his camp, the warrior planted the Spirit Banner outside the entrance to proclaim his identity and to stand as his perpetual guardian. The Spirit Banner always remained in the open air beneath the Eternal Blue Sky that the Mongols worshiped. As the strands of hair blew and tossed in the nearly constant breeze of the steppe, they captured the power of the wind, the sky, and the sun, and the banner channeled this power from nature to the warrior. The wind in the horsehair inspired the warrior's dreams and encouraged him to pursue his own destiny. The streaming and twisting of the horsehair in the wind beckoned the owner ever onward, luring him away from this spot to seek another, to find better pasture, to explore new opportunities and adventures, to create his own fate in his life in this world. The union between the man and his Spirit Banner grew so intertwined that when he died, the warrior's spirit was said to reside forever in those tufts of horsehair. While the warrior lived, the horsehair banner carried his destiny; in death, it became his soul. The physical body was quickly abandoned to nature, but the soul lived on forever in those tufts of horsehair to inspire future generations.

Genghis Khan had one banner made from white horses to use in peacetime and one made from black horses for guidance in war. The white one disappeared early in history, but the black one survived as the repository of his soul. In the centuries after his death, the Mongol people continued to honor the banner where his soul resided. In the sixteenth century, one of his descendants, the lama Zanabazar, built the monastery with a special mission to fly and protect his banner. Through storms and blizzards, invasions and civil wars, more than a thousand monks of the Yellow Hat sect of Tibetan Buddhism guarded the great banner, but they proved no match for the totalitarian politics of the twentieth century. The monks were killed, and the Spirit Banner disappeared.

Fate did not hand Genghis Khan his destiny; he made it for himself. It seemed highly unlikely that he would ever have enough horses to create a Spirit Banner, much less that he might follow it across the world. The boy who became Genghis Khan grew up in a world of excessive tribal violence, including murder, kidnapping, and enslavement. As the son in an outcast family left to die on the steppes, he probably encountered no more than a few hundred people in his entire childhood, and he received no formal education. From this harsh setting, he learned, in dreadful detail, the full range of human emotion: desire, ambition, and cruelty. While still a child he killed his older half brother, was captured and enslaved by a rival clan, and managed to escape from his captors.

Under such horrific conditions, the boy showed an instinct for survival and self-preservation, but he showed little promise of the achievements he would one day make. As a child, he feared dogs and he cried easily. His younger brother was stronger than he was and a better archer and wrestler; his half brother bossed him around and picked on him. Yet from these degraded circumstances of hunger, humiliation, kidnapping, and slavery, he began the long climb to power. Before reaching puberty, he had already formed the two most important relationships of his life. He swore eternal friendship and allegiance to a slightly older boy who became the closest friend of his youth but turned into the most dedicated enemy of his adulthood, and he found the girl whom he would love forever and whom he made the mother of emperors. The dual capacity for friendship and enmity forged in Genghis Khan's youth endured throughout his life and became the defining trait of his character. The tormenting questions of love and paternity that arose beneath a shared blanket or in the flickering firelight of the family hearth became projected onto the larger stage of world history. His personal goals, desires, and fears engulfed the world.

Year by year, he gradually defeated everyone more powerful than he was, until he had conquered every tribe on the Mongolian steppe. At the age of fifty, when most great conquerors had already put their fighting days behind them, Genghis Khan's Spirit Banner beckoned him out of his remote homeland to confront the armies of the civilized people who had harassed and enslaved the nomadic tribes for centuries. In the remaining years of life, he followed that Spirit Banner to repeated victory across the Gobi and the Yellow River into the kingdoms of China, through the central Asian lands of the Turks and the Persians, and across the mountains of Afghanistan to the Indus River.

In conquest after conquest, the Mongol army transformed warfare into an intercontinental affair fought on multiple fronts stretching across thousands of miles. Genghis Khan's innovative fighting techniques made the heavily armored knights of medieval Europe obsolete, replacing them with disciplined cavalry moving in coordinated units. Rather than relying on defensive fortifications, he made brilliant use of speed and surprise on the battlefield, as well as perfecting siege warfare to such a degree that he ended the era of walled cities. Genghis Khan taught his people not only to fight across incredible distances but to sustain their campaign over years, decades, and, eventually, more than three generations of constant fighting.

In twenty-five years, the Mongol army subjugated more lands and people than the Romans had conquered in four hundred years. Genghis Khan, together with his sons and grandsons, conquered the most densely populated civilizations of the thirteenth century. Whether measured by the total number of people defeated, the sum of the countries annexed, or by the total area occupied, Genghis Khan conquered more than twice as much as any other man in history. The hooves of the Mongol warriors' horses splashed in the waters of every river and lake from the Pacific Ocean to the Mediterranean Sea. At its zenith, the empire covered between 11 and 12 million contiguous square miles, an area about the size of the African continent and considerably larger than North America, including the United States, Canada, Mexico, Central America, and the islands of the Caribbean combined. It stretched from the snowy tundra of Siberia to the hot plains of India, from the rice paddies of Vietnam to the wheat fields of Hungary, and from Korea to the Balkans. The majority of people today live in countries conquered by the Mongols; on the modern map, Genghis Kahn's conquests include thirty countries with well over 3 billion people. The most astonishing aspect of this achievement is that the entire Mongol tribe under him numbered around a million, smaller than the workforce of some modern corporations. From this million, he recruited his army, which was comprised of no more than one hundred thousand warriors—a group that could comfortably fit into the larger sports stadiums of the modern era.

In American terms, the accomplishment of Genghis Khan might be understood if the United States, instead of being created by a group of educated merchants or wealthy planters, had been founded by one of its illiterate slaves, who, by the sheer force of personality, charisma, and determination, liberated America from foreign rule, united the people, created an alphabet, wrote the constitution, established universal religious freedom, invented a new system of warfare, marched an army from Canada to Brazil, and opened roads of commerce in a free-trade zone that stretched across the continents. On every level and from any perspective, the scale and scope of Genghis Khan's accomplishments challenge the limits of imagination and tax the resources of scholarly explanation.

As Genghis Khan's cavalry charged across the thirteenth century, he redrew the boundaries of the world. His architecture was not in stone but in nations. Unsatisfied with the vast number of little kingdoms, Genghis Khan consolidated smaller countries into larger ones. In eastern Europe, the Mongols united a dozen Slavic principalities and cities into one large Russian state. In eastern Asia, over a span of three generations, they created the country of China by weaving together the remnants of the Sung dynasty in the south with the lands of the Jurched in Manchuria, Tibet in the west, the Tangut Kingdom adjacent to the Gobi, and the Uighur lands of eastern Turkistan. As the Mongols expanded their rule, they created countries such as Korea and India that have survived to modern times in approximately the same borders fashioned by their Mongol conquerors.

Genghis Khan's empire connected and amalgamated the many civilizations around him into a new world order. At the time of his birth in 1162, the Old World consisted of a series of regional civilizations each of which could claim virtually no knowledge of any civilization beyond its closest neighbor. No one in China had heard of Europe, and no one in Europe had heard of China, and, so far as is known, no person had made the journey from one to the other. By the time of his death in 1227, he had connected them with diplomatic and commercial contacts that still remain unbroken.

As he smashed the feudal system of aristocratic privilege and birth, he built a new and unique system based on individual merit, loyalty, and achievement. He took the disjointed and languorous trading towns along the Silk Route and organized them into history's largest free-trade zone. He lowered taxes for everyone, and abolished them altogether for doctors, teachers, priests, and educational institutions. He established a regular census and created the first international postal system. His was not an empire that hoarded wealth and treasure; instead, he widely distributed the goods acquired in combat so that they could make their way back into commercial circulation. He created an international law and recognized the ultimate supreme law of the Eternal Blue Sky over all people. At a time when most rulers considered themselves to be above the law, Genghis Khan insisted on laws holding rulers as equally accountable as the lowest herder. He granted religious freedom within his realms, though he demanded total loyalty from conquered subjects of all religions. He insisted on the rule of law and abolished torture, but he mounted major campaigns to seek out and kill raiding bandits and terrorist assassins. He refused to hold hostages and, instead, instituted the novel practice of granting diplomatic immunity for all ambassadors and envoys, including those from hostile nations with whom he was at war.

Genghis Khan left his empire with such a firm foundation that it continued growing for another 150 years. Then, in the centuries that followed its collapse, his descendants continued to rule a variety of smaller empires and large countries, from Russia, Turkey, and India to China and Persia. They held an eclectic assortment of titles, including khan, emperor, sultan, king, shah, emir, and the Dalai Lama. Vestiges of his empire remained under the rule of his descendants for seven centuries. As the Moghuls, some of them reigned in India until 1857, when the British drove out Emperor Bahadur Shah II and chopped off the heads of two of his sons and his grandson. Genghis Khan's last ruling descendant, Alim Khan, emir of Bukhara, remained in power in Uzbekistan until deposed in 1920 by the rising tide of Soviet revolution.

History has condemned most conquerors to miserable, untimely deaths. At age thirty-three, Alexander the Great died under mysterious circumstances in Babylon, while his followers killed off his family and carved up his lands. Julius Caesar's fellow aristocrats and former allies stabbed him to death in the chamber of the Roman Senate. After enduring the destruction and reversal of all his conquests, a lonely and embittered Napoleon faced death as a solitary prisoner on one of the most remote and inaccessible islands on the planet. The nearly seventy-year-old Genghis Khan, however, passed away in his camp bed, surrounded by a loving family, faithful friends, and loyal soldiers ready to risk their life at his command. In the summer of 1227, during a campaign against the Tangut nation along the upper reaches of the Yellow River, Genghis Khan died—or, in the words of the Mongols, who have an abhorrence of mentioning death or illness, he "ascended into heaven." In the years after his death, the sustained secrecy about the cause of death invited speculation, and later inspired legends that with the veneer of time often appeared as historic fact. Plano di Carpini, the first European envoy to the Mongols, wrote that Genghis Khan died when he was struck by lightning. Marco Polo, who traveled extensively in the Mongol Empire during the reign of Genghis Khan's grandson Khubilai, reported that Genghis Khan succumbed from an arrow wound to the knee. Some claimed that unknown enemies had poisoned him. Another account asserted that he had been killed by a magic spell of the Tangut king against whom he was fighting. One of the stories circulated by his detractors asserted that the captured Tangut queen inserted a contraption into her vagina so that when Genghis Khan had sex with her, it tore off his sex organs and he died in hideous pain.

Contrary to the many stories about his demise, his death in a nomad's *ger*, essentially similar to the one in which he had been born, illustrated how successful he had been in preserving the traditional way of life of his people; yet, ironically, in the process of preserving their lifestyle, he had transformed human society. Genghis Khan's soldiers escorted the body of their fallen khan back to his homeland in Mongolia for secret burial. After his death, his followers buried him anonymously in the soil of his homeland without a mausoleum, a temple, a pyramid, or so much as a small tombstone to mark the place where he lay. According to Mongol belief, the body of the dead should be left in peace and did not need a monument because the soul was no longer there; it lived on in the Spirit Banner. At burial, Genghis Khan disappeared silently back into the vast landscape of Mongolia from whence he came. The final destination remained unknown, but in the absence of reliable information, people freely invented their own history, with many dramatic flourishes to the story. An often repeated account maintains that the soldiers in his funeral cortege killed every person and animal encountered on the forty-day journey, and that after the secret burial, eight hundred horsemen trampled repeatedly over the area to obscure the location of the grave. Then, according to these imaginative accounts, the horsemen were, in turn, killed by yet another set of soldiers so that they could not report the location of the site; and then, in turn, those soldiers were slain by yet another set of warriors.

After the secret burial in his homeland, soldiers sealed off the entire area for several hundred square miles. No one could enter except members of Genghis Khan's family and a tribe of specially trained warriors who were stationed there to kill every intruder. For nearly eight hundred years, this area— the *Ikh Khorig,* the Great Taboo, deep in the heart of Asia—remained closed. All the secrets of Genghis Khan's empire seemed to have been locked up inside his mysterious homeland. Long after the Mongol Empire collapsed, and other foreign armies invaded parts of Mongolia, the Mongols prevented anyone from entering the sacred precinct of their ancestor. Despite the eventual conversion of the Mongols to Buddhism, his successors nevertheless refused to allow priests to build a shrine, a monastery, or a memorial to mark his burial.

In the twentieth century, to assure that the area of Genghis Khan's birth and burial did not become a rallying point for nationalists, the Soviet rulers kept it securely guarded. Instead of calling it the Great Taboo or using one of the historic names that might hint at a connection to Genghis Khan, the Soviets called it by the bureaucratic designation of Highly Restricted Area. Administratively, they separated it from the surrounding province and placed it under the direct supervision of the central government that, in turn, was tightly controlled from Moscow. The Soviets further sealed it off by surrounding 1 million hectares of the Highly Restricted Area with an equally large Restricted Area. To prevent travel within the area, the government built neither roads nor bridges during the Communist era. The Soviets maintained a highly fortified MiG air base, and quite probably a storehouse of nuclear weapons, between the Restricted Area and the Mongolian capital of Ulaanbaatar. A large Soviet tank base blocked the entrance into the forbidden zone, and the Russian military used the area for artillery practice and tank maneuvers.

The Mongols made no technological breakthroughs, founded no new religions, wrote few books or dramas, and gave the world no new crops or methods of agriculture. Their own craftsmen could not weave cloth, cast metal, make pottery, or even bake bread. They manufactured neither porcelain nor pottery, painted no pictures, and built no buildings. Yet, as their army conquered culture after culture, they collected and passed all of these skills from one civilization to the next.

The only permanent structures Genghis Khan erected were bridges. Although he spurned the building of castles, forts, cities, or walls, as he moved across the landscape, he probably built more bridges than any ruler in history. He spanned hundreds of streams and rivers in order to make the movement of his armies and goods quicker. The Mongols deliberately opened the world to a new commerce not only in goods, but also in ideas and knowledge. The Mongols brought German miners to China and Chinese doctors to Persia. The transfers ranged from the monumental to the trivial. They spread the use of carpets everywhere they went and transplanted lemons and carrots from Persia to China, as well as noodles, playing cards, and tea from China to the West. They brought a metalworker from Paris to build a fountain on the dry steppes of Mongolia, recruited an English nobleman to serve as interpreter in their army, and took the practice of Chinese fingerprinting to Persia. They financed the building of Christian churches in China, Buddhist temples and stupas in Persia, and Muslim Koranic schools in Russia. The Mongols swept across the globe as conquerors, but also as civilization's unrivaled cultural carriers.

The Mongols who inherited Genghis Khan's empire exercised a determined drive to move products and commodities around and to combine them in ways that produced entirely novel products and unprecedented invention. When their highly skilled engineers from China, Persia, and Europe combined Chinese gunpowder with Muslim flamethrowers and applied European bell-casting technology, they produced the cannon, an entirely new order of technological innovation, from which sprang the vast modern arsenal of weapons from pistols to missiles. While each item had some significance, the larger impact came in the way the Mongols selected and combined technologies to create unusual hybrids.

The Mongols displayed a devoutly and persistently internationalist zeal in their political, economic, and intellectual endeavors. They sought not merely to conquer the world but to institute a global order based on free trade, a single international law, and a universal alphabet with which to write all languages. Genghis Khan's grandson, Khubilai Khan, introduced a paper currency intended for use everywhere and attempted to create primary schools for universal basic education of all children in order to make everyone literate. The Mongols refined and combined calendars to create a ten-thousand year calendar more accurate than any previous one, and they sponsored the most extensive maps ever assembled. The Mongols encouraged merchants to set out by land to reach their empire, and they sent out explorers across land and sea as far as Africa to expand their commercial and diplomatic reach.

In nearly every country touched by the Mongols, the initial destruction and shock of conquest by an unknown and barbaric tribe yielded quickly to an unprecedented rise in cultural communication, expanded trade, and improved civilization. In Europe, the Mongols slaughtered the aristocratic knighthood of the continent, but, disappointed with the general poverty of the area compared with the Chinese and Muslim countries, turned away and did not bother to conquer the cities, loot the countries, or incorporate them into the expanding empire. In the end, Europe suffered the least yet acquired all the advantages of contact through merchants such as the Polo family of

Venice and envoys exchanged between the Mongol khans and the popes and kings of Europe. The new technology, knowledge, and commercial wealth created the Renaissance in which Europe rediscovered some of its prior culture, but more importantly, absorbed the technology for printing, firearms, the compass, and the abacus from the East. As English scientist Roger Bacon observed in the thirteenth century, the Mongols succeeded not merely from martial superiority; rather, "they have succeeded by means of science." Although the Mongols "are eager for war," they have advanced so far because they "devote their leisure to the principles of philosophy."

Seemingly every aspect of European life—technology, warfare, clothing, commerce, food, art, literature, and music—changed during the Renaissance as a result of the Mongol influence. In addition to new forms of fighting, new machines, and new foods, even the most mundane aspects of daily life changed as the Europeans switched to Mongol fabrics, wearing pants and jackets instead of tunics and robes, played their musical instruments with the steppe bow rather than plucking them with the fingers, and painted their pictures in a new style. The Europeans even picked up the Mongol exclamation *hurray* as an enthusiastic cry of bravado and mutual encouragement.

With so many accomplishments by the Mongols, it hardly seems surprising that Geoffrey Chaucer, the first author in the English language, devoted the longest story in *The Canterbury Tales* to the Asian conqueror Genghis Khan of the Mongols. He wrote in undisguised awe of him and his accomplishments. Yet, in fact, we are surprised that the learned men of the Renaissance could make such comments about the Mongols, whom the rest of the world now view as the quintessential, bloodthirsty barbarians. The portrait of the Mongols left by Chaucer or Bacon bears little resemblance to the images we know from later books or films that portray Genghis Khan and his army as savage hordes lusting after gold, women, and blood.

Despite the many images and pictures of Genghis Khan made in subsequent years, we have no portrait of him made within his lifetime. Unlike any other conqueror in history, Genghis Khan never allowed anyone to paint his portrait, sculpt his image, or engrave his name or likeness on a coin, and the only descriptions of him from contemporaries are more intriguing than informative. In the words of a modern Mongolian song about Genghis Khan, "we imagined your appearance but our minds were blank."

Without portraits of Genghis Khan or any Mongol record, the world was left to imagine him as it wished. No one dared to paint his image until half a century after his death, and then each culture projected its particular image of him. The Chinese portrayed him as an avuncular elderly man with a wispy beard and empty eyes who looked more like a distracted Chinese sage than a fierce Mongol warrior. A Persian miniaturist portrayed him as a Turkish sultan seated on a throne. The Europeans pictured him as the quintessential barbarian with a fierce visage and fixed cruel eyes, ugly in every detail.

Mongol secrecy bequeathed a daunting task to future historians who wished to write about Genghis Khan and his empire. Biographers and historians had so little on which to base an account. They knew the chronology of cities conquered and armies defeated; yet little reliable information existed regarding his origin, his character, his motivation, or his personal life. Through the centuries, unsubstantiated rumors maintained that soon after his death, information on all these aspects of Genghis Khan's life had been written in a secret document by someone close to him. Chinese and Persian scholars referred to the existence of the mysterious document, and some scholars claimed to have seen it during the apex of the Mongol Empire. Nearly a century after Genghis Khan's death, the Persian historian Rashid al-Din described the writings as an "authentic chronicle" written "in the Mongolian idiom and letters." But he warned that it was guarded in the treasury, where "it was hidden and concealed from outsiders." He stressed that "no one who might have understood and penetrated" the Mongol text "was given the opportunity." Following the collapse of Mongol rule, most traces of the secret document seemed to have disappeared, and in time, many of the best scholars came to believe that such a text never existed, that it was merely one more of the many myths about Genghis Khan.

Just as the imaginative painters of various countries portrayed him differently, the scholars did likewise. From Korea to Armenia, they composed all manner of myths and fanciful stories about Genghis Khan's life. In the absence of reliable information, they projected their own fears and phobias onto these accounts. With the passage of centuries, scholars weighed the atrocities and aggression committed by men such as Alexander, Caesar, Charlemagne, or Napoleon against their accomplishments or their special mission in history. For Genghis Khan and the Mongols, however, their achievements lay forgotten, while their alleged crimes and brutality became magnified. Genghis Khan became the stereotype of the barbarian, the bloody savage, the ruthless conqueror who enjoyed destruction for its own sake. Genghis Khan, his Mongol horde, and to a large extent the Asian people in general became unidimensional caricatures, the symbol of all that lay beyond the civilized pale.

By the time of the Enlightenment, at the end of the eighteenth century, this menacing image appeared in Voltaire's *The Orphan of China,* a play about Genghis Khan's conquest of China: "He is called the king of kings, the fiery Genghis Khan, who lays the fertile fields of Asia waste." In contrast to Chaucer's praise for Genghis Khan, Voltaire described him as "this destructive tyrant . . . who proudly . . . treads on the necks of kings," but "is yet no more than a wild Scythian soldier bred to arms and practiced in the trade of blood" (Act I, scene I). Voltaire portrayed Genghis Khan as a man resentful of the superior virtues of the civilization around him and motivated by the basic barbarian desire to ravish civilized women and destroy what he could not understand.

The tribe of Genghis Khan acquired a variety of names—*Tartar, Tatar, Mughal, Moghul, Moal,* and *Mongol*—but the name always carried an odious curse. When nineteenth-century scientists wanted to show the inferiority of the Asian and American Indian populations, they classified them as *Mongoloid.* When doctors wanted to account for why mothers of the superior white race could give birth to retarded children, the children's facial characteristics made "obvious" that one of the child's ancestors had been raped by a Mongol warrior. Such blighted children were not white at all but members of the Mongoloid race. When the richest capitalists flaunted their wealth and showed antidemocratic or antiegalitarian values, they were derided as *moguls,* the Persian name for Mongols.

In due course, the Mongols became scapegoats for other nations' failures and shortcomings. When Russia could not keep up with the technology of the West or the military power of imperial Japan, it was because of the terrible Tatar Yoke put on her by Genghis Khan. When Persia fell behind its neighbors, it was because the Mongols had destroyed its irrigation system. When China lagged behind Japan and Europe, the cause was the cruel exploitation and repression by its Mongol and Manchu overlords. When India could not resist British colonization, it was because of the rapacious greed of Moghul rule. In the twentieth century, Arab politicians even assured their followers that Muslims would have invented the atomic bomb before the Americans if only the Mongols had not burned the Arabs' magnificent libraries and leveled their cities. When American bombs and missiles drove the Taliban from power in Afghanistan in 2002, the Taliban soldiers equated the American invasion with that of the Mongols, and therefore, in angry revenge, massacred thousands of Hazara, the descendants of the Mongol army who had lived in Afghanistan for eight centuries. During the following year, in one of his final addresses to the Iraqi people, dictator Saddam Hussein made similar charges against the Mongols as the Americans moved to invade his country and remove him from power.

Amidst so much political rhetoric, pseudoscience, and scholarly imagination, the truth of Genghis Khan remained buried, seemingly lost to posterity. His homeland and the area where he rose to power remained closed to the outside world by the Communists of the twentieth century, who kept it as tightly sealed as the warriors had done during the prior centuries. The original Mongolian documents, the so-called *Secret History of the Mongols*, were not only secret but had disappeared, faded into the depths of history even more mysteriously than Genghis Khan's tomb.

In the twentieth century, two developments gave the unexpected opportunity to solve some of the mysteries and correct part of the record about Genghis Khan. The first development was the deciphering of manuscripts containing the valuable lost history of Genghis Khan. Despite the prejudice and ignorance regarding the Mongols, scholars throughout the centuries had reported occasional encounters with the fabled Mongol text on the life of Genghis Khan. Like some rare animal or precious bird thought to have been extinct, the rumored sightings provoked more skepticism than scholarship. Finally, in the nineteenth century, a copy of the document written in Chinese characters was found in Beijing. Scholars easily read the characters, but the words made no sense because they had been recorded in a code that used Chinese characters to represent Mongolian sounds of the thirteenth century. The scholars could read only a small Chinese language summary that accompanied each chapter; these offered tantalizing hints at the story in the text, but otherwise the document remained inexplicable. Because of the mystery surrounding the document, scholars referred to it as *The Secret History of the Mongols*, the name by which it has continued to be known.

Throughout most of the twentieth century, the deciphering of the *Secret History* remained mortally dangerous in Mongolia. Communist authorities kept the book beyond the hands of common people and scholars for fear that they might be improperly influenced by the antiquated, unscientific, and nonsocialist perspective of the text. But an underground scholarly movement grew around the *Secret History*. In nomadic camps across the steppe, the whispered story of the newfound history spread from person to person, from camp to camp. At last, they had a history that told their story from the Mongol perspective. The Mongols had been much more than barbarians who harassed the superior civilizations around them. For the Mongol nomads, the revelations of the *Secret History* seemed to come from Genghis Khan himself, who had returned to his people to offer them hope and inspiration. After more than seven centuries of silence, they could, at last, hear his words again.

Despite official Communist repression, the Mongol people seemed determined that they would not lose these words again. For a brief moment, the liberalization of political life following the death of Stalin in 1953 and the admission of Mongolia to the United Nations in 1961 emboldened the Mongol people, and they felt free to reexplore their history. The country prepared a small series of stamps in 1962 to commemorate the eight hundredth anniversary of the birth of Genghis Khan. Tomor-ochir, the second highest ranking member of the government, authorized the erection of a concrete monument to mark the birthplace of Genghis Khan near the Onon River, and he sponsored a conference of scholars to assess the good and the bad aspects of the Mongol Empire in history. Both the stamp and the simple line drawing on the monument portrayed the image of the missing *sulde* of Genghis Khan, the horsehair Spirit Banner with which he conquered and the resting place of his soul.

Still, after nearly eight centuries, the *sulde* carried such a deep emotional meaning to both the Mongols and to some of the people they had conquered that the Russians treated its mere display on a stamp as an act of nationalist revival and potential aggression. The Soviets reacted with irrational anger to the fear that their satellite state might pursue an independent path or, worse yet, side with Mongolia's other neighbor, China, the Soviet Union's erstwhile ally turned enemy. In Mongolia, the Communist authorities suppressed the stamps and the scholars. For his traitorous crime of showing what party officials labeled as "tendencies directed at idealizing the role of Genghis Khan," the authorities removed Tomor-ochir from office, banished him to internal exile, and finally hacked him to death with an ax. After purging their own party, the Communists focused attention on the work of Mongolian scholars, whom the party branded as *anti-party elements, Chinese spies, saboteurs,* or *pests.* In the antinationalist campaign that followed, authorities dragged the archaeologist Perlee off to prison, where they kept him in extremely harsh conditions merely for having been Tomor-ochir's teacher and for secretly researching the history of the Mongol Empire. Teachers, historians, artists, poets, and singers stood in danger if they had any association with the history of Genghis Khan's era. The authorities secretly executed some of them. Other scholars lost their jobs, and together with their families were expelled from their homes in the harsh Mongolian climate. They were also denied medical care, and many were marched off into internal exile at various locations in the vast open expanse of Mongolia.

During this purge, the Spirit Banner of Genghis Khan disappeared completely, and was possibly destroyed by the Soviets as punishment of the Mongolian people. But despite this brutal repression, or perhaps because of it, numerous Mongol scholars independently set out to study the *Secret History,* putting their lives at risk, in search of a true understanding of their maligned and distorted past.

Outside of Mongolia, scholars in many countries, notably Russia, Germany, France, and Hungary, worked to decipher the text and translate it into modern languages. Without access to the resources within Mongolia itself, they labored under extremely difficult conditions. In the 1970s, one chapter at a time appeared in Mongolian and English under the careful supervision and analysis of Igor de Rachewiltz, a devoted Australian scholar of the ancient Mongol language. During the same time, American scholar Francis Woodman Cleaves independently prepared a separate, meticulous translation that Harvard University Press published in 1982. It would take far more than deciphering the code and translating the documents, however, to make them comprehensible. Even in translation the texts remained difficult to comprehend because they had obviously been written for a closed group within the Mongol royal family, and they assumed a deep knowledge not only of the culture of thirteenth-century Mongols but also of the geography of their land. The historical context and biographical meaning of the manuscripts remained nearly inaccessible without a detailed, on-the-ground analysis of where the events transpired.

The second major development occurred unexpectedly in 1990 when Communism collapsed and the Soviet occupation of Mongolia ended. The Soviet army retreated, the planes flew away, and the tanks withdrew. The Mongol world of Inner Asia was, at last, opened to outsiders. Gradually a few people ventured into the protected area. Mongol hunters snuck in to poach the game-filled valleys, herders came to graze their animals along the edges of the area, occasional adventurers trekked in. In the 1990s, several teams of technologically sophisticated foreigners came in search of the tombs of Genghis Khan and his family; although they made many fascinating finds, their ultimate goal eluded them.

My research began as a study of the role of tribal people in the history of world commerce and the Silk Route connecting China, the Middle East, and Europe. I traveled to archaeological sites, libraries, and meetings with scholars across the route from the Forbidden City in Beijing through central Asia to the Topkapi Palace in Istanbul. Beginning in 1990 with the first trip into Buryatia, the Mongol district of Siberia, I pursued the trail of the Mongols through Russia, China, Mongolia, Uzbekistan, Kazakhstan, Tajikistan, Kyrgystan, and Turkmenistan. I devoted one summer to following the ancient migration path of the Turkic tribes as they spread out from their original home in Mongolia as far as Bosnia on the Mediterranean. Then I encircled the old empire by the approximate sea route of Marco Polo from South China to Vietnam, through the Strait of Malacca to India, the Arab states of the Persian Gulf, and on to Venice.

The extensive travel produced a lot of information but not as much understanding as I had hoped. Despite this lack, I thought that my research was nearly finished when I arrived in Mongolia in 1998 to finalize the project with some background on the area of Genghis Khan's youth in what, I assumed, would be a final, brief excursion. That trip turned into another five years of far more intensive research than I could have imagined. I found Mongolians to be delirious at their freedom from centuries of foreign rule, and much of the excitement centered on honoring the memory of their founding father, Genghis Khan. Despite the rapid commercialization of his name on vodka bottles, chocolate bars, and cigarettes, as well as the release of songs in his honor, as a historical person he was still missing. Not only was his soul missing from the monastery, but his true face was still missing from their history as much as from ours. Who was he?

Through no credit or skill of my own, I arrived in Mongolia at a time when it suddenly seemed possible to answer those questions. For the first time in nearly eight centuries, the forbidden zone of his childhood and burial were open at the same time that the coded text of the *Secret History* had finally been deciphered. No single scholar could complete the task, but working together with a team from different backgrounds, we could begin to find the answers.

As a cultural anthropologist, I worked closely with the archaeologist Dr. Kh. Lkhagvasuren, who had access to much of the information collected by his professor and mentor Dr. Kh. Perlee, the most prominent archaeologist of twentieth-century Mongolia. Gradually, through Lkhagvasuren, I met other researchers who had spent many years working secretly and, almost always, alone on studies they could never write down or publish. Professor O. Purev, a Communist Party member, had used his position as an official researcher of party history to study the shamanist practices of the Mongols and to use that as a guide to interpreting the hidden meanings in the *Secret History*. Colonel Kh. Shagdar of the Mongolian army took advantage of his station in Moscow to compare the military strategies and victories of Genghis Khan as described in the *Secret History* with those in Russian military archives. A Mongolian political scientist, D. Bold-Erdene, analyzed the political techniques Genghis Khan used in getting and acquiring power. The most extensive and detailed studies of all had been made by the geographer O. Sukhbaatar, who had covered over a million kilometers across Mongolia in search of the history of Genghis Khan.

Our team began working together. We compared the most important primary and secondary texts from a dozen languages with the accounts in the *Secret History*. We hunched over maps and debated the precise meaning of different documents and much older analyses. Not surprisingly, we found vast discrepancies and numerous contradictions that were difficult to reconcile. I soon saw that Sukhbaatar was a literalist, an extreme empiricist for whom every statement in the *Secret History* was true, and he had taken the job of proving it with scientific evidence. But Purev thought nothing in the history should be taken at its literal meaning. According to him, Genghis Khan was the most powerful shaman in history, and the text was a manuscript of mysteries that chronicled, in symbolic ways, his rise to that position. If it could be unlocked, it would again provide a shaman's blueprint for conquering and controlling the world.

From the beginning of our combined work, it was apparent that we could not sift through the competing ideas and interpretations without finding the places where the events happened. The ultimate test of each text's veracity would come when it lay spread out on the ground at the place where the events allegedly happened. Books can lie, but places never do. One quick and exhausting overview of the main sites answered some questions but presented many more. We realized that not only did we have to find the right place, but to understand the events there, we had to be there in the right weather conditions. We returned repeatedly to the same places in different seasons of the year. The sites lay scattered across a landscape of thousands of square miles, but the most significant area for our research lay in the mysterious and inaccessible area that had been closed since the time of Genghis Khan's death. Because of the nomadic life of Genghis Khan, our own work became a peripatetic project, a sort of archaeology of movement rather than just place.

Satellite images showed a Mongolian landscape void of roads yet crisscrossed with thousands of trails leading in seemingly every direction over the steppe, across the Gobi, and through the mountains; yet they all stopped at the edge of the *Ikh Khorig,* the closed zone. Entry into the homeland of Genghis Khan required crossing the buffer zone that had been occupied and fortified by the Soviets to keep everyone out. When they fled Mongolia, the Soviets left behind a surreal landscape of artillery craters strewn with the metal carcasses of tanks, wrecked trucks, cannibalized airplanes, spent artillery shells, and unexploded duds. Strange vapors filled the air and peculiar fogs came and went. Twisted metal sculptures rose several stories high, strange remnants from structures of unknown purpose. Collapsed buildings, which once housed secret electronic equipment, now squatted empty among lifeless dunes of oil-drenched sand. Equipment from old weapons programs lay abandoned across the scarred steppe. Dark and mysterious ponds of unidentified chemicals shimmered eerily in the bright sun. Blackened debris of unknown origin floated in the stagnant liquid, and animal bones, dried carcasses, swatches of fur, and clumps of feathers littered the edges of the ponds. Beyond this twentieth-century graveyard of horrors lay—in the sharpest imaginable contrast—the undisturbed, closed homeland of Genghis

Khan: several hundred square miles of pristine forest, mountains, river valleys, and steppes.

Entry into the Highly Restricted Area was more than just a step backward in time; it was an opportunity to discover Genghis Khan's world almost precisely as he left it. The area had survived like a lost island surrounded, yet protected, by the worst technological horrors of the twentieth century. Clogged with fallen trees, thick underbrush, and giant boulders, much of it remained impenetrable, and the other parts had seen only occasional patrols of soldiers over the last eight centuries. This restricted region is a living monument to Genghis Khan; as we traveled through the area, it seemed that at any moment he might come galloping up the river or over the ridge to pitch his camp once again in the places he had loved, to fire his arrow at a fleeing gazelle, to chip a fishing hole in the ice covering the Onon River, or to bow down and pray on Burkhan Khaldun, the sacred mountain that continued to protect him in death, as it had in life.

Our research team approached the *Ikh Khorig* like detectives searching a fresh crime scene. With *The Secret History of the Mongols* as our primary guide, we navigated the plain and surveyed the primeval landscape from various small hills and mounds. On the open steppe away from the clear landmarks of mountains, rivers, and lakes, we relied heavily on the herders who were accustomed to navigating across the grass like sailors crossing the sea. A constantly changing cluster of Mongolian students, scholars, local herders, and horsemen accompanied us, and they intently debated among themselves the answers to the questions I was researching. Their judgments and answers were always better than mine, and they asked questions that had never occurred to me. They knew how herders thought, and although they were in unknown territory, they easily identified where their ancestors would have camped or in which direction they would have traveled. They readily identified places as having too many mosquitoes for summer camp or being too exposed for winter camp. More important, they were willing to test their ideas, such as racing a horse from one point to another to see how long it took or how the soil and grass reverberated the sound of horse hooves in this particular place versus another. They knew how thick the ice needed to be in order to cross a frozen river on horseback, when to cross on foot, and when to break the ice and wade through the cold water.

The descriptive quality of some Mongol place-names permitted us to restore them to Mongolian and apply them to the landscape around us with ease. The text recounts that Genghis Khan first became a clan chief at Khokh Lake by Khara Jirugen Mountain, which meant a Blue Lake by Back-Heart-Shaped Mountain. The identity of that place had been preserved for centuries and was easily found by anyone. Other names associated with his birth, such as Udder Hill and Spleen Lake, proved more challenging because of uncertainty whether the name applied to a visual characteristic of the place or to an event that took place there, and because the shape of hills and lakes can vary over eight centuries in this area of wind erosion and dryness.

Gradually, we pieced together the story as best we could with the evidence we had. By finding the places of Genghis Khan's childhood and retracing the path of events across the land, some misconceptions regarding his life could be immediately corrected. Although we debated the precise identity of the hillock along the Onon River where he had been born, for example, it was obvious that the wooded river with its many marshes differed greatly from the open steppe where most nomads lived and where most historians had assumed Genghis Khan grew up. This distinction highlighted the differences between him and other nomads. It immediately became clear why the *Secret History* mentioned hunting more often than herding in Genghis Khan's childhood. The landscape itself tied the early life of Genghis Khan more firmly into the Siberian cultures, from which the *Secret History* said the Mongols originated, than into the Turkic tribes of the open plains. This information in turn greatly influenced our understanding of Genghis Khan's field methods and how he treated hostile civilians as animals to be herded but hostile soldiers as game to be hunted.

Our team went out repeatedly over a five-year period under a great variety of conditions and situations. Temperatures varied by more than 150 degrees—from highs of over 100 degrees in tracts of land without shade to a low of minus 51 degrees, not counting the chill of the fierce wind, in Khorkhonag steppe in January 2001. We experienced the usual assortment of mishaps and opportunities of travel in such areas. Our vehicles became stuck in snow in the winter, mud in spring, and sand in the summer; one even washed away in a flash flood. At different times our camps were destroyed by wind and snow or by drunken revelry. We enjoyed the wonderful bounty of endless milk and meat in the final summers of the twentieth century. But in the opening years of this century, we also experienced some of the worst years of animal famine, called *zud,* when horses and yaks literally dropped dead around us and animals of all sizes froze standing during the night.

Yet there was never a moment of doubt or danger in our work. Compared to the difficulty of daily life for the herders and hunters living permanently in those areas, ours were only the smallest of irritations. Invariably an unplanned episode that started as an inconvenience ended by teaching me something new about the land or people. From riding nearly fifty miles in one day on a horse, I learned that the fifteen feet of silk tied tightly around the midriff actually kept the organs in place and prevented nausea. I also learned the importance of having dried yogurt in my pocket on such long treks, when there was no time to stop and cook a meal, as well as the practicality of the thick Mongol robe, called a *deel,* when riding on wooden saddles. An encounter with a wolf near the sacred mountain of Burkhan Khaldun became a blessing in the eyes of our companions rather than a threat, and countless episodes of getting lost or of breaking down brought new lessons about directions, navigation, and the patience of waiting until someone came along. Repeatedly, I learned how intimately the Mongols know their own world and how consistently and completely I could trust in their astute judgment, physical ability, and generous helpfulness.

This book presents the highlights of our findings without recounting any more of the minutia of weather, food, parasites, and ailments encountered, nor the personality quirks of the researchers and the people we met along the way. The focus remains on the mission of our work: to understand Genghis Khan and his impact on world history.

The first part of the book tells the story of Genghis Khan's rise to power on the steppe and the forces that shaped his life and personality from the time of his birth in 1162 until he unified all the tribes and founded the Mongol nation in 1206. The second part follows the Mongol entrance onto the stage of history through the Mongol World War, which lasted five decades (from 1211 to 1261), until Genghis Khan's grandsons went to war with one another. The third section examines the century of peace and the Global Awakening that laid the foundations of the political, commercial, and military institutions of our modern society.

PART I

The Reign of Terror on the Steppe: 1162–1206

Nations! What are nations? Tartars! and Huns! and Chinamen!

Like Insects they swarm. The historian strives in vain to make them memorable.

It is for want of a man that there are so many men. It is individuals that populate the world.

HENRY DAVID THOREAU,
journal entry for May 1, 1851

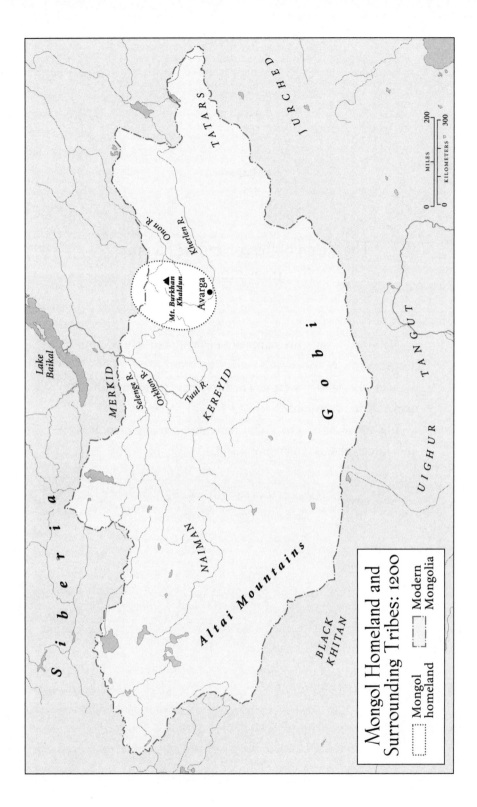

Mongol Homeland and
Surrounding Tribes: 1200

Mongol
homeland

Modern
Mongolia

1

—⚬—

The Blood Clot

There is fire in his eyes and light in his face.
THE SECRET HISTORY OF THE MONGOLS

O F THE THOUSANDS OF cities conquered by the Mongols, history only mentions one that Genghis Khan deigned to enter. Usually, when victory became assured, he withdrew with his court to a distant and more pleasant camp while his warriors completed their tasks. On a March day in 1220, the Year of the Dragon, the Mongol conqueror broke with his peculiar tradition by leading his cavalry into the center of the newly conquered city of Bukhara, one of the most important cities belonging to the sultan of Khwarizm in what is now Uzbekistan. Although neither the capital nor the major commercial city, Bukhara occupied an exalted emotional position throughout the Muslim world as Noble Bukhara, the center of religious piety known by the epithet "the ornament and delight to all Islam." Knowing fully the propaganda value of his actions by conquering and entering the city, Genghis Khan rode triumphantly through the city gates, past the warren of wooden houses and vendors' stalls, to the large cluster of stone and brick buildings at the center of the city.

His entry into Bukhara followed the successful conclusion of possibly the most audacious surprise attack in military history. While one part of his army

3

took the direct route from Mongolia to attack the sultan's border cities head-on, he had secretly pulled and pushed another division of warriors over a distance longer than any other army had ever covered—two thousand miles of desert, mountains, and steppe—to appear deep behind enemy lines, where least expected. Even trade caravans avoided the Kyzyl Kum, the fabled Red Desert, by detouring hundreds of miles to avoid it; and that fact, of course, was precisely why Genghis Khan chose to attack from that direction. By befriending the nomads of the area, he was able to lead his army on a hitherto unknown track through the stone and sand desert.

His targeted city of Bukhara stood at the center of a fertile oasis astride one of the tributaries of the Amu Darya inhabited mostly by Tajik or Persian people, but ruled by Turkic tribesmen in the newly created empire of Khwarizm, one of the many transitory empires of the era. The sultan of Khwarizm had, in a grievously fatal mistake, provoked the enmity of Genghis Khan by looting a Mongol trade caravan and disfiguring the faces of Mongol ambassadors sent to negotiate peaceful commerce. Although nearly sixty years old, when Genghis Khan heard of the attack on his men, he did not hesitate to summon his disciplined and experienced army once again to their mounts and to charge down the road of war.

In contrast to almost every major army in history, the Mongols traveled lightly, without a supply train. By waiting until the coldest months to make the desert crossing, men and horses required less water. Dew also formed during this season, thereby stimulating the growth of some grass that provided grazing for horses and attracted game that the men eagerly hunted for their own sustenance. Instead of transporting slow-moving siege engines and heavy equipment with them, the Mongols carried a faster-moving engineer corps that could build whatever was needed on the spot from available materials. When the Mongols came to the first trees after crossing the vast desert, they cut them down and made them into ladders, siege engines, and other instruments for their attack.

When the advance guard spotted the first small settlement after leaving the desert, the rapidly moving detachment immediately changed pace, moving now in a slow, lumbering procession, as though they were merchants coming to trade, rather than with the speed of warriors on the attack. The hostile force nonchalantly ambled up to the gates of the town before the residents realized who they were and sounded an alarm.

Upon emerging unexpectedly from the desert, Genghis Khan did not race to attack Bukhara immediately. He knew that no reinforcements could leave the border cities under attack by his army, and he therefore had time to play on the surprise in a tortured manipulation of public fear and hope. The objective of such tactics was simple and always the same: to frighten the enemy into surrendering before an actual battle began. By first capturing several small towns in the vicinity, Genghis Khan's army set many local people to flight toward Bukhara as refugees who not only filled the city but greatly increased the level of terror in it. By striking deeply behind the enemy lines, the Mongols immediately created havoc and panic throughout the kingdom. As the Persian chronicler Ata-Malik Juvaini described his approach, when the people saw the countryside all around them "choked with horsemen and the air black as night with the dust of cavalry, fright and panic overcame them, and fear and dread prevailed." In preparing the psychological attack on a city, Genghis Khan began with two examples of what awaited the people. He offered generous terms of surrender to the outlying communities, and the ones that accepted the terms and joined the Mongols received great leniency. In the words of the Persian chronicler, "whoever yields and submits to them is safe and free from the terror and disgrace of their severity." Those that refused received exceptionally harsh treatment, as the Mongols herded the captives before them to be used as cannon fodder in the next attack.

The tactic panicked the Turkic defenders of Bukhara. Leaving only about five hundred soldiers behind to man the citadel of Bukhara, the remaining army of twenty thousand soldiers fled in what they thought was still time before the main Mongol army arrived. By abandoning their fortress and dispersing in flight, they sprung Genghis Khan's trap, and the Mongol warriors, who were already stationed in wait for the fleeing soldiers, cut them down at a nearly leisurely pace.

The civilian population of Bukhara surrendered and opened the city gates, but the small contingent of defiant soldiers remained in their citadel, where they hoped that the massive walls would allow them to hold out indefinitely against any siege. To more carefully assess the overall situation, Genghis Khan made his unprecedented decision to enter the city. One of his first acts on reaching the center of Bukhara, or upon accepting the surrender of any people, was to summon them to bring fodder for his horses. Feeding the Mongol warriors and their horses was taken as a sign of submission by the conquered;

more important, by receiving the food and fodder, Genghis Khan signaled his acceptance of the people as vassals entitled to Mongol protection as well as subject to his command.

From the time of his central Asian conquests, we have one of the few written descriptions of Genghis Khan, who was about sixty years old. The Persian chronicler Minhaj al-Siraj Juzjani, who was far less kindly disposed toward the Mongols than the chronicler Juvaini, described him as "a man of tall stature, of vigorous build, robust in body, the hair on his face scanty and turned white, with cats' eyes, possessed of dedicated energy, discernment, genius, and understanding, awe-striking, a butcher, just, resolute, an overthrower of enemies, intrepid, sanguinary, and cruel." Because of his uncanny ability to destroy cities and conquer armies many times the size of his own, the chronicler also goes on to declare that Genghis Khan was "adept at magic and deception, and some of the devils were his friends."

Eyewitnesses reported that upon reaching the center of Bukhara, Genghis Khan rode up to the large mosque and asked if, since it was the largest building in the city, it was the home of the sultan. When informed that it was the house of God, not the sultan, he said nothing. For the Mongols, the one God was the Eternal Blue Sky that stretched from horizon to horizon in all four directions. God presided over the whole earth; he could not be cooped up in a house of stone like a prisoner or a caged animal, nor, as the city people claimed, could his words be captured and confined inside the covers of a book. In his own experience, Genghis Khan had often felt the presence and heard the voice of God speaking directly to him in the vast open air of the mountains in his homeland, and by following those words, he had become the conqueror of great cities and huge nations.

Genghis Khan dismounted from his horse in order to walk into the great mosque, the only such building he is known to have ever entered in his life. Upon entering, he ordered that the scholars and clerics feed his horses, freeing them from further danger and placing them under his protection, as he did with almost all religious personnel who came under his control. Next, he summoned the 280 richest men of the city to the mosque. Despite his limited experience inside city walls, Genghis Khan still had a keen grasp of the working of human emotion and sentiment. Before the assembled men in the mosque, Genghis Khan took a few steps up the pulpit stairs, then turned to face the elite of Bukhara. Through interpreters, he lectured them sternly on the sins and misdeeds of their sultan and themselves. It was not the common people who were to blame for these failures; rather, "it is the great ones among you who have committed these sins. If you had not committed great sins, God would not have sent a punishment like me upon you." He then gave each rich man into the control of one of his Mongol warriors, who would go with him and collect his treasure. He admonished his rich prisoners not to bother showing them the wealth above the ground; the Mongols could find that without assistance. He wanted them to guide them only to their hidden or buried treasure.

Having begun the systematic plundering of the city, Genghis Khan turned his attention to attacking the Turkic warriors still defiantly sealed inside the citadel of Bukhara. Although not familiar with the Mongols in particular, the people in the urbanized oases of central Asian cities like Bukhara and Samarkand had seen many barbarian armies come and go through the centuries. Prior tribal armies, no matter how brave or disciplined, never posed a severe threat because urban armies, so long as they had food and water, could hold out indefinitely behind the massive walls of their forts. By most measures, the Mongols should have been no match for the professionally trained career soldiers they encountered at Bukhara. Although the Mongols had excellent bows in general, each man was responsible for making or acquiring his own, and the quality of workmanship varied. Similarly, the Mongol army was composed of all the males of the tribe, who depended on the ruggedness of their upbringing herding animals for their training; and while they were hardy, disciplined, and devoted to their tasks, they lacked the professional selection and training of the defenders of Bukhara. The greatest factor in favor of the soldiers holed up behind the massive stone walls of the citadel was that no tribal army had ever mastered the complex technology of siege warfare, but Genghis Khan had something to show them.

The attack was designed as a show of overwhelming strength for which the audience was not the already conquered people of Bukhara, but the still distant army and people of Samarkand, the next city on his march. The Mongol invaders rolled up their newly constructed siege engines—catapults, trebuchets, and mangonels that hurled not only stones and fire, as besieging armies had done for centuries, but also pots of burning liquids, exploding devices, and incendiary materials. They maneuvered immense crossbows mounted on wheels, and great teams of men pushed in portable towers with retractable ladders from which they could shoot down at the defenders of the walls. At the same time that they attacked through the air, miners went to work digging into the earth to undermine the walls by sapping. During this awesome display of technological prowess in the air, on the land, and beneath the earth, Genghis Khan heightened the psychological tension by forcing prisoners, in some cases the captured comrades of the men still in the citadel, to rush forward until their bodies filled the moat and made live ramparts over which other prisoners pushed the engines of war.

The Mongols devised and used weapons from the different cultures with whom they had contact, and through this accumulation of knowledge they created a global arsenal that could be adapted to whatever situation they encountered. In their flaming and exploding weapons, the Mongols experimented with early forms of armaments that would later become mortars and cannons. In the description of Juvaini, we sense the confusion of the witnesses in accounting for exactly what happened around them. He described the Mongol assault as "like a red-hot furnace fed from without by hard sticks thrust into the recesses, while from the belly of the furnace sparks shoot into the air." Genghis Khan's army combined the traditional fierceness and speed of the steppe warrior with the highest technological sophistication of Chinese civilization. Genghis Khan used his fast-moving and well-trained cavalry against the enemy's infantry on the ground, while negating the protective power of the fortress walls with the new technology of bombardment using firepower and unprecedented machines of destruction to penetrate the fortress and terrorize its defenders. With fire and death raining down on the men in the citadel, the warriors of the sultan, in Juvaini's words, quickly "drowned in the sea of annihilation."

Genghis Khan recognized that warfare was not a sporting contest or a mere match between rivals; it was a total commitment of one people against another. Victory did not come to the one who played by the rules; it came to the one who made the rules and imposed them on his enemy. Triumph could not be partial. It was complete, total, and undeniable—or it was nothing. In battle, this meant the unbridled use of terror and surprise. In peace, it meant the steadfast adherence to a few basic but unwavering principles that created loyalty among the common people. Resistance would be met with death, loyalty with security.

His attack on Bukhara ranked as a success, not merely because the people of that city surrendered, but because when word of the Mongol campaign reached the capital of Samarkand, that army surrendered as well. The sultan fled his kingdom, and the Mongol juggernaut pushed onward. Genghis Khan himself took the main part of the army across the mountains of Afghanistan and on to the Indus River, while another detachment circled around the Caspian Sea, through the Caucasus Mountains, and onto the plains of Russia. For precisely seven hundred years, from that day in 1220 until 1920, when the Soviets moved in, Genghis Khan's descendants ruled as khans and emirs over the city of Bukhara in one of the longest family dynasties in history.

Genghis Khan's ability to manipulate people and technology represented the experienced knowledge of more than four decades of nearly constant warfare. At no single, crucial moment in his life did he suddenly acquire his genius at warfare, his ability to inspire the loyalty of his followers, or his unprecedented skill for organizing on a global scale. These derived not from epiphanic enlightenment or formal schooling but from a persistent cycle of pragmatic learning, experimental adaptation, and constant revision driven by his uniquely disciplined mind and focused will. His fighting career began long before most of his warriors at Bukhara had been born, and in every battle he learned something new. In every skirmish, he acquired more followers and additional fighting techniques. In each struggle, he combined the new ideas into a constantly changing set of military tactics, strategies, and weapons. He never fought the same war twice.

The story of the boy who was destined to become the world's greatest conqueror began six decades before the Mongol conquest of Bukhara in one of the most remote places in the inner expanse of Eurasia, near the border of modern Mongolia and Siberia. According to legend, the Mongols originated in the mountain forest when Blue-Gray Wolf mated with Beautiful Red Doe on the shores of a great lake. Because the Mongols permanently closed this homeland to outsiders when Genghis Khan died, we have no historical descriptions of it. The names of its rivers and mountains are virtually unknown in the historical literature, and even modern maps give conflicting names to its features, in a great variety of spellings.

This territory of the Mongol clans occupied only a small part in the northeast of the country now known as Mongolia. Most of the country now spreads across a high plateau in north-central Asia, beyond the range of the Pacific Ocean's moisture-bearing winds that water the lush coastal plains of Asia's agricultural civilizations. By contrast, the winds that reach the Mongolian plateau mostly blow from the Arctic in the northwest. These winds release what little moisture they carry onto the northern mountains and leave the southern part of the country dry, a terrain known as *govi*, or to foreigners as the Gobi. Between the harsh Gobi and the moderately watered mountains to the north lie vast stretches of steppe that turn green in the summer if they get rain. It is along these steppes that the herders move in the summer, searching for grass.

Although reaching only about ten thousand feet above sea level, Mongolia's Khentii Mountain Range consists of some of the oldest mountains on the planet. Unlike the jagged, youthful Himalayas, which can only be ascended with climbing gear, the ancient Khentii Mountains have been smoothed by millions of years of erosion so that, with only moderate difficulty, a horse and rider can reach all but a few of the peaks in summer. Marshes dot their sides; in the long winter, these freeze into a solid mass. The deeper indentations in the mountainsides collect snow and water that freeze into what looks like glaciers in the winter, but in the brief summer, they turn into beautiful lakes of cobalt blue. The spring thaw of ice and snow overflows the lakes and spills off the mountains to form a series of small rivers that flow out onto the steppe that in the best of summers shimmers with grass as green as emeralds, but in the worst of times can remain a burned brown for several consecutive years.

The rivers that flow out of the Khentii Mountains are small and remain frozen for much of the year—even in May, when the ice is usually thick enough to support a team of mounted horses and sometimes even a loaded jeep. The long, broad steppes that stretch out along these small rivers served as the highways for the Mongols toward the various regions of Eurasia. Spurs of this grassland reach west all the way into Hungary and Bulgaria in eastern Europe. To the east, they reach Manchuria and would touch the Pacific Ocean if not barred by a thin ridge of coastal mountains that cut off the Korean

Peninsula. On the southern side of the Gobi, the grasslands slowly pick up again and join the heart of the Asian continent, connecting with the extensive agricultural plains of the Yellow River.

Despite the gentle roll of the landscape, the weather can be fierce, and changes abruptly. This is a land of marked extremes, where humans and their animals face constant challenges from the weather. The Mongols say that you can experience all four seasons in a single day in the Khentii. Even in May, a horse might sink into snowbanks so deep that it could barely keep its head up.

On this, the land by the side of the Onon River, the boy destined to become known as Genghis Khan was born. In contrast to the natural beauty of the place, its human history was already one of constant strife and hardship long before he was born in the spring of 1162, the Year of the Horse by the Asian calendar. On an isolated and bald hillock overlooking the remote Onon River, Hoelun, a young, kidnapped girl, struggled to give birth to him, her first child. Surrounded by strangers, Hoelun labored far away from the family that had raised her and the world she knew. This place was not her home, and the man who now claimed her as his wife was not the man whom she had married.

Only a short time before, her destiny had seemed so different; she had been the wife of another young warrior, Chiledu of the Merkid tribe. He had traveled to the eastern steppe to find and woo her from the Olkhunuud, a tribe noted for the beauty of its women. According to steppe tradition, he would have given her parents gifts and worked for them, perhaps for several years, before taking their daughter back to his tribe as his bride. Once married, the two had set out alone for the trek of many weeks back to his homeland. According to the *Secret History,* she rode in a small black cart pulled by an ox or a yak, and her proud husband rode beside the cart on his dun horse. Hoelun was probably no more than sixteen years old.

They traveled easily over the steppe, following the course of the Onon River, and then prepared to enter the mountainous range that divided them from the Merkid lands. Only a few hard days of travel through the isolated mountain valleys lay ahead of them before they would drop down into the fertile grassland of the Merkid's herds. The young bride sat in the front of her small black cart unaware of the horsemen about to swoop down upon her, a violent assault that would not only forever change her life, but alter the course of world history.

A solitary horseman out hunting with his falcon looked down on Hoelun and Chiledu from his unobserved perch at the top of a nearby cliff. Hoelun and her cart promised greater game than he could capture with his bird.

Without letting the newlyweds see him, the hunter rode back to his camp to find his two brothers. Too poor to afford the presents necessary to make a marriage with a wife such as Hoelun, and perhaps unwilling to perform the traditional bride-service for her parents, the hunter chose the second most common way of obtaining a wife on the steppes: kidnapping. The three brothers set out in pursuit of their unsuspecting prey. As they swooped down toward the couple, Chiledu immediately galloped off to draw the attackers away from the cart, and, as expected, they chased after him. He tried in vain to lose them by circling around the base of the mountain to return to his bride, but even then Hoelun knew that her husband had not fooled the attackers, not on their own land, and that they would soon be back. Although only a teenage girl, she decided that in order to give her husband a chance to live, she must stay and surrender to her kidnappers. If she fled with Chiledu on one horse, they would be captured and he would be killed. But if he fled alone, only she would be captured.

The *Secret History* recounts that to convince her husband to cooperate with her plan, she told him, "If you but live, there will be maidens for you on every front and in every cart. You can find another woman to be your bride, and you can call her *Hoelun* in place of me." Hoelun then quickly slipped out of her blouse and commanded her new husband to "flee quickly." She thrust her blouse into his face as a parting gesture and said, "Take this with you so that you may have the smell of me with you as you go."

Smell holds a deep, important place within steppe culture. Where people in other cultures might hug or kiss at meeting or departing, the steppe nomads sniff one another in a gesture much like a kiss on the cheek. Smelling carries deeply emotional meanings on different levels that vary from the familial sniff between parent and child to the erotic sniff between lovers. Each person's breath and unique body aroma is thought to constitute a part of that person's soul. By thrusting her blouse at her husband, Hoelun offered him a deeply important reminder of her love.

After that day, Hoelun would have a long and eventful life ahead of her, but she was indeed destined never again to see her first love. As he fled his wife's kidnappers, Chiledu clutched her blouse to his face and turned back to look at her so many times that his long black braids beat like whips back and forth from his chest to his shoulders. As she saw her husband ride over the pass and slip forever from her sight, Hoelun gave vent to the full emotion of her heart. She screamed out so loudly, according to the *Secret History,* that "she stirred up the Onon River" and "shook the woods and valley."

Her captor and the man destined to be her new husband was Yesugei of the small and insignificant band that would one day be known as the Mongols, but at this time he was simply a member of the Borijin clan, subservient to its more powerful Tayichiud relatives. Even more troubling for Hoelun than the status of her captor was that he already had a wife or concubine, Sochigel, and a son with her. Hoelun would have to struggle for her position within the family. If she was lucky the two women probably lived in separate *gers,* the domed tent homes made of felt blankets tied around a lattice framework, but they would have been in close daily proximity even if not in the same *ger.*

Hoelun grew up on the wide, open grassland where one could see over vast expanses in any direction and where great herds of horses, cows, sheep, and goats grazed and grew fat during the summer. She was accustomed to the abundant and rich diet of meat and milk offered by the life of the steppe. By contrast, the small tribe of her new husband subsisted on the northern edge of the herding world, where the steppes pushed up against the wooded mountains, without enough grassland to feed large herds. She would now have to eat harsher hunter's foods: marmots, rats, birds, fish, and the occasional deer or antelope. The Mongols claim no ancient and glorious history among the steppe tribes. They were considered scavengers who competed with the wolves to hunt down the small animals, and, when the opportunity arose, steal animals and women from the herders of the steppe. Hoelun would rank as little more than captured chattel by them.

According to an often repeated account, Hoelun's first baby supposedly struggled into the world tightly clutching something mysterious and ominous in the fingers of his right hand. Gently, but nervously, his young mother pried back his fingers one by one to find a large, black blood clot the size of a knucklebone. From somewhere in his mother's warm womb, this boy had grasped the blood clot and brought it with him from that world into this one. What could an inexperienced, illiterate, and terribly lonely young girl make of this strange sign in her son's hand? More than eight centuries later, we still struggle to answer the same questions that she had about her son. Did the blood clot represent a prophecy or a curse? Did it foretell good fortune or evil? Should she be proud or alarmed? Hopeful or fearful?

In the twelfth century, dozens of tribes and clans lived on the steppe in, as is characteristic of nomadic people, shifting combinations. Of all the steppe tribes, the Mongols' closest relatives were Tatars and Khitan to the east, the Manchus yet farther to the east, and the Turkic tribes of central Asia to the west. These three ethnic groups shared a common cultural and linguistic heritage with some of the tribes of Siberia, where they possibly all originated. Located between the Tatars and the Turkic tribes with whom outsiders often confused them, the Mongols were sometimes known as Blue Turks or as Black Tatars. As speakers of Altaic languages, named for the Altai Mountain range in western Mongolia, their languages bore a distant similarity with Korean and Japanese, but none with Chinese or the other tonal languages of Asia.

Although the Turkic tribes and Tatars had coalesced into several tribal confederacies, the Mongols were divided into many small bands headed by a chief, or *khan*, and loosely based on kinship ties. The Mongols themselves claim a distinct identity from the Turkic and Tatar groups. They asserted, then and now, a direct descent from the Huns, who founded the first empire on the high steppe in the third century. *Hun* is the Mongolian word for human being, and they called their Hun ancestors *Hun-nu*, the people of the sun. In the fourth and fifth centuries, the Huns spread out from the Mongolian steppes to conquer countries from India to Rome, but they were unable to sustain contact among the various clans and were quickly assimilated into the cultures they conquered.

Shortly after he had kidnapped Hoelun, Yesugei had gone on a campaign against the Tatars and killed a warrior called Temujin Uge. Returning just after the birth of his son, he named the boy Temujin. Since people of the steppe received only one name in life, its selection carried much symbolism, often on several levels; the name imparted to the child its character, fate, and destiny. The bestowal of the name Temujin may have stressed the lingering enmity between Mongols and Tatars, but much scholarly and imaginative discussion has surrounded the precise meaning of Temujin's name or what was being conferred upon him by his father. The best hint of the intended meaning comes from the Mongol practice of giving several children names derived from a common root word. Of her four subsequent children born after Temujin, Hoelun's youngest son bore the name Temuge, and the youngest child and only daughter was named Temulun. All three names seem to have the common root of the verb *temul*—which occurred in several Mongol words meaning to rush headlong, to be inspired, to have a creative thought, and even to take a flight of fancy. As one Mongolian student explained to me, the word was best exemplified by "the look in the eye of a horse that is racing where it wants to go, no matter what the rider wants."

Despite the isolation of the Mongolian world, the tribes who lived there were not cut off entirely from the currents of world events. For centuries before the birth of Genghis Khan, Chinese, Muslim, Hindu, and Christian civilizations filtered into the Mongol homeland; little of their culture proved adaptable, however, to the harsh environment of the high steppes. The nomadic tribes had distant but complex commercial, religious, and military relations with the constantly changing configuration of states in China and central Asia. Living so far to the north, the Mongols were essentially out of range of the trade routes that later became known as the Silk Route, which ran south of the Gobi, tenuously and sporadically connecting Chinese and Muslim societies. Yet enough trade goods filtered north to make the Mongols aware of the treasures that lay in the south.

For the nomads, trading with their neighbors and fighting with them constituted an interrelated part of the yearly rhythm of life, as customary and predictable as tending the newborn animals in the spring, searching for pastures in the summer, or drying meat and dairy products in the fall. The long, cold winter was the season for hunting. The men left home in small parties to roam the mountains and penetrate the forests hunting rabbits, wolves, sables, elks ibex, argali (wild sheep), boars, bears, foxes, and otters. Sometimes the whole community participated in hunts, where they would encircle as large an area as they could and drive the game toward a central slaughtering point. The animals provided not only meat, leather, and fur, but also antlers, horns, tusks, teeth, and bones that the nomads fashioned into a variety of tools, weapons, and decorations, and various dried organs that were used as medicines. The forest also supplied other goods for trade and daily life, including hunting birds that were taken from their nests in infancy.

The nomads traded the forest products, from family to family, *ger* to *ger*, toward the south, while manufactured products such as metal and textiles slowly moved north from the trading centers south of the Gobi. The Mongols survived on the most northern edge of this world, just at the juncture of the steppe and the northern Siberian forest. They lived as much through hunting in the forest as by herding animals on the steppe, and they exemplified the most extreme characteristics of both groups. They clung to the frayed ends of thin, delicate threads of trade connecting the northern tundra and the steppe with the agricultural fields and workshops of the south. So few goods penetrated the far north that it was said that among the Mongols the man with a pair of iron stirrups ranked as the highest lord.

Some years the hunting was poor, and the people would grow hungry early in the winter, without a supply of forest products to trade. In those years, the Mongols still organized their hunting parties. Only instead of heading north into the forest to hunt animals, they moved out across the steppe to hunt for humans. If the Mongols had nothing to trade, they raided the herders they could find out on the steppe or in isolated valleys. The attackers used the same tactics in approaching human prey as animals, and at first sign of attack, the targeted victims usually fled, leaving behind most of their animals, the material goods of their homes, and whatever else the attackers might want. Since the object of the attack was to secure goods, the attackers usually looted the *gers* and rounded up the animals rather than pursuing the fleeing people. Because the raiders wanted goods, casualties in this type of struggle remained low. Young women were kidnapped as wives and young boys as slaves. Older women and the youngest children were usually exempt from harm, and the men of fighting age usually fled first on the swiftest and sturdiest horses since they stood the greatest chance of being killed and the future livelihood of the entire group depended so heavily on them.

If the escaping men managed to summon allies quickly enough, they set off in pursuit of their attackers in an attempt to track them and recover their goods. If not, the defeated tribesmen rounded up as many of their animals as had managed to elude the captors, and they reorganized their lives as they nourished plans for their counterattack at a more propitious time.

For the Mongols, fighting functioned as more of a cyclical system of raiding than of true warfare or even sustained feuding. Revenge often served as the pretext for a raid, but it rarely acted as the true motivator. Success in battle carried prestige for the victor based on the goods brought back and shared with family and friends; fighting did not revolve around the abstract prestige of honor on the battlefield. Victorious warriors showed pride in their kills and remembered them, but there was no ostentatious collecting of heads or scalps, nor making notches or other emblems to represent the number of men killed in battle. Only the goods mattered, not the kill.

Hunting, trading, herding, and fighting formed a seamless web of subsistence activities in the lives of the early Mongol tribes. From the time that he could ride, every male began to learn the skills for each of these pursuits, and no family could live off only one activity without the others. Raiding followed a geographic pattern originating in the north. The southern tribes that lived closest to the trade cities of the Silk Route always had more goods than the more distant northern tribes. The southern men had the best weapons, and to succeed against them, the northern men had to move quicker, think more cleverly, and fight harder. This alternating pattern of trade and raiding supplied a slow, but steady, trickle of metal and textile goods moving northward, where the weather was always worse, the grazing more sparse, and men more rugged and violent.

Only a few details have survived from Temujin's earliest childhood, and they do not suggest that he was highly valued by his father. His father once accidentally left him behind when they moved to another camp. The Tayichiud clan found him, and their leader, Targutai, the Fat Khan, took him into his own household and kept him for some time. Later in life, when Temujin became powerful, Targutai boasted that he had trained Temujin with the same careful attention and loving discipline that he would train a colt, a herder's most prized possession. The details and sequence are unknown, but eventually the child and his family were reunited, either because the Fat Khan returned the boy to them or because the family joined the camp of the Fat Khan.

The next known episode in Temujin's life occurred when his father took him in search of a wife at the early age of nine by the Mongol count, eight by the Western count. Yesugei and Temujin set out alone on the quest to find Hoelun's family in the east, since, perhaps, Hoelun wanted her son to marry a woman of her own tribe or at least to know her family. More important than Hoelun's preferences, however, Yesugei seemed to have wanted to be rid of him. Perhaps the father sensed the coming struggle that would erupt between his son Temujin and Begter, the slightly older son born to him by Sochigel, his first wife. By taking Temujin far away at this early age, the father probably sought to prevent the full eruption of the rivalry into trouble for his small family.

With only a single extra horse to present to the parents of the prospective bride, Yesugei needed to find a family that would accept Temujin as a laborer for several years, in return for which they would give him their daughter in marriage. For Temujin, this trip probably was his first venture away from his homeland along the Onon River. It was easy to become lost in unfamiliar territory, and the traveler faced the triple dangers of wild animals, harsh weather, and, most of all, other humans. As things turned out, the father did not bother taking Temujin all the way to Hoelun's family. Along the way, they stayed with a family whose daughter, Borte, was only slightly older than Temujin. The children apparently liked each other, and the fathers agreed to betroth them. During his time of apprenticeship, or bride-service, Temujin was expected to live and work under the protective eyes of his in-laws. Gradually, the intended couple would become ever more intimate. Because the girl was normally slightly older than the boy, as was the case with Borte and Temujin, she would initiate him into sexual intimacy at the rate and in the timing that seemed appropriate to the two of them.

On the long ride home alone after leaving Temujin, Yesugei happened upon an encampment where the Tatars were celebrating a feast. The *Secret History* explains that he wanted to join the party, but he knew that he must not reveal his identity as the enemy who had killed their kinsman, Temujin Uge, in battle eight years earlier. Despite his attempted deceit, someone is said to have recognized him and secretly poisoned him. Although quite ill from the poison, Yesugei managed to leave the Tatars and return home to his family's camp, whereupon he immediately sent a man to find and bring back Temujin, who had to leave Borte behind in the rush to his father's deathbed.

By the time the boy arrived back at his family encampment, his father lay dead. Yesugei left behind two wives and seven children under the age of ten. At the time, the family still lived along the Onon River with the Tayichiud clan. For the last three generations the Tayichiud had dominated Yesugei's Borijin clan. Without Yesugei to help them fight and hunt, the Tayichiud decided they had little use for his two widows and their seven young children. In the harsh environment of the Onon River, the clan could not possibly feed nine extra people.

By steppe tradition, one of Yesugei's brothers, who helped to kidnap Hoelun, should have taken her as a wife. Under the Mongol system of marriage, even one of Yesugei's sons by his other wife, Sochigel, would have been an appropriate husband for her if he had been old enough to support the family. Mongol women often married much younger men in their deceased husband's family because it gave the younger man the opportunity to have an experienced wife without having to pay an elaborate set of gifts to her family or to put in the years of hard bride-service. Although still a young woman, probably in her mid-twenties, Hoelun already had too many children for most men to support. As a captive wife far from her homeland, she offered a potential husband neither family wealth nor beneficial family ties.

With her husband dead and no other man willing to take her, Hoelun was now outside the family, and as such no one had any obligation to help her. The message that she was no longer a part of the band came to her, the way Mongols always symbolize relationships, through food. In the spring, when two old crones, the widows of a previous khan, organized the annual ceremonial meal to honor the family's ancestors, they did not inform Hoelun, thereby cutting her off not only from the food itself but from membership in the family. She and her family were therefore left to feed and protect themselves. As the clan prepared to move down the Onon River toward summer grounds, they planned to leave Hoelun and her children behind.

According to the *Secret History,* as the band moved out, deserting the two women and seven children, only a single old man, from a low-ranking family in the band, objected loudly to what they were doing. In an incident that apparently made a deep impression on Temujin, one of the deserting Tayichiud bellowed back to the old man that he had no right to criticize them, turned back, and speared the old man to death. Upon seeing this, Temujin, at this point a boy of no more than ten years, is said to have dashed up to try to help the dying man; unable to do anything, he just sobbed in hurt and anger.

Hoelun, who had shown such clearheadedness during her kidnapping a decade earlier, showed the same determination and strength during this new crisis. She made a violent and defiant last effort to shame the Tayichiud into keeping her family. As the clan deserted their encampment, she grabbed up the horsehair Spirit Banner of her dead husband, mounted her horse, and chased after them. Raising the Spirit Banner over her head and waving it furiously in the air, she circled the fleeing people. For Hoelun to wave the banner of her dead husband was not merely to wave his emblem but to parade his very soul in front of the deserting tribesmen. They indeed felt such shame in the presence of his soul, and fear of possible supernatural retribution from it, that they temporarily returned to the camp. They then awaited nightfall and, one by one, sneaked away, taking with them the family's animals, thereby condemning to a nearly certain winter death both widows and their seven children.

But the family did not die. In a monumental effort, Hoelun saved them—all of them. As related in the *Secret History,* she covered her head, tucked up her skirt, and ran up and down the river searching for food day and night in order to feed her five hungry children. She found small fruits, and used a juniper stick to dig up the roots of the plants growing along the river. To help feed the family, Temujin made wooden arrows tipped with sharpened bones to hunt rats on the steppe, and he bent his mother's sewing needles into fishhooks. As the boys grew older, they hunted larger game. In the words of the Persian chronicler Juvaini, who visited the Mongols fifty years later and wrote one of the first foreign accounts of the life of Temujin, the family wore clothing "of the skins of dogs and mice, and their food was the flesh of those animals and other dead things." Whether precisely accurate or not, the description shows the desperate, isolated struggle of these social outcasts on the verge of starvation, living almost as much like animals as like the other tribes around them. In the land of harsh lives, they had fallen to the lowest level of steppe life.

How could an outcast child rise from such a lowly station to become the Mongols' Great Khan? Searching through the account of Temujin's coming of age in the *Secret History,* we find crucial clues about the powerful role these early traumatic events must have played in shaping his character, and, in turn, his rise to power. The tragedies his family endured seemed to have instilled in him a profound determination to defy the strict caste structure of the steppes, to take charge of his fate, and to rely on alliances with trusted associates, rather than his family or tribe, as his primary base of support.

The first of these powerful associations was with a slightly older boy named Jamuka, whose family camped repeatedly nearby Temujin's on the banks of the Onon River and as a member of the Jadaran clan was distantly related to the clan of Temujin's father. In the ideals of Mongol culture, kinship reigned above all other social principles. Anyone outside the kinship network was automatically an enemy, and the closer the kin, the closer the tie should be. Temujin and Jamuka were distant relatives, but they wished to be closer, to become brothers. Twice in their childhood, Temujin and Jamuka swore an oath of eternal brotherhood, becoming blood brothers according to Mongol tradition. The story of this fated friendship, and the pivotal events of his life in this early period, reveal many telling details about Temujin's extraordinary ability to rise above adversity and marshal the resources he needed to ultimately tame the unbridled violence of tribe against tribe that ruled the steppe.

Temujin and Jamuka formed a close friendship as they hunted, fished, and played the games the children were taught to improve their everyday skills. Mongol children, both boys and girls, grew up on horses. From infancy, they learned to ride with their parents or older siblings until, after only a few years, they managed to hold on by themselves and ride alone. Usually by age four, children had mastered riding bareback, and eventually how to stand on a horse's back. While standing on the horse, they often jousted with one another to see who could knock the other off. When their legs grew long enough to reach the stirrups, they were also taught to shoot arrows and to lasso on horseback. Making targets out of leather pouches that they would dangle from poles so that they would blow in the wind, the youngsters practiced hitting the targets from horseback at varying distances and speeds. The skills of such play proved invaluable to horsemanship later in life.

Other games included playing knucklebones, a type of dice made from the anklebones of a sheep. Every boy carried a set of four such knucklebones with him, and they could be used to forecast the future, to settle disagreements, or simply as a fun game. In addition, Jamuka and Temujin also played a more vigorous game on the frozen river that was somewhat like curling. Although the *Secret History* does not mention their use of skates, a European visitor in the next century wrote that hunters in the area frequently tied bones onto their feet to be able to race across frozen lakes and rivers both for sport and in pursuit of animals.

These skills later gave the Mongols a great advantage because, unlike almost every other army, the Mongols easily rode and even fought on frozen rivers and lakes. The frozen rivers that Europeans relied upon as their protection from invasion, such as the Volga and the Danube, became highways for the Mongols, allowing them to ride their horses right up to city walls during the season that found the Europeans least prepared for fighting.

Most of Temujin's youth was consumed by the work of helping his family survive. The games Temujin and Jamuka played on the Onon River are the only known frivolities mentioned in any source on the life of the boy who became the great conqueror. The first time that Temujin and Jamuka swore loyalty to one another was when Temujin was about eleven years old. The boys exchanged toys as a symbol of this oath. Jamuka gave Temujin a knucklebone from a roebuck, and Temujin gave Jamuka one inlaid with a small piece of brass, a rare treasure that must have traveled a long distance. The next year they exchanged the adult gift of arrowheads. Jamuka took two pieces of a calf's horn and, by drilling a hole through them, made a whistling arrowhead for Temujin, who, in turn, gave Jamuka an elegant arrowhead crafted from cypress. Like hunters had done for generations, Temujin learned early how to use the whistling arrow to communicate secretly through sounds that other people ignored or simply could not decipher.

As part of the second oath-swearing ceremony, boys often swallowed a small amount of each other's blood, thereby exchanging a part of their soul. In the case of Jamuka and Temujin, the *Secret History* quotes Jamuka as saying that the two of them spoke to each other words that could not be forgotten and together they ate the unnamed "food that could not be digested." With this oath, two boys became *andas*, a bond that was supposed to be stronger even than that between biological brothers because *andas* freely chose their tie. Jamuka was the only *anda* Temujin had in his life.

Jamuka's clan did not return the following winter, and the coming years separated the boys. This bond forged in childhood, however, would later become a major asset and a major obstacle in Temujin's rise to power.

In contrast with the early intimacy shared with Jamuka, at home Temujin chafed under the sometimes bullying authority of his older half brother Begter, and the sibling rivalry grew more intense as the two approached adolescence. A strict hierarchy normally ruled the family life of Mongol herders then, as it does now. In the face of so many daily dangers from both predators and weather, Mongols developed a system in which children had to obey their parents unquestioningly. In the absence of a father, whether for a few hours or for months, the eldest son assumed that role. The elder brother had the right to control their every action, to assign them any task, and to take from them or give them whatever he pleased. He exercised complete power over them.

Begter was slightly older than Temujin, and gradually after the father was killed, he began to exercise the power prerogatives of the eldest male. In an account known only from the *Secret History,* Temujin's resentment erupted in an episode that initially appears quite trivial. Begter, it seems, seized a lark that Temujin had shot. Begter may have taken it for no other reason than to enforce his claim as the head of the family; if so, he would have done well not to have lorded his power over Temujin. Soon thereafter, Temujin and his full brother Khasar, who was next to him in age, sat together with their two half brothers Begter and Belgutei fishing in the Onon River. Temujin caught a small fish, but the half brothers snatched it from him. Angered and frustrated, Temujin and Khasar ran to their mother, Hoelun, to tell her what had happened. Instead of taking the side of her own sons, however, she sided with Begter, telling them they should be worrying about their enemies, the Tayichiud, who had abandoned them, and not fighting with their older brother.

Hoelun's siding with Begter portended a future that Temujin could not abide. As the eldest son, Begter not only could command the actions of his younger siblings, but he had wide prerogatives, including rights of sexual access, to any widow of his father, aside from his own mother. As a widow not taken in marriage by one of her late husband's brothers, Hoelun's most likely partner would be Begter, since he was her husband's son by another wife.

At this moment of tremendous family tension and potential disruption, Hoelun angrily reminded her own sons of the story of Alan the Beautiful, the founding ancestress of the Mongols, who bore several more sons after her husband died and left her living with an adopted son. The implication of the story seemed clear; Hoelun would accept Begter as her husband when he became old enough, thereby making him the head of the family in every sense. Temujin, however, decided not to tolerate such a situation with Begter. After the emotional confrontation with his mother over Begter, Temujin threw aside the felt covering over the doorway, a highly offensive gesture in Mongol culture, and angrily rushed off, followed by his younger brother Khasar.

The two brothers found Begter sitting silently on a small knoll overlooking the steppe, and approached him cautiously through the grass. Temujin instructed Khasar, who was the best shot in the family, to circle toward the front of the knoll while he himself climbed up the back side. They crept up on Begter quietly, as if stalking a resting deer or grazing gazelle. When they came within easy striking distance, each silently placed an arrow in his bow, and then suddenly rose out of the grass with bows drawn. Begter did not run, or even attempt to defend himself; he would not deign to show fear in front of his younger brothers. Admonishing them, in the same words as their mother had, that their real enemy was the Tayichiud clan, he is reported to have said, "I am not the lash in your eye, the impediment in your mouth. Without me you have no companion but your own shadow." He sat cross-legged and still as his two younger brothers continued to approach him. Knowing clearly what fate lay ahead, Begter still refused to fight. Instead, he made one final request of them, that they spare the life of his younger full brother, Belgutei.

Maintaining their distance from him, Temujin and Khasar shot their arrows straight into Begter, Temujin striking him in the back, while Khasar hit him from the front. Rather than approach him and risk contamination from his blood, which was flowing onto the earth, they turned and abandoned him to die alone. The author of the *Secret History* does not state whether he died quickly or bled to death in a long, lingering end. According to Mongol tradition, mere mention of blood or death violates a taboo, but this killing was deemed of such importance to Temujin's life that it was recorded in detail.

When Temujin and Khasar returned home, Hoelun is said to have read immediately in their faces what they had done and screamed out at Temujin: "Destroyer! Destroyer! You came from my hot womb clutching a clot of blood in your hand." She turned to admonish Khasar: "And you like a wild dog gnawing its own afterbirth." Her screaming rage at Temujin is vented in one of the longest monologues in the *Secret History,* during which, in repeated insults, she compares her sons to animals—"like an attacking panther, like a lion without control, like a monster swallowing its prey alive." At the end, exhausted, she repeated Begter's earlier warning as though it were a curse: "Now, you have no companion other than your shadow."

Already, at this young age, Temujin played the game of life, not merely for honor or prestige, but to win. He stalked his brother as if he were hunting an animal, just as he would later prove to have a genius for converting hunting skills into war tactics. By putting Khasar, who was the better shot, in front while he himself took the rear, he also showed his tactical acumen. Like the horse that must be first in every race, Temujin had determined he would lead, not follow. In order to achieve this primacy of place, he proved himself willing to violate custom, defy his mother, and kill whoever blocked his path, even if it was his own family member.

While the killing of Begter freed Temujin from the grip of his half brother's dominance, he had committed a taboo act that put his family in still greater jeopardy. They would have to immediately flee the area, and did so. According to Mongol tradition, they left Begter's body to rot in the open, and avoided returning to that spot for as long as any trace of him might remain. Just as both Begter and Hoelun had admonished, Temujin now found himself with no protector or ally, and he would soon be hunted. He was head of a household, but he was also in danger as a renegade.

Until this time Hoelun's family had been a band of outcasts, but not criminals. The killing changed all that and gave anyone who wanted it an excuse to hunt them down. The Tayichiud considered themselves the aristocratic lineage of the Onon River and sent a party of warriors to punish Temujin for the killing in their territory and to forestall what he might do next. With no place to hide on the open steppe, Temujin fled toward the safety of the mountains, but his pursuers still captured him. The Tayichiud took him back to their main camp where, in an effort to break his will, they strapped him into a cangue, a device something like an ox yoke, which permitted him to walk but immobilized his hands and prevented him from feeding himself or even getting a drink of water unaided. Each day a different family assumed responsibility for guarding and caring for him.

The Tayichiud band had several households of subordinate lineages, as well as war captives, living with them as their servants, and it was to these servant families that Temujin was turned over as a prisoner. Unlike the Tayichiud, who treated him with disdain, he found sympathy and comfort among these families when they took him into their *gers* at night. Protected from the view of the Tayichiud leaders, they not only shared food with him, but in one episode highlighted in the *Secret History,* an old woman gently tended the raw wounds cut into his neck by the cangue. The children of the family also persuaded their father to violate his orders by removing the cangue at night, to let Temujin rest more peacefully.

The story of Temujin's escape from this impossible situation is further testament to his character, which would shape his rise to power. One day while the Tayichiud men got drunk and Temujin had been assigned to the care of a simpleminded and physically weak boy, the captive suddenly swung the cangue around violently, struck the boy's head with it, and knocked him out. Rather than face almost certain death by fleeing on foot across the steppe wearing the cangue, he hid in a clump of weeds in a nearby river. Shortly after a search began, he was quickly spotted by the father of the family that had treated him kindly. Rather than sounding an alarm, the old man told him to flee when darkness fell. After dark, Temujin left the river, but did not flee. He slowly made his way to the old man's *ger* and entered it, much to the horror, and danger, of the family. But despite the great risk to their own lives, the reluctant hosts removed the cangue and burned it. They hid Temujin in a pile of wool during the next day when the Tayichiud resumed their hunt for him. That night, they sent him on his way, and despite their poverty, cooked a lamb for him and gave him a horse with which he managed to elude his trackers for the long flight back to his mother's distant and isolated camp.

For a poor family to risk their lives to help him and to give him such valuable resources, Temujin must have had some special attraction or ability. Meanwhile, this humble family impressed him as well. The Tayichiud, with whom he shared a close kinship tie, had once put his family out to die and now appeared eager to kill him. This other family, which had no kinship tie to him, proved willing to risk their lives to help him. This episode seems to have instilled in him not only a distrust of higher-ranking people, but also the conviction that some people, even those outside his clan, could indeed be trusted as if they were family. In later life, he would judge others primarily by their actions toward him and not according to their kinship bonds, a revolutionary concept in steppe society.

Mongol traditions and sources acknowledge only this one brief period of capture and enslavement of Temujin, but a contemporary Chinese chronicler wrote that Temujin endured more than ten years in slavery. He may have been repeatedly enslaved, or this episode may have lasted much longer than the *Secret History* suggests. Some scholars suspect that such a long period of enslavement accounts for the glaring absence of detailed information on his childhood. In later years, the time of enslavement would have been an episode of shame for Genghis Khan, but even more importantly would have been a tremendous danger to the descendants of the families that had enslaved him. Virtually everyone associated with the slavery episode had good reason to keep silent about that connection, and to make it seem briefer would be in keeping with Mongol sensibilities that would dictate only barely mentioning the bad while emphasizing instead the heroic nature of the escape.

In 1178, Temujin turned sixteen. He had not seen his intended wife, Borte, since his father's death seven years earlier, but he felt confident enough in the matter to go out to find her again. Accompanied by his surviving half brother, Belgutei, he set off down the Kherlen River in search of her family. When they found the *ger* belonging to Borte's father, Dei-sechen, Temujin was pleased to discover that Borte still waited for him, even though at age seventeen or eighteen she was now nearly past the age of marriage. Dei-sechen knew of Temujin's troubles with the Tayichiud clan, but was nevertheless still amenable to the match.

Temujin and Belgutei set off toward home with Borte. By custom, a new bride brought a gift of clothing to her husband's parents when she came to live with them. For nomads, large gifts are impractical, but high-quality clothing carries high prestige and also serves a valuable practical function. Borte brought a coat of the most prized fur on the steppe, black sable. Under normal circumstances, Temujin would have presented such a gift to his father, but in the absence of a father, he perceived a greater value to which he could put the coat. He decided to use the sable coat to revive an old friendship of his father's, and thereby make an alliance that might offer him and his now growing family some security.

The man was Torghil, more commonly known later as Ong Khan, of the Kereyid tribe that lived on some of the most luxuriant steppes in central

Mongolia between the Orkhon River and the Black Forest of larch trees along the Tuul River. Unlike the scattered lineages and clans of the Mongols, the Kereyid constituted a powerful tribal confederacy that embraced a large group of tribes united under a single khan. The great expanse of the steppe north of the Gobi fell, at this time, under the rule of three major tribes. The center was controlled by Ong Khan and his Kereyid tribe, the west was dominated by the Naiman tribe under their ruler Tayang Khan, and the Tatars occupied the area to the east as vassals of the Jurched of North China under their ruler Altan Khan. The rulers of the three large tribes made and broke alliances and waged wars with the smaller tribes along their borders in a perpetual effort to enlist them in campaigns against their more important enemies. Thus, Temujin's father, Yesugei, had no kinship tie with the Kereyid, but he had once been the *anda* of Ong Khan, and they had fought together against many enemies. The tie between the men had been stronger than merely patron and vassal because when they were quite young, Yesugei helped Ong Khan become khan of the Kereyid people by overthrowing his uncle, the Gur-khan, or supreme ruler. In addition, they had fought together against the Merkid and were allied at the time of Temujin's birth, when Yesugei was on the campaign against the Tatars.

According to steppe culture, politics were conducted through the idiom of male kinship. To be allies, men had to belong to the same family, and therefore every alliance between men not connected through biology had to be transformed into ceremonial or fictive kinship. Thus, with Temujin's father and the would-be Kereyid leader having been ceremonial brothers as *andas,* Temujin now sought to be treated as a son to the old man. By giving Ong Khan the wedding gift, Temujin was recognizing him as his father; and if Ong Khan accepted, he would be recognizing Temujin as his son and therefore entitled to protection. For most steppe men, such forms of ceremonial kinship stood as adjuncts to their real kin relations, but for Temujin, such chosen forms of fictive kinship were already proving more useful than the ties of biological kinship.

The Kereyid, and the Naiman to the west, represented not just larger political units but more developed cultures tied, ever so tentatively, into the commercial and religious networks of central Asia via their conversion to Christianity several centuries earlier by missionaries of the Assyrian Church of the East. Without churches or monasteries among the nomads, the tribal branch of Christianity claimed descent from the Apostle Thomas and relied on wandering monks. They practiced their religion in sanctuaries located in *gers,* and de-emphasized theology and rigidity of belief in favor of a varied reading of the Scriptures combined with general medical care. Jesus exercised a strong fascination for the nomads because he healed the sick and survived death. As the only human to triumph over death, Jesus was considered an important and powerful shaman, and the cross was sacred as the symbol of the four directions of the world. As a pastoral people, the steppe tribes felt very comfortable with the pastoral customs and beliefs of the ancient Hebrew tribes as illustrated in the Bible. Perhaps above all, the Christians ate meat, unlike the vegetarian Buddhists; and in contrast to the abstemious Muslims, the Christians not only enjoyed drinking alcohol, they even prescribed it as a mandatory part of their worship service.

After leaving his bride, Borte, with his mother in their *ger,* Temujin set out with his brother Khasar and half brother Belgutei to take the coat to the Christian Ong Khan, who eagerly accepted the gift, thereby signifying that he acknowledged each of them as a sort of stepson. The khan offered to make Temujin a local leader over other young warriors, but in a telling display of his lack of interest in the traditional system, Temujin declined. Instead, he seemed only to want the khan's protection for his family, and with that assured, he and his brothers returned to their encampment on the Kherlen River. There, the young groom sought to enjoy his hard-earned time with his bride and family.

The many troubles of Temujin's early years must have seemed behind him and his family now that everyone was old enough to work in some way. In addition to his brothers, Temujin's household expanded to include two other young men. Boorchu had joined the group after a chance encounter while Temujin was tracking some stolen horses; Jelme was apparently given to Temujin by his father, although the *Secret History* does not explain why. With these two additions, the camp consisted of seven teenage boys to hunt and protect the group. In addition to his bride, Borte, Temujin's household also included his sister and three older women: his mother, Hoelun, who was matriarch, as well as Sochigel, the mother of Temujin's half brother Belgutei, and yet another old woman of unknown origin who stayed with them.

According to the account of the *Secret History,* Temujin would have preferred to remain simply the ruler of this intimate clan, but the roiling world of tribal attack and counterattack all around them would not allow so idyllic a life. For generations stretching back through hundreds of years, the tribes of the steppes had been preying on one another mercilessly. The memory of past transgressions lingered. An injury inflicted on any family within a tribe served as a license for retribution, and it could serve as a pretext for a raid even after many years. No matter how isolated they might attempt to be, no group such as Temujin's could go unaccounted for, or untouched, in this world of continual turmoil.

After all his family had already suffered, now, after eighteen years, the tribe from which Temujin's mother had been abducted, the Merkid, decided to seek their vengeance for that slight. The Merkid came not to reclaim Hoelun, the widow who had grown old struggling to raise her five children, but after Borte, Temujin's young bride, who would serve to repay the kidnapping of Hoelun from them. The alliance he had so shrewdly made with Ong Khan was to prove decisive in Temujin's response to this crisis, and the challenges of the Merkid would prove the decisive contest that would set him on his path to greatness.

2

———❧———

Tale of Three Rivers

The banner of Chingiz-Khan's fortune
was raised and they issued forth.
ATA-MALIK JUVAINI,
Genghis Khan: The History of the
World Conqueror

EARLY ONE MORNING AS the family slept in their *ger*, which stood alone on an isolated steppe in the upper reaches of the Kherlen River, a raiding party of Merkids raced toward them. The old woman the family had taken in lay with her head on the ground, but as old women often do, she passed much of the predawn hours drifting in and out of a fitful sleep. As the horses drew nearer, she sensed the vibrations of their hooves on the ground. Suddenly snapping out of her sleep, she shouted with alarm to rouse the others. The seven boys sprang up, scrambled frantically to put on their boots, and raced out to their horses, hobbled nearby. Temujin fled with his six companions and his mother and sister, leaving behind his new bride, his stepmother, Sochigel, and the old woman who had saved them all. In the desperate tribal world where daily life skirted so close to potential tragedy and annihilation, no one had the luxury of artificially chivalrous codes of behavior. In the quick decision of their utilitarian calculus, leaving these three women as booty would at least slow the raiders enough so that the others might have time to escape. For Temujin's fleeing band, the open steppe offered no refuge; they would have to ride hard to reach safety in the mountains to the north.

By the time the attackers reached the *ger*, Temujin and his small group had raced off into the early morning darkness, but they quickly found Borte hiding in an oxcart that the old woman was leading away. For several desperate days while the Merkid prowled the vicinity, Temujin stayed constantly on the move, hiding along the slopes and wooded crevices of Mount Burkhan Khaldun. Finally, the Merkid abandoned their roaming, and headed off northwest, toward their home on the distant Selenge River, a tributary of Siberia's Lake Baikal. Fearing that the withdrawal might have been a trap to lure him out of hiding, Temujin sent Belgutei and their two friends, Boorchu and Jelme, to track the kidnappers for three days to make sure that they did not double back to surprise him.

Hiding in the forest of Mount Burkhan Khaldun, Temujin faced the pivotal decision of his life: deciding what to do about the kidnapping of his wife. He could have chosen to abandon any hope of recapturing Borte, and that would surely have been the expected course, as his small group could not possibly take on the much more powerful Merkid. In due time, Temujin could find another wife, but he would have to kidnap her, as his father had done to his mother, because no family would voluntarily bestow their daughter on a man who had already lost one wife to more powerful men.

In the past, Temujin had relied upon his quick wits to fight or flee, but the decisions had been spontaneous ones in response to a sudden danger or opportunity. Now he had to think carefully and devise a plan of action that would influence the whole of his life. He had to choose his own destiny. In the belief that he had just been saved by the mountain where he was hiding, he turned in prayer to the spirit of the mountain. Unlike the other steppe tribes that had embraced the scriptural and priestly traditions of Buddhism, Islam, or Christianity, the Mongols remained animists, praying to the spirits around them. They worshiped the Eternal Blue Sky, the Golden Light of the Sun, and the myriad spiritual forces of nature. The Mongols divided the natural world into two parts, the earth and the sky. Just as the human soul was contained not in the stationary parts of the body but in the moving essences of blood, breath, and aroma, so, too, the soul of the earth was contained in its moving water. The rivers flowed through the earth like the blood through the body, and three of those rivers began here on this mountain. As the tallest mountain, Burkhan Khaldun, literally "God Mountain," was the khan of the area, and it was the earthly place closest to the Eternal Blue Sky. And as the source of three rivers, Burkhan Khaldun was also the sacred heart of the Mongol world.

The *Secret History* relates that Temujin, grateful for having escaped death at the hands of the Merkid, first offered a prayer of thanks to the mountain that protected him and to the sun that rode across the sky. He made special thanks to the captured old woman who had saved the others by hearing like a weasel. To thank the spirits around him, as was Mongol practice, he sprinkled milk into the air and on the ground. Unwinding his belt from his robe, he hung it around his neck. The sash or belt, traditionally worn only by men, was the center of a Mongol man's identity. For Temujin to remove his sash in this way was to remove his strength and to appear powerless before the gods around him. He then removed his hat, put his hand on his breast, and dropped down onto the ground nine times to kowtow before the sun and before the sacred mountain.

For the steppe tribes, political, worldly power was inseparable from supernatural power since both sprang from the same source, the Eternal Blue Sky. In order to find success and to triumph over others, one must first be granted supernatural power from the spirit world. For his Spirit Banner to lead to victory and power, it had to first be infused with supernatural power. Temujin's three days of prayer while hiding on Burkhan Khaldun marked the beginning of a long and intimate spiritual relationship he would maintain with this mountain and the special protection he believed it provided. This mountain would be the source of his strength.

Rather than merely giving him the power, Burkhan Khaldun seems to first test him with a difficult choice. Each of the three rivers that flowed out from the mountain offered him an alternate choice of action. He could return to the southeast, downstream to the Kherlen River, where he had been living on the steppe, but no matter how many animals or wives he managed to accumulate as a herder, he would always risk losing them in another raid to the Merkid, the Tayichiud, or whoever else came along. The Onon River, along which he himself had been born, flowed to the northeast and offered another option. Because it meandered through more wooded and isolated land than the Kherlen River, the Onon offered more shelter, but it lacked pastures for the animals. Living there would require the group to scrape by, as in his childhood, while fishing, trapping birds, and hunting rats and other small mammals. Life on the Onon would be safe but without prosperity or honor. The third option was to follow the Tuul River, which flowed toward the southwest, to seek the help of Ong Khan, to whom he had given the sable coat. At that time, Temujin had declined the offer to make him a subordinate leader under Ong Khan's authority. Now, only a year later, with the life he had chosen instead shattered by the Merkid raiders, Temujin still seemed reluctant to plunge into the internecine struggle of khan against khan, but there seemed no other way to get back his bride.

Though he had sought to create a quiet life apart from the constant turmoil of steppe warfare, the Merkid raid had taught him that such a life was simply not to be had. If he did not want to live the life of an impoverished outcast, always at the mercy of whatever raiders chose to swoop down on his encampment, he would now have to fight for his place in the hierarchy of steppe warriors; he would have to join in the harsh game of constant warfare he had thus far avoided.

Aside from all the issues of politics, hierarchy, and spiritual power, Temujin showed how desperately he missed Borte, the one person in a short and tragedy-laden life who brought him happiness. Despite the emotional reserve that Mongol men were expected to show in public, particularly in the presence of other men, Temujin made a strong emotional affirmation of his love for Borte and of his pain without her. He lamented that not only had the attackers left his bed empty, but they had cut open his chest, broken his heart.

Temujin chose to fight. He would find his wife, or he would die trying. After those three difficult days of pondering, praying, and planning on the mountain, Temujin followed the Tuul River down to search for the camp of Ong Khan and seek his help. But he would do so not as a lonely outcast; he would do so as the rightful son who had already brought the powerful Ong Khan a prize sable coat and allegiance.

When Temujin found Ong Khan and explained that he wanted to launch a raid on the Merkid, the old khan immediately agreed to help. Had he not wanted to fight, Ong Khan could easily have deferred and instead offered Temujin another wife from the women in his own encampment. The old khan, however, had a lingering feud of his own with the Merkid, and Temujin's request offered him a pretext to attack and loot them once again.

Ong Khan also sent Temujin to seek additional support from a rising young Mongol ally of the khans, one who had been proving himself an adept warrior and had attracted a sizable following. This man was none other than Temujin's sworn *anda*, Jamuka of the Jadaran clan. Jamuka readily agreed to the summons from his khan to help his young blood brother fight against the Merkid. Together they would form the steppe ideal of a good army, with Ong Khan leading the Right (west) Wing, and Jamuka leading the Left (east) Wing. The armies of Ong Khan and Jamuka gathered with Temujin's small band at the source of the Onon River near Burkhan Khaldun, from whence they would cross the mountains and drop down on the steppes into Merkid territory along the Selenge River, in the direction of Lake Baikal.

Temujin had survived many difficult scrapes in his short life, without engaging in an actual raid. In this raid, he would prove himself up to the task, though the raid was really more of a rout. Some Merkid on a night hunt in the mountains saw the attacking army and rushed word back to alarm their people, arriving only a little ahead of the invading horsemen. The Merkid began fleeing for safety downstream, and panic overtook the whole string of encampments. As the raiders began their looting of the Merkid's *gers*, Temujin is said to have raced from camp to camp among those left behind crying out Borte's name, but Borte, who had been given as a wife to an older Merkid warrior, was loaded into a cart and sent away from the battle. She did not know who was attacking her new home and did not want to be kidnapped again; she had no reason to suspect that the attack was launched to rescue her.

The *Secret History* describes in detail how suddenly, from amid the confusion and turmoil around her, Borte heard a voice crying out her name and recognized it as Temujin's. Jumping from the cart, she raced through the darkness toward the voice. Temujin twisted frantically in his saddle as he peered out at the night and shouted her name again and again. He became so distraught that he did not know her as she ran toward him, and when she grabbed the reins of his horse and snatched them from this hand, he almost attacked her before he recognized her, whereupon they "threw themselves upon each other" in an emotional embrace.

Although the other two women were not rescued, Temujin had won his wife back again, and nothing else mattered now. He had inflicted upon the Merkid the same pain that they had caused him, and he was ready to return home. The *Secret History* reports that he said to the attacking troops, "We have made their breasts to become empty. . . . And we have made their beds to become empty. . . . And we have made an end of the men and their descendants. . . . And we have ravished those who remained. . . . The Merkid people being so dispersed, let us withdraw ourselves."

After the decisive victory over the Merkid and Borte's emotional reunion with Temujin, the newly reunited couple, still well under twenty years of age, might have hoped to live joyously together, at least for awhile. But as happens in life, the solution to one problem can create another. Temujin found that Borte was pregnant. Rather than describing the tremendous happiness for the couple at being together again, the *Secret History* falls silent about Borte and their life together for the duration of her pregnancy. This silence would reverberate through Mongol politics for the next century in a long debate over who had fathered Borte's eldest child. Borte gave birth to her first son in 1179, and Temujin named the boy Jochi, which means "visitor" or "guest." Many scholars accept that as evidence that Temujin did not believe the child was his own, but he may just as easily have given that name to signify that they were all the guests of Jamuka's band at the time of the baby's birth.

The relationship that the *Secret History* dwells on in detail at this time is Temujin's renewed allegiance with Jamuka. After the dramatic rescue of Borte, Temujin decided to join his small camp with Jamuka's larger group of followers. Temujin led his small band to Jamuka's encampment in the large fertile area known as the Khorkhonag Valley, located between Temujin's ancestral Onon River and the Kherlen River.

For the third time in their young lives, Temujin and Jamuka made their vows of sworn brotherhood. This time they swore their friendship as two grown men in a public ceremony with their followers as witnesses. Standing before a tree at the edge of a cliff, they exchanged golden sashes and strong horses. By exchanging clothing, each shared his body smell and, therefore, the essence of his soul with the other; the sash, in particular, embodied the symbol of their manhood. They swore a public oath to "let us love one another" and make two lives into one, never to forsake each other. Celebrating their pledges with a feast, including much drinking, Temujin and Jamuka publicly symbolized their brotherhood by sleeping apart from the others under a single blanket, just as true brothers grow up sharing a single blanket.

By moving his small group away from the protection of the mountains and out onto the steppe with Jamuka, Temujin was trading the life of a hunter for that of a herder. Although he loved hunting throughout his life, Temujin's family never again depended exclusively on it for their subsistence, enjoying a higher standard of living with a more consistent supply of meat and dairy products as part of Jamuka's group. Temujin had much to learn from Jamuka's people about the herding way of life, in which well-established customs governed all aspects of the yearly routine, and rightly specialized knowledge of the animals revolved around the management of cows, yaks, horses, goats, sheep, and camels, which the Mongols called the Five Snouts, since they counted yaks and cows together. Every animal provided crucial subsistence materials in addition to food, with the horse being the aristocrat of them, not being used for work other than riding.

Of course, given the constant feuding among the clans, in joining with Jamuka, Temujin was also electing to assume the life of a steppe warrior, a role at which he would come to excel. Their *anda* relationship allowed Temujin a special status within the larger hierarchy, so that he did not join as a regular follower, and for a year and a half, so the *Secret History* says, Temujin seemed content to follow Jamuka's lead and learn from him. But perhaps for the young man who had killed his older half brother rather than submit to his dominance, any such arrangement would inevitably become irritating, and in this case, old steppe customs of caste hierarchy also came into play.

Under the kinship hierarchy, each lineage was known as a bone. The closest lineages, those with whom no intermarriage was allowed, were known as white bones. More distant kin with whom intermarriage was allowed were the black-boned lineages. Since they were all interrelated, each lineage claimed descent from someone of importance, but the strength of the claim depended on their ability to enforce it. Temujin and Jamuka were distant cousins, but of different bones, because they traced their ancestry back to a single woman but to two different husbands. Jamuka descended from her first husband, who was a steppe herder. Temujin descended from the forest hunter known in their oral history as Bodonchar the Fool, who had kidnapped the woman after killing her husband. According to this descent,

Jamuka could claim that because he descended from the firstborn son and had been fathered by a steppe man, his lineage was higher. Such stories are used in steppe society to emphasize bonds when needed, but they may also provide the pretext for animosity, and in the relationship between Temujin and Jamuka, the story of their kinship would play both ways. Kinship was not so much the determinant of relationships as it was a general idiom through which people made, negotiated, and enforced their social claims.

As long as Temujin was a part of Jamuka's band, then Jamuka's family ranked as a white bone, and Temujin was a part of the distant, black-boned kin. Only if he established his own band with himself and his lineage at the center could he be considered white-boned. As the months passed with Temujin following Jamuka's leadership, the account in the *Secret History* suggests that Jamuka began to treat Temujin less like an *anda* and more like a younger brother, also emphasizing that Jamuka's clan descended from the eldest son of their common ancestor. As already evidenced in his family relations, Temujin was not one to accept being treated as an inferior for long, and soon enough this situation proved unacceptable to him.

The *Secret History* recounts that in the middle of May in the year 1181, Jamuka called for the breaking of winter camp and headed toward more distant summer pastures. Jamuka and Temujin rode together, as usual, at the front of the long train of their followers and animals. But that day Jamuka decided that he was no longer willing to share his leadership position with Temujin. Perhaps Jamuka realized that Temujin had proven very popular with the other members of the band, or perhaps Jamuka had simply grown tired of his presence. Jamuka told Temujin that he himself should take the horses and camp closer to the mountains, while Temujin should take the less prestigious sheep and goats and set up another camp closer to the river. The white-boned Jamuka seemed to be asserting his authority as the horse herder and was treating Temujin as the black-boned shepherd boy.

According to the *Secret History,* when Temujin received the order, he dropped back where his own family and animals were traveling in the rear of the train, and consulted with Hoelun. He seemed confused and unsure how to respond. Upon overhearing Temujin describe the situation to his mother, however, Borte interrupted and insisted angrily that her husband break with Jamuka and that they and whoever wished to follow them set out on their own. Later in the day, when Jamuka stopped to pitch camp and rest for the night, Temujin and his small entourage fled in secret and continued moving throughout the night in order to put as much distance as possible between them and Jamuka in case he decided to pursue them. Either by plan or spontaneous choice, many of Jamuka's followers fled with Temujin, taking, of course, their animals. Despite this fission of the band, Jamuka did not pursue them.

The rift between the two young men on that early summer night in 1181 evolved into two decades of warfare as Temujin and Jamuka both rose in stature as leading Mongol warriors and hardened into the bitterest of enemies. After his split with Jamuka, at the age of nineteen, Temujin seems to have determined to become a warrior leader of his own, to attract his own followers and build a base of power, eventually aiming to become a khan, the leader and unifier of the unruly Mongol tribe. In that pursuit, his chief rival would be Jamuka, and their feud would gradually engulf all of the Mongols in a civil war. The two rivals spent the next quarter of a century stealing animals and women from each other, raiding and killing each other's followers, and struggling to see which one would eventually rule all the Mongols.

Over the coming years, Jamuka and Temujin each acquired a following of families and clans among the Mongol people in a constantly shifting set of ephemeral alliances and pragmatic loyalties; yet neither proved able to unite all the lineages into a single tribe like the more powerful Kereyid, Tatars, and Naiman. According to Mongol oral history, they had once before been united under a single khan; but in recent generations, no one had been able to reunite them. In the summer of 1189, the Year of the Cock, and eight years after his break from Jamuka, twenty-seven-year-old Temujin decided to make a play for the title of khan, the chief of the Mongols, with the hope that once he claimed the title, he would attract more of Jamuka's followers and make the claim into a self-fulfilling prophecy. If not, the claim might, at least, provoke a final struggle between the two and lead to a more definitive solution to the rival claims.

He summoned his followers to a steppe beside the Blue Lake at the foot of the Heart-Shaped Mountain where they held the traditional council called a *khuriltai*. Families, lineages, and clans voted merely by showing up. Their presence served as an official endorsement of Temujin as khan; not appearing counted as voting against him. Merely attracting a quorum constituted a victory. On such an occasion, a list would usually be made and memorized as a form of election verification, but no tally survives, possibly indicating a modest turnout. A large number of the steppe lineages, perhaps even a majority, still supported Jamuka.

Temujin's tribe, which now consisted of his family, a loyal coterie of friends, and scattered families, was small by comparison to the other steppe tribes, and he was still a vassal to Ong Khan. To show that his new office was not meant as a challenge to Ong Khan, Temujin sent an envoy to the Kereyid leader to reassert his loyalty and to ask his blessing. Temujin's envoy explained carefully that all he sought was to unite the scattered Mongol clans under the leadership of Ong Khan and his Kereyid tribe. Ong Khan agreed and seemed to worry little about the unification of the Mongols so long as they remained loyal. Ong Khan kept the subservient Mongols divided. By encouraging the ambitions of both young men, Ong Khan was playing the two leaders against each other in order to keep both weak and under his control as the khan of the Kereyid.

Having received the support he deemed sufficient to function as the khan of a minor group, Temujin began a radical process of erecting a novel power structure within his tribe, calling on the lessons of his youth for guidance. A chief's complex of *gers* that served as his tribal center or his chiefly court was called an *ordu*, or *horde*. In most steppe tribes, the khan's *ordu* consisted of his relatives and served as a sort of aristocracy over the tribe, managing it and leading it. Temujin, however, assigned some dozen responsibilities to various followers according to the ability and loyalty of the individual without regard to kinship. He gave the highest positions as his personal assistants to his first two followers, Boorchu and Jelme, who had shown persistent loyalty to him for more than a decade. Temujin Khan exercised a decisive ability to assess a man's talents and assign him to precisely the right task based on his ability rather than his genealogy.

The first appointments went to trusted men to serve as cooks, a job that consisted largely of slaughtering animals, butchering meat, and moving large cauldrons for boiling it, but which Temujin also considered his first line of defense because of a fear he had developed of being poisoned as his father had been. Other followers became archers, and several received responsibility for guarding the herds, which often had to be taken great distances from the main camp. He appointed his large and strong brother Kasar as one of the warriors charged to protect the camp, and he placed his half brother, Belgutei, in charge of the large reserve of geldings that always stayed close to the main camp for use as mounts. He also created an elite bodyguard of 150 warriors: 70 day guards and 80 night guards to surround his camp at all hours. Under Temujin, the administration of the nascent Mongol tribe became an extension of Temujin's own household.

Despite Temujin's success in becoming recognized as a khan and in establishing his administrative court, Jamuka still commanded his own following, steadfastly refusing to acknowledge Temujin as the khan of all the Mongol clans. For Jamuka and the aristocratic white-boned lineages, Temujin was no more than an insolent upstart whom the black-boned people idolized but who needed to be taught a lesson and put back in his place. In 1190, only one year following Temujin's election, Jamuka used the killing of one of his kinsmen by one of Temujin's followers during a cattle raid as an excuse to summon all of his followers to battle. Each side rallied an army, probably numbering no more than several hundred on each side, but estimates of size are only conjectures at this point in the story. In the ensuing battle, Jamuka's forces routed Temujin's followers across the steppe. To prevent their regrouping against him, Jamuka then perpetrated one of the cruelest shows of revenge ever recorded on the steppe. First, he cut off the head of one of the captured leaders and tied it to the tail of his horse. The spilling of the blood and the disgrace to the head, the most ritually sacred part of the body, defiled the dead man's soul, and tying it to the most obscene part of the horse shamed his whole family.

Reportedly, Jamuka then boiled seventy young male captives alive in cauldrons, a form of death that would have destroyed their souls and thus completely annihilated them. Since seven represents an unlucky number for the Mongols, this story of seventy cauldrons may well have been an embellishment for dramatic effect, but the *Secret History* makes clear that whatever he really did, in the wake of this victory, Jamuka horrified people greatly and harmed his image. This display of unwarranted cruelty by Jamuka further emphasized the divisions between the old aristocratic lineages based on inherited power and the abused lower-ranking ones based on ability and personal loyalty. The episode proved a decisive turning point for Temujin, who had lost the battle but gained public support and sympathy among the Mongols, who were increasingly fearful of the cruelty of Jamuka. Temujin's warriors had been routed, but they would slowly collect together again behind their young khan.

His rivalry with Jamuka was not yet resolved, but in 1195, when Temujin was thirty-three, an unexpected opportunity arose for a foreign raid and substantial plunder that would greatly increase his military prestige and his economic power among the Mongols. The civilized Jurched rulers of Cathay, to the south of the Gobi, frequently delved into steppe politics as a way of keeping the tribes at war with one another and thus too weak to threaten their own power. Although traditionally the allies of the Tatars, the Jurched feared the Tatars were growing too strong, and they instigated Ong Khan to raise an army to attack them. Ong Khan again enlisted the aid of Temujin in a quickly arranged alliance with the Golden Khan of the Jurched so that they might jointly attack and plunder the much richer Tatar tribe.

In the winter of 1196, the Kereyid ruler Ong Khan and Temujin with his Mongol followers set out on their campaign against the Tatars; their raid, carried out according to the same tactics used in typical steppe raids, but on a larger scale, brought quick and easy success. Temujin was profoundly impressed by the sumptuous booty that warfare could yield. Because of their proximity to the Jurched kingdom and the more sophisticated manufactured goods of the Chinese empire, the Tatars owned more trade goods than any other tribe on the steppe. Among the goods seized, the *Secret History* mentions the impression made on the Mongols by a cradle embossed with silver and covered by a silken blanket embroidered with golden threads and pearls. Even captured Tatar children wore satin clothes decorated with golden threads; in one case, a young boy wore a gold ring in his nose and one in each ear. The ragged Mongols had never seen such luxurious goods worn by anyone, much less a child.

Temujin saw clearly how the powerful Jurched kingdom used one border tribe to fight another. One year, they might ally with the Tatars against the Kereyid, but the next year with the Kereyid and Mongols against the Tatars. Today's allies could be tomorrow's enemies, as in the case of Jamuka, and a tribe conquered today would have to be conquered again and again in a ceaseless cycle of warfare and feuding. No victory was ever decisive, no peace permanent. This lesson would eventually have a profound effect on the new world Temujin would fashion out of this havoc, but for now the vicissitudes of this particular war had brought an unprecedented number of goods to his people and had improved his standing among them.

Temujin still had a struggle ahead of him against Jamuka for control of the Mongols. The wealth looted from the Tatars attracted more followers; he now began to increase his power over other Mongol lineages and to expand into their territories. He could not expand into the area of the great tribes, but he could push out the smaller ones such as the Jurkin, a small Mongol lineage located immediately to the south of Temujin's group along the Kherlen River.

When Temujin had agreed to fight the Tatars, he had enlisted the help of his Jurkin relatives, who had initially agreed to join him. But when Temujin was prepared to leave for the campaign, he waited for six days for the Jurkin to arrive, and they never did. Just as with a *khuriltai*, where showing up counted as a vote of support, not showing up to organize raids constituted a vote of no confidence in the raid's leader—in this case Temujin. Relations between the Jurkin and Temujin's followers had been strained before. Like almost everyone around them, the Jurkin lineage outranked Temujin's lineage, and they often treated Temujin and his followers with scorn. One colorful story told in the *Secret History* reveals the animosity that had developed between the groups.

Temujin had invited the Jurkin to a feast, shortly before the Tatar campaign was to begin, but a chaotic brawl erupted when Temujin's half brother was assaulted in an especially demeaning way. Belgutei was the appointed guardian of the horses for Temujin's band, and he stood watch over them as the feast got under way. When a man, apparently from the Jurkin group, attempted to steal one of the horses, Belgutei chased him, but was stopped by another Jurkin known as Buri the Wrestler. As a sign that he stood ready to fight Buri, Belgutei pulled the top of his clothing down, leaving most of his upper body exposed. Rather than wrestle Belgutei, as would have been the custom in a disagreement among equals, Buri treated Belgutei with contempt as a lesser by unsheathing his sword and slicing Belgutei across the shoulder with it. To draw blood in this manner, even with just a small cut, constituted a grave insult. Learning of what had taken place outside by the horses, the drunken guests began fighting among themselves. As was customary, they had entered the feast without their weapons; so the guests began throwing the dishes of food at one another, and clubbing each other with the paddles used to stir the fermented mare's milk that had been consumed in great quantity.

Not only had the Jurkin failed to join Temujin's force in the fight against the Tatars, they now took advantage of Temujin's absence by raiding his base camp, killing ten of his followers and stripping the remainder of their clothes and other possessions. So when Temujin sought to expand his territory of rule in the wake of victory against the Tatars, the Jurkin were the first he struck out against. He launched his campaign against them in 1197, and in a testament to his now well-honed skills as a warrior and commander, he easily defeated them. At this point, Temujin instituted the second radical change in ruling style—the first being the appointment of loyal allies as opposed to family members to key positions in his entourage—that would mark his rise to power.

In the long history of steppe warfare, a defeated tribe was looted, some members taken prisoner, and the rest left again to their own devices. Defeated groups regularly reorganized and counterattacked, or broke away and joined rival tribes. In his defeat of the Jurkin, however, Temujin followed a radical new policy that revealed his ambition to fundamentally alter the cycle of attack and counterattack and of making and breaking alliances. He summoned a *khuriltai* of his followers to conduct a public trial of the Jurkin's aristocratic leaders for having failed to fulfill their promise to join him in war and for having, instead, raided his camp in his absence. Finding them guilty, he had them executed as a lesson about the value of loyalty to allies, but also as a clear warning to the aristocrats of all lineages that they would no longer be entitled to special treatment. He then took the unprecedented step of occupying the Jurkin lands and redistributing the remaining members of their group among the households of his own clan. Though some among both clans apparently interpreted this as the Jurkin being taken as slaves, as would have been more in keeping with steppe custom, according to the account in the *Secret History,* Temujin took them into his tribe not as slaves but as members of the tribe in good standing. He symbolized this by adopting an orphan boy from the Jurkin camp and presenting him to Hoelun to raise in her *ger* not as a slave but as her son. By having his mother adopt the Jurkin boy, as he had her previously adopt one each from the defeated Merkid, Tayichiud, and Tatars, Temujin was accepting the boys as his younger brothers. Whether these adoptions began for sentimental reasons or for political ones, Temujin displayed a keen appreciation of the symbolic significance and practical benefit of such acts in uniting his followers through this usage of fictive kinship. In the same way that he took these children into his own family, he accepted the conquered people into his tribe with the possibility that they would share fairly in the future conquests and prosperity of his army.

In a final display of his new power, Temujin ended the Jurkin episode with a feast for both the victorious Mongols and their newly adopted relatives. For the feast, he summoned Buri the Wrestler, who had cut Belgutei at the feast the year before, and ordered a wrestling match between the two men. No one had ever defeated Buri, but in his fear of Temujin's wrath, he allowed Belgutei to throw him. Normally, at this point the match would have been finished, but Temujin and Belgutei apparently worked out a different plan. Belgutei seized Buri's shoulders and mounted his rump like a horse, and upon receiving a signal from Temujin, he plunged his knee into Buri's back and snapped his spinal cord. Belgutei then dragged Buri's paralyzed body outside the camp, leaving him to die alone.

Temujin had rid himself of all the leaders of the Jurkin. The messages were clear to all their related clans on the steppe. To those who followed Temujin faithfully, there would be rewards and good treatment. To those who chose to attack him, he would show no mercy.

After defeating the Jurkin, he moved his followers downstream on the Kherlen into their territory. Temujin made his new base camp near the confluence of the smaller Tsenker River with the Kherlen. Eventually, this became his capital known as Avarga, but at this time, it was only a remote camp. The land between two rivers was called *aral*, "island," in Mongolian. Because the island between the Tsenker and Kherlen Rivers offered a wide open pasture, they called it the Khodoe Aral, which in modern Mongolian means "Country Island" but in classical Mongolian carried the meaning "Barren Island," and that name is an apt description for this isolated place in the midst of a large, open, and treeless prairie.

Barren as Avarga may have been, it constitutes on a grand scale the steppe herder's ideal home territory. Herders desire a *ger* that faces south in order to admit the light and warmth of the southern sun through the entryway as well as to prevent the cold northern winds from entering. They want to face water, but not be too close. A thirty-minute walk from the river seems to be the right distance to avoid polluting it with too much human waste. That distance also provides protection from the summer insects and flash floods that sometimes rage along the river plains. In addition to these advantages, Avarga was still close to the place of Temujin's birth and to the sacred mountain Burkhan Khaldun, which rose about 130 miles upstream at the headwaters of the Kherlen River. Avarga offered all of this, and from 1197 to the end of his life, it served as Temujin's operations base.

Although Temujin's followers prospered for four years in their new home as the size of his tribe continued to grow, Jamuka refused to recognize his leadership, and increasingly became the rallying figure for the aristocratic clans who did not like the changes Temujin was bringing to their traditional way of life. In 1201, the Year of the Cock, Jamuka made a play, with their support, for the position of ruler of all the Mongol people. In a challenge to both Temujin and Ong Khan, Jamuka summoned a *khuriltai* that conferred upon him the ancient and honored title of Gur-ka or Gur-khan, which meant chief of all chiefs or khan of all khans. His people swore a new oath of loyalty to him, and to sanctify the oath, they cut up one stallion and one mare in sacrifice.

Jamuka had not chosen the ancient title merely because it was old; he had a more directly sinister motive. The last khan to bear the title of Gur-Khan had been Ong Khan's uncle, who had ruled the Kereyid people until Ong Khan revolted against him and killed him and his brothers. It was during this revolt that Temujin's father, Yesugei, became the ally of Ong Khan. By choosing this title, Jamuka was publicly challenging the power of Ong Khan as well as his subordinate, Temujin.

If Jamuka could win this war, he would be the supreme ruler of the central steppe. He had on his side the important and aristocratic clans such as the Tayichiud, to which Temujin's family had once been subservient and who had enslaved Temujin when he was a boy. The struggle that began to shape up between the two Mongol factions portended to be more than just a series of raids for loot and captives; it would be a death struggle between Jamuka and Temujin for leadership of all the Mongols. As the sponsor for Temujin, Ong

Khan organized his warriors and came out to personally lead the campaign against Jamuka.

The primary objective of such campaigns was never to have to actually fight a battle at all but instead to frighten the other side by overwhelming force so that they would flee. To induce this fear, the steppe warriors relied on many tactics. One of those was the display of the Spirit Banners of the opposing leaders and their ancestors. Before battle, the warriors made animal sacrifices before the Spirit Banners as an offering to their guiding spirits and to their ancestors. Such spiritual dramas whipped up emotions and heightened tension. A lineage on one side would find it very difficult to fight if kinsmen on the other side had paraded the Spirit Banner of their common ancestor. That would be tantamount to attacking one's own grandfather.

The prebattle propaganda also involved shamans with their drums and all their ritual paraphernalia. Before the battle, the rival shamans foretold the future by reading the cracks in the burned shoulder bones of sheep. The presence of a shaman showed that he had forecast victory for his side, and the power of that forecast depended on his past reputation for choosing the winning side. Temujin had already attracted a number of shamans who revealed dreams to him, including one named Teb Tengeri, who would later play an important role. The shamans added to the occasion by climbing up on a promontory to pound their drums and beat magical rocks with which they could summon supporting spirits and control the weather. The objective was to entice warriors on the other side to defect to the superior side or to flee.

When Jamuka pitted his army against the Kereyid, the numerical advantage clearly belonged to Ong Khan and Temujin. The psychological advantage of Temujin's cadre of respected shamans strengthened his position, especially after a tremendous storm erupted with intense thunder and lightning that both sides attributed to the magic of the shamans. Many of Jamuka's followers fled in fright, forcing Jamuka to retreat. Ong Khan's warriors chased after Jamuka and the main part of his army, and he ordered Temujin to follow the Tayichiud as they fled back toward the Onon River, the land where Temujin had grown up and which he knew well.

When Temujin caught up with the Tayichiud, they proved more difficult to defeat than expected. The steppe mode of warfare consisted primarily of shooting arrows at one another from horseback or from fixed positions behind the protection of rocks—or in the case of the wooded Onon area, hastily assembled log barricades. When fighting, the steppe warriors sought to avoid being splattered by blood, so they rarely fought close to one another in hand-to-hand combat. The breath or odor of the enemy carried a part of his soul, and thus warriors sought to avoid the contamination of even smelling their enemy. The attackers swarmed down toward their enemies on horseback, firing arrows rapidly as they approached, then turned and continued firing as they fled. Sometimes the defenders rode out with long poles with which they tried to dismount their opponents and then shoot them as they stumbled back to their feet.

Temujin's army and the Tayichiud fought all day without either side gaining a clear advantage, though Temujin's forces apparently instilled the greater fear of defeat in their foes. According to the account in the *Secret History*, late in the day, an arrow pierced Temujin Khan's neck. As darkness fell, the two opposing armies laid down their arms and made camp close to each other on the same field where they had spent the day fighting. Though this may seem strange, by staying close together during the night, they could more effectively watch each other and prevent a surprise attack.

Though Temujin's wound was not deep, he lost consciousness after sunset. Such wounds carried a high risk of infection, or possibly poison had been applied to the arrow. His loyal follower Jelme, the next in command, stayed by his side throughout the evening and sucked the blood from the wound. In order to prevent offending the earth by spitting the blood on the ground, Jelme swallowed it. In addition to the religious reasons for his acts, hiding the blood had the practical value of preventing the other warriors from seeing how great the blood loss was. Only when Jelme was too full to swallow any more and the blood began trickling down from his mouth did he begin to spit it onto the ground.

After midnight, Temujin temporarily regained consciousness and begged to drink *airak*, fermented mare's milk. Because they had camped on the battlefield, Jelme had nothing but a little water, but he knew that in the middle of their camp, the Tayichiud had several supply wagons drawn up in a defensive circle. He stripped off his clothes, slipped across the battlefield, and walked naked among the enemy soldiers in search of *airak*. For a Mongol, public nakedness is a great sign of debasement, and had one of the Tayichiud seen him going through the camp naked at night, they probably would have assumed that he was one of their own getting up to relieve himself. Out of politeness, they probably would have looked away for fear of shaming one of their own warriors. Had they looked carefully and recognized him, Jelme planned to claim that he had just been stripped and humiliated by his fellow Mongols and had escaped to the Tayichiud. They would probably have believed him because of the unlikelihood that any proud Mongol warrior would intentionally allow himself to be captured naked.

The Tayichiud did not awaken, and although Jelme could not find *airak*, he did find a bucket of fermenting curds and took them. He brought the curds back, mixed them with water, and fed them to Temujin throughout the night. As the morning light came, Temujin's sight cleared, and he saw the blood around him and his half-dressed companion; he was confused and asked what had happened. Upon hearing the account of the night, his discomfort at the sight of his own blood on the ground so close to him made him ask, "Couldn't you have spit it somewhere else?" Despite the apparent lack of gratitude, Temujin never forgot how Jelme saved him from the Tayichiud, and he later entrusted Jelme with some of the most important expeditions of the Mongol conquests.

The episode of the neck wound is emblematic of the deep bonds of loyalty that Temujin seemed to have a gift of inspiring. Though the steppe tribes of his time changed sides at the least provocation and soldiers might desert their leaders, none of Temujin's generals deserted him throughout his six decades as a warrior. In turn, Temujin never punished or harmed one of his generals. Among the great kings and conquerors of history, this record of fidelity is unique.

The Tayichiud did not know of Temujin's wound, and during the night many of them began to sneak off the battlefield. By the next morning, most of the warriors had fled, and Temujin sent his warriors in pursuit. As he had done with the defeated Jurkin, Temujin killed off most of their leaders but accepted the rest as his own followers. Some thirty years after his initial capture by the Tayichiud and imprisonment in the cangue, he rewarded the family that had helped him to escape by freeing them from bondage.

While Temujin had been defeating the Tayichiud, Jamuka escaped from the army of Ong Khan. Although Jamuka had lost the Tayichiud, he still had many other clans loyal to him, and as he fled to more distant parts of the steppe, he would enlist new allies, as well, to join his cause. The final show-down between him and Temujin had not yet come.

In 1202, the Year of the Dog, the year following Temujin's defeat of the Tayichiud, Ong Khan sent Temujin on another campaign to plunder the Tatars in the east while he, the aging khan, stayed closer to home on another campaign against the Merkid.

In this campaign against the Tatars, Temujin would institute yet another set of radical changes to the rules that had long governed steppe life, and these changes would both antagonize some of his followers, those of the aristocratic lineages, and deepen the loyalty felt for him by many others, those of the lower lineages whose lives he enriched with his reforms and distribution of goods. While conducting raid after raid, Temujin had realized that the rush to loot the *gers* of the defeated served as an impediment to more complete victory. Rather than chasing down the warriors of the raided camps, attackers generally allowed them to flee and focused instead on immediately looting their camps. This system allowed many defeated warriors to escape and eventually return for a counterattack. So on this raid, his second conquest of the Tatars, Temujin decided to order that all looting would wait until after a complete victory had been won over the Tatar forces; the looting could then be carried out in a more organized fashion, with all the goods being brought under his central control and then redistributed among his followers as he determined fit. He distributed the goods along the same lines by which the hunting men of the forest traditionally distributed the kill at the end of a group hunt.

In another innovation, he ordered that a soldier's share be allocated to each widow and to each orphan of every soldier killed in the raid. Whether he did this because of the memory of his own mother's predicament when the Tatars killed his father, or for more political purposes, it had a profound effect. This policy not only ensured him of the support of the poorest people in the tribe, but it also inspired loyalty among his soldiers, who knew that even if they died, he would take care of their surviving families.

After routing the Tatars, some of Temujin's followers ignored his order against individual looting, and he demonstrated how serious he was about this reform by exacting a tough but appropriate punishment. He stripped those men of all their possessions and deprived them of the goods seized in the campaign. By controlling the distribution of all the looted goods, he had again violated the traditional rights of the aristocratic lineages under him to disperse the goods among their followers. The radical nature of his reforms angered many of them, and some deserted him to join the forces of Jamuka at this point, further drawing a line between the higher-prestige lineages and the common herders. Again, he had shown that rather than relying on the bonds of kinship and tradition, members of his tribe could now look to Temujin for direct support; with this move, he greatly centralized the power of his rule while at the same time strengthening the commitment of his followers.

Despite the minority discontent from within the Mongol ranks, Temujin's new system proved immediately effective. By postponing the looting until the end of the campaign, Temujin's army amassed more goods and animals than ever before. But the new wealth system also posed a new problem; the Mongols had not only defeated the Tatars, they had also captured almost the entire army and all the civilians.

In traditional steppe systems of thought, everyone outside the kinship network was an enemy and would always be an enemy unless somehow brought into the family through ties of adoption or marriage. Temujin sought an end to the constant fighting between such groups, and he wanted to deal with the Tatars the same way that he had dealt with the Jurkin and the Tayichiud clans—kill the leaders and absorb the survivors and all their goods and animals into his tribe. Although this policy had worked with clans of hundreds, however, the Tatars were a tribe of thousands. For such a massive social transformation, he needed the full support of his followers, and to achieve that support he summoned a *khuriltai* of his victorious warriors.

The members of the *khuriltai* agreed to the plan, determining to kill Tatar males taller than the linchpin holding the wheels on a cart, which was not only a measure of adulthood but a symbolic designation of the nation itself, in much the same way that maritime people often use the ship as a symbol of their state. Once again, as a counter to the killing, Temujin wanted the surviving Tatars taken in as full members of his tribe, not as slaves. To stress this, he not only adopted another Tatar child for his mother, but also encouraged intermarriage. Until this time he had only one official wife, Borte, who bore him four sons and an unknown number of daughters, but he now took the aristocratic Tatar Yesugen and her elder sister Yesui as additional wives. The

Tatars had had a much greater reputation than the Mongols, and after this battle, the Mongols took in so many Tatars, many of whom rose to high office and great prominence in the Mongol Empire, that the name *Tatar* became synonymous with, and in many cases better known, than the name *Mongol*, leading to much historic confusion through the centuries.

Intermarriage and adoption would not suffice, however, to achieve Temujin's goal of merging the two large groups into one people. If kin groups were allowed to remain essentially intact, the larger group would eventually fragment. In 1203, therefore, the year after the Tatar conquest, Temujin ordered yet another, and even more radical, reformation of the Mongol army and tribe.

He organized his warriors into squads, or *arban,* of ten who were to be brothers to one another. No matter what their kin group or tribal origin, they were ordered to live and fight together as loyally as brothers; in the ultimate affirmation of kinship, no one of them could ever leave the other behind in battle as a captive. Like any family of brothers in which the eldest had total control, the eldest man took the leadership position in the Mongol *arban,* but the men could also decide to chose another to hold this position.

Ten of the squads formed a company, or *zagun,* of one hundred men, one of whom they selected as their leader. And just as extended families united to form lineages, ten Mongol companies formed a battalion, or *mingan,* of one thousand men. Ten *mingan* were then organized into a *tumen,* an army of ten thousand; the leader of each *tumen* was chosen by Temujin, who knew the qualities needed in such a leadership position. He allowed fathers and sons and brothers and cousins to stay together when practical, but by forcing them into new units that no man could desert or change, under penalty of death, he broke the power of the old-system lineages, clans, tribes, and ethnic identities. At the time of his reorganization, he reportedly had ninety-five *mingan,* units of a thousand, but since some of the units were not staffed to capacity, the total number of troops may have been as low as eighty thousand.

The entire Mongol tribe became integrated by means of the army. Under this new system, all members of the tribe—regardless of age or gender—had to perform a certain amount of public service. If they could not serve in the military, they were obliged to give the equivalent of one day of work per week for public projects and service to the khan. This included caring for the warriors' herds, gathering dung for fuel, cooking, making felt, repairing weapons, or even singing and entertaining the troops. In the new organization, all people belonged to the same bone. Temujin the boy, who had faced repeated rejections ascribed to his lower-status birth, had now abolished the distinction between black bone and white bone. All of his followers were now one united people.

Historical speculation abounds as to how Temujin adopted the decimal organization of his people. Some of the earlier Turkic tribes used a similar military organization based on units of ten, and Temujin may well have borrowed it from them. Temujin, however, not only utilized the system as a military tactic for war, but he also employed it as the permanent structure for the whole society.

Temujin's solution was quite similar to that of the Athenian lawgiver Cleisthenes nearly two thousand years earlier, though there is no reason to believe that Temujin had ever heard of this piece of history. In order to cut through traditional rivalries and feuds in Athens, Cleisthenes abolished the tribes and reassigned everyone to ten units of ten, thereby transforming a tribal city into a city-state that grew into the strongest military, commercial, artistic, and intellectual power along the eastern shore of the Mediterranean Sea. Virtually the same reform would produce even more astonishing results for the Mongols on the steppes of Inner Asia.

After reorganizing his army, Temujin instituted one further, seemingly small, reform. While keeping his main camp at Avarga on the Kherlen River, he decided to create a closed territory as the homeland of the Mongol tribe at the headwaters of the Onon, Kherlen, and Tuul Rivers around the holy mountain Burkhan Khaldun, where he found refuge from the Merkid. "Let no one set up camp at the source of the Three Rivers," he commanded. With that order, the Mongol homeland was closed to all outsiders except for the Mongol royal family, who buried their dead there for the next two centuries and who returned there for familial ceremonies and closed family meetings without outsiders. The Mongols had always considered the mountains where the three rivers originated as their homeland, but with this new law, it became the secret ritual center of what would eventually be the Mongol Empire. The land around Burkhan Khaldun now became officially sacred in the Mongol cosmography, occupying not only the center of the earth, but the center of the universe.

Instead of using a single ethnic or tribal name, Temujin increasingly referred to his followers as the People of the Felt Walls, in reference to the material from which they made their *gers*. The adoption of this term after the defeat of the Tatars offers, perhaps, the first indication that he had an ambition to unite all the people on the steppe.

With the defeat and incorporation of the mighty Tatars, as well as the lesser groups of Tayichiud and Jurkin, Temujin gained significant prestige in the world of the steppes, a degree of power unanticipated by Ong Khan, his longtime overlord. Even as Temujin consolidated his rule over his greatly enlarged following, he would confront yet another great challenge that would put his new system to a decisive test. His next move would drive his lifelong rival Jamuka into an alliance with his ritual father Ong Khan to combat Temujin's growing might and popularity.

3

≈⟨⟩≈

War of the Khans

All the tribes were of one color and
obedient to his command.
ATA-MALIK JUVAINI,
Genghis Khan: The History of the
World Conqueror

EVERYONE REALIZED THAT ONG Khan was nearing the end of his career, but no one knew who would take over for him. After more than twenty years of struggle, Temujin controlled most of the Mongols, but he had not yet conquered his rival Jamuka. Ong Khan, while generally siding with Temujin, had continued to play the two subordinate khans off against one another. In 1203, the Year of the Pig and one year after the Tatar victory, Temujin decided to bring the issue out into the open and resolve it by requesting a marriage between Ong Khan's daughter and Temujin's eldest son, Jochi. If Ong Khan accepted the proposed marriage, it would be acknowledgment of Temujin as the favorite over Jamuka.

With urging from Senggum, his biological son, who had little talent and no following of his own, Ong Khan haughtily refused the marriage. Even if Temujin fancied his followers as the People of the Felt Walls and refused to recognize the distinction between clans, in the eyes of the aristocratic Kereyid royal family, Temujin, no matter how useful he may have been to them, was a common upstart. Nearly a century later, Marco Polo, assuming that Temujin had asked for the bride for himself, recorded the tone, if not the actual words, of Ong Khan as later recounted to him by the Mongols: "Is not Genghis Khan ashamed to seek my daughter in marriage? Does he not know that he is my vassal and my thrall? Go back to him and tell him that I would sooner commit my daughter to the flames than give her to him as his wife."

The aging khan, however, quickly regretted his impetuous refusal and grew fearful of how Temujin would respond. Without question Temujin now ranked as the best military leader on the steppe, and Ong Khan knew that he could not risking coming against Temujin in battle. Instead, he devised a plan to rid himself of the potential danger posed by Temujin through trickery, just as the Tatars had killed Temujin's father. Ong Khan dispatched a message to Temujin informing him that he had changed his mind and would welcome a marriage between their families. He set a date and invited Temujin to come with his family to celebrate the wedding between their offspring. Apparently, Temujin trusted the khan, who had been his ritual father for more than two decades, and set out with a small party toward the designated rendezvous for the wedding feast, leaving his army behind. This marriage, if he successfully concluded it, could be the zenith of his career by uniting all the people already under his rule with the Kereyid under Ong Khan, and the marriage would put him in the strongest position to succeed Ong Khan as the future ruler of the central steppes.

Only about one day's ride from Ong Khan's court, Temujin learned that the wedding invitation was a plot against him. Ong Khan had assembled his army secretly and intended to kill him and wipe out his family. Just at the moment of Temujin's anticipated triumph, he found that not only was the union not to take place, but that his very life and the survival of his family were endangered. With only a small contingent of warriors and far away from his main body of supporters, Temujin could not risk a fight. Instead, he did what steppe people had always done in the face of overwhelming odds: Temujin ordered his small group to disperse quickly in all directions, while he himself and a few companions fled rapidly toward the east before Ong Khan's army began the pursuit.

Temujin now faced a crisis that would be the greatest test of his abilities. His flight before the warriors of Ong Khan must have seemed so much like his flight, more than two decades earlier, from the Merkid when they kidnapped Borte. The endless cycle of steppe raids seemed to never end. Despite everything he had done in his life, little had really changed as he, once again, fled from those who were ranked socially higher above him and politically far more powerful.

With their unprepared leader on the run, Temujin's newly amalgamated tribe of the People of the Felt Walls faced its first major threat. Could it hold? Would the people of so many different tribes and families keep their allegiance and confidence in Temujin, wherever he was now fleeing? Or would they flee back to their original homelands or hastily seek to make arrangements for themselves under the protection of Ong Khan or Jamuka? The events that followed became legendary among the Mongols as the greatest trial and triumph in Temujin's life.

Exhausted and without provisions after days of constant flight, Temujin reached the distant shores of muddy Lake Baljuna. He looked around him to see how many men had survived the flight. He counted only nineteen of his men, and they now faced the possibility of starvation in this remote exile. As they paused to recuperate by the waters of Baljuna and decide what to do, a wild horse unexpectedly appeared from the north, and Temujin's brother Khasar set out in pursuit of it. He brought the horse down, and the men quickly skinned it. Without flaming wood over which to roast meat or pots in which to boil it, they relied on their ancient cooking technique. After skinning the horse, they cut up the meat and made a large bag from the horsehide into which they put the meat and some water. They gathered dried dung to make a fire, but they could not put the hide kettle directly on the fire. Instead, they heated rocks in the fire until glowing hot, then they dropped the hot rocks into the mixture of meat and water. The rocks heated the water, but the water prevented the rocks from burning through the bag. After a few hours, the starving men feasted on boiled horseflesh.

Aside from Khasar, the men gathered with him were his friends, not his relatives. Some of his family members were temporarily lost on the steppe, but other relatives had deserted Temujin to join Ong Khan or Jamuka. In particular his uncle, one of his father's two brothers who had helped him to kidnap Temujin's mother from her Merkid husband, had joined Ong Khan against his own nephew.

With little to comfort them or offer encouragement for the future, the exhausted men seized upon the appearance of the horse as a supernatural gift that offered them more than just food for their empty bellies. As the most important and honored animal in the Mongol world, the horse solemnized the occasion and served as a sign of divine intervention and support. The horse symbolized the power of Temujin's destiny, and its sacrifice, as before any major battle or *khuriltai*, not only fed the men, but further empowered Temujin's Spirit Banner. With only the muddy water of Baljuna to drink at the end of the horseflesh meal, Temujin Khan raised one hand to the sky, and with the other he held up the muddy water of Baljuna in a toast. He thanked his men for their loyalty and swore never to forget it. The men shared in drinking the muddy waters and swore eternal allegiance to him. In the retelling of the episode in oral history, it became known in history as the Baljuna Covenant, and acquired a mythic aura as the lowest point in the military fortunes of Temujin Khan but also as the event out of which the identity and form of the Mongol Empire would arise.

The event acquired a symbolic representation of the diversity of the Mongol people based on mutual commitment and loyalty that transcended kinship, ethnicity, and religion. The nineteen men with Temujin Khan came from nine different tribes; probably only Temujin and his brother Khasar were actually from the Mongol clans. The others included Merkid, Khitan, and Kereyid. Whereas Temujin was a devout shamanist who worshiped the Eternal Blue Sky and the God Mountain of Burkhan Khaldun, the nineteen included several Christians, three Muslims, and several Buddhists. They were united only in their devotion to Temujin and their oath to him and each other. The oaths sworn at Baljuna created a type of brotherhood, and in transcending kinship, ethnicity, and religion, it came close to being a type of modern civic citizenship based upon personal choice and commitment. This connection became a metaphor for the new type of community among Temujin's followers that would eventually dominate as the basis of unity within the Mongol Empire.

After hiding at Baljuna, Temujin formulated his plan to counterattack. He knew that he had to move quickly while Ong Khan was still basking in his false confidence of having permanently rid himself of Temujin's threat. Temujin dispatched word of his plan to his followers scattered across the steppe, and the story probably contained all the details of the miraculous appearance of the horse that saved him and his men. In the following days, to a degree that Temujin himself possibly had not expected, his newly organized army units of tens and hundreds reassembled themselves across the steppe. As Temujin marched westward from Baljuna back toward the lands of Ong Khan, his men returned to him from all directions. In addition, some of Temujin's relatives through his mother and through his wife Borte, ones who had been loyal followers of Ong Khan, now deserted their Kereyid leader and came searching for Temujin's camp.

Meanwhile, to celebrate his victory over Temujin, the still unsuspecting Ong Khan organized a large feast in his palatial golden *ger* that he took wherever he went. Overconfident in his own power over his followers and unaware of what was happening out on the steppe, Ong Khan celebrated in the illusion that Temujin's followers had been disbanded and that Temujin himself was far away in the east.

Temujin's army raced toward the place of the feast. Loyal followers had gone ahead of them to station reserves of horses so that as one set tired out, another awaited his men. With these remounts, his army raced, without pause, through the dead of night, in what he called the Lightning Advance. Rather than approaching the Kereyid court directly across the steppe, which would have been the easy approach, Temujin took his men over a more remote and difficult pass that he knew would not be guarded.

Suddenly, Temujin, who was thought to be several days' ride away, swooped down on the revelers; his men had surrounded the entire camp. Over the next three days of hard fighting the Kereyid retreated before the advancing army of Temujin. Many of the followers of Ong Khan deserted to Temujin's banner, and, as was his known policy, he accepted them so long as they had not committed any act of treachery or harm to their former leader other than to abandon him in favor of Temujin.

Ong Khan's army was not so much defeated as swallowed by Temujin's forces. The Kereyid court fled in different directions, with each man for himself. Ong Khan's son fled south and, after being abandoned by his own servants, died of thirst in the desert, while Jamuka and his shrinking followers fled west toward the territory of the Naiman, the last of the three great steppe tribes not yet defeated by Temujin. Ong Khan also tried to make his way alone to the sanctuary of the Naiman tribe.

Having failed to capture the leader of his enemies, or even the son of the old khan, the Mongols had to account for this failure and dismiss its importance. Temujin's supporters spread stories to denigrate Ong Khan's reputation and to assure people on all sides he was dead and no longer a threat. According to the account circulated by the Mongols, after arriving safely at the Naiman border, Ong Khan encountered a border guard who, refusing to believe that the solitary old man was the renowned warrior khan of the Kereyid, killed him. They said that to atone for the killing of Ong Khan, the Naiman queen had his head brought to her and placed on a sacred white cloth of felt in the position of honor at the back of the *ger,* opposite the door, where she could make offerings and prayers to it. Nothing could be more offensive to Mongol sensibilities than such a bloody item inside the home, and nothing could be more dangerous than the head, the seat of Ong Khan's soul. According to the story, however, she ordered a musician to play the *morin huur,* the horsehead fiddle, while her daughters-in-law sang and danced for the head and she made ceremonial offerings of wine to it as though Ong Khan were still alive and an honored guest in her *ger.* When Tayang Khan, the Naiman ruler, entered and saw the severed head, he panicked and shouted in horrified anger that the head had smiled at him. Whereupon, he kicked the head off the sacred felt cloth and then trampled it to pieces.

Such stories offered assurance that the old khan was truly dead, and at the same time they heaped shame and opprobrium on the court of the Naiman, the next target of Temujin's campaign. Propaganda and control of public opinion were quickly emerging as Temujin's primary weapons of choice. The Mongols spread stories among their supporters accusing the aging Tayang Khan of having disintegrated into an imbecile and weakling whose wife and son despised and shamed him in public. To build anger among their followers against the enemy, the Mongol leaders spread the story that the Naiman queen despised Mongols as dirty and smelly savages. Using gossip as a way to build confidence in their own men and to weaken the enemy's resolve, the Mongols reported that the son of Tayang Khan mockingly called him Old Woman Tayang, and that he would not venture any farther from his *ger* than would a pregnant woman going to piss.

At the same time that they spread such strange stories about the Naiman court, the Mongols boosted their own spirits with stories of how afraid the Naiman were of them. Since Jamuka had joined the Naiman, stories circulated of how he would terrify them with descriptions of Temujin's warriors. The *Secret History* recounted the horrific description of the Mongols in proud detail: "They have chisels for noses and sharp awls for tongues. They can live by eating the dew and riding the wind." They compared Temujin to a starved falcon, but also said that "his whole body is made from copper and iron fastened so tightly together that no awl could penetrate it."

By contrast to this description, the first Mongol captured by a Naiman advance guard rode a horse so skinny with a saddle so primitive that the captors sent the horse and saddle from camp to camp in mockery to convince their fellow Naiman of how pathetic the Mongols had become. Temujin responded to the captured horsemen episode with another trick. Since he had far fewer soldiers than the Naiman, Temujin ordered each man to set five campfires every night on the hills where his army camped. From a distance, the small army appeared much larger, since they seemed to have "more fires than the stars in the sky."

The final battle for control of Mongolia came in 1204, the Year of the Rat, about three hundred miles west of Burkhan Khaldun. In the days leading up to the battle, Temujin tested his new military organization based on squads of ten. Rather than committing to an all-out battle, which he might easily lose because of his smaller numbers, Temujin picked at the Naiman with small and unpredictable hit-and-run skirmishes. In the first episode, Temujin ordered his men to advance in what was called the Moving Bush or Tumbleweed Formation just before daylight. Rather than large units racing in to attack, the dispersed squads of ten advanced severally and silently from different directions while keeping their profiles low in the predawn darkness. This prevented the enemy from seeing how many there were or from preparing for an attack from a single direction. After attacking, the squads fled in different directions, leaving the enemy wounded but unable to retaliate before the attackers disappeared.

Temujin followed the sporadic attacks of the Moving Bush with the Lake Formation, in which a long line of troops advanced, fired its arrows, and then was replaced by the next line. Like waves, they struck and then disappeared as quickly as they had appeared, each wave, in turn, returning to the rear and forming another wave. The use of the Lake Formation caused the Naiman to spread out in a long, thin line to meet the long line of attacking men. Once the Naiman spread out, Temujin switched to his third tactic. He regrouped his squads one behind the other in the Chisel Formation, which was narrow across the front but extremely deep, allowing the attackers to channel maximum force to one point on the now thinned Naiman lines and chisel through them.

The tactics seemed to be, at least in part, an amalgamation of older fighting techniques and hunting strategies; yet the consistent inability of the perplexed enemy to respond effectively to this form of warfare indicated that Temujin had introduced enough innovation to make these strategies uniquely his own. Temujin had produced a new type of steppe army based on a greater variety of tactics and, most important, close cooperation among the men and complete obedience to their commanders. They were no longer an attacking swarm of individuals; they were now a united formation. Temujin used a set of maneuvers that each man had to know and to which each responded precisely and without hesitation. The Mongols had a saying: "If he sends me into fire or water I go. I go for him." The saying reflected not just an ideal, but the reality, of the new Mongol warfare, and it made short order of the Naiman.

The Mongols were gaining the advantage, but Temujin did not race to victory. The night before what everyone expected would be the decisive battle, he told his men to sleep soundly. On the other side, confused, disoriented, and their line of communication broken, the Naiman began to flee during the night. Temujin, however, held his soldiers in check and did not pursue them. The night was dark and moonless, and the only escape route was on the steep back side of the mountain. Unable to see, the fleeing men and their horses slipped and fell into the gorge. In the words of the *Secret History,* their bodies piled up like "rotten logs" at the bottom of the cliff

The next morning, the Mongol forces easily defeated the few remaining Naiman and "finished Tayang Khan." Among the warriors who had successfully escaped, Tayang Khan's son Guchlug fled to the distant Tian Shan Mountains of the Black Khitan, while Jamuka disappeared into the forest. There was no group left where Jamuka might find refuge, and his end would come with a slow whimper, not with a climactic final struggle. Even the few remaining bands of Merkid were quickly swallowed by the growing Mongol nation, and the forty-year-old Jamuka lived as an outcast bandit with a small number of followers who fed themselves on wild animals. In an odd reversal of fate, the once aristocratic Jamuka had been reduced to the same state of existence that the young Temujin had faced when his father died. In 1205, the Year of the Ox, a year after the victory over the Naiman, Jamuka's followers, desperate and resigned to defeat, seized him and delivered him to Temujin. Despite the animosity between the two men, Temujin valued loyalty above all else. Rather than reward the men who brought Jamuka to him, Temujin had all of them executed in front of the leader whom they had betrayed.

The final meeting between the two men, who had fought each other for more than twenty years, formed an emotional highpoint of the *Secret History*. Rather than seek revenge against Jamuka, now that he was past posing a threat to him, Temujin offered to unite with him again: "Let us be companions. Now, we are joined together once again, we should remind each other of things we have forgotten. Wake each other from our sleep. Even when you went away and were apart from me, you were still my lucky, blessed sworn brother. Surely, in the days of killing and being killed, the pit of your stomach and your heart pained for me. Surely, in the days of slaying and being slain, your breast and your heart pained for me."

Jamuka seemed moved by the plea and by the emotion of his erstwhile junior partner who now ruled all that Jamuka once had and much more. He seemed for a moment to fall into Temujin's sentimental nostalgia for the brotherhood of their youth. Jamuka responded, "We ate the food that is not to be digested, and we spoke to each other the words that are not to be forgotten" while "sharing together the quilt under which we slept." Jamuka then blamed their separation on the influence of another, unnamed person: "We have been provoked by one who cuts across us. We have been goaded by one who came from the side."

The *Secret History* offers a lengthy confession and repentance by Jamuka, but both the grandiose prose and the detail of its account invite suspicion regarding its accuracy. "Now, when the world is ready for you," the text quotes Jamuka as saying, "what use is there in my becoming a companion to you? On the contrary, sworn brother, in the black night I would haunt your dreams, in the bright day I would trouble your heart. I would be the louse in your collar, I would become the splinter in your door-panel."

Almost like a modern lawyer pleading for mercy based on psychological problems and emotional disability, Jamuka reflected back on their youth, searching for an explanation of why he had been so drawn to Temujin and why he had betrayed him. Jamuka explained laconically that he himself had lost both of his parents, had no siblings or trusted companions, and had a shrew for a wife. But rather than asking for mercy in the end, Jamuka asked for death, with a single request—that they kill him in the aristocratic way without shedding his blood on the earth or exposing it to the sun and sky.

Although he had failed Temujin in life, Jamuka offered to be a better friend to him in death. He vowed that if Temujin would place his body in a high place, he would watch over Temujin and all of his descendants: "Kill me and lay down my dead bones in the high ground. Then eternally and forever, I will protect the seed of your seed, and become a blessing for them." Legend says that Temujin buried Jamuka in the golden belt that he had given to Jamuka when they swore the oath of *andas*.

Jamuka had been Temujin's first rival, and now he ended his life as the last of the Mongol aristocrats opposing him. In Temujin's long quest for control of the Mongol clans, Temujin had defeated every tribe on the steppe and removed the threat of every aristocratic lineage by killing off their men and marrying their women to his sons and other followers. He chafed under the authority of anyone who stood above him. He killed Begter to rule over his family. He destroyed the Merkid because they took his wife. He killed off the Tatars who had killed his father and looked down on the Mongols as little more than steppe rats. He overthrew the nobles of his own Mongol people and eliminated one by one the higher-ranking Mongol clans of the Tayichiud and the Jurkin. When his own ally and father figure refused to allow a marriage between their respective families, Temujin destroyed him and his tribe. When the Naiman queen mocked the Mongols as her inferiors, he attacked the tribe, killed her husband, and gave her to one of his men as a wife. Finally, he killed Jamuka, one of the people whom he most loved in life, and thereby destroyed the aristocratic Jadaran clan.

Temujin now ranked as undisputed ruler of a vast land, controlling everything from the Gobi in the south to the Arctic tundra in the north, from the Manchurian forests in the east to the Altai Mountains of the west. His empire was grass and contained far more animals than humans. Victory on the battlefield alone did not confer legitimacy of rule until it was publicly acclaimed at a *khuriltai* of representatives from every part of the territory. If a group chose not to send anyone, then they rejected the rule of the khan who called it. The khan could not claim to rule them, and, more important, they could not claim his protection.

Temujin allowed another year to restore peace and mend relations before he called the *khuriltai* to install him in office. In 1206, the Year of the Tiger, Temujin returned to the headwaters of the Onon River near his sacred mountain of Burkhan Khaldun and summoned a *khuriltai,* probably the largest and most important ever held in steppe history. Tens of thousands of animals grazed nearby to provide milk and meat for the festivities. The lines of *gers* stretched for miles in every direction from the camp of Temujin, and at the center of all stood the horsehaired *sulde,* the Spirit Banner that had guided Temujin to this event. Days of great solemnity and massive ceremony alternated with days of celebration, sports, and music. The court shamans, including Teb Tengeri, pounded their drums and sang by day, and musicians performed at dusk. The night air filled with the mesmerizing drone of the distinctive type of Mongolian throat singing, or overtone singing, in which men make sounds from so deep inside their bodies that they can follow two musical lines simultaneously. As with every major political event, young people competed in wrestling, horse racing, and archery, the traditional games of the Mongol known as *naadam.*

Temujin controlled a vast territory roughly the size of modern western Europe, but with a population of about a million people of the different nomadic tribes under his control and probably some 15 to 20 million animals. He ruled not merely as the khan of the Tatars, the Kereyid, or the Naiman. He was to be the ruler of all the People of the Felt Walls, and for this new empire, he chose a new official name derived from his own tribe. He named his people *Yeke Mongol Ulus,* the Great Mongol Nation. After uniting all the people, he abolished inherited aristocratic titles in their lineages, clans, and tribes. All such offices belonged to the state, not to the individual or his family, and they would be distributed at the will of the new ruler. For himself, Temujin rejected the older tribal titles such as Gur-Khan or Tayang Khan and chose instead the title that his own followers probably already used for him, Chinggis Khan, a name that later became known in the West through the Persian spelling as Genghis Khan. The Mongolian word *chin* means strong, firm, unshakable, and fearless, and it is close to the Mongolian word for wolf, *chino,* the ancestor from whom they claimed descent. It was a simple, but fitting, title for the new khan.

Like most successful rulers, Genghis Khan understood the political potential of solemn ceremony and grand spectacle. Unlike most rulers confined within the architecture of buildings such as palaces or temples, however, the installation of Genghis Khan took place on the vast open steppe, where hundreds of thousands of people participated.

Mongol public ceremonies created a marked impression on visitors and chroniclers who described them in detail. The fullest surviving account available comes from the seventeenth-century French biographer François Pétis de la Croix, who had access to now-lost Persian and Turkish documents of the era. According to Pétis, Genghis Khan's followers "placed him upon a black Felt Carpet, which they had spread on the Ground; and the Person who was order'd to give the Peoples Voice, pronounc'd to him aloud the Peoples Pleasure." The speaker admonished Genghis Khan "that whatever Authority of Power he had given him, was derived from Heaven, and that God would not fail to bless and prosper his Designs if he govern'd his Subjects well and justly; but that, on the contrary he would render himself miserable if he abused that power."

The ceremony provided an unmistakable sign of support from his followers, who publicly demonstrated their submission by raising him up on a carpet above their heads and literally carrying him to the throne. Then they "bow'd their knees nine times before this new Emperor, to shew the Obedience they promised to him." Just as the presence of each lineage committed its support to Genghis Khan, the presence of each shaman showed that his spirits and dreams had instructed him to do likewise. Without an organized religion, the shamans conferred a spiritual blessing on the event and made it more than just a political occasion. Through their presence, the event became a sacred proclamation of Temujin's spiritually ordained destiny from the Eternal Blue Sky.

Shamans beat the drums, chanted to the spirits of nature, and sprinkled *airak* into the air and on the ground. The assembled throngs of people prayed, standing in uniform ranks with the palms of their hands facing upward toward the Eternal Blue Sky. They concluded their prayers and sent them skyward with the ancient Mongol phrase *"huree, huree, huree"* that ended all prayers, similar to the Christian use of amen. This spiritual act made each of them a part of the election and sealed a religious covenant not just between themselves and their leader but also with the spiritual world.

Most leaders, whether kings or presidents, grew up inside the institutions of some type of state. Their accomplishments usually involved the reorganization or revitalization of those institutions and the state that housed them. Genghis Khan, however, consciously set out to create a state and to establish all the institutions necessary for it on a new basis, part of which he borrowed from prior tribes and part of which he invented. For his nation-state to survive, he needed to build strong institutions, and for Genghis Khan this began with the army that brought him to power; he made it even stronger and more central to government. Under Genghis Khan, cowherds, shepherds, and camel boys advanced to become generals and rode at the front of armies of a thousand or ten thousand warriors. Every healthy male aged fifteen to seventy was an active member of the army. Just as he had done when first elected tribal khan, he appointed his most loyal followers as the heads of groups of one thousand soldiers and their households, and his oldest followers, such as Boorchu, took charge of units of ten thousand. He rewarded men who came from lowly black-boned lineages and placed them in the highest positions based on their achievements and proven loyalty to him on and off the battlefield. Compared with the units of ten thousand that he gave to his loyal friends, those assigned to the control of members of his own family were more meager—five thousand each to his mother, his youngest brother, and his two youngest sons, Ogodei and Tolui. With only eight thousand for Chaghatai and nine thousand for Jochi, even his two eldest sons did not receive a full *tumen* of ten thousand. Genghis Khan appointed trusted friends of his own to oversee the administration for several family members, particularly for his mother, youngest brother, and Chaghatai. He explained the need for such overseers by stating that Chaghatai was "obstinate and has a petty, narrow mind." He warned the advisers to "stay beside him morning and evening to advise him."

In order to maintain peace in this large and ethnically diverse set of tribes that he had forged into one nation, he quickly proclaimed new laws to suppress the traditional causes of tribal feuding and war. The Great Law of Genghis Khan differed from that of other lawgivers in history. He did not base his law on divine revelation from God; nor did he derive it from an ancient code of any sedentary civilization. He consolidated it from the customs and traditions of the herding tribes as maintained over centuries; yet he readily abolished old practices when they hindered the functioning of his new society. He allowed groups to follow traditional law in their area, so long as it did not conflict with the Great Law, which functioned as a supreme law or a common law over everyone.

The Great Law, however, did not represent a single codification of the law so much as an ongoing body of legal work that he continued to develop throughout the remaining two decades of his life. Genghis Khan's law did not delve into all aspects of daily life; instead, he used it to regulate the most troublesome aspects. As long as men kidnapped women, there would be feuding on the steppes. Genghis Khan's first new law reportedly forbade the kidnapping of women, almost certainly a reaction to the kidnapping of his wife Borte. The persistent potential for strife originating in such kidnappings still plagued Genghis Khan within his own family in the uncertainty of whether his eldest son had been fathered by him or by Borte's kidnapper, and the uncertainty would cause increasingly more severe problems as Genghis Khan grew older.

Concomitant with an end to kidnapping, he forbade the abduction and enslavement of any Mongol. From his own capture and enslavement by the Tayichiud, he knew the individual and personal anguish of being abducted and forced to work as a slave, but he also recognized how detrimental the practice was to the entire social fabric and what strong animosities and violence it perpetrated throughout the tribes of the steppe.

Genghis Khan sought to remove every source of internal dissension within the ranks of his followers. Based upon his own experiences over the disruptions that surrounded questions of the legitimacy of children, he declared all children legitimate, whether born to a wife or a concubine. Because haggling over the value of a wife as though she were a camel could provoke lingering dissension among his men, he forbade the selling of women into marriage. For the same reasons, he outlawed adultery, an act that the Mongols' defined differently than most people. It did not include sexual relations between a woman and her husband's close relatives, nor those between a man and female servants or the wives of other men in his household. In keeping with Genghis Khan's dictum that matters of the *ger* should be decided within the *ger* and matters of the steppe decided on the steppe, adultery applied to relations between married people of separate households. As long as it did not cause a public strife between families, it did not rank as a crime.

Theft of animals had always been considered wrong, but it had been commonplace in the raiding culture of the steppes, and had also been the cause of lingering animosity and discord. Perhaps remembering the great harm caused to his family when their eight geldings were stolen, Genghis Khan made animal rustling a capital offense. Additionally, he required anyone finding a lost animal to return it to the rightful owner. For this purpose, he instituted a massive lost-and-found system that continued to grow as his empire spread. Any person who found such goods, money, or animals and did not turn them in to the appropriate supervisor would be treated as a thief; the penalty for theft was execution.

Aside from fighting over lost animals, the steppe people argued frequently over hunting rights for wild animals. Genghis Khan codified existing ideals by forbidding the hunting of animals between March and October during the breeding time. By protecting the animals in the summer, Genghis Khan also provided a safety net for the winter, and hunters had to limit their kill to what they needed for food and no more. The law also specified how animals should be hunted as well as the manner of butchering, so as to waste nothing.

In addition to sex, property, and food, Genghis Khan recognized the disruptive potential of competing religions. In one form or another, virtually every religion from Buddhism to Christianity and Manichaeanism to Islam had found converts among the steppe people, and almost all of them claimed not only to be the true religion but the only one. In probably the first law of its kind anywhere in the world, Genghis Khan decreed complete and total religious freedom for everyone. Although he continued to worship the spirits of his homeland, he did not permit them to be used as a national cult.

To promote all religions, Genghis Khan exempted religious leaders and their property from taxation and from all types of public service. To promote related professions, he later extended the same tax exemptions to a range of professionals who provided essential public services, including undertakers, doctors, lawyers, teachers, and scholars.

Genghis Khan made a number of laws designed specifically to prevent fighting over the office of khan. According to his law, the khan must always be elected by a *khuriltai*. He made it a capital offense for any member of his family to claim the office without election. To prevent rival candidates from killing each other, he ordered that the death penalty would be applied to members of his family only through a *khuriltai* of the whole family and not through any individual member. In so doing, he outlawed the very means that he himself had used to begin his rise to power—killing his half brother.

Mongol law, as codified by Genghis Khan, recognized group responsibility and group guilt. The solitary individual had no legal existence outside the context of the family and the larger units to which it belonged; therefore, the family carried the responsibility of ensuring the correct behavior of its members. A crime by one could bring punishment to all. Similarly, a tribe or a squad of soldiers bore the same liability for one another's actions, and thereby the entire nation, not just the army or just the civil administration, bore responsibility for upholding and enforcing the law. To be a just Mongol, one had to live in a just community.

Enforcement of the law and the responsibility to abide by it began at the highest level, with the khan himself. In this manner, Genghis Khan had proclaimed the supremacy of the rule of law over any individual, even the sovereign. By subjugating the ruler to the law, he achieved something that no other civilization had yet accomplished. Unlike many civilizations—and most particularly western Europe, where monarchs ruled by the will of God and reigned above the law—Genghis Khan made it clear that his Great Law applied as strictly to the rulers as to everyone else. His descendants proved able to abide by this rule for only about fifty years after his death before they discarded it.

To run the empire in general, but most specifically to record the many new laws and to administer them over the vast stretches of land now under his control, Genghis Khan ordered the adoption of a writing system. Although writing had been introduced to the steppes many centuries earlier by Muslim merchants and itinerant Christian monks, few of the native people learned the skill, even those among the most sophisticated tribes of Tatars, Naiman, and Kereyid; and so far as is known, no Mongol had learned it. In his conquest of the Naiman in 1204, Genghis Khan discovered that Tayang Khan kept a scribe who wrote down his pronouncements and then embossed them with an official state seal. The scribe came from the Uighur people, who had originated on the Mongol steppe, but in the ninth century had migrated to the oases of what is now the Xinjiang region of western China. The Uighur language was closely related and proved relatively easy to adapt for writing in the Mongolian language. Derived from the Syriac alphabet used by the missionary monks who brought Christianity to the steppe tribes, the writing was made from letters rather than characters, but it flowed vertically down the page in columns, like Chinese.

To keep track of his laws, Genghis Khan created the position of supreme judge for his adopted brother Shigi-Khutukhu, the Tatar boy with the golden earrings and nose ring whom he had found and given to his mother to raise. Genghis Khan charged him to "punish the thieves and put right the lies," as well as to keep a record of his decisions on white paper bound in blue books, the sacred color of the Eternal Sky. This close association between writing and the keeping of the law in Genghis Khan's administration probably accounts for why the Mongolian word for book, *nom,* was derived from the Greek *nomos,* meaning "law." In the Mongol world of the thirteenth century, the law and the written word were one and the same.

In maintaining loyalty and cohesion in the vast apparatus of his state, Genghis Khan innovated on an ancient political practice of hostage taking. He demanded that each of the commanders of the units of one thousand and ten thousand send their own sons and their sons' best friends to him personally to make his own unit of ten thousand. Instead of threatening to kill them if their relatives misbehaved, Genghis Khan introduced a far more effective strategy. Genghis Khan trained the would-be hostages as administrators and kept them as a ready reserve to replace any ineffective or disloyal official. The threat of such potential replacement probably did much more to ensure loyalty in the field than the threat that the relative might be killed. Genghis Khan thus changed the status of hostages, transforming them into an integral part of his government that gave almost every family a direct and personal connection to the imperial court.

Genghis Khan divided the elite unit into the day guard and the night guard. As the name indicated, they formed a permanent watch over him and his encampment, but they functioned as much more than a bodyguard. They controlled the boys and girls who worked in the court, and they organized the herders of the different animals. They oversaw the movement of the camp, together with all the weapons and accoutrements of the state: banners, pikes, and drums. They also controlled the cooking vessels and the slaughter of animals, and they ensured the proper distribution of meat and dairy products. The guard helped to adjudicate legal hearings, carry out punishments, and generally enforce the law. Because they controlled the entrance to and egress from the royal tents, they formed the basis of government administration.

All members of Genghis Khan's own regiment held the rank of elder brother to the other nine units of ten thousand, and therefore they could issue orders to any of them and expect to be obeyed without question. Unlike other armies in which each individual held a rank, in the Mongol army, the entire unit held a rank. The lowest-ranking man in Genghis Khan's *tumen* of ten thousand outranked the highest-ranking men of the other *tumen*. In turn, within each *tumen,* every member of the commander's unit of one thousand outranked every man in the other nine units of one thousand.

To facilitate communication so that the orders got to the intended recipient, Genghis Khan relied on a system of fast riders known as arrow messengers. The military supplied the riders, but the local people supplied the stations. The postal service ranked alongside the military in importance for the Mongols, and individual Mongols were allowed to serve in it in lieu of regular military service. Depending on local terrain, the stations were set approximately twenty miles apart, and each station required about twenty-five families to maintain and operate it. Although the stations were open for public use, much of the information on the individual stations and the total number at any given time remained a carefully guarded secret, and therefore the information has not survived. Some idea of its expanse can be derived from the eighteenth century, however, when the system still operated and required approximately sixty-four stations to cross Mongolia from the Altai Mountains in the west to the entrance through the Great Wall into China in the east.

Genghis Khan adapted a variety of older methods of communication over shorter distances, such as the use of torches, whistling arrows, smoke, flares, and flags, for even more rapid transmission of information during maneuvers, hunts, and military movements. The herders had earlier developed a complicated system of arm signals that could be used long after individuals had passed out of hearing range, and under Genghis Khan these, too, were built upon to make an ever more elaborate system of rapid and efficient communication for use in battle or troop maneuvers.

Peace and prosperity bred their own problems for Genghis Khan. Six years of peace allowed, or possibly encouraged, the intrigues and the petty rivalries that threatened to undo Genghis Khan's hard-fought unification of the tribes. The more powerful he became, the more disagreements sparked among his followers—particularly within his own family, whose members felt entitled to substantially larger shares of goods and power than his allies outside the family. Genghis Khan's court of trusted advisers included almost none of his own relatives. He sent his mother to live with her youngest son, Temuge, who by steppe tradition was called *Otchigen,* the Prince of the Hearth, and had the responsibility of caring for his parents in their old age.

With a steadfastly loyal army and without family or old aristocrats as rivals, new trouble arose from an unexpected source: Teb Tengeri, Genghis Khan's shaman. He had proclaimed time and again that the Eternal Blue Sky favored Genghis Khan and would make him ruler of the world; he interpreted dreams and all kinds of signs in favor of Genghis Khan's success and as indications of his great importance. Genghis Khan exploited not only the supernatural value that Teb Tengeri contributed to his court but his practical value as well, as when he appointed him to oversee the estates of Hoelun and Temuge Otchigen. Teb Tengeri used his position to enrich himself and his six brothers, who formed a powerful coalition and, because of his supernatural power, had a following within the newly created Mongol nation second only to that of Genghis Khan himself.

On one occasion the seven brothers ganged up on Genghis Khan's brother Khasar and beat him. Afterward, Khasar went to Genghis Khan's *ger,* fell to his knees, and begged his brother to help him. Never completely trustful of his own family, Genghis Khan rebuked his brother and mockingly asked how it was that he, who had once been renowned as the strongest man in the tribe, could now be beaten by these men. According to the *Secret History,* Khasar broke into tears of shame as he knelt before his brother. He left the *ger,* and in his anger, fear, and humiliation, he did not speak to Genghis Khan for three days.

Apparently emboldened by this small success against Khasar, Teb Tengeri reported to Genghis Khan shortly thereafter that a dream had come to him in which he saw that Genghis Khan would rule the nation, but that in another dream he saw that Khasar would rule it. He urged Genghis Khan to strike quickly and firmly against his brother to prevent any threat to his own rule. Genghis Khan immediately ordered Khasar arrested and stripped of his small contingent of followers.

Genghis Khan's mother lived a day's journey away from his court with her youngest son, but she quickly heard of the trouble. She already resented Teb Tengeri's power over her as one of the administrators of her estate, and she became enraged at hearing of the strife he had caused between her sons. Despite the late hour, Hoelun hitched her white camel to her black cart and rode through the night to reach her son's royal encampment at sunrise.

According to the *Secret History,* Genghis Khan froze in surprise as his mother charged unexpectedly into his *ger,* untied Khasar, put his hat back on his head, and helped him to tie the sash around his waist. Working herself into ever greater anger against her eldest son, she sat down cross-legged, ripped open her *deel,* and pulled out her breasts that were now so old, wrinkled, and worn from nourishing five children that, according to the *Secret History,* even as she held them up in her hands, they still rested on her knees.

"Have you seen these?" she demanded angrily of Genghis Khan as she held up her withered breasts with both hands. "These are the breasts that you sucked!" She then launched into a long tirade against her son. In much the same words that she had used when he killed his half brother Begter, she accused him of acting like an animal that gnaws its own umbilical cord and chews its own afterbirth. To calm and appease her, Genghis Khan agreed to restore Khasar's freedom and his control over some of his followers.

Soon after the fight with her son, Hoelun, who was probably in her late fifties, died. Her property should have passed, according to tradition, to her youngest son, who wanted to add it to his own, giving him control over a total of ten thousand people, more than any other family member. The shaman Teb Tengeri and his six brothers, perhaps with Genghis Khan's implied consent, pushed Temuge Otchigen aside and seized the estate of Hoelun and her followers. When Temuge tried to get back his followers, Teb Tengeri and his brothers publicly humiliated Genghis Khan's youngest brother by making him kneel on the ground behind Teb Tengeri's backside and beg for his life.

Despite the repeated outcries from relatives, Genghis Khan continued to ally himself with Teb Tengeri rather than his own family. The only family member to whom Genghis Khan still seemed willing to listen was his wife Borte. She understood more clearly than her husband the danger posed by seven powerful brothers who stood firmly united and now had their own following within the Mongol nation. After hearing of the latest episode, the humiliation of his youngest brother, Borte angrily explained to Genghis Khan that by allowing Teb Tengeri so much power, Genghis Khan's own sons were in danger. Just as she had been the one to advise Temujin to break with Jamuka back when they had combined their followers, she now demanded that he break with Teb Tengeri and his family. If Teb Tengeri could do these things to the Great Khan's brothers while the khan still lived, she asked her husband, what would he do to the sons or widows after the khan died?

The next time Teb Tengeri appeared in court with his six brothers and their father, Monglik, Temuge Otchigin was waiting inside the *ger* with Genghis Khan. As soon as Teb Tengeri was seated, Temuge came up to him and grabbed him by the collar of his *deel*. Genghis Khan, pretending that the two men were merely about to wrestle, ordered them to take the contest outside the *ger*. Temuge, however, was not seeking a wrestling contest with Teb Tengeri; he was seeking punishment against him. As soon as Temuge pulled Teb Tengeri through the doorway of the *ger*, three men waited to grab and snap his back. Genghis Khan ordered that a small tent be erected over the dying man, and everyone deserted the area.

Teb Tengeri was the last rival Genghis Khan had to face from the steppe tribes. What he could not control he had destroyed. He had neutralized the power of his own relatives, killed the lineages of aristocrats and all rival khans, abolished the old tribes, redistributed the people and, finally, allowed the most powerful shaman on the steppe to be killed.

Genghis Khan appointed a new shaman to take Teb Tengeri's place, but he was an older, less ambitious, and more tractable character. Genghis Khan's followers also learned a lesson. They interpreted his victory as a sign that not only did Genghis Khan have military power but that his spiritual power was greater than that of the most powerful shaman. In the eyes of many followers, Genghis Khan had shown himself to be a powerful shaman, a belief that many Mongols have retained until today.

With all the nomadic tribes united and Genghis Khan securely ensconced as their ruler, it seemed uncertain what should happen next. He had spent so many years locked into the drama with Jamuka and Ong Khan that without them, his large tribe seemed to lack an objective or purpose. Without enemies, they lacked a reason to hold together. Genghis Khan seemed to be searching for new ones, but he found no tribe worthy of the distinction. With no other potential targets, in 1207 he sent his eldest son, twenty-eight-year-old Jochi, and his *tumen* on a campaign into the area the Mongols called *Sibir,* from which derives the modern name of Siberia, to secure the submission of the forest tribes and the reindeer herders. Jochi returned successfully with thousands of new recruits for the Mongol army, as well as tribal leaders with whom Genghis Khan negotiated a number of alliance marriages, including one with Jochi's daughter. In addition to the people, Jochi brought back valuable tribute, including rare furs such as black sable, hunting birds, and other forest products.

Expansion into the north offered little attraction beyond furs and feathers. It was the south that captured Genghis Khan's greatest attention with its far greater variety of manufactured goods—metal, textiles, and novelties. He received the first infusion of goods from the Uighur people who farmed the oases of the great deserts of the Taklimakan and surrounding areas in what is now Xinjiang Autonomous Region in China. Genghis Khan accepted their submission and, in the only way of making an alliance, sought to bring them into his family. He offered his daughter to the Uighur khan in marriage, thereby making him his son-in-law.

In the extension of kinship to the Siberian tribes and the Uighur, Genghis Khan was not merely making alliances between his family and their ruling families. He was accepting the entire tribe or nation into his empire as familial members, since, in the political idiom of the tribes, granting kinship to the khan was tantamount to recognizing family ties with the whole nation. In this way, the idiom of kinship had expanded into a type of citizenship. As Genghis Khan continued to utilize and expand that idiom in the coming years, it came to be a form of universal citizenship based not on a common religion, as among Christian and Muslim people, or just on biology, as in traditional tribal culture. It was based simply on allegiance, acceptance, and loyalty. In time, all the non-Mongol kingdoms in the Mongol Empire became known as *Khari,* derived from the word for *black* and connoting in-laws. Thus, select nations such as the Uighur and the Koreans, as well as select

Turkic groups, would have the honor of being in-laws to the Mongols, whereas intermarriage outside of the "black-kin" would not be permitted.

When the Uighur khan came to the Mongol court for his wedding in approximately 1209, he arrived laden with a camel caravan of lavish gifts, including gold, silver, and pearls of many sizes, shapes, and colors. Without the craft of weaving, the Mongols had only leather, fur, and felt made from pressed wool, so the most important gifts to them were the incredible woven textiles, including silk, brocade, damask, and satin. The visit of the Uighurs highlighted the contrast between the wealth of the agricultural civilization and the poverty of the steppe tribes. Genghis Khan commanded a great army but presided over a largely impoverished people, while to the south, beyond the Gobi, there flowed an intermittent but impressive stream of goods along the Silk Route. He was ready for the opportunity to redress this imbalance of goods and to test his army against others, but such an endeavor carried great risks. Genghis Khan was eager to take the chance, and soon the opportunity, as though delivered in answer to his prayers, presented itself.

No one had yet taken any notice of this upstart ruler and his newly proclaimed nation of Mongols. Outside of the high, inner steppe of Asia, at the time, few people paid attention to the killing of one barbarian chief and the crowning of a newcomer, nor did they relate the destruction of one savage tribe and the rise of its rival. The battles of petty tribes fighting over horses, women, and bolts of cloth lacked the apparent importance of the much more momentous struggles of real civilizations. All of that was about to change.

PART II

The Mongol World War: 1211–1261

By the arms of Zingis and his descendants the globe was shaken: the sultans were overthrown: the caliphs fell, and the Cæsars trembled on their throne.

EDWARD GIBBON,
Decline and Fall of the Roman Empire

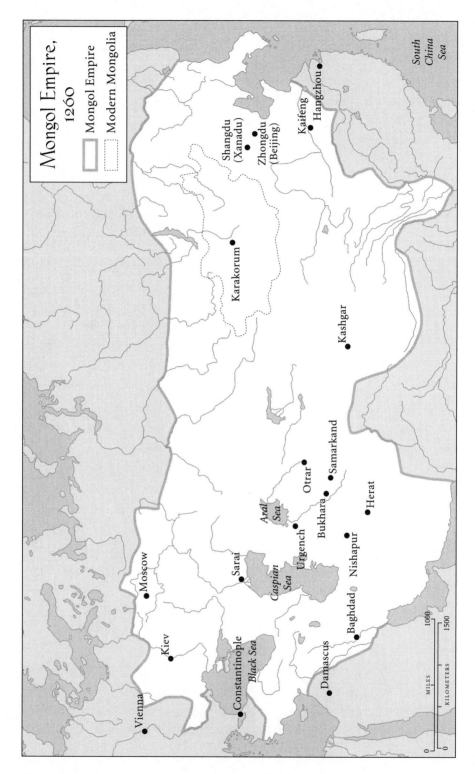

Mongol Empire, 1260

☐ Mongol Empire
☐ Modern Mongolia

South China Sea

Hangzhou
Kaifeng
Shangdu (Xanadu)
Zhongdu (Beijing)
Karakorum
Kashgar
Otrar
Aral Sea
Samarkand
Bukhara
Herat
Urgench
Nishapur
Sarai
Caspian Sea
Baghdad
Moscow
Kiev
Constantinople
Black Sea
Damascus
Vienna

MILES
KILOMETERS

0   1000
0   1500

4

Spitting on the Golden Khan

The hooves of our Mongol horses go everywhere.
They climb to the heaven and plunge into the sea.
Y E L Ü   C H U C A I ,   1 2 3 7

IN 1210, THE YEAR of the Horse and the forty-eighth year of the life of Genghis Khan and the fourth year of his new nation, a delegation arrived at the Mongol encampment to proclaim the ascension of a new Golden Khan to the Jurched throne and demand the submission of Genghis Khan and the Mongols as a vassal nation. From their capital city of Zhongdu, where modern Beijing now rises, the Jurched dynasty, founded nearly a century earlier in 1125, ruled Manchuria and much of modern-day Inner Mongolia and northern China. As a tribal people themselves from the forests of Manchuria, they claimed sovereignty over all the tribes of the steppe. Ong Khan had offered allegiance to them in the past, and the Jurched seemed eager to reassert their superiority over Genghis Khan, who had replaced Ong Khan as the dominant figure among the nomads of the steppe.

Jurched power over the steppe rested not from military prowess as much as from their tight control of goods flowing to the pastoralists from the workshops and cities across China. The position of a steppe khan rested on his ability to win in battle and to ensure a steady supply of trade goods. Usually the two coincided when battlefield victory provided an opportunity to loot the defeated. Genghis Khan's unprecedented success in defeating and uniting all the tribes had the inadvertent consequence of ending the looting and thereby stifling the flow of goods. Since all manufactured goods originated in the south, Genghis Khan could either offer allegiance to one of the southern rulers and receive goods as a vassal warrior, or he could attack them and seize the goods.

Genghis Khan placed no trust in the Jurched. The Mongols had much closer ethnic and linguistic affinity with the Khitan, whom the Jurched had defeated and now dominated. Sensing the power of the new Mongol ruler, many Khitan had fled from Jurched territory to find sanctuary under Genghis Khan. In 1208, four high court officials deserted to the Mongols and urged them to attack the Jurched, but, fearful of a trap or some other nefarious scheme, Genghis Khan refused.

The unexpected death of the Golden Khan of the Jurched and the ascension of his young son to the throne in 1210 offered the Jurched court an opportunity to assess Genghis Khan by sending the envoy to him to announce the change of events and demand a strong show of submission from him. An idea of the type of ceremony expected is contained in an 1878 report in the *Peking Gazette* describing the investiture of a Mongol official by an envoy from the court of the Manchus, descendants of the Jurched. The young Mongol knelt "reverently upon the ground" and, "with the deepest gratitude," acknowledged himself "to be a Mongol slave of inferior ability, perfectly unable to repay in the slightest degree the Imperial favours of which his family have been the recipients for generations past, he declares his intention of performing his duties to the best of his feeble powers." He then "turned himself toward the Palace and beat his head upon the ground . . . in grateful acknowledgement of the Imperial bounty."

Genghis Khan knew full well how to kowtow—he had done it on Mount Burkhan Khaldun in repeated homage to the Eternal Blue Sky—but now, at nearly fifty years of age, he would kowtow to no man. Nor was he anyone's Mongol slave. Upon receiving the order to demonstrate submission, Genghis Khan is reported to have turned to the south and spat on the ground; then he unleashed a line of vindictive insults to the Golden Khan, mounted his horse, and rode toward the north, leaving the stunned envoy choking in his dust. Genghis Khan's defiance of the envoys of the Golden Khan was tantamount to a declaration of war between the Mongols and the Jurched. Genghis Khan's need for trade goods already gave him a reason to make war on the Jurched, and the demand from the Golden Khan for submission now presented him with the pretext for attacking.

After the encounter with the Jurched envoy, Genghis Khan returned to his home base on the Kherlen River and, in the spring of 1211, the Year of the Sheep, summoned a *khuriltai*. Since everyone knew the issue to be decided, the people could exercise a veto simply by not showing up; if too few people came to the *khuriltai*, Genghis Khan would not have been able to proceed. By organizing a long public discussion, everyone in the community was included into the process, and, most important, everyone understood why they were fighting the war. Although on the battlefield the soldiers were expected to obey without question, even the lowest ranking were treated as junior partners who were expected to understand the endeavor and to have some voice in it. The senior members met together in large public meetings to discuss the issues, then individually went to their own units to continue the discussion with the lower-ranking warriors. To have the full commitment of every warrior, it was important that each of them, from the highest to the lowest, participate and know where he stood in the larger plan of events.

By including representatives from the allied Uighur and Tangut nations, Genghis Khan solidified his relations with them and thereby protected the exposed underbelly and rear of his land when he launched his invasion. On the home front, he also needed to inspire his people with the courage and understanding of this war. Toward both goals, Genghis Khan appealed to the honor of his followers and to their need to avenge past wrongs, but he also held out to them a much broader opportunity of unlimited goods from the great wealth of the cities of the Jurched. According to the *Secret History*, once he felt confident that his people and allies stood firmly with him, Genghis Khan publicly withdrew from the assembled delegates of the *khuriltai* to pray privately on a nearby mountain. He removed his hat and belt, bowed down before the Eternal Blue Sky, and stated his case to his supernatural guardians. He recounted the generations of grievances his people held against the Jurched and detailed the torture and killing of his ancestors. He explained that he had not sought this war against the Golden Khan and had not initiated the quarrel.

In his absence, the Mongol people divided into three separate groups, one each of men, women, and children, in order to fast and pray. For three nervous days and nights, the assembled Mongol nation awaited, bareheaded and hungry, the decision of the Eternal Blue Sky and the orders of Genghis Khan. Night and day they mumbled their ancient Mongol prayer of *"huree, huree, huree"* to the Eternal Blue Sky.

At dawn on the fourth day, Genghis Khan emerged with the verdict: "The Eternal Blue Sky has promised us victory and vengeance."

As the Mongol army set out south toward the splendid cities of the south, their overly confident Jurched enemies awaited them and mocked the Mongol advance. "Our empire is like the sea; yours is but a handful of sand," a Chinese scholar recorded the Jurched khan as saying in reference to Genghis Khan. "How can we fear you?" he asked.

He would soon have his answer.

In the thirteenth century, the area south of Mongolia now occupied by China consisted of many independent states and kingdoms containing perhaps a third of the world population. With some 50 million people, the Jurched kingdom was only the second largest of the many kingdoms occupying the territory now included in modern China. The largest and most important territory was under the administration of the Sung dynasty, heir to centuries of Chinese civilization, based in Hangzhou and ruling some 60 million people in southern China. A string of nomadic buffer states separated the Mongolian plateau from the Sung, each buffer state consisting of a hybrid of agricultural and grazing regions ruled over by a former nomadic tribe that had conquered and settled among its subjects in order to more efficiently exploit them. Frequently, a new tribe emerged from the steppes to displace the older tribe that had grown weak and dissipated from several generations of soft city life. In a long-established cycle, a nomadic army swept down from the steppe, conquered the peasants and cities to the south, created a new dynasty, and, after a few years, fell to the attack of another marauding tribe. Although the identities of the ruling tribe changed from century to century, the system had already been in place for thousands of years.

To the west of the Jurched were the kingdoms of the Tangut, then the

Uighur, and finally, in the Tian Shan mounts, the Black Khitan. The Uighur had already made their commitment to Genghis Khan, and, in what seemed to be a practice war, he had recently subdued the Tangut. The conquest of the Tangut took place through a series of raids between 1207 and 1209. The campaign was like a thorough dress rehearsal of the coming battle against the much stronger Jurched, complete with a crossing of the Gobi. The Tangut, a Tibetan people who had created an empire of farmers and herders along the upper reaches of the Yellow River in what is the modern Gansu Province in China, occupied a weak link along the line of oases in the interior desert that controlled the flow of trade goods from the Muslim West to the Chinese East. The routes stretched like thin, delicate ribbons across the deserts of the interior and provided the only links, albeit fragile ones, between the great civilizations of the East and the West. The Tangut raids had spurred Genghis Khan to learn a new type of warfare against walled cities, moats, and fortresses. Not only were the Tangut well fortified, but they had some 150,000 soldiers, nearly twice the size of the army Genghis Khan brought with him. Unlike generals who had grown up with cities and had access to centuries-old besieging techniques, Genghis Khan had to invent his own methods. He quickly learned the simple tactics, such as cutting off the Mongols' enemies from the surrounding food supply, but he soon attempted more unorthodox methods, such as when he attacked the fortified Tangut capital by diverting a channel of the Yellow River to flood it. With their inexperience in engineering, the Mongols succeeded in diverting the river, but they wiped out their own camp instead of the Tangut. Nevertheless, the Mongols survived their dangerous mistake. Genghis Khan learned from it and went on to conquer the city. In the future, the Mongols would use this method again, but each time they would be more adept at it and use it more successfully.

With Genghis Khan's decision to cross the Gobi and invade the Jurched in 1211, he had begun not just another Chinese border war: He had lit a conflagration that would eventually consume the world. No one, not even Genghis Khan, could have seen what was coming. He showed no sign of any global ambitions inasmuch as he fought only one war at a time, and for him the time had come to fight the Jurched. But starting from the Jurched campaign, the well-trained and tightly organized Mongol army would charge out of its highland home and overrun everything from the Indus River to the Danube, from the Pacific Ocean to the Mediterranean Sea. In a flash, only thirty years, the Mongol warriors would defeat every army, capture every fort, and bring down the walls of every city they encountered. Christians, Muslims, Buddhists, and Hindus would soon kneel before the dusty boots of illiterate young Mongol horsemen.

Crossing the vast Gobi required extensive preparation. Before the army set out, squads of soldiers went out to check the water sources and to report on grass conditions and weather. A Chinese observer remarked how the advance group scouted out every hill and every spot before the main army arrived. They wanted to know everyone in the area, every resource, and they always sought to have a ready path of retreat should it be needed.

The Mongol was ideally suited to travel long distances; each man carried precisely what he needed, but nothing more. In addition to his *deel,* the traditional wool robe that reached to his ankles, he wore pants, a fur hat with earflaps, and riding boots with thick soles. In addition to clothes designed to protect him in the worst weather, each warrior carried flints for making fires, leather canteens for water and milk, files to sharpen arrowheads, a lasso for rounding up animals or prisoners, sewing needles for mending clothes, a knife and a hatchet for cutting, and a skin bag into which to pack everything. Each squad of ten carried a small tent.

The movement and formation of the Mongol army were determined by two factors that set them clearly apart from the armies of every other traditional civilization. First, the Mongol military consisted entirely of cavalry, armed riders without a marching infantry. By contrast, in virtually all other armies, the majority of the warriors would have been foot soldiers. Approximately sixty-five thousand Mongol horsemen left on the Jurched campaign to confront an army with about the same number of horsemen, as well as another eighty-five thousand infantry soldiers, giving the Jurched an advantage of well over two to one but without the mobility of the Mongol force.

The second unique characteristic of the Mongol army was that it traveled without a commissary or cumbersome supply train other than its large reserve of horses that always accompanied the soldiers. As they moved, they milked the animals, slaughtered them for food, and fed themselves from hunting and looting. Marco Polo alleged that the Mongol warriors could travel ten days without stopping to make a fire or heat food, that they drank horses' blood, and that each man carried with him ten pounds of dried milk paste, putting one pound of it in a leather flask of water each day to make his meal. The warrior carried strips of dried meat and dried curd with him that he could chew while riding; and when he had fresh meat, but no time to cook it, he put the raw flesh under his saddle so it would soon be softened and edible.

The Chinese noted with surprise and disgust the ability of the Mongol warriors to survive on little food and water for long periods; according to one, the entire army could camp without a single puff of smoke since they needed no fires to cook. Compared to the Jurched soldiers, the Mongols were much healthier and stronger. The Mongols consumed a steady diet of meat, milk, yogurt, and other dairy products, and they fought men who lived on gruel made from various grains. The grain diet of the peasant warriors stunted their bones, rotted their teeth, and left them weak and prone to disease. In contrast, the poorest Mongol soldier ate mostly protein, thereby giving him strong teeth and bones. Unlike the Jurched soldiers, who were dependent on a heavy carbohydrate diet, the Mongols could more easily go a day or two without food.

Traditional armies moved in long columns of men marching the same route with their large supplies of food following them. By contrast, the Mongol army spread out over a vast area to provide sufficient pasture for the animals and to maximize hunting opportunities for the soldiers. Genghis Khan moved at the center, flanked by the Army of the Right to the west and the Army of the Left to the east. A smaller unit took positions as advance guard and another as guard of the rear, where the Mongols also carried their reserve animals. The decimal organization of Genghis Khan's army made it highly mutable and mobile. Each unit of ten thousand functioned like a miniature version of Genghis Khan's camp. The commander of ten thousand moved at the center of his unit of one thousand, and he stationed the other nine units around him—to the left, the right, the back, and the front—as needed. Rather than a hierarchy of military units, Genghis Khan organized his men into a set of concentric circles.

Although the Mongols moved their military camps frequently, the central camp for each unit was laid out in a precise pattern so that newly arriving soldiers always knew where to report and how to find whatever they needed. Each Mongol unit of one thousand traveled with its own medical unit, usually composed of Chinese doctors, to care for the sick and wounded. The tents were lined up in specific formations, each formation with its name and purpose, and even the insides of the tents were arranged in precisely the same way. After a day of travel, fighting, or hunting, the army camped with the officers at the center of the camp surrounded by guards and other soldiers. At night, horses were kept ready in case they might be needed, and a perimeter was set up at the edge of the camp.

By contrast to the well-structured and neatly organized center of the camp, most of the common warriors broke up into their small bands and spread out over the countryside to camp at night. At dusk they made small fires, preferably when it was too light for the fire to show up clearly at a distance, yet too dark for the smoke to be seen from very far away. With the fire, they quickly prepared their only hot meal of the day. After eating, they did not linger or sleep by the fire; they dispersed into yet smaller groups of three to five men who slept in hidden recesses spread throughout the area. As soon as daylight broke the next morning, they began the day with a careful reconnaissance of the right, the left, the back, and the front.

With his men spread out over such a large area, communications became more important, yet more difficult. Conventional armies moved and camped in massive columns, and the commanders could easily communicate with one another through written messages. For the Mongols, the troops were more spread out, and even the officers were illiterate. All communication at every level had to be oral, not written. Orders moved by word of mouth from man to man. The problem with an oral system of communication lay in the accuracy of the message; the message had to be repeated precisely each time to each person and then remembered exactly as spoken. To ensure accurate memorization, the officers composed their orders in rhyme, using a standardized system known to every soldier. The Mongol warriors used a set of fixed melodies and poetic styles into which various words could be improvised according to the meaning of the message. For a soldier, hearing the message was like learning a new verse to a song that he already knew.

The soldiers, like bands of riders on the steppe still do today, frequently sang as they rode in their small groups. In addition to singing about what soldiers always sing about—home, women, and fighting—the Mongol soldiers sang their laws and rules of conduct, which had also been set to music so that every man might know them. By memorizing the laws and constantly practicing the format of their message-songs, every man was ready, at any moment's notice, to learn a new message, in the form of a new verse to these well-rehearsed songs, and take it where ordered.

Despite the disadvantages of fighting on alien land outnumbered by enemies, Genghis Khan had the advantage of lessons learned from a lifetime of warfare, and he knew his troops and his officers intimately. He had fought with many of them for more than a quarter of a century, and a few of the generals, such as Boorchu and Jelme, had been with him for nearly forty years. He knew that he could trust them on long campaigns far away from his oversight. He also understood each general's strengths and weaknesses. Jebe, one of his commanders, would fight fast and furiously, taking unusual chances and inspiring resolute courage among his men in battle; while Muhali, another commander, moved slowly and methodically but could sustain longer and broader assignments.

The Mongols, no matter how rigorous their training, how precise their discipline, or how determined their will, could not conquer fortified cities by conventional warfare. In facing the Jurched, Genghis Khan employed the basic strategy of his earlier steppe wars by trying to win the battle before the first arrow was shot across the battlefield, to defeat the enemy by first creating confusion and then instilling fear to break his spirit. Because the Mongols initially lacked the weapons or knowledge to break down the massive city walls, they wreaked havoc in the surrounding countryside and then disappeared, only to reappear again just when it seemed that the city was safe.

Genghis Khan sought to further undermine his enemies by exploiting any internal social turmoil or rift he could identify. In the Jurched campaign, his first effort was to divide the Khitan from their Jurched rulers while breaking the confidence that the Chinese subjects had that the Jurched could defend them. In a masterful propaganda campaign, the Mongols entered Jurched territory announcing themselves as a liberating force intent on restoring the older Khitan royal family that had ruled before the Jurched overthrew them a century earlier. Before the fighting began, many Khitan fled to join the Mongols, whom they saw as relatives speaking the same language. In one of the first actions of the war, Jebe, accompanied by Genghis Khan's brother Khasar, led a Mongol army straight for the Khitan homeland along the Liao River. The Mongol soldiers found enthusiastic support from the Khitan, and they quickly located a descendant of the Yelü dynasty, the former Khitan royal family. The following year, 1212, Genghis Khan officially restored the Khitan monarchy as a vassal state within the Mongol Empire. Of course, the Mongols had not yet conquered all the Jurched lands, but by creating the vassal state, he managed to further divide the Jurched and attract more deserters to the Mongol side.

Throughout his campaign he found members of the old Khitan aristocracy anxious to help him understand the land he had invaded. One of the most important would be Yelü Chucai, a young man in his twenties from the royal family of the Khitan. He attracted Mongol attention because of his training in astrology and the esoteric art of scapulimancy, divining the future by reading the cracks in the heated shoulder blade of a sacrificed sheep or goat. Because he was a native Khitan and spoke that language, he could easily communicate with the Mongols, but he also had extensive knowledge of Chinese culture. With their understanding of the Mongolian and Chinese languages, as well as their skill in writing and knowledge of law and tradition among the settled populace, the Khitan scholars proved so useful in administering the Mongol Empire that Genghis Khan concentrated more attention on attracting or capturing scholars of all sorts in an effort to apply their knowledge to benefit the empire. Thereafter, everywhere he went, he had such men brought to him for interrogation to see what skill they might have and where in his empire it might be applied.

The Mongol way of fighting was a refinement of the traditional steppe system that had been developed in Mongolia over many thousands of years. Superior weapons, in the end, did not account for the Mongol success. Weapon technology does not remain secret for long, and whatever works for one side can be readily adopted for use by the enemy after just a few battles. The Mongol's success arose from their cohesion and discipline, bred over millennia as nomads working in small groups, and from their steadfast loyalty to their leader.

Warriors everywhere have been taught to die for their leader, but Genghis Khan never asked his men to die for him. Above all else, he waged war with this strategic purpose in mind: to preserve Mongol life. Unlike other generals and emperors in history who easily ordered hundreds of thousands of soldiers to their death, Genghis Khan would never willingly sacrifice a single one. The most important rules that he created for his army concerned the loss of soldiers. On and off the battlefield, the Mongol warrior was forbidden to speak of death, injury, or defeat. Just to think of it might make it happen. Even mentioning the name of a fallen comrade or other dead warrior constituted a serious taboo. Every Mongol soldier had to live his life as a warrior with the assumption that he was immortal, that no one could defeat him or harm him, that nothing could kill him. At the last moment of life, when all had failed and no hope remained, the Mongol warrior was supposed to look upward and beckon his fate by calling out the name of the Eternal Blue Sky as his final earthly words. In fighting on the steppe, the nomads left the corpses of fallen soldiers and their possessions on the field to be disposed of by animals and to decompose naturally.

In the cultivated lands far from home, the Mongols feared that the body would not be allowed a natural decomposition and that local people might desecrate it. In another change from the normal pattern for steppe battles during the Jurched campaign, the Mongols began sending home the dead warriors for interment on the steppe. War captives transported the dead bodies by some means, probably sewing them in leather bags put on camels or in carts drawn by oxen. On the few occasions when this proved impossible, the Mongols had the bodies taken to a grassy area nearby and secretly buried each man with all of his belongings. They then drove animals over the grave to obscure it and prevent the peasants from finding it and exhuming the possessions.

The Mongols did not find honor in fighting; they found honor in winning. They had a single goal in every campaign—total victory. Toward this end, it did not matter what tactics were used against the enemy or how the battles were fought or avoided being fought. Winning by clever deception or cruel trickery was still winning and carried no stain on the bravery of the warriors, since there would be plenty of other occasions for showing prowess on the field. For the Mongol warrior, there was no such thing as individual honor in battle if the battle was lost. As Genghis Khan reportedly said, there is no good in anything until it is finished.

Nowhere did Mongol ingenuity show itself more clearly than in their ability to transform the Jurched's greatest asset, their large population, into their greatest liability. Before attacking a city, the Mongols typically cleared out all the surrounding villages. They forcefully conscripted the local labor through an extension of their decimal organization of the military. Each Mongol warrior had to round up ten local men to work under his command; if any of them died, he had to replace the worker so that he always had ten men at his disposal. As an extension of the army, these captives performed the daily tasks of getting food and water for the animals and soldiers, as well as gathering needed material, such as stones and dirt, to fill in the moat in the upcoming siege. These conscripted men would also maneuver and operate the siege engines that pounded the walls with wooden or stone missiles and would push the movable towers built to breach the city walls.

For the Mongols, the lifestyle of the peasant seemed incomprehensible. The Jurched territory was filled with so many people and yet so few animals; this was a stark contrast to Mongolia, where there were normally five to ten animals for each human. To the Mongols, the farmers' fields were just grasslands, as were the gardens, and the peasants were like grazing animals rather than real humans who ate meat. The Mongols referred to these grass-eating people with the same terminology that they used for cows and goats. The masses of peasants were just so many herds, and when the soldiers went out to round up their people or to drive them away, they did so with the same terminology, precision, and emotion used in rounding up yaks.

Traditional armies of the era treated villages as resources to be looted and the peasants as a nuisance to be raped, killed, or disposed of in any convenient way. By contrast, the Mongols, who were always low in numbers compared with the place they invaded, put the massive number of people to strategic uses. The Mongol warriors modified the traditional steppe strategy of rounding up the enemy's herds and stampeding them toward their owners' battle lines or homes, thereby creating great confusion before the soldiers raced in to attack. In the Jurched campaign, the Mongols adapted this tactic to the herds of the peasant farmers. The Mongol army divided into small units that attacked undefended villages, set them afire, and chased out the residents. The frightened peasants fled in all directions. They clogged the highways and made it difficult for the Jurched supply convoys to move. In the Jurched campaign, more than a million refugees fled the countryside in desperation and poured into the cities; they ate up huge stores of food, and caused chaos wherever they went.

Instead of being followed by mobs of refugees as was typical for the armies of the time, the Mongols were preceded by them, and the Mongols also used the displaced peasants in a more direct way as shields and as living battering rams against the city gates. The Mongols showed little concern for the loss of enemy life so long as it preserved Mongol life. As the captives fell in battle, their bodies helped to fill in the moats and form pathways over defensive holes and structures made by the enemies. Trapped inside their cities, the Jurched and their subjects starved; and in one city after another, they resorted to cannibalism. Discontent grew, and urban mutinies and peasant rebellions broke out against the Jurched officials, who proved unable to protect, feed, or manage the massive numbers of refugees. In the worst such rebellion, the Jurched army ended up killing some thirty thousand of their own peasants.

In contrast to the massive infantry armies that moved slowly and fought along a particular front or on a specific battlefield, the Mongols practiced warfare across the entire territory, and the ensuing turmoil and confusion allowed the Mongols to employ clever trickery of all sorts. In one episode, the Mongols captured a convoy with a high-ranking official en route to relieve the besieged city of Dading. One of the Mongols dressed in the envoy's clothes, took his official papers, and proceeded to the enemy city in disguise. As he arrived, by prearrangement, the Mongol army lifted its siege and departed. Once inside the city, the Mongol pretender fooled the local officials into believing that they had just defeated the Mongols. The pretender then oversaw the painstaking dismantling of the city's defenses and the withdrawal of troops. After several weeks of disarmament, he sent word to the Mongols, who returned like lightning and easily took the city.

The Mongols not only took advantage of such trickery, but in their relentless use of propaganda, they spread stories to foment anxiety and fear among the enemy. In one apocryphal account circulated to create anxiety among the enemy, the Mongols supposedly promised to retreat from a besieged city if the Jurched defenders would give them a large number of cats and birds as booty. According to the story, the starving residents eagerly gathered the animals and gave them to the Mongols. After receiving all the birds and animals, the Mongols attached burning torches and banners to their tails and released them, whereupon the frightened animals raced back into the city and set it on fire. The story supplied a dramatic dose of war propaganda.

After all the reconnaissance, organization, and propaganda, when the attack finally came, the Mongol army sought to create as much confusion and havoc for the enemy as possible. One of the most common forms of attack, similar to the Bush Formation, was the Crow Swarm or Falling Stars attack. At the signal of a drum, or by fire at night, the horsemen came galloping from all directions at once. In the words of a Chinese observer of the time, "they come as though the sky were falling, and they disappear like the flash of lightning." The enemy was shaken and unnerved by the sudden assault and equally sudden disappearance, the roaring wave of noise followed by a greater silence. Before they could respond properly to the attack, the Mongols were gone and left the enemy bleeding and confused.

Beginning with the Tangut campaigns, Genghis Khan had discovered that Chinese engineers knew how to build siege machines that could batter city walls with massive stones from far away. The Chinese had already developed a number of those devices: the catapult hurled stones, flaming liquids, and other harmful substances at or across city walls; and the trebuchet, a catapult powered by the drop of a heavy counterweight, threw objects even faster than the torsion catapult. The ballista was a mechanical device that shot large arrows that could damage buildings and structures and kill any person or animal in its path. Although quite old in the military history of siege warfare, the weapons were new to the Mongols, but they soon became a permanent part of the arsenal of Genghis Khan, who appreciated the efficiency and ingenuity behind them. More than merely using the weapons, Genghis Khan acquired the engineering intelligence needed to create them. The Mongols eagerly rewarded engineers who defected to them and, after each battle, carefully selected engineers from among the captives and impressed them into Mongol service. Genghis Khan made engineering units a permanent part of the Mongol army, and with each new battle and each conquest, his war machinery grew in complexity and efficiency.

The siege engines exercised a particular fascination for the Mongols because they allowed the attackers to stay well outside of the city and away from the danger of the person-to-person combat that they so abhorred. At some point, the Mongols encountered the Jurched use of the firelance, a bamboo tube stuffed with gunpowder, which when lit produced a slow burn that spewed sparks, flames, and smoke out of the end of the tube like a flamethrower. Developed from firecrackers, this weapon was used to ignite fires and as a device to disorient the enemy and their horses; in later refinements, the Mongols would adapt it for many more military purposes.

When he could not overtake their fortifications, Genghis Khan tried to draw the enemy out from their stronghold through strategems such as pretending to retreat, as illustrated in Jebe's siege of Liaoyang during the Jurched campaign. In a movement known as the Dog Fight tactic, he feigned a withdrawal, ordering his troops to leave behind a lot of their equipment and stores as though they had fled in great fearful haste. The city officials sent soldiers out to gather up the booty, and they quickly clogged the open gates with carts and animals transporting all the goods. With the soldiers on the open field, and the city gates opened, the Mongols fell upon them and raced through the open doors to capture the city.

As lifelong nomads, the Mongols learned early to fight on the move. For the soldier farmer, to flee meant to lose; to chase meant to win. The sedentary soldier sought to drive the attacker away from the place. The nomad sought to kill the enemy, and it mattered not at all whether he killed the enemy while attacking toward him or fleeing from him. For the Mongol, both directions represented fighting; a fleeing conquest was just as good as a stationary one. Once Mongols lured their opponents out of their walled cities, they applied the techniques they had learned for managing the movement of large groups of animals. Most commonly, they either strung their pursuers out in a long line that became increasingly defenseless and was easily attacked as soon as the Mongols had lured them into a trap, or the fleeing Mongols divided into their small squads and led their pursuers off in small groups that could be more easily overcome.

Even when routed or pursued by a determined enemy, the Mongols employed still more tricks with which to save themselves. If they were surprised and overtaken while on patrol, they usually carried some valuable items with them to strew on the ground as they escaped. The enemy invariably broke ranks to retrieve the goods, often fighting among themselves to do so, and thereby allowed the Mongols to escape. At other times, the Mongols threw sand in the wind or tied tree branches to their horses' tails to whip up the dust in order to obscure their movements or to make the pursuers think that the Mongols were in much greater numbers than they actually were.

After the first year of the Jurched campaigns, it became clear that the worst danger for the Mongols derived not from battle but from the unpleasant climate. The lower altitude and closeness to great rivers and the ocean made the air hold its moisture, and in the summer, the heat and humidity became nearly unbearable for the Mongols and their shaggy horses. Repeatedly, they reported falling ill with a horrible variety of maladies when in the agricultural and urban areas. Campaigning nearly halted in the summer, when large numbers of the Mongols and their horse herds withdrew the relatively short distance to the higher and cooler grasslands of Inner Mongolia.

In 1214, Genghis Khan, at last, besieged the court of the Golden Khan himself in Zhongdu (Beijing). The court had just been through a palace coup, and the new Golden Khan had endured so much internal strife that rather than face a prolonged siege and war, he agreed to a settlement with the Mongols to make them withdraw. He gave them massive amounts of silk, silver, and gold, as well as three thousand horses and five hundred young men and women. To seal the arrangement, the Golden Khan recognized himself as a vassal of Genghis Khan and gave him one of his royal princesses as a wife.

In response, Genghis Khan broke his siege of Zhongdu and began the long trek back toward Outer Mongolia on the north side of the Gobi. The Khitan had received back much of their land, and their royal family had been restored; the Jurched would be allowed to keep a smaller kingdom for themselves. He evidenced no intention of ruling these areas or setting up a Mongol government so long as he could get the goods he wanted. Just as he had left the Uighur and the Tangut in charge of their own lands, he was glad to leave the Jurched and the Khitan to administer their kingdom in whatever way they saw fit so long as they remained subservient to the Mongols and supplied them with tribute.

Since both the Khitan and the Jurched acknowledged Genghis Khan as the supreme emperor over all of them, he had no further reason to stay in their lands. The summer was just beginning, but already the heat and dryness prevented his army crossing the Gobi back toward home. Instead, they made camp on the south side of the Gobi at a place called Dolon Nor (Seven Lakes). As they awaited the cooler days of autumn, the troops could enjoy games, feasting, and the talents of the musicians and singers whom they had captured and were taking home with them.

As soon as the Mongols withdrew from the newly conquered territory, however, the Jurched authorities began to renege on their agreement. Mistrusting his own subjects, whom he suspected of secretly siding with the Mongol invaders, the Golden Khan, whom Genghis Khan had left on the throne, evacuated his capital at Zhongdu and the entire court fled south to Kaifeng, where they thought they would be well beyond the ability of the Mongol army to penetrate. For Genghis Khan, the flight of the Golden Khan was an act of betrayal of their new alliance, and he considered it rebellion. Although he had been away from his homeland between the Onon and Kherlen Rivers for more than three years, Genghis Khan prepared to return to fight again. He organized his army for a fourth year of fighting, marched down from Inner Mongolia, and headed back toward the capital that had surrendered to him and his army only a few months previously.

The Golden Khan had left a contingent of soldiers to guard the old capital city, but the soldiers and the people knew that they had been deserted. Genghis Khan's victories in the previous year's campaign inspired a mounting wave of support from within the enemy ranks, particularly those abandoned by the Golden Khan. In the traditional Chinese view, victory in war came to those whom Heaven favored—and with an increasingly long list of victories to his credit, it became apparent to Chinese peasants and Jurched warriors alike that Genghis Khan fought under the clear mandate of Heaven, and to fight against him risked offending Heaven itself. Many Jurched and other tribal soldiers in the service of the Golden Khan also discerned in Genghis Khan a true steppe warrior, like their own ancestors were prior to conquering and settling in cities. They had more in common with him and his soldiers than with the effete and debauched rulers who had, in any event, abandoned them to their fate against the invaders. Entire regiments, with their officers and weapons, deserted to join the Mongol forces.

Genghis Khan and his newly incorporated allies easily took the city. This time, however, he presented no opportunity for the defeated Jurched to submit tribute; the city would be punished and looted. The Mongols would take everything. Once it became clear that the city would soon fall, Genghis Khan turned over the final assault to his subordinates. Irritated by the increasing summer heat and disgusted by the filth of sedentary life, Genghis Khan left Zhongdu to return to the higher, drier, and more open lands of Inner Mongolia. He delegated the looting of the city to Khada, a Khitan commander, and his troops since they were more accustomed to managing cities and would know best how to extract the wealth. Mongol officials would wait outside the city some distance away for the loot to be brought to them and recorded. Genghis Khan expected the sacking to be executed in the usual and efficient Mongol manner that he had insisted upon since the defeat of the Tatars. In the Mongol way, soldiers treated the collection of loot as they did the harvesting of animals on the group hunt, distributing it among all the Mongols according to their rank. Down to the last brass button or final grain of silver, all of it was allocated according to a precise formula, from the 10 percent for the khan to the specified share for orphans and widows.

The new Mongol allies, however, either did not understand the system or simply refused to abide by it. Many of them, particularly the Khitan and the Chinese, who had suffered great repression and had many complaints against the Jurched, lusted after revenge and destruction. They felt that each soldier had the right to keep what he seized. They stripped gold from the walls of palaces, pried precious stones out of their settings, and seized chests filled with gold and silver coins. They loaded the precious metals into oxcarts and tied bundles of silk on their camels' backs.

Genghis Khan considered plunder to be an important matter of state, and as such he sent the chief Mongol judge, Shigi-Khutukhu, to the city to oversee the methodical looting and compile a meticulous inventory. Instead of an orderly process, Shigi-Khutukhu encountered chaos. Mongol officials outside the city, including the royal cook, had accepted silk embroidered with gold as bribes to allow the chaotic looting by the allied soldiers to continue; and when Shigi-Khutukhu arrived, he, too, was offered a personal share of the goods. He refused and returned to Genghis Khan to report the misconduct.

Genghis Khan became angry, rebuked the Khitan, and confiscated the goods, but no record of the punishment survives.

As the Mongol warriors withdrew from the cities of the Jurched, they had one final punishment to inflict upon the land where they had already driven out the people and burned their villages. Genghis Khan wanted to leave a large open land with ample pastures should his army need to return. The plowed fields, stone walls, and deep ditches had slowed the Mongol horses and hindered their ability to move across the landscape in any direction they wished. The same things also prevented the free migration of the herds of antelope, asses, and other wild animals that the Mongols enjoyed hunting. When the Mongols left from their Jurched campaign, they churned up the land behind them by having their horses trample the farmland with their hooves and prepare it to return to open pasture. They wanted to ensure that the peasants never returned to their villages and fields. In this way, Inner Mongolia remained a grazing land, and the Mongols created a large buffer zone of pastures and forests between the tribal lands and the fields of the sedentary farmers. The grassy steppes served as ready stores of pasturage for their horses that allowed them easier access in future raids and campaigns, and they provided a ready store of meat in the herds of wild animals that returned once the farmers and villagers had been expelled.

Through the first half of 1215, the Year of the Pig, the Mongols slowly set out with caravans of people, animals, and goods from the smoldering ruins of Zhongdu to the high, arid plateau of Inner Mongolia. They gathered again at Dolon Nor, where Genghis Khan had waited unsuccessfully to cross back home one year earlier, and they waited for the summer to pass before venturing across the Gobi. Genghis Khan had, once again, shown his ability to win in war, and now he demonstrated, on a scale unprecedented in the history of steppe khans, his ability to bring the goods home to his people.

A river of brightly colored silk flowed out of China. It was as though Genghis Khan had rerouted all the different twisting channels of the Silk Route, combined them into one large stream, and redirected it northward to spill out across the Mongol steppes. The caravans of camels and oxcarts carried so much of the precious cloth that the Mongols used silk to wrap their other goods and as packing material. They threw away their rawhide ropes and used twisted cords of silk instead. They bundled robes embroidered with silver and golden thread in the designs of blooming peonies, flying cranes, breaking waves, and mythical beasts, and they packed silk slippers sewn with tiny pearls. The Mongols filled carts with silk rugs, wall hangings, pillows, cushions, and blankets, as well as silk sashes, braid, fringe, and tassels. They carried bolts of raw silk, silken threads, and cloth worked into every imaginable type of clothing or decorations and in more colors than the Mongol language could identify.

In addition to silk, satin, brocade, and gauze, the bundles contained whatever objects the Mongol eye fancied and could be moved, including lacquered furniture, paper fans, porcelain bowls, metal armor, bronze knives, wooden puppets, iron kettles, brass pots, board games, and carved saddles. The Mongols carried jugs of perfume and makeup made from ocher, yellow lead, indigo, flower extracts, fragrant waxes, balsam, and musk. They brought hair ornaments and jewelry crafted from precious metals, ivory, or tortoiseshell and studded with turquoise, pearls, cornelian, coral, lapis lazuli, emeralds, and diamonds. Wagons loaded with skins of wine, casks of honey, and bricks of black tea followed camels that smelled of incense, medicines, aphrodisiacs, and special woods of cinnabar, camphor, and sandalwood.

Long lines of clerks laboriously cataloged, checked, and rechecked the goods of each caravan of camels and oxcarts. Musicians played and sang to delight their captors as the caravan moved. Whenever the caravan paused, acrobats, contortionists, and jugglers performed while young girls gathered dried dung for the fire, milked the animals, cooked a meal, and offered whatever else might be asked of them. Boys tended the animals and lifted the heavy loads. Behind the animals came the endless lines of marching captives—thousands upon thousands. Princes and priests. Tailors and pharmacists. Translators and scribes. Astrologers and jewelers. Artists and soothsayers. Magicians and goldsmiths. Anyone evidencing a skill had been rounded up, together with those who merely attracted the attention of one of the Mongols for whatever reason or fancy.

In all the centuries of raiding and trading, no leader had brought back to his homeland nearly the amount of goods as Genghis Khan. But vast as the quantities were, the appetites of his own people were insatiable. As he returned from his campaigns, his caravans were laden with valuable goods, but each load created the desire for yet more. Every Mongol could sit in his *ger* on lacquered furniture draped in silk; every maiden was perfumed, painted with makeup, and bejeweled. Every riding horse was fixed with metal fittings, and every warrior with bronze and iron weapons. To work their crafts, the thousands of new craftsmen needed more raw materials— everything from wood, clay, and cloth to bronze, gold, and silver. To feed these workers, constant supplies of barley, wheat, and other food commodities had to be hauled across the vast wasteland separating the herders' pastures and the agricultural fields of the south; and the more captives Genghis Khan brought home, the more food and equipment he had to obtain to supply them. Novelties became necessities, and each caravan of cargo stimulated a craving for more. The more he conquered, the more he had to conquer.

The steppes could no longer be isolated. Genghis Khan had to organize supply lines, maintain production, and coordinate the movement of goods and people on an unprecedented scale. What began as a quick raid on cities south of the Gobi for silks and baubles had turned into three decades of the most extensive war in world history. Genghis Khan would spend the next fifteen years of his life fighting across the face of Asia, and at his death, he bequeathed the war to his descendants to expand into new countries and against new people for two more generations.

After the Jurched campaigns, the Great Khan returned directly to his steppes of Khodoe Aral between the Kherlen and the Tsenker Rivers. In keeping with his prior practices, Genghis Khan immediately began to distribute the accumulated booty to his generals and officers, who in turn made the appropriate divisions among their own men. For the first time in his career, however, he simply had too much loot and material to distribute, and he needed to find ways to administer it and store it until needed. To solve this problem of affluence, Genghis Khan allowed the construction of some buildings. He situated them near the small Avarga Stream, somewhat to the side of the steppe where a spring bubbled up out of the ground. According to tradition, Borte treated her young son Ogodei with the water from this spring in order to cure a disease. Collectively, the buildings were named the Yellow Palace, and they served mostly as warehouses for the goods brought back from the campaigns. With rivers on both sides and a small clump of hills in the middle, the area was easily protected, and made a surprise attack virtually impossible.

After his long absence, Genghis Khan had many pending problems to solve, not only among his Mongol subjects, but also with the Siberian tribes of the north and the Uighur farmers of the south. Some of the Siberian tribes that had first submitted to Mongol rule during Jochi's invasion of 1207 used Genghis Khan's lengthy absence on the Jurched campaign to quit sending tributary furs, forest products, and young women. When a Mongol envoy arrived to investigate, however, he found that in keeping with the fame of their women, they now had a woman chief whom they called Botohui-tarhun, a name that meant roughly Big and Fierce. Rather than surrender thirty maidens to the Mongols as wives, she took the Mongol himself captive. When the messenger did not return, Genghis Khan eventually sent another negotiator, and she took him captive as well.

In 1219, the Year of the Hare, Genghis Khan sent a trusted general with a detachment of good soldiers to find out what had happened. Accustomed to campaigning on the open steppes and in the farmlands, the Mongols had little experience fighting or traveling in the dense forest. Usually, the Mongols crossed the steppe by spreading out and moving forward on a broad front. In the forest, however, they had to follow one another along the narrow trails. Botohui-tarhun's forces heard them coming long before they arrived in her territory, and like any experienced forest hunter, she set a trap for them. She sent a contingent of her troops to seal off the trail behind the men to prevent their escape, then she ambushed them from the front. Botohui-tarhun's forces triumphed—and in the battle, her warriors killed the Mongol general.

Such a loss was highly unusual, and it enraged Genghis Khan. At first, he threatened to lead the army himself in vengeance against the victorious queen. His advisers soon convinced him otherwise. They prepared a large expedition, and this time the Mongols were determined to win by whatever means necessary. A small detachment of Mongol warriors moved out as a decoy pretending to guard the frontier trail and passes between the Mongols and the queen's territory. Meanwhile, the Mongol soldiers in the main force of the army secretly cut a new road through the forest from another direction. With axes, adzes, saws, chisels, and all the tools and

weapons they could muster, the Mongols laboriously cleared a path by following the mountain trail of the "red bull," probably the large reddish deer
or elk. After completing the secret road, the Mongol soldiers swooped down
on the queen's headquarters so fast that in the words of the *Secret History*,
it seemed as though they had descended "through the top of the smoke-
holes of their tents."

The victorious Mongols freed their envoys and brought back the tribe as
prisoners to be divided up as servants and mates. Genghis Khan gave the
queen Botohui-tarhun in marriage to the second of the envoys, whom she
may have already taken as her husband since she had kept him as her prisoner
and had not killed him.

The forest tribes provided only a brief distraction for Genghis Khan
compared to the more serious issues among the Uighurs of the desert oases,
who ranked among his most steadfast subjects. They supported him so
strongly that other Muslim Uighurs, living further to the west in the
foothills of the Tian Shan Mountains of what is modern-day Kyrgyzstan
and Kazakhstan, wished to overthrow their Buddhist rulers and join
Genghis Khan as well. Envoys came to the Mongol country from the
Muslim people of Kashgar, a trading city in what is now the province of
Xinjiang, in western China. At the beginning of the thirteenth century,
these people were ruled by another group of Khitan that originated in
Manchuria; but they had been driven out of the east by the Jurched, and
settled in the Tian Shan Mountains. To differentiate them from the Khitan
who had stayed in the east, the Mongols called them Kara Khitan, the
"Black Khitan," since black both signified distant kin and was, in particular,
the color that symbolized the west.

While many of the Uighurs had voluntarily joined the Mongols, others
remained under the control of the Black Khitan, who were now ruled by
Guchlug, the son of the Tayang Khan of the Naiman, Genghis Khan's erstwhile enemy. After the defeat of his people, Guchlug fled to the south,
where he married the daughter of the Black Khitan ruler and then usurped
his power. Although Guchlug was originally a Christian and the Black
Khitan were Buddhists, they shared a common mistrust of the Uighur subjects, who were Muslims. In his newly acquired position as ruler of the
kingdom, Guchlug began to persecute his Muslim subjects by limiting the
practice of their religion. He forbade the call to prayer and prohibited pub-

lic worship or religious study. When Guchlug left the capital of Balasagun on a campaign, his subjects closed the city gates behind him and tried to prevent his return. In retaliation, he besieged the capital, conquered it, and then razed it.

Without a Muslim ruler willing to protect them, the Muslims of Balasagun turned to Genghis Khan to overthrow their oppressive king. Though the Mongol army was stationed twenty-five hundred miles away, Genghis Khan ordered Jebe, the general who restored the Khitan monarchy, to lead twenty thousand Mongol soldiers across the length of Asia and defend the Muslims. Genghis Khan's refusal to take to the battlefield himself indicates how low a priority these lands held for him. His world was in Mongolia, and he wanted to spend as much time as he could with his family at the Avarga encampment along the banks of the Kherlen River. The distant oasis cities of the desert and mountains held little attraction for him. This particular invasion offered him little more than an opportunity to finally deal with his old enemy Guchlug.

Because the Mongols conducted the campaign at the request of the Uighur Muslims, they did not allow plunder, destroy property, or endanger the lives of civilians. Instead, Jebe's army defeated the army of Guchlug and, in a punishment befitting his crimes, had him beheaded on a plain near the modern borders of Afghanistan, Pakistan, and China. Following the execution, the Mongols sent a herald to Kashgar to proclaim the end of religious persecution and the restoration of religious freedom in each community. According to the Persian historian Juvaini, the people of Kashgar proclaimed the Mongols "to be one of the mercies of the Lord and one of the bounties of divine grace."

Although Persian and other Muslim chroniclers recorded the episode in tremendous detail, the *Secret History* summed up the entire campaign in one simple sentence. "Jebe pursued Guchlug Khan of the Naiman, overtook him at the Yellow Cliff, destroyed him, and came home." From the Mongol perspective, that is probably all that mattered. Jebe had done his duty: He killed the enemy and returned home safely. The campaign tested and proved the ability of the Mongol army to successfully operate over thousands of miles from the home base and apart from Genghis Khan himself.

More important than acquiring new subjects or building his reputation as the defender of persecuted religions, the victory over the Black Khitan gave Genghis Khan complete control over the Silk Route between the Chinese and the Muslims. He now had vassal states among the Tangut, the Uighurs, the Black Khitan, and the northern Jurched lands; and although he controlled neither the primary production area of the Sung dynasty nor the primary purchasing areas in the Middle East, he controlled the links between. With his control over large amounts of Chinese trade goods, he saw tremendous opportunities for trade with the Muslim countries of central Asia and the Middle East.

In 1219, with many military and commercial accomplishments behind him, Genghis Khan neared sixty years of age. As Juvaini describes, "He had brought about complete peace and quiet, and security and tranquillity, and had achieved the extreme of prosperity and well-being; the roads were secure and disturbances allayed." He seemed content to live out his days in peace, to enjoy his family and horses, and to bask in the new prosperity he had brought to his people.

He had far more goods now than he could possibly use or distribute to his people, and he wanted to use this vast amount of new resources to stimulate trade. In addition to the thriving supply of traditional Asian goods, other commodities sometimes trickled in from the more distant and exotic western lands of the Middle East. The Muslims in that part of the world produced the finest of all metals, the magnificent gleaming steel. They had cottons and other fine textiles, and they knew the mysterious process of making glass. The vast area from the mountains of modern Afghanistan to the Black Sea fell under the power of the Turkic sultan Muhammad II, whose empire was called Khwarizm. Genghis Khan wanted these exotic commodities, and toward this end he sought a trading partnership with the distant sultan.

The French historian Pétis explained Genghis Khan's situation at the time: ". . . this Emperor having nothing more to fear either from the East, West, or Northern Parts of Asia, endeavour'd to cultivate a sincere Friendship with the King of Carizme. He therefore toward the latter end of this Year 1217 sent three Ambassadors to him with Presents . . . to ask . . . that their People might trade together with Safety, and find in a perfect Union with one another, that Repose and Plenty which are the chief Blessings that can be wished for in all Kingdoms."

To negotiate a trade treaty and formalize their commercial relations, Genghis Khan sent an envoy to the sultan of Khwarizm: "I have the greatest desire to live in peace with you. I shall look on you as my son. For your part, you are not unaware that I have conquered North China and subjected all the tribes of the north. You know that my country is an ant heap of warriors, a mine of silver, and that I have no need to covet other dominions. We have an equal interest in fostering trade between our subjects."

With some suspicion and reluctance, the sultan agreed to the treaty. Since the Mongols themselves were not merchants, Genghis Khan turned to the Muslim and Hindu merchants already operating in his newly acquired territories of the Uighur; from among them, he assembled 450 merchants and retainers whom he sent from Mongolia to Khwarizm with a caravan loaded with the luxury commodities of white camel cloth, Chinese silk, silver bars, and raw jade. He sent an Indian at the head of the delegation with another message of friendship to the sultan, inviting trade so that "henceforth the abscess of evil thoughts may be lanced by the improvement of relations and agreement between us, and the pus of sedition and rebellion removed."

When the caravan entered Khwarizm in the northwestern province of Otrar, now located in southern Kazakhstan, the arrogant and greedy governor seized the goods and killed the merchants and their drivers. He had no idea what a grievous response would follow. As the Persian observer Juvaini explained, the governor's attack not only wiped out a caravan, it "laid waste a whole world."

Hearing of the episode, Genghis Khan sent envoys to request that the sultan punish the local official for the attack; instead, the sultan rebuked the khan in the most publicly dramatic and offensive manner he knew. He killed some of the envoys and mutilated the faces of the others, whom he sent back to their master. It only took a few weeks for word of the rebuke to fly across the steppes and reach the Mongol court, where, in the words of Juvaini, "the whirlwind of anger cast dust into the eyes of patience and clemency while the fire of wrath flared up with such a flame that it drove the water from his eyes and could be quenched only by the shedding of blood." In anger, humiliation, and frustration, Genghis Khan withdrew once again to his mountaintop of Burkhan Khaldun, where he uncovered "his head, turned his face toward the earth and for three days and nights offered up prayer, saying 'I was not the author of this trouble; grant me strength to exact vengeance.' Thereupon he descended from the hill, meditating action and making ready for war."

5

Sultan Versus Khan

War for the nomadic people was a sort of production.
For the warriors it meant success and riches.

SECHEN JAGCHID,

Essays in Mongolian Studies

ENGHIS KHAN SET OUT to the west, heading for Khwarizm in 1219, the Year of the Rabbit, and arrived with the following spring in the Year of the Dragon, when he crossed the desert to suddenly appear deep behind enemy lines at Bukhara. Before the year ended, the Mongols had taken every major city in the Khwarizm empire, and its sultan lay abandoned and dying on a small island out in the Caspian Sea where he had sought refuge from the relentless hounding by Genghis Khan's warriors.

The Mongols carried the fighting deeper into the new lands, and in a campaign of four years, they conquered the cities of central Asia as though swatting flies. The names seem to run together in a numbing sequence of syllables in a dozen languages: Bukhara, Samarkand, Otrar, Urgench, Balkh, Banakat, Khojend, Merv, Nisa, Nishapur, Termez, Herat, Bamiyan, Ghazni, Peshawar, Qazvin, Hamadan, Ardabil, Maragheh, Tabriz, Tbilisi, Derbent, Astrakhan. The armies of Genghis Khan crushed every army wherever they found them, from the Himalayan Mountains to the Caucasus Mountains, from the Indus

River to the Volga River. Each conquered city had its own story that followed a mildly different course of events, but the results never varied. No city withstood their onslaught. No citadel survived untaken. No prayers could save the people. No officials could bribe or talk their way out of submission. Nothing could slow, much less stop, the Mongol juggernaut.

By riding against Khwarizm, Genghis Khan attacked a newly formed kingdom only twelve years older than his own Mongol nation, but he attacked not just an empire, but an entire ancient civilization. The Muslim lands of the thirteenth century, combining Arabic, Turkic, and Persian civilizations, were the richest countries in the world and the most sophisticated in virtually every branch of learning from astronomy and mathematics to agronomy and linguistics, and possessed the world's highest levels of literacy among the general population. Compared with Europe and India, where only priests could read, or China, where only government bureaucrats could, nearly every village in the Muslim world had at least some men who could read the Koran and interpret Muslim law. While Europe, China, and India had only attained the level of regional civilizations, the Muslims came closest to having a world-class civilization with more sophisticated commerce, technology, and general learning, but because they ranked so high above the rest of the world, they had the farthest to fall. The Mongol invasion caused more damage here than anywhere else their horses would tread.

Just as in northern China, where the formerly nomadic Khitan, Jurched, and Tangut tribes ruled over peasant populations, across the Middle East the formerly nomadic Turkic tribes such as the Seljuks and the Turkoman had conquered and ruled various kingdoms populated mostly by farmers. A series of Turkic states dominated the political landscape from the territories of modern-day India, Pakistan, and Afghanistan, across Persia, and into the heart of the Anatolia region of modern Turkey along the Mediterranean. The civilization of the area rested on an ancient bed of Persian cultures, heavily augmented by influences from the Arab world and from earlier classical civilizations from Rome to India. The cultural mosaic of the Middle East included sizable minority populations of Jews, Christians, and other religious and linguistic groups. Overall, however, the scholars, judges, and religious leaders spoke Arabic and quoted the Koran. The soldiers spoke the Turkic dialects of their warrior tribe. The peasants spoke and sang in the many dialects of Persian.

Despite the wealth of the area at the time of Genghis Khan's sudden appearance, the complexity of its social life left its many kingdoms riven with political rivalries, religious tensions, and cultural hatreds. As an upstart Turk, the sultan of Khwarizm could scarcely claim any allies among his fellow Muslims, mostly Arabs and Persians, who looked upon him as little more than a barbarian conqueror himself. Relations between the sultan of Khwarizm and the Arab Caliph in Baghdad were so strained that according to several chronicles, the Caliph supposedly petitioned Genghis Khan to attack the sultan by sending him a secret message tattooed onto a man's head, who then passed undetected through Khwarizm territory to reach the Mongols. Although apocryphal, the story of the tattooed messenger circulated widely in the Muslim world and conferred a certain legitimacy on Genghis Khan's war against the sultan for those Muslims looking for a religious reason to side with the infidel against a Muslim sultan. According to a possibly true story, the Caliph further aided the Mongol attack by sending Genghis Khan a gift of a regiment of Crusaders captured in the Holy Land. Since Genghis Khan had no need for infantry, he freed them, and some of them eventually made their way home to Europe with the first rumors of the previously unknown Mongol conquerors.

In addition to the strains with his Muslim neighbors, the sultan of Khwarizm faced numerous divisions within his own lands and family. The sultan quarreled constantly with his mother, who held virtually as much power as he did, and the threat of a Mongol invasion heightened their disagreement on everything from how to run the empire to how to prepare for war. It was her brother who had seized the first Mongol caravan that precipitated the war, but in refusing to allow her son to punish him and thereby avoid war, she exacerbated the tensions with the Mongols. If the stresses within the ruling family were not menacing enough, the masses of Persian and Tajik subjects showed little connection to their rulers and even less to the Turkic soldiers who were stationed in their cities to exploit them rather than defend them. In turn, the soldiers had minimal vested interest in protecting the lands where they were stationed, and they showed little inclination to risk their lives to save people whom they despised.

When Genghis Khan dropped down on the cities of Khwarizm, he commanded an army of about 100,000 to 125,000 horsemen, supplemented by Uighur and other Turkic allies, a corps of Chinese doctors, and engineers for a total of 150,000 to 200,000 men. By comparison, the Khwarizm ruler had some 400,000 men under arms across his empire, and they were fighting with the home advantage on their own territory.

The Mongols promised justice to those who surrendered, but they swore destruction to those who resisted. If the people accepted and acted as relatives should by reciprocating the offer of kinship by offering food, then the Mongols would treat them as family members with a guarantee of protection and certain basic familial rights; if they refused, they would be treated as enemies. Genghis Khan's offer to the besieged was as simple as it was horrifying, as when he sent this message to the citizens of Nishapur: "Commanders, elders, and commonality, know that God has given me the empire of the earth from the east to the west, whoever submits shall be spared, but those who resist, they shall be destroyed with their wives, children, and dependents." The same sentiment found expression in many documents of the era, one of the clearest in the Armenian chronicle that quotes Genghis Khan as saying that "it is the will of God that we take the earth and maintain order" to impose Mongol law and taxes, and to those who refused them, the Mongols were obligated to "slay them and destroy their place, so that the others who hear and see should fear and not act the same."

Some cities surrendered without fighting. Others fought for a few days or weeks, and only the hardiest of defenders held out for more than a few months. Genghis Khan had learned much from his campaigns against the Jurched cities: not only how to capture heavily fortified cities, but how to treat them afterward, in particular how to most efficiently plunder them. He did not want to repeat the mistakes of the chaotic plunder of Zhongdu. In Khwarizm, he introduced the new and more efficient system of first emptying the city of all people and animals before beginning to loot, thereby minimizing the danger to his men as they plundered.

Before the plundering began, the Mongol warriors followed a similar procedure toward the enemy population in each hostile city. First, they killed the soldiers. The Mongols, dependent on cavalry, had little use for an infantry trained to defend fortress walls, and, more important, they did not want to leave a large army of former enemies blocking the route between them and their homeland in Mongolia. They always wanted a clear, open way home. After executing the soldiers, the Mongol officers sent clerks to divide the civilian population by profession. Professional people included anyone who could read and write in any language—clerks, doctors, astronomers, judges, soothsayers, engineers, teachers, imams, rabbis, or priests. The Mongols particularly needed merchants, cameleers, and people who spoke multiple languages, as well as craftsmen. These workers would be put to use by the Mongols, who themselves practiced no crafts other than war, herding, and hunting. Their growing empire needed skilled workers in almost every service imaginable, including smiths, potters, carpenters, furniture makers, weavers, leather workers, dyers, miners, papermakers, glassblowers, tailors, jewelers, musicians, barbers, singers, entertainers, apothecaries, and cooks.

People without occupations were collected to help in the attack on the next city by carrying loads, digging fortifications, serving as human shields, being pushed into moats as fill, or otherwise giving their lives in the Mongol war effort. Those who did not qualify even for these tasks, the Mongol warriors slaughtered and left behind.

In Genghis Khan's conquest of central Asia, one group suffered the worst fate of those captured. The Mongol captors slaughtered the rich and powerful. Under the chivalrous rules of warfare as practiced in Europe and the Middle East during the Crusades, enemy aristocrats displayed superficial, and often pompous, respect for one another while freely slaughtering common soldiers. Rather than kill their aristocratic enemy on the battlefield, they preferred to capture him as a hostage whom they could ransom back to his family or country. The Mongols did not share this code. To the contrary, they sought to kill all the aristocrats as quickly as possible in order to prevent future wars against them, and Genghis Khan never accepted enemy aristocrats into his army and rarely into his service in any capacity.

Genghis Khan had not always pursued this policy. In the first conquests of the cities of the Jurched, the Tangut, and the the Black Khitan, Genghis Khan had often protected the rich and even allowed rulers to stay in office after he defeated them. But the Jurched and the Tangut had betrayed him as soon as his army withdrew. By the time Genghis Khan arrived in the Muslim countries of central Asia, he had learned his lesson about the loyalty, dependability, and usefulness of the rich and powerful. In his keen awareness of public attitudes and opinions, he also recognized that the common people cared little about what befell the idle rich.

By killing the aristocrats, the Mongols essentially decapitated the social system of their enemies and minimized future resistance. Some of the cities never recovered enough to rebuild after the loss of aristocrats on the battlefield or from the annihilation of their families. Genghis Khan wanted officeholders who were loyal and indebted to the Mongols alone for their positions of power and prestige, and for this reason he recognized no titles other than those granted by him. Even an allied prince or king who wished to retain an older title had to have it reconferred on him by the Mongol authorities. In his report on his trip to Mongolia from 1245 to 1247, the papal envoy Giovanni Di Plano Carpini complained frequently about the lack of respect that Mongols showed the aristocratic people. The lowest-ranking Mongol could walk in front of visiting kings and queens and speak rudely to them.

The fate of the sultan's mother, who had been the most powerful woman in the empire, showed the Mongol attitude toward aristocratic women. They captured her and killed most members of her court and some two dozen members of her family. Then they sent her off to live the remaining decade of her life in ignominious servitude in Mongolia, where she disappeared from history. Such a woman earned no prestige or consideration by virtue of her birth; she, like a captured man, was only as good as her skills, work, and service.

When the Mongols passed through a city, they left little of value behind them. In a letter written just after the invasion, the geographer Yaqut al-Hamawi, who barely escaped the Mongols, wrote glowingly of the beautiful and luxurious palaces that the Mongols had "effaced from off the earth as lines of writing are effaced from paper, and those abodes became a dwelling for the owl and the raven; in those places the screech-owls answer each other's cries, and in those halls the winds moan."

Genghis Khan epitomized ruthlessness in the eyes of the Muslims. Chroniclers of the era attribute to Genghis Khan the highly unlikely statement that "the greatest joy a man can know is to conquer his enemies and drive them before him. To ride their horses and take away their possessions. To see the faces of those who were dear to them bedewed with tears, and to clasp their wives and daughters in his arms." Rather than finding such apocalyptic descriptions derogatory, Genghis Khan seemed to have encouraged them. With his penchant for finding a use for everything he encountered, he devised a powerful way to exploit the high literacy rate of the Muslim people, and turned his unsuspecting enemies into a potent weapon for shaping public opinion. Terror, he realized, was best spread not by the acts of warriors, but by the pens of scribes and scholars. In an era before newspapers, the letters of the intelligentsia played a primary role in shaping public opinion, and in the conquest of central Asia, they played their role quite well on Genghis Khan's behalf. The Mongols operated a virtual propaganda machine that consistently inflated the number of people killed in battle and spread fear wherever its words carried.

By August 1221, only a year into the campaign, Mongol officials sent their Korean subjects a demand for one hundred thousand sheets of their famous paper. The volume of paper shows how rapidly Mongol record keeping was increasing as the size of the empire grew, but the order also symbolized the Mongol emphasis on writing their history. Increasingly, paper was the most potent weapon in Genghis Khan's arsenal. He showed no interest in having his accomplishments recorded or in panegyrics to his prowess; instead, he allowed people to freely circulate the worst and most incredible stories about him and the Mongols.

From every conquered city, the Mongols sent forth delegations to the other cities to tell them of the unprecedented horrors inflicted by the nearly supernatural abilities of Genghis Khan's warriors. The power of those words can still be felt in the accounts of eyewitnesses recorded by chroniclers such as the historian Ibn al-Athir, who lived through the era of the conquest in Mosul, a city now located in Iraq, but at that time close to but slightly beyond the Mongol campaign. He recorded the accounts of refugees in his book *al-Kamil fi at-tarikh,* known in English as *The Perfect History* or *The Complete History.* At first, Ibn al-Athir seemed disinclined to believe the accounts: "Stories have been related to me, which the hearer can scarcely credit, as to the terror of the Tatars." But he quickly warmed to the retelling. "It is said that a single one of them would enter a village or a quarter wherein were many people, and would continue to slay them one after another, none daring to stretch forth his hand against this horseman." From another account, he heard that "one of them took a man captive, but had not with him any weapon wherewith to kill him; and he said to his prisoner, 'Lay your head on the ground and do not move,' and he did so, and the Tatar went and fetched his sword and slew him therewith."

Each victory released a flood of new propaganda, and the belief in Genghis

Khan's invincibility spread. As absurd as the stories appear from a reasoned distance and safety in time, they had a tremendous impact across central Asia. Ibn al-Athir lamented the Mongol conquests as "the announcement of the death-blow of Islam and the Muslims." With a touch of the dramatic, he added, "O would that my mother had not born me or that I had died and become a forgotten thing ere this befell!" He agreed to write out the gory details only because "a number of my friends urged me to set it down in writing." He declared the invasion as the "greatest catastrophe and the most dire calamity . . . which befell all men generally, and the Muslims in particular . . . since God Almighty created Adam until now." By comparison, he noted that the worst slaughters in pre-Mongol history had been unleashed upon the Jews, but the attack of the Mongols on the Muslims was worse because of the toll of Muslims whom "they massacred in a single city exceeded all the children of Israel." Lest the reader prove too suspicious, Ibn al-Athir promised details about the Mongol "deeds which horrify all who hear of them, and which you shall, please God, see set forth in full detail in their proper connection." The impassioned rhetoric, however, seems to have been more an effort to arouse his fellow Muslims than to accurately chronicle their conquest.

Although the army of Genghis Khan killed at an unprecedented rate and used death almost as a matter of policy and certainly as a calculated means of creating terror, they deviated from standard practices of the time in an important and surprising way. The Mongols did not torture, mutilate, or maim. War during that time was often a form of combat in terror, and other contemporary rulers used the simple and barbaric tactic of instilling terror and horror into people through public torture or gruesome mutilation. In an August 1228 battle with Jalal al-Din, the son of the sultan, four hundred Mongol prisoners fell into enemy hands, and they knew well that they would die. The victors took the Mongol warriors to nearby Isfahan, tied them behind horses, and dragged them through the streets of the city to entertain the city's residents. All the Mongol prisoners were thus killed as public sport and then fed to dogs. Because of this public torture, the Mongols never forgave the civilized people of that city, and it, too, would eventually pay a price. In another case where a Mongol army lost a battle, the Persian victors killed the captives by driving nails into their heads, the seat of their souls according to Mongol belief. This episode was echoed a century later in 1305, when the sultan of Delhi turned the deaths of other Mongol prisoners into public entertainment by having them crushed by elephants. He then built a tower from the severed heads of the Mongols who had been killed or captured in battle.

Civilized rulers and religious leaders from China to Europe depended upon these gruesome displays to control their own people through fear and to discourage potential enemies through horror. When the Byzantine Christian emperor Basil defeated the Bulgarians in 1014, he had fifteen thousand Bulgarian war captives blinded. He left one man out of each hundred with one eye in order that he might lead the other ninety-nine homeward and thereby spread the terror. When the Christian Crusaders took cities such as Antioch in 1098 and Jerusalem in 1099, they slaughtered the Jews and Muslims without regard for age or gender, but merely because of their religion.

Holy Roman Emperor Frederick Barbarossa, who ranks as one of Germany's greatest historical and cultural heroes, best exemplified the use of terror in the West. When he tried to conquer the Lombard city of Cremona in the north of modern Italy in 1160, he instituted an escalating series of violent acts of terror. His men beheaded their prisoners and played with the heads outside the city walls, kicking them like balls. The defenders of Cremona then brought out their German prisoners on the city walls and pulled their limbs off in front of their comrades. The Germans gathered more prisoners and executed them in a mass hanging. The city officials responded by hanging the remainder of their prisoners on top of the city walls. Instead of fighting each other directly, the two armies continued their escalation of terror. The Germans then gathered captive children and strapped them into their catapults, which were normally used to batter down walls and break through gates. With the power of these great siege machines, they hurled the living children at the city walls.

By comparison with the terrifying acts of civilized armies of the era, the Mongols did not inspire fear by the ferocity or cruelty of their acts so much as by the speed and efficiency with which they conquered and their seemingly total disdain for the lives of the rich and powerful. The Mongols unleashed terror as they rode east, but their campaign was more noteworthy for its unprecedented military success against powerful armies and seemingly impregnable cities than for its bloodlust or ostentatious use of public cruelty.

Those cities that surrendered to the Mongols at first found their treatment so mild and benign, in comparison with the horrific stories that circulated, that they naively doubted the abilities of the Mongols in other areas as well. After surrendering, a large number of the cities waited obediently until the Mongols had passed well beyond their country, and then revolted. Since the Mongols left only a few officials in charge and stationed no military detachment to guard a city, the inhabitants misinterpreted the Mongol withdrawal as weakness and presumed that the main Mongol army would never return that way. For these cities, the Mongols showed no mercy; they returned quickly to the rebels and destroyed them utterly. An annihilated city could not revolt again.

One of the worst slaughters was unleashed on the citizens of Omar Khayyám's home city of Nishapur. The residents revolted against the Mongols, and in the ensuing battle an arrow fired from walls of the city killed Genghis Khan's son-in-law, Tokuchar. In revenge for the revolt and as a lesson to other cities, Genghis allowed his widowed daughter, who was pregnant at the time, to administer whatever revenge she wished upon the captured city. She reportedly decreed death for all, and in April 1221, the soldiers carried out her command. According to widely circulated but unverified stories, she ordered the soldiers to pile the heads of the dead citizens in three separate pyramids—one each for the men, the women, and the children. Then she supposedly ordered that the dogs, the cats, and all other living animals in the city be put to death so that no living creature would survive the murder of her husband.

The most painful episode for Genghis Khan personally occurred during a battle in the beautiful valley of Bamiyan in Afghanistan, a Buddhist pilgrimage site and home of the largest statues in the world. Ancient devotees had carved giant images of Buddha in the mountainside, and one can only wonder what the Mongols thought of such large images. During the battle there, an arrow struck and killed young Mutugen, Genghis Khan's favorite grandson. Genghis Khan received word of the death before the boy's father, Chaghatai, was informed. Genghis Khan summoned his son, and before telling him what had happened, ordered Chaghatai not to weep or mourn.

Genghis Khan had cried publicly many times in his life and at the least provocation. He had cried in fear, in anger, and in sadness, but faced with the death of one whom he loved more than any other, Genghis Khan did not allow himself or his sons to show their pain and anguish through tears or mourning. Whenever faced with great difficulty or personal pain, Genghis Khan funneled it into combat. Kill, don't mourn. He transformed the painful sorrow into a great fury that he poured out over the people of the valley. No one—rich or poor, beautiful or ugly, good or bad—would survive. The valley was eventually resettled by the Hazara, a name that meant "ten thousand" in Persian, who claimed to be descendants from one of Genghis Khan's regiments of that size.

While the destruction of many cities was complete, the numbers given by historians over the years were not merely exaggerated or fanciful—they were preposterous. The Persian chronicles reported that at the battle of Nishapur, the Mongols slaughtered the staggeringly precise number of 1,747,000. This surpassed the 1,600,000 listed as killed in the city of Herat. In more outrageous claims, Juzjani, a respectable but vehemently anti-Mongol historian, puts the total for Herat at 2,400,000. Later, more conservative scholars place the number of dead from Genghis Khan's invasion of central Asia at 15 million within five years. Even this more modest total, however, would require that each Mongol kill more than a hundred people; the inflated tallies for other cities required a slaughter of 350 people by every Mongol soldier. Had so many people lived in the cities of central Asia at the time, they could have easily overwhelmed the invading Mongols.

Although accepted as fact and repeated through the generations, the numbers have no basis in reality. It would be physically difficult to slaughter that many cows or pigs, which wait passively for their turn. Overall, those who were supposedly slaughtered outnumbered the Mongols by ratios of up to fifty to one. The people could have merely run away, and the Mongols would not have been able to stop them. Inspection of the ruins of the cities conquered by the Mongols show that rarely did they surpass a tenth of the population enumerated as casualties. The dry desert soils of these areas preserve bones for hundreds and sometimes thousands of years, yet none of them has yielded any trace of the millions said to have been slaughtered by the Mongols.

Genghis Khan would be more accurately described as a destroyer of cities than a slayer of people, because he often razed entire cities for strategic reasons in addition to revenge or to provoke fear. In a massive and highly successful effort to reshape the flow of trade across Eurasia, he destroyed cities on the less-important or more inaccessible routes to funnel commerce into more routes that his army could more easily supervise and control. To stop trade through an area, he demolished the cities down to their very foundations.

In addition to the organized destruction of some cities, he depopulated expansive areas of land by the laborious destruction of the irrigation system. Without irrigation, the villagers and farmers left, and the fields reverted to grazing land. This allowed large areas to be set aside for the herds that accompanied the army and were kept as reserves for future campaigns. Just as when he churned up the agricultural land when he left northern China to return to Mongolia, Genghis Khan always wanted a clear area of retreat or advancement where his army could always find adequate pasturage for the horses and for the other animals on which their success depended.

After four years of campaigning in central Asia, Genghis Khan was in his sixties. He was at the height of his power without competition from any rival within his tribe or threat from any enemy external to it. Yet in contrast to this overwhelming success on the battle front, his family was already, even before he died, tearing itself apart. Leaving the Mongol homeland in the care of his youngest brother, Temuge Otchigen, he had brought all four of his sons with him on the central Asian campaign, where he hoped that they would not only learn to be better warriors, but also how to live and work together. Unlike conquerors who came to think of themselves as gods, Genghis Khan knew clearly that he was mortal, and he sought to prepare his empire for a transition. In the tradition of the steppe, each son in a herding family received some of each kind of animal that the family owned, as well as the use of some portion of the grazing lands. Similarly, Genghis Khan planned to give each son a miniature empire reflecting, to the degree practical, the diverse holdings of the whole empire. Each son would be the khan of a large number of people and herds on the steppe as well as owner of a large section of territory with cities, workshops, and farms in the sedentary zones. Above the other three, however, one son would be the Great Khan who would administer the central government, provide a final court of appeal, and, together with the advice of his other brothers, have responsibility for foreign affairs, particularly for making war. The system depended on the ability and willingness of the brothers to work together and to cooperate under the leadership of the Great Khan.

Even before he left on the Khwarizm campaign, the plan encountered difficulty when, despite the strong taboos against discussing or preparing for death, he summoned a family *khuriltai* to deal precisely with that subject. The meeting turned into one of the pivotal episodes of Mongol history by bringing together all the rivalries of the past and foreshadowing the way in which his empire would eventually be broken apart.

In addition to his sons, Genghis Khan had several of his most trusted men with him to be a part of the discussion, since their agreement and support would also be necessary to guarantee the succession after his death. As the meeting began, the two eldest sons, Jochi and Chaghatai, seemed tensely poised, like steel traps ready to snap. If Ogodei, the third son, arrived true to character, he would have already had a few drinks and been mildly inebriated, although it seems unlikely that he would have been completely drunk in his father's presence. Tolui, the youngest, remained quiet and seemed to have disappeared into the folds of the tent while his older brothers dominated center stage.

Genghis Khan opened the family *khuriltai* by explaining the business of selecting a successor. He was quoted as saying that "if all my sons should wish to be Khan and ruler, refusing to serve each other, will it not be as in the fable of the single-headed and the many-headed snake." In this traditional fable, when winter came, the snake's competing heads quarreled among themselves and disagreed about which hole was better for them to find refuge in from the cold wind and snow. One head preferred one hole and pulled in that direction, and the other heads pulled in other directions. The other snake— with many tails but only one head—went immediately into one hole and stayed warm throughout the winter, while the snake with many heads froze to death.

After explaining the seriousness and importance of the issue, Genghis Khan asked his eldest son, Jochi, to speak first on the matter of succession. Order of seating, walking, speaking, drinking, and eating all carry heavy symbolic value among Mongols even today. By setting this order of speaking, the khan was publicly emphasizing that Jochi ranked as his eldest son, and this set him up as the likely successor. If the younger sons accepted this order of speaking, it would be tantamount to accepting Jochi's legitimacy and seniority over them.

Chaghatai, the second son, refused to allow that assumption to pass unstated and untested. Before Jochi could answer his father, Chaghatai spoke up loudly. "When you tell Jochi to speak," he defiantly asked his father, "do you offer him the succession?" Then he blurted out the rhetorical question that was intended as a statement of fact, no matter how much Genghis Khan disagreed, about the suspicious paternity of Jochi, who had been born forty years earlier, but too soon after Borte's rescue from her Merkid kidnappers. "How could we allow ourselves to be ruled by this bastard son of a Merkid?" demanded Chaghatai of his father and brothers.

Jochi snapped at being called a bastard by his brother. He let loose a scream, lunged across the tent, and seized Chaghatai by the collar. The two men pummeled each other. In painfully emotional words that were probably spoken by Genghis Khan himself, but which the *Secret History* attributes to an adviser in an effort to preserve the dignity of the khan, Chaghatai was reminded how much his father loved and respected him. The father pleaded in obviously painful words with his sons to understand how different things were in the old days, before the boys were born, when terror ruled the steppes, neighbors fought neighbors, and no one was safe. What happened to their mother when she was kidnapped was not her fault: "She didn't run away from home. . . . She wasn't in love with another man. She was stolen by men who came to kill."

Genghis Khan almost meekly implored his sons to remember that despite the circumstances of their birth, they all sprang "from a single hot womb," and that "if you insult the mother who gave you your life from her heart, if you cause her love for you to freeze up, even if you apologize to her later, the damage is done." The councillor reminded the sons how hard both parents worked to create their new nation, and he listed the sacrifices that both of them made to make a better world for their sons.

After the long, emotional scene, Genghis Khan knew that he could not impose a choice on his sons that they would reject after his death. He had to negotiate a compromise agreement that all of them would be willing to accept. He invoked his limited parental authority by reasserting that he himself accepted Jochi as his eldest son, and he commanded his other sons to accept this as fact and not to repeat suspicions about his paternity again.

Chaghatai submitted to the command of his father but made it clear that even in abiding by his edict, words could not make it true. Chaghatai grinned and said that the "game killed by mouth cannot be loaded onto a horse. Game slaughtered by words cannot be skinned." Outwardly, the sons would all recognize Jochi's legitimacy as long as their father lived; but inwardly, they would never do so. Recognizing the legitimacy of Jochi as the eldest son, however, did not guarantee him the succession to the office of Great Khan because such an important office was supposed to be based upon ability and support from the others, not on age.

Having incurred so much anger from his father, Chaghatai knew that the father would not then agree to his taking the office of Great Khan, but he still wanted to prevent Jochi from having it. So Chaghatai offered the family a compromise, which may have been spontaneously conceived or already agreed upon by the younger siblings. He said that neither he nor Jochi should become khan; instead, the succession should to fall to their third brother, the mellow, good-natured, hard-drinking Ogodei.

With no other option open to him other than war, Jochi agreed to this compromise and endorsed Ogodei as the successor. Genghis Khan then allotted personal lands and herds to each son by doing what parents always do to quarreling youngsters: He separated Jochi and Chaghatai. "Mother Earth is broad and her rivers and waters are numerous. Make up your camps far apart and each of you rules your own kingdom. I'll see to it that you are separated." He then warned the sons not to behave so that people would laugh at or insult them.

The Muslim scholars serving at the Mongol court evidenced a tortured difficulty in recording this event, since for them a man's honor rested on his control of the sexuality of the women around him. It was almost inconceivable that a man as powerful as Genghis Khan might have had a son sired by another man, or even be accused of such a thing by his own sons. Unlike the *Secret History,* written by a Mongol and including a full account of the family fight, the first Persian chronicler, Juvaini, wrote the conflict out of his history completely by making the family *khuriltai* into a gathering of serene decorum and complete unanimity. In his version of events, Genghis Khan delivered a beautiful speech on the admirable qualities of Ogodei, and all of his sons agreed. The sons obediently "laid the knee of courtesy upon the group of fealty and submission and answered with the tongue of obedience, saying 'Who hath the power to oppose the word of Genghis Khan and who the ability to reject it?' . . . All Ogodei's brothers obeyed his commandment and made a statement in writing."

With a little more distance from the original events, Rashid al-Din offered a slightly more honest account, but his manuscript has blanks in crucial places that would impugn the honor of Genghis Khan or his wife. He wrote that "because of _____, the path of unity was trodden upon both sides between them," but the good members of the family "never uttered that taunt but regarded his _____ as genuine." Whether the blanks were entered into the original work by Rashid al-Din or made by later scribes copying it, they show the symbolic and political importance of the issue of Jochi's paternity for generations to come.

At the end of the emotionally intense family encounter between Genghis Khan and his sons, it is doubtful that anyone knew how far-reaching the effects of this meeting would be. In this family *khuriltai,* the victors had just carved up the world in a way that would presage the Vienna Congress following the Napoleonic Wars, the Versailles Conference after World War I, and the meetings of the World War II Allies at Yalta and Potsdam.

Although repeatedly mentioned in the family conference, Borte was absent, but presumably still alive. It is not known if she heard of what went on among her sons, and no reliable information exists on exactly what happened to her. Oral tradition maintains that during this time, she continued to live in the beautiful steppe at Avarga on the Kherlen River, only a few days ride from where she and her husband had lived in the first days of their marriage. She likely died there, or in the vicinity, sometime between 1219 and 1224.

The unpleasant episode cast a pall over the remaining years of Genghis Khan's life and particularly over the central Asian campaign. The fighting among his sons made him keenly aware of how much work he needed to do to preserve the empire after his death. His sons did not match up to the needs of the empire. While pursuing his great quest to unite the steppe tribes and conquer every threat around him, he had never devoted the attention he should have to his sons, and now they were all reaching middle age and were still unproven men. In his mistrust of his own relatives and his lifelong reliance on his companions and friends from youth, he had not built a working relationship among his own sons nor trained them to replace him.

Throughout his final years of life, Genghis Khan sought, without success, to mend the relations between Jochi and Chaghatai by assigning them to a joint campaign against the city of Urgench, a former capital of the sultan south of the Aral Sea. The tension seething between the two brothers nearly erupted into fighting against each other during the siege. Both brothers knew that the city would belong to Jochi as a part of his patrimony, and because of this they could not agree on the tactics to conquer it. Jochi suspected that because Urgench would belong to him, his brother was trying to destroy it utterly. Chagahatai, in turn, suspected that Jochi's greed made him want to protect the buildings and structures of the city even at the risk of killing more Mongol soldiers.

Whereas most cities had fallen in a matter of days or weeks, the Mongol conquest of Urgench required an unprecedented six months. The city's defenders fought fiercely. Even after the Mongols broke through the city walls, the defenders continued to fight from house to house. Uncomfortable with fighting in the claustrophobic confines of a nearly destroyed city, the Mongols set fires to burn down the city. The defenders continued fighting from the charred ruins. Finally, the Mongols built a dam, diverted the river, and flooded the city, thereby killing the remaining warriors and destroying nearly everything in it. Urgench never rose again, and although allotted to Jochi, nothing remained there for him and his descendants to rule over.

Angry with the quarreling between his sons, Genghis Khan summoned them, momentarily ostracized them by refusing to admit them to the court, then, when he finally admitted them, alternately berated, scolded, and pleaded with them. More conversations and quotes survive from this phase of Genghis Khan's life than any other, and they show a growing concern but lessening power to control his family. After too long a neglect of their education, he tried to teach his sons everything at once, and in doing so he struggled to articulate lessons he had learned and ideas he had but had not verbalized clearly. He was accustomed to giving orders, not making explanations.

He tried to teach them that the first key to leadership was self-control, particularly the mastery of pride, which was something more difficult, he explained, to subdue than a wild lion, and anger, which was more difficult to defeat than the greatest wrestler. He warned them that "if you can't swallow your pride, you can't lead." He admonished them never to think of themselves as the strongest or smartest. Even the highest mountain had animals that step on it, he warned. When the animals climb to the top of the mountain, they are even higher than it is.

In keeping with the laconic Mongol traditions, he warned his sons not to talk too much. Only say what needs to be said. A leader should demonstrate his thoughts and opinions through his actions, not through his words: "He can never be happy until his people are happy." He stressed to them the importance of vision, goals, and a plan. "Without the vision of a goal, a man cannot manage his own life, much less the lives of others," he told them.

Some thoughts seem to contradict others. As much as he emphasized the importance of seizing the mantle of leadership, he seemingly sought to impart cautious conservatism in that "the vision should never stray far from the teaching of the elders." As he explained it, "the old tunic, or *deel,* fits better and is always more comfortable; it survives the hardships of life in the bush, while the new or untried *deel* is quickly torn." In keeping with his own sober manner and simple style of living, Genghis Khan warned them against the pursuit of a "colorful" life with material frivolities and wasteful pleasures. "It will be easy," he explained, "to forget your vision and purpose once you have fine clothes, fast horses, and beautiful women." In that case, "you will be no better than a slave, and you will surely lose everything."

In one of his most important lessons, he told his sons that conquering an army is not the same as conquering a nation. You may conquer an army with superior tactics and men, but you can conquer a nation only by conquering the hearts of the people. As idealistic as that sounded, he followed with the even more practical advice that even though the Mongol Empire should be one, the subject people should never be allowed to unite as one: "People conquered on different sides of the lake should be ruled on different sides of the lake." Like so many of his teachings, this, too, would be ignored by his sons and their successors.

The Mongol conquest stopped at the city of Multan, in the center of modern-day Pakistan, in the summer of 1222, the Year of the Horse. After descending from the mountains of Afghanistan onto the plains of the Indus River earlier that year, Genghis Khan had considered conquering all of northern India, circling around south of the Himalayas, and heading north across the Sung territory of China. Such a plan well suited the Mongol sensibility that one should never return by exactly the same route that one came. However, the geography and climate stopped him. As soon as the Mongols left the dry and colder region of the mountains, both warriors and horses weakened and grew sick. Even more alarming, the Mongol bows that were so well adapted to the extreme cold and heat of the steppe homeland also weakened in the damp air and seemed to lose the powerful accuracy that made the Mongol warrior such a dreaded shot. Facing these obstacles, Genghis Khan headed back into the mountains in February, and despite the tremendous loss of lives among the prisoners who cleared the snow-filled passes, he took his army to more comfortable and colder terrain. He left behind two *tumen,* some twenty thousand men, to continue the India campaign, but by summer illness and heat had so depleted their ranks that the survivors withdrew and limped back to the benign and healthful environment of Afghanistan.

Despite the aborted invasion of India, the campaign had achieved its main goals of conquering the Khwarizm empire and bringing central Asia and much of the Middle East under Mongol control. Before leaving the newly conquered lands, Genghis Khan called for a celebration that featured what was probably the largest hunt in history. During months of preparation during the winter of 1222–1223, his men cordoned off a large area by planting posts in the ground and stringing long pieces of horsehair twine between them. They hung strips of felt on the twine, and when the wind blew, as it almost always did, it frightened the animals away from the edges and toward the center of the area. At the appointed time, different armies began to converge on the area from different directions. Tens of thousands of soldiers took part in the ensuing hunt, which lasted for several months. They bagged all manner of animals from rabbits and birds to large herds of gazelle, antelope, and wild asses.

The hunt was part celebration, but it also seemed an effort to use the conviviality of the hunts and the entertainment that followed them to mellow relations among his sons, soothe over the hotheaded anger of the battlefield, and end the campaigns on a cooperative note. Still smarting from the wounds inflicted by his brothers and apparently alienated from his father as well,

Jochi, the most beloved of the sons, claimed to be ill and refused to come even when summoned by direct order of Genghis Khan. Relations between the father and son nearly erupted into armed conflict when Genghis Khan heard that the supposedly ill Jochi had organized rival hunts in a celebration for his men.

The father and son never met again. Instead of returning to Mongolia, Jochi stayed in the newly conquered territory. He would soon die there, leaving as much mystery surrounding his death as his birth. The timing of his death, while his father still lived, sparked rumors that Genghis Khan may have killed Jochi in order to ensure political peace among his sons and for the Mongol Empire; but as with so many parts of Mongol history, only the rumors survived without convincing evidence one way or another.

Despite the tensions within Genghis Khan's family, for most Mongols the victorious return of the army marked a high point in their lives. The triumphant spirit of the group hunt was continued throughout the long trek back to Mongolia, where the mood of pride and success erupted in a joyous homecoming and victory celebration, or *naadam*. Long caravans of captives preceded the main part of Genghis Khan's army. For nearly five years, a steady flow of camel caravans lumbered out of the Muslim lands carrying packs of looted goods to Mongolia, where the population eagerly awaited each load of exotic luxuries. Mongol girls who had spent their days milking goats and yaks when the army left soon wore garments of silk and gold, while their newly acquired servants milked the animals for them. Old people who had rarely seen metal in their childhood cut meat with knives of engraved Damascus steel set in handles of sculpted ivory, and they served *airak* from silver bowls while their musicians sang to them.

Although Genghis Khan was once again in the land that he loved, he could hardly stop to rest before setting out on another campaign. Perhaps knowing that he was nearing the end of his life, he did not have time to stop, or perhaps he realized that his empire depended upon constant conquest. If he paused, factionalism within his own family threatened to rip the empire apart. Probably even more pressing, his followers had grown dependent on a steady flow of goods. They would not willingly return to the simple goods that he had known as a child. In order to feed this voracious appetite, he had to move on to new conquests.

He launched the final campaign in his long life against the Tangut, the first foreign enemies he had invaded in 1207, the year following the creation of the Mongol Empire. Despite their initial surrender, Genghis Khan had nourished a lingering grudge against their khan for refusing to furnish troops for the Khwarizm invasion. The Tangut king smugly sent word that if Genghis Khan could not defeat Khwarizm alone, then he should not go to war. Although irritated, Genghis Khan kept his immediate focus on the Khwarizm campaign; but once finished with it, he turned back toward the Tangut. As he again moved his army south, he almost certainly had plans for yet one more major campaign in which the Tangut war would only be an opening move. He probably intended to secure a base in the Tangut kingdom and then move on south toward the final goal of the Sung dynasty, a prize that had eluded the army he had left fighting in northern China when he invaded Khwarizm.

During the winter of 1226–1227, while en route across the Gobi to make war on the Tangut, Genghis Khan paused to hunt wild horses. He rode a reddish gray horse that shied when the wild horses charged him, and the skittish horse threw the Great Khan to the ground. Despite internal injuries, a raging fever, and the concerned advice of his wife Yesui, Genghis Khan refused to return home and instead pressed on with the Tangut campaign. Although his health never recovered after the fall, he continued the campaign against the Tangut king, whose name, by an odd coincidence, was Burkhan, which meant "god," as in the sacred mountain Burkhan Khaldun. The name was so sacred to Genghis Khan that once he defeated the Tangut, he ordered that the king's name be changed before he was executed.

Six months later and only a few days before the final victory over the Tangut, Genghis Khan died. The *Secret History* states clearly that he died at the end of summer, but although the text describes in great detail each horse that he rode, it falls suddenly silent regarding the circumstances of his death. Other sources maintain that when death finally arrived, his Tatar wife Yesui prepared the body for burial in a simple way befitting the manner in which Genghis Khan had lived. Attendants cleaned and dressed the body in a plain white robe, felt boots, and a hat, then wrapped it in a white felt blanket filled with sandalwood, the valuable aromatic wood that repelled insects and infused the body with a pleasant perfume. They bound the felt coffin with three golden straps.

On the third day, a procession set out toward Mongolia with the Great Khan's body on a simple cart. The Spirit Banner of Genghis Khan led the mourners, followed by a woman shaman, and behind her followed a horse with a loose bridle and Genghis Khan's empty saddle.

It is difficult to imagine what kind of image Genghis Khan thought he was leaving to the world. Only a small hint of how he saw himself can be found in the chronicle of Minhaj al-Siraj Juzjani, who called Genghis Khan accursed and described his death as his descent into hell. Yet Juzjani recorded a conversation that an imam claimed to have had with the infamous conqueror. The cleric served in Genghis Khan's court and, at least according to his own boastful claim, became a special favorite of the Mongol khan. One day during a conversation, Genghis Khan supposedly said, "A mighty name will remain behind me in the world."

With some hesitation, the imam told Genghis Khan that he was killing so many people that there might not be anyone left to remember his name. The khan did not like this response and told the cleric, "It has become evident to me that [you do] not possess complete understanding, and that [your] comprehension is but small. There are many kings in the world," he explained to the learned man. In reference to his future reputation, he added that there are many more people in other parts of the world and many more sovereigns and many more kingdoms. Genghis Khan confidently declared, "They will relate my story!"

We find an unusual and more informative glimpse into the mind of Genghis Khan and into his image of himself near the end of his life, which survives in the text of a letter Genghis Khan sent to a Taoist monk in China, a copy of which was made by some of the old monk's followers. Unlike the *Secret History,* which mostly records deeds and spoken words, this letter recorded Genghis Khan's analysis of himself. Although the letter is available to us only in the form written in classical Chinese by a scribe, almost certainly one of the Khitan traveling with the Mongol court, the sentiments and perceptions of Genghis Khan himself come out quite clearly in the document.

His voice comes through as simple, clear, and informed by common sense. He ascribed the fall of his enemies more to their own lack of ability than to his superior prowess: "I have not myself distinguished qualities." He said that the Eternal Blue Sky had condemned the civilizations around him because of their "haughtiness and their extravagant luxury." Despite the tremendous wealth and power he had accumulated, he continued to lead a simple life: "I wear the same clothing and eat the same food as the cowherds and horse-herders. We make the same sacrifices, and we share the riches." He offered a simple assessment of his ideals: "I hate luxury," and "I exercise moderation." He strove to treat his subjects like his children, and he treated talented men like his brothers, no matter what their origin was. He described his relations with his officials as being close and based on respect: "We always agree in our principles and we are always united in mutual affection."

Although he sent the letter on the eve of his invasion of the Muslim world and it was written in Chinese, he clearly did not see himself as the heir of kingdoms or cultural traditions in either area. He acknowledged only one preceding empire from which he personally took inspiration—his ancestors, the Huns. It is clear that he did not wish to rule in either the Muslim or the Chinese style. He wanted to find his own way as befitted a steppe empire descended from the Huns.

He claimed that his victories had been possible only through the assistance of the Eternal Blue Sky, "but as my calling is high, the obligations incumbent on me are also heavy." He did not, however, feel that he had been as successful in peace as he had been in war: "I fear that in my ruling there may be something wanting." He said that good officials over the state are as important as a good rudder to a boat. While he managed to find men of talent to serve as his generals, he admitted he had unfortunately not been able to find men as good in administration.

Most important, the letter shows a shift in the political thinking of Genghis Khan. After admitting to his shortcomings, Genghis Khan nevertheless shows in this document a rising sense of himself and his mission on earth. He had begun his campaign against the Jurched—his first major campaign beyond the steppe—as a series of raids for plunder, but by the end of it he had installed a vassal state. His words reveal a deeper and wider plan than mere raiding and controlling trade networks. He acknowledged that he went south to accomplish something that no one else in history had done. He was pursuing "a great work," because he sought to "unite the whole world in one empire." He was no longer a tribal chief, and now he sought to be the ruler of all people and all lands from where the sun rises to where the sun sets.

Perhaps the most fitting description of Genghis Khan's passing was penned in the eighteenth century by Edward Gibbon, the British historian of the Romans and a great scholar on the history of empires and conquest. He wrote simply that Genghis Khan "died in the fullness of years and glory, with his last breath, exhorting and instructing his sons to achieve the conquest of the Chinese empire." To fulfill the wishes and commands of Genghis Khan, there still remained much to be done.

6

The Discovery and
Conquest of Europe

For our sins, unknown tribes came.
CHRONICLE OF NOVGOROD, 1224

IN THE SPIRIT OF inebriated generosity at the celebration of his installation as Great Khan, Ogodei threw open his father's treasury and riotously distributed all the riches stored there. He passed out pearls, the gem most admired by the Mongols, by the casket loads. Bolts of silk cloth were thrown out among the people. Horses and camels were decorated in great finery, and all the Mongols had new silk *deels* embroidered with golden threads. They had so many beautiful colors that each day the courtiers could all wear the same color, and then the next day a different color was prescribed. They drank, feasted, and played games throughout the summer of 1229 at Avarga, where storehouses had been erected to serve as a treasury for some of the tremendous amount of loot sent back from Genghis Khan's campaigns. The days of blue and green and white and yellow silks rolled one into the other, as the most powerful family in the world celebrated itself. To lubricate the event, the alcohol flowed without pause. Men and women drank until they passed out; they slept a while, and then resumed drinking when they awoke.

About this time, the family took on the name of the Golden Family or Golden Lineage. Gold symbolized royalty for the steppe people, but it could just have easily represented the vast wealth that the family held and that they quickly began to use up. Without Genghis Khan to moderate the celebration, his heirs now ruled the empire, drunk with riches they had not earned and with the alcohol that they had come to love. The drunken revelry of Ogodei Khan's inauguration set the standard and the model for his rule, and, at least momentarily, it controlled the spirit of the empire as well. As Ata-Malik Juvaini wrote soon thereafter, Ogodei "was ever spreading the carpet of merrymaking and treading the path of excess in constant appreciation to wine and the company of beautiful women."

In the interim after Genghis Khan's death and during the Mongol distraction with the celebration of Ogodei's election, some of the newly conquered subjects broke away and stopped sending tribute. Ogodei had to send large armies back into northern China and central Asia to reassert Mongol dominance. As soon as he was installed in 1230, he sent a force of three *tumens,* nearly thirty thousand soldiers, to strengthen the Mongol hold on central Asia, but most of the wealth had already been taken. He sent in an occupying army, one that even took its families along, not a conquering one. The level of tribute remitted back to Mongolia from both northern China and central Asia, however, remained modest compared to the wealth taken in the original looting.

Ogodei did not accompany his army; conquest was not his priority. As part of his enjoyment of his empire, Ogodei decided that like all great sovereigns he should have a permanent capital city—not just a collection of *gers,* but real buildings with walls and roofs, windows and doors. Contrary to the thinking of his father, Ogodei had become convinced that a kingdom conquered on horseback could not be ruled on horseback, when, of course, rule from horseback and a mobile center of power had in fact been one of the primary factors behind Mongol success. In the first of several bad mistakes in what would be a short reign, Ogodei abandoned this policy and tried to create a fixed center of power and administration for the empire.

Since the old homeland on the Onon and Kherlen Rivers now belonged, as was the Mongol custom, to Tolui, the youngest son, Ogodei decided to build his capital on his own territory farther west. He chose an area in the middle of the Mongol lands on the Orkhon River in the territory that had earlier belonged to Ong Khan's Kereyid tribe and before that had been the capital of the early Turkic kingdoms. He chose the site according to the nomadic standards for a good camp. It was on an open steppe, with good wind to keep down mosquitoes, with ample water far enough away that it would not be polluted by the people living in the city, and with mountains nearby as a winter sanctuary for the herds. In all these regards the site of Karakorum, as it came to be known, was perfect, the only problem being that a city with a permanent population has much different requirements than a good, but temporary, camp. They needed a constant supply of food throughout the year, and without any way of producing it, the city would be constantly dependent on goods brought at great expense from hundreds of miles south of the Gobi. Its location on the open steppe provided no shelter from the extremely bitter winter wind. Unlike the herds that could withdraw to the protection of the mountains, the city could not be so easily relocated each season. These problems would plague, and ultimately doom, this Mongol capital.

Ogodei probably began construction of his palace in a typically Mongol style by shooting an arrow across the steppe and then building the first wing following the arrow shot. In keeping with the Mongol system of measuring space, the building stretched the length of a standard bowshot. He built another wing in the same way, and placed a tall pavilion in the middle to connect them. He built a sturdy wall to enclose the palaces, and from these walls the place acquired the name of Karakorum, meaning "black stones" or "black walls." Rashid al-Din described Ogodei's new palace as "exceedingly tall in structure and with lofty pillars, such as was in keeping the high resolve of such a king. The craftsmen finished the buildings by painting them with colorful designs and pictures."

The Mongols continued to live in their *gers* around Karakorum as they had on the open steppe. The royal court moved from area to area with the seasons—often several days' or a week's journey away from the capital. Chinese architects and craftsmen designed and built the structures of Karakorum, but the private palace Ogodei built for his family at Kerchagan, a day's ride from Karakorum, was in the Muslim style. Unlike other world capitals that functioned as showpieces for the power, grandeur, and majesty of the ruling family, Karakorum served primarily as a large warehouse and workshop, ignored by most Mongols, including Ogodei, through most of the year. They used it as a base where they kept their goods, and their goods included craftsmen who worked for them. The city produced little, but it collected tribute from across the empire. One-third of the city was reserved to house the newly recruited clerks needed to run the empire. These included scribes and translators from every nation in the empire so that they could manage the correspondence with each country.

The oldest visitor's account we have of the city comes from Juvaini, who described a garden enclosed within a compound with a gate facing each of the cardinal directions. Within the garden, Chinese artisans built "a castle with doors like the gates of the garden; and inside it a throne having three flights of steps, one for [Ogodei] alone, another for his ladies and a third for the cup-bearers and table-deckers." In front of the palace, Ogodei built a series of lakes "wherein many water fowl used to gather." He would watch the hunting of these birds and afterward would give himself up to the joys of drinking. As befitted a man so fond of alcohol, the centerpiece of the palace complex was a series of gold and silver vats so large that he reportedly kept camels and elephants on hand so that "when a public feast was held they might lift up the various beverages."

In addition to the palaces for himself and other members of the Golden Family, Ogodei erected several houses of worship for his Buddhist, Muslim, Taoist, and Christian followers. Of these, the Christians seemed to be gaining dominance at the Mongol court because Ogodei, like his three brothers, had taken Christian wives when they conquered the Kereyid and Naiman, and some of his descendants were Christian, particularly his favorite grandson, Shiremun (the Mongol version of the biblical name Solomon). Part of the attraction of the Mongols to Christianity seemed to be in the name of Jesus, Yesu, which sounded like the Mongolian word for nine, their sacred number, and the name of Genghis Khan's father, Yesugei, who was the founder of the whole dynasty. Despite the high status of Christians, the small city of Karakorum was probably the most religiously open and tolerant city in the world at that time. Nowhere else could followers of so many different religions worship side by side in peace.

To encourage trade caravans to seek out his new capital, Ogodei paid extremely high prices for all manner of goods whether he needed them or not and whether they were of high or low quality. Rashid al-Din wrote that Ogodei "would sit, every day, after he had finished his meal, on a chair outside his Court, where every kind of merchandise that is to be found in the world was heaped up in piles. These wares he used to give away to all classes of Mongols and Muslims, and it would often happen that he would command persons of great size to take as many of the wares they wanted as they could lift up." In addition to animals and a variety of foods, merchants arrived with loads of textiles, ivory tusks, pearls, hunting falcons, golden goblets, jeweled belts, willow whip handles, cheetahs, bows and arrows, garments, hats, and exotic animal horns. People also came to entertain, including actors and musicians from China, wrestlers from Persia, and a jester from Byzantium.

Ogodei Khan frequently paid twice the asking price for imported goods as a show of appreciation for the effort the merchant made in reaching his realm and as an inducement for other merchants to do the same. Ogodei also decreed that whatever price the merchants asked should be paid to them plus a 10 percent bonus. The Mongols also provided the capital backing to finance caravans when needed. In an effort to improve trade, Ogodei introduced a standardized system of weights and measures to replace the various types used in different countries and cities. Because bullion and coins proved so bulky to transport, the Mongols created a system of paper money exchanges that made trade much easier and safer.

Ogodei's army managed to reassert Mongol rule in central Asia and, under the able leadership of old general Subodei, allied with the Sung dynasty to pick apart the remaining wealth and land of the Jurched. His father had kept a steady supply of goods coming by living in the field at war and shipping home the loot; Ogodei, however, increasingly used the might of his army to make the routes safe for merchants to bring in more goods. He stationed permanent garrisons to protect the roads and merchants, and he abolished the complex system of local taxes and extortion that had added to the difficulty and expense of trade. The Mongols planted trees along the sides of roads to shade the travelers in summer and to mark the road during winter snows. In areas where trees would not grow, they erected stone pillars to mark the way. Juvaini stated that the Mongol roads were to ensure "that wherever profit or gain was displayed, in the uttermost West or the farthermost East, thither merchants would bend their steps."

The dismounting of Ogodei at Karakorum, and the building of stone walls so hated by his father, marked a major step away from the policies of Genghis Khan. Thereby began a process of co-optation that over the next four decades transformed the Mongols from a nation of mounted warriors to a sedentary court with all the trappings of civilized decadence that was so contrary to Genghis Khan's legacy.

By 1235, Ogodei had squandered most of his father's wealth. Ogodei's city was expensive to build and operate, and his habits expensive to meet. Tribute still poured in from across the empire, but it did not come in quite the volume of his father's day. No matter what he did to build a capital or reform the administration, in the end the Mongol Empire rested on conquest. He desperately needed an infusion of wealth to continue in the lifestyle to which he and the Mongols had become accustomed. The Mongol people grew no crops and manufactured no products, and they were loath to trade away the horses that they bred in such copious numbers. If the Mongol Empire were to survive, Ogodei had to take them to war against a new target, one that had not yet been looted. But which, and where?

To decide the targets of future conquest, Ogodei summoned a *khuriltai* to the steppes near his newly built capital of Karakorum. Each participant seemed to support a different course of action. Some wanted the army to head south into the vast subcontinent of India that Genghis Khan had merely glimpsed from the northern mountains but had declined to invade because of its wretched heat. Others advocated a prolonged push farther into Persia and then on to the fabled Arab cities of Baghdad and Damascus, and still others advocated a full-scale assault on the Sung, with whom the Mongols had recently been allies of convenience.

One man, however, had a different proposal. Subodei, fresh from his victory over the Jurched, had been the greatest general in Genghis Khan's army, and with his shrewd knowledge of siege warfare and the use of large attack machines, he had played a major role in every important campaign the Mongols had fought. He was now sixty years old, probably blind in one eye, and according to some reports so fat that he could no longer ride a horse and had to be hauled around in an iron chariot. Despite these physical limitations, his mind was sharp and vigorous, and he was eager to return to war.

Rather than returning to fight against the Muslim or Chinese armies over which he had many victories, Subodei favored a break with the policies of Genghis Khan by organizing a massive campaign to the west, toward Europe, a previously unknown civilization that he had recently discovered quite by accident. He insisted that like China, India, and the Muslim countries, Europe also held the promise of great wealth. Subodei had tested the European armies, and he knew how they fought and how easily they could be defeated.

For most of the participants in the *khuriltai*, Europe was a great unknown. Subodei was the only surviving commander who had been there, and he had originally probed it with only a small force. His discovery of Europe happened more than a decade earlier, in 1221, during Genghis Khan's invasion of central Asia, when Subodei and Jebe had circled the Caspian in pursuit of the Khwarizm sultan. After the sultan's death, they asked and received permission to continue to see what lay to the north. There they discovered the small Christian kingdom of Georgia, ruled by Giorgi III the Brilliant.

Jebe led the probe of their defenses. After centuries of warfare with the Muslims around it, Georgia boasted a highly skilled and professional army, and operating on their home territory, the defenders moved out to meet the attacking Mongols as they had met numerous Turkic and Muslim armies before them. Jebe's Mongols charged the Georgians, fired a few volleys, and then turned to flee in what appeared to the Georgians to be a panicked rout; but, of course, it was no more than the Dog Fight strategy of the feigned retreat. The overconfident Georgian forces broke ranks and began to eagerly chase the Mongols, who barely managed to stay ahead of their pursuers. The Georgian horses gradually began to tire under their heavy loads and the strain of the long pursuit; they began to thin out as the weaker ones fell farther behind.

Then, suddenly, with the Georgian forces spread out and beginning to tire, Jebe's retreating warriors led them straight into the ranks of the other Mongol regiment waiting under Subodei's command. While Subodei's men began to pick off the Georgians, Jebe's soldiers mounted fresh horses and struck out to rejoin the fight. Within hours, the Mongols had completely destroyed the Georgian army and the small nation's aristocracy. Subodei made the country a vassal state, the first in Europe, and it proved to be one of the most loyal and supportive Mongol vassals in the generations ahead.

With this test complete, Subodei and Jebe set out down the mountains to explore the plains of eastern Europe and see what the rest of these unknown people were like on the battlefield. Systematically but persistently, the Mongols probed the area. With the usual emphasis on reconnaissance and information gathering, they determined the number of people, the location of cities, the political divisions, and the rivalries among them. The Mongols found some Turkic tribes, known as the Kipchak, living on the plains between the northern shores of the Black and Caspian Seas. The Kipchak practiced a herding lifestyle very familiar to the Mongols. Playing on their similarities as fellow dwellers within felt walls and speaking related languages, the Mongols learned much from them and enticed some Kipchak to join them as allies. The real object of Subodei's interest was in the agricultural lands farther north and west. The area contained many cities, and although all shared the Orthodox religion and the Russian language, rival and ambitious lords ruled them. Subodei moved his forces toward them to see how they would respond. He reached the banks of the Dnieper River, north of the Black Sea, at the end of April 1223.

The Christian cities of the plain managed to unite enough against the heathen invaders to send out their armies. Hastily assembled troops set out from all the small kingdoms and city-states of the area—Smolensk, Galich, Chernigov, Kiev, Volhynia, Kursk, Suzdal, and some of the Kipchak. Three of the armies—from Galich, Chernigov, and Kiev—came under the command of princes, all of whom were named Mstislav. The most impressive of the three Mstislavs was Prince Mstislav Romanovitch of Kiev, the largest and richest of all the cities, who arrived with the most impressive army, including his two sons-in-law. As the Russian armies gradually trickled in, the Mongols sent an envoy of ten ambassadors to negotiate a surrender or alliance. The Russians haughtily executed them all without any awareness of what a serious breach of Mongol diplomatic etiquette they had committed and what a high price their princes, and all Russians, would soon pay for their crime.

The Mongols began the confrontation with a small skirmish, after which they immediately began to fall back toward the east, from whence they had come, as though they might have been afraid to fight such a large and powerful foe. The Russian troops and some of their Kipchak allies gleefully followed them, but day after day the Mongols remained a little beyond the reach of the pursing Russians. While some of the regiments had not yet arrived to join the pursuit, the slower regiments fell behind, and the faster ones raced on nipping at the heels of the fleeing Mongols. The Russians feared that the Mongols might escape and thereby deprive the Russians of the large number of horses and other booty they carried from their earlier raids across Persia, Georgia, and Azerbaijan. In the competition for glory and loot, the Russian princes began pushing their soldiers on to get the glory of being the first to attack the Mongols; but in a crucial mistake, they made no plans for an organized retreat, regrouping, or withdrawal. After nearly two weeks of chase, the vanguard of the Russian army finally caught up with the Mongols on the Kalka River, which empties into the Sea of Azov, and here at last they would force the invaders to fight, at the place Jebe and Subodei had selected as most advantageous to the Mongols. Without pausing to allow their men to recover from the long forced march, and in fear that the Mongols might escape once again, the confident Russian princes drew up the battle lines for attack.

The later chronicles varied greatly on the number of Russian soldiers present, but somewhere between forty and eighty thousand men fought on the Russian side; the Russians fielded at least twice as many soldiers as the Mongols. But the Russian soldiers had been recruited mostly from the grainfields and small villages of the countryside. They were peasants who, when healthy and properly nourished, were quite strong and experienced in episodic campaigns, but they could scarcely be considered a professional army, particularly at the end of winter when they were poorly nourished. Most of them had more expertise in swinging a scythe to cut hay or cracking a whip to spur on an ox than using the weapons of war. Yet assured of easy victory by their aristocratic officers, the peasants lined up dutifully in military ranks behind their shields. Each man carried whatever weapon he had found or adapted from his farm tools—a makeshift sword, spear, mace, or club. A smaller number of better-trained archers stood nearby, and the elite officers proudly perched atop their steeds in the rear behind their infantry.

The Russian soldiers braced themselves, standing solidly shoulder to shoulder, unsure what kind of attack would come, but they remained determined not to break ranks. But the attack seemed not to come. Instead of attacking, the Mongols starting singing and beating their drums, and then, just as suddenly, the Mongol rank fell into an eerie but absolute quiet. Since it was a clear spring day without too much dust, the Mongols had chosen a Silent Attack to be controlled and coordinated by the waving of flags, at which signal the mounted Mongol archers raced silently forward toward the Russian infantry lines. The pounding of their hoofs on the earth reverberated across the lines and into the legs of the nervous soldiers waiting for the brunt of their charge. But the opposing sides failed to clash. The Mongol horsemen halted just beyond reach of the Slav's hand weapons, and from there, the Mongols fired their arrows straight into the Russian infantry ranks. All around them, the Russian soldiers saw their comrades falling in pools of blood, yet they had no one within reach to counterattack. They had no one with whom to have a sword fight. No one at whom to throw a spear or chase with a club. All they had was a barrage of arrows, and the Mongols had purposefully made the arrows so that they could not be nocked onto their adversaries' bowstrings. In their angry frustration, all the Russian soldiers could do was break the fallen arrows to make sure that the Mongols could not retrieve them to use again.

With their infantry cut to pieces, the Russian archers took aim and began to return the volley of arrows, but with the shorter range of the less-powerful European bows, few hit their mark. In mockery, the Mongols chased down the Russian arrows; but rather than breaking them, they fired them back at their original owners, since the notches of the arrow easily fit the Mongol bowstring. The stunned Russian forces quickly began to fall back in panic. The Mongols followed them, picking them off one by one as they would a herd of fleeing gazelle or panicked deer. As the retreating Russians bumped into the columns of soldiers that had not yet arrived, they began to fall over one another, jamming the route of retreat and increasing the chaos and the slaughter.

The mounted princes of Russia sat astride their massive warhorses with their shiny javelins, glistening swords, colorful flags and banners, and boastful coats of arms. Their European warhorses had been bred for a massive show of strength—to carry the weight of their noble rider's armor on the parade ground—but they had not been bred for speed or agility on the battleground. In their heavy metal armor, the Russians normally had little to fear on the battlefield from other European aristocrats mounted on similar show horses, but with their infantry routed all around them, they, too, had to flee—but beautiful as their horses were, they could not carry the heavy loads for long. The Mongols overtook the ironclad warriors, and one by one killed the reigning princes of the city-states of Russia. The Mongols continued chasing and slaughtering the Russians all the way back to the Black Sea, where the campaign began. In the words of the Novgorod Chronicle entry for 1224, of the large army sent out to fight the Mongols, only "every tenth returned to his home." For the first time since the attack of the Huns on Europe nearly a thousand years earlier, an Asian force had invaded Europe and utterly annihilated a major army.

At the end of the campaign, Subodei and Jebe led their soldiers down to spend a relaxing spring in the Crimea on the Black Sea. They celebrated their victory with a great drunken party that lasted for days. The guest of honor was the defeated Prince Mstislav and his two sons-in-law, but their treatment showed how much the Mongols had changed since the time of Genghis Khan. The Mongols wrapped the three of them in felt rugs, as befitted high-ranking aristocrats, and stuffed them beneath the floorboards of their *ger*, thereby slowly, but bloodlessly, crushing the men as the Mongols drank and sang through the night on the floor above them. It was important to the Mongols that the Russians understand the severe penalty for killing ambassadors, and it was equally as important for the Mongol leaders to reaffirm to their own men the extent to which they would always be willing to go to avenge the unjust killing of a Mongol.

Although the chroniclers of Armenia, Georgia, and the trading cities of ancient Russia recorded the appearance of the Mongols, they were totally mystified as to who these people were, and where they went when they left. The chroniclers interpreted their own defeat at the hands of these strangers as a punishment from God. Since the Mongols did not stay to occupy the land but continued on their trek back to Mongolia, the Europeans quickly forgot the Mongol victories and returned to their own squabbles. In the Christian interpretation, the Mongols had fulfilled God's wish to chastise the people, so God sent them home again. As explained by the Novgorod Chronicle, "the Tartars turned back from the river Dnieper, and we know not whence they came, nor where they hid themselves again; God knows whence he fetched them against us for our sins."

Twelve years after Subodei's first victory over the Russians, participants at Ogodei's *khuriltai* reviewed the information about the earlier Mongol victory. Ogodei's primary interest was the wealth accrued from the European campaign, not the battle tactics. Despite the stunning victory on the battlefield, the expedition had produced little loot compared with the Chinese or Muslim campaigns. Because Subodei's force had not had time or the numbers to organize a campaign against the walled cities, they had brought back little, but his reconnaissance revealed that there were many cities. More important, during their rest to fatten the horses in the Crimea, the Mongols discovered trading centers manned by the merchants of Genoa, some of which the Mongols had raided.

Ogodei seemed to dislike, and perhaps mistrust, Subodei, and the feelings seemed largely mutual. Subodei's position was most strongly supported by the family of Jochi, who lived in the far western steppe and had inherited the lands conquered by Subodei around the Volga River. After Jochi's death, he had been succeeded in the office of khan of his lineage by his son Batu. As the second eldest and one of the most capable of Genghis Khan's grandsons, Batu Khan was in the best position to be elected Great Khan when Ogodei died, and a campaign against Europe would add greatly to his wealth, prestige, and ultimate candidacy.

For much the same reasons that Batu wanted the campaign, Ogodei Khan resisted it. He personally stood much more to gain from a campaign against the Sung. In his position at the center of the Mongol Empire, the lands of two of his brothers' families separated him from Europe, but only the land of his youngest brother, Tolui, lay between him and the Sung dynasty. Conveniently for Ogodei, only three years earlier—in the fall, when the most fermented mare's milk was available—forty-year-old Tolui had staggered drunk out of his tent one morning after a drinking binge and dropped dead. Ogodei immediately moved to annex his dead brother's property, which included the ancestral homeland and Burkhan Khaldun, by arranging a marriage between his son Guyuk and Tolui's widow, Sorkhokhtani, who was the Kereyid niece of the late Ong Khan. She refused, however, on grounds that her four young sons needed her undivided attention, a decision that later proved one of the most important in the history of the empire; but for now, her untested sons lacked the power to compete with their uncle, the Great Khan.

By moving south against the Sung, Ogodei would be increasing his presence in and surrounding the holdings of Sorkhokhtani, and he used the invasion as a pretext to assume command of some of the warriors who had been granted to her husband. Thus, for Ogodei, a campaign against the Sung could have the double benefit of bringing more wealth from China while giving him the chance to annex the lands and armies of his deceased brother from his widow.

With the family divided between those who wanted to invade Europe and those favoring an attack on the Sung dynasty, they reached a remarkable and unprecedented decision: The Mongol army would push out in all directions; it would divide and attack the Sung dynasty and Europe simultaneously. The Mongol army would fight campaigns that would stretch it out over a distance of five thousand miles and more than one hundred degrees of latitude, a feat unmatched by any army until World War II, when the United States and the Allies fought campaigns simultaneously in Europe and in Asia. Ogodei Khan sent three armies—mostly under the command of his favored sons—to attack the Sung from different directions. The European campaign would operate under the command of Batu Khan, who would be guided by Subodei; but in a move probably designed to minimize Batu's power, grandsons from all four branches of the family would be sent to command different aspects of it. Ogodei sent Guyuk, his least-favorite and most-annoying son.

Daring as the decision was, it was probably the worst in the history of the Mongol Empire. Despite many successes in the Sung campaign, the Mongols ultimately failed to conquer the main territory of the Sung—and in the process, Ogodei lost his favorite son. This was probably due to the division in their focus and the lack of Subodei's guidance. Because of the half-staffed invasion, the Sung empire managed to limp along for another four decades before finally capitulating to the Mongols. By contrast, the European campaign, despite prolonged bickering among the different princes of the family, achieved tremendous military success, but once again produced very little of value compared with the wealth in the cities conquered earlier by Genghis Khan.

Preparation for the campaign toward Europe required two years. Messengers went out in all directions to deliver the decision and distribute assignments. The system of post stations established by Genghis Khan were renewed and expanded by decision at the *khuriltai* of 1235; with a war on such a vast front, swift and reliable communication became more important than ever. Before the actual invasion, the Mongols sent in small squads to probe enemy defenses and to locate appropriate pasturelands and water sources for the Mongol animals. They identified valleys and plains that would best feed sheep or goats and those that would support cattle and horses. Where the natural grassland seemed inadequate, the Mongols opened up farmland for pasture by sending in small detachments of soldiers to burn villages and farm settlements in their future path. Without farmers to plow and plant the land, it reverted to grassland before the main Mongol army arrived.

The five-year European campaign marked the zenith of Mongol military ability, and almost everything went according to plan on the battlefield. The army for the invasion of Europe consisted of some fifty thousand Mongols and another one hundred thousand allies. Subodei embodied the accumulated knowledge of the old steppe hunter and warrior who had followed Genghis Khan closely and knew how he thought and fought. In addition, Mongke and Batu, the two smartest and most capable grandsons of Genghis Khan, helped to command the European war effort. By the start of the campaign, the Mongol army had absorbed the best of Chinese and Muslim technology and military knowledge, making it an incredible fighting force that probably surpassed the army commanded by Genghis Khan himself.

Subodei set the conquest of the Volga River, occupied by the Bulgars, as his initial objective. In 1236, the Year of the Monkey, the main army set out. They moved with a party of about two hundred scouts in front and with a rear guard of another two hundred warriors. Once they reached the Volga, the real invasion began. At this point, the Mongols enacted their unusual but, for them, tried-and-true strategy of dividing their army and invading on at least two fronts at once. In this way, the enemy could not tell which city or prince would be the main target. If any prince took his army from his home city to help another prince, then the other Mongol army could attack the undefended one. With such uncertainty and danger to his home base, every prince kept his army at home to guard his own territory, and none came to the aid of the others.

Subodei led his forces north up the Volga toward the homeland of the Bulgars, while Mongke, the eldest son of the deceased Tolui, led another force south toward the Kipchak Turks. Some of the Kipchak fled from him, but others agreed to join the Mongols in attacking the Russian cities. After the quick routing of the Volga Bulgars, the Mongols used their territory for the base camp and a reserve of millions of animals pastured on the steppes for hundreds of miles to the east. Some of the nomadic tribes already living in the eastern European plains joined with the Mongols, while others fled from them and spread fear and panic ahead of the invaders.

From the Volga, they began a three-year campaign across what would later become Russia and Ukraine. In their probes, they found the city-states and principalities still as divided and antagonistic toward one another as they had been when the Mongols invaded nearly two decades earlier. The Mongols followed the same protocols in every case. They began the campaign in each territory by sending official envoys to request the capital city to surrender, join the Mongol family, and become the vassals of the Great Khan. If they agreed, the envoy offered protection to the new vassals from their enemies and allowed them to keep their ruling family and their religion. In return for such protections, the people had to agree to commit tribute of 10 percent of all wealth and goods to the Mongols. Few cities took the offer.

The Mongols made the city of Riazan one of the first targets. The Chronicle of Novgorod for 1238 recorded that "Tartars came in countless numbers, like locusts." First, small units of Mongol warriors divided to scourge the countryside. Each Mongol warrior seized a set number of civilians for the jobs ahead, such as digging fortifications, cutting trees, and hauling supplies. They then burned the villages and sent the remaining peasants scrambling toward safety within the city's wooden walls. When the Mongol army finally reached the city, they sent, much to the consternation and horror of the people gathered inside, a woman ambassador to deliver their terms and demand surrender. Fearing that she was a witch, the city officials refused to admit her for any negotiation, and the Mongols prepared for attack.

Everything about the invading Mongols must have seemed horrifying to the Russians. "They have hard and robust breasts," wrote an observer, "lean and pale faces, stiff high shoulders, and short distorted noses; their chins are sharp and prominent, the upper jaw low and deep, the teeth long and few, their eyebrows stretch from the hair to the nose, their eyes are black and restless, their countenances long and grim, their extremities bony and nervous, their legs thick but short below the knee." When attacking, the Mongol warriors wore a light leather armor that was thick in the front but thin at the back so "that they might not be tempted to run away." In battle, "they use darts, clubs, battle-axes, and swords . . . and fight bravely and unyieldingly, but their chief prerogative is their use of the bow." If captured, "they never ask for mercy, and themselves never spare the vanquished." It is their "intention and fixed purpose of reducing all the world under their dominion."

Instead of attacking the walls of Riazan, the Mongols used their massive number of conscripted laborers in a project that confused and terrified the citizens even more. The workers cut down trees, hauled them to the Mongol lines outside the city, and rapidly began building a wall completely surrounding the already walled city. The Mongol wall formed a strong stockade that surrounded the city completely, sealed off the gates, and prevented the city's defenders from sending out forays of troops to attack the Mongols or to destroy their siege machines. The wall was a wooden form of the traditional line, the *nerge*, used to enclose the animals in a group hunt. The Mongol wall cut off routes for reinforcements to arrive in the city or to bring food or supplies. Probably the most psychologically horrifying effect of the wall was that it sealed the people into their own city without hope of escape. Behind their wall, the Mongols remained out of range of the bows fired from the city wall, and they could set up their siege engines and other equipment without being seen.

From the safety of catwalks behind their own newly built wall, the Mongol warriors now looked down upon the city of Riazan exactly as generations of Mongol hunters had looked down at their tightly bunched hunting prey from behind the safety of their ropes strung from trees and hung with felt blankets. Already accustomed to attackers using catapults and battering rams, the city dwellers had not experienced the innovations in bombardment that the Mongols had developed into a new form of warfare. Their catapults rained down rocks, chunks of wood, flaming pots of naphtha, gunpowder, and other unknown substances. The Mongols used these as incendiaries to spread fires, but also as smoke bombs and to create terrible smells, which, at that time in Europe, were thought to be both acts of evil magic and the source of disease. In addition to shooting fire, the firelances could launch a small incendiary rocket or hurl exploding grenades over enemy walls. The mysterious devices provoked such terror that the victims later reported that the Mongols traveled not only with horses but with trained attack dragons as well.

In the bombardment of the city, the fire, smoke, and confusion caused by these unknown substances from an unseen invader demoralized the people as much as it destroyed their defenses. After five terrorizing and highly destructive days of bombardment, the Mongols finally emerged from behind their wall and attacked the damaged city walls with scaling ladders and battering rams. Within the day, they had taken the city. The civilians sought refuge in their church, where many of them died in the conflagration ignited by the Mongol attack. The victors rounded up the ruling aristocrats and executed them all. As a contemporary Russian chronicler wrote of the carnage, after the Mongol army passed "no eye remained open to cry for the dead." The Mongols culled the captives to be kept for labor and forced large numbers of people to flee on to the next city. Not only did the refugees carry gory details of the attack to terrify the residents of the next city, but the increasing number of refugees would, once again, strain the capacity of that city before the Mongols arrived to attack it as well.

While the new prisoners dismantled the stockade wall and began transporting the logs on toward the next targeted city, a cadre of Mongol census takers followed the army to record the number of people, animals, and products seized. They divided the goods and the captives into lots according to the laws of shares for everyone from orphans and widows to the Golden Family. Then they sent thousands of prisoners to transport the goods back to Karakorum.

The refugees spread information about the Mongols across Europe, as can be seen from the chronicle written by Matthew Paris, a monk of the Benedictine abbey at St. Albans in Hertfordshire, England. In 1240 he recorded the oldest known mention of the Mongols in western Europe, calling them "an immense horde of that detestable race of Satan" and "like demons loosed from Tartarus." He wrote, incorrectly, that "they are called Tartars, from a river called Tartar, which runs through their mountains." *Tartarus* was the Greek name for Hell, the lowest cavern beneath Hades, where the Titans had been condemned after creating a war among the gods.

Paris wrote that the Mongols "ravaged the eastern countries with lamentable destruction, spreading fire and slaughter wherever they went." He then described in specific detail the horror of these invaders who "razed cities to the ground, burnt woods, pulled down castles, tore up the vine-trees, destroyed gardens, and massacred the citizens and husbandmen; if by chance they did spare any who begged their lives, they compelled them, as slaves of the lowest condition, to fight in front of them against their own kindred. And if they merely pretended to fight, or perhaps warned their countrymen to flee, the Tartars following in their rear, slew them; and if they fought bravely and conquered, they gained no thanks by way of recompense, and thus these savages ill-treated their captives as though they were horses."

Matthew Paris's diatribe against the Mongol invaders escalated from frenzied alarm to hysterical loathing: "The men are inhuman and of the nature of beasts, rather to be called monsters than men, thirsting after and drinking blood, and tearing and devouring the flesh of dogs and human beings." Interspersed in the contemptuous vitriol, he did relay some important and accurate information: "They clothe themselves in the skins of bulls, and are armed with iron lances; they are short in stature and thickset, compact in their bodies, and of great strength; invincible in battle, indefatigable in labour; they wear no armour on the back part of their bodies, but are protected by it in front; they drink the blood which flows from their flocks, and consider it a delicacy; they have large powerful horses, which eat leaves and even the trees themselves, and which owing to the shortness of their legs, they mount by three steps instead of stirrups." Other parts of his description have a kernel of truth mixed with some odd misperceptions: "They have no human laws, know no mercy, and are more cruel than lions or bears; they have boats made of the hides of oxen, ten or twelve having one amongst them; they are skilful in sailing or swimming, hence they cross the largest and most rapid rivers without any delay or trouble; and when they have no blood, they greedily drink disturbed and even muddy water."

At the same time in 1240 that Matthew Paris recorded these observations, the Mongols had finished capturing most of the regional cities of Russia and were preparing to capture the largest and most important political and religious center in the Slavic world—Kiev. Taking advantage of early ice to cross the rivers in November 1240, the Year of the Rat, Mongol envoys arrived at the gates of Kiev. Not unexpectedly, the city authorities murdered them and arrogantly pinioned the bodies above the city gate.

Under the leadership of Mongke, the Mongol army amassed around the city in the early winter in what the Russian priests recorded as "clouds of Tatars." The noise of the Mongols was said to be so loud that people inside the city could not hear one another talk. As the soldiers fought to hold the walls, the civilians sought refuge in the magnificent Church of the Virgin. When no room remained to take in anyone else, the people closed the doors. Still hoping to find protective proximity to the virgin's shrine, many other terrified refugees clambered up the church walls seeking sanctuary on the roof. The number grew so large that their weight caused the entire building to collapse, crushing the throngs inside.

When the Mongol forces took the city on December 6, 1240, they looted and burned it to the ground. The Kievan commander Dmitri had fought so hard, even after being abandoned by many of the city's aristocrats, that Batu, with great appreciation of his military talent and tenaciousness, released him and let him live. The Russian phase of the Mongol invasion was coming to a successful close. Only a little more than one year later, in the entry for 1242, the Novgorod Chronicle began referring to the new ruler not only as Khan Batu of the Mongols, but also as *Tsar* Batu, a title that literally meant *Caesar* Batu, signifying a newly united rule over the many warring princely families of Russia. As Prince Michael said on being presented before Batu Khan, "To thee, Tsar, I bow, since God hath granted thee the sovereignty of this world."

With the fall of Kiev, the Mongol conquest of the European east was complete. The Mongols evicted more refugees to flee toward the west and begin terrorizing central Europe with their tales before the Mongols arrived. The refugees barely had time to get away before Subodei sent out new scouting squads in February 1241, while the rivers were still frozen and the riders could more easily and quickly reach the plains of Hungary. On the battlefields of Europe, future control of the Mongol Empire and the world was being fought over—not in the battles themselves, which proved relatively easy for the Mongols to win, but in the political skirmishing behind the scene among the grandsons of Genghis Khan. The compromised selection of Ogodei as the Great Khan after the death of his father had not settled the issue of succession; it had merely postponed it for a generation, and that generation was now in command of the Mongol armies across Europe and already vying for leadership.

Subodei was accompanied by representatives from the family of each of Genghis Khan's four sons. After the death of Ogodei's favorite son, one of these young men would become the next Great Khan, but which one? Under Mongol law, the person would have to be elected at a *khuriltai,* and the campaign in Europe was the proving ground and the election campaign for each of them. The grandsons jockeyed for leadership and for precedence in the emerging hierarchy, and part of this involved seizing credit for the military victories. As with many Mongol political processes, they reach a climactic expression in a fight over who took precedence. At a victory banquet, Batu stood and offered the opening toast. By drinking first, he demonstrated his position as the eldest and the highest ranking of the grandsons, tantamount to publicly proclaiming that he expected be the next Great Khan. Guyuk objected vehemently, claiming that he should be served before Batu because his father was the Great Khan. Another, named Buri, who was "headstrong and brave" but who "uttered harsh words when he drank," resurrected the oldest and most painful issue in the family when he angrily denounced Batu as not really a member of the family because his father was a Merkid bastard.

According to a report that later made its way back to the Great Khan, the three princes spent a long time shouting and screaming at one another. "You are nothing more than an old woman with a beard," Buri screamed at Batu. "Batu is just an old woman with a quiver," echoed Guyuk. Outraged at their treatment by the rest of the family, Guyuk and Buri stormed out of the banquet, mounted their horses, and rode away swearing and cursing. When word reached Ogodei Khan of the incident, he was livid. Ogodei summoned the young men back to court. He initially refused to see them and threatened to have his son Guyuk executed. "May he rot like an egg!" Ogodei said of his ill-behaved son.

When he calmed down and finally admitted Guyuk into his *ger,* he reprimanded him harshly for fighting within the family and for mistreating his soldiers. "You broke the spirit of every man in your army," he charged. In insightful questioning into the proper way to treat one's own troops, Ogodei Khan asked his son, "Do you think that the Russians surrendered because of how mean you were to your own men? Do you think that they surrendered because they were afraid of you?" he added mockingly. "Because you captured one or two warriors, you think that you won the war. But you did not capture even a single kid goat."

Ogodei continue his tirade against his son: "This was your first time out of the *ger,* and so you try to flaunt your manhood. You act as though you achieved everything. You shout and scream at people as though they were animals." He finally calmed down with soothing words from the sons of his other brothers. He quoted a saying of his father's about the need to let army matters be settled out on the steppe, then sent all the boys back to continue the conquest of Europe.

Europe had heard little of the earlier conquests of Genghis Khan in Asia and had only the faintest glimmer of information about his destruction of the Khwarizm empire—but suddenly, with the fall of Kiev, a mass of refugees and stories came pouring out of eastern Europe. Right behind them came the feared Mongol horsemen, seemingly from every direction. Matthew Paris wrote that the Mongols invaded the West "with the force of lightning into the territories of the Christians, laying waste the country, committing great slaughter, and striking inexpressible terror and alarm into every one." This reference to "lightning" warfare was possibly the first mention of the style that later acquired the German name *Blitzkrieg*.

Subodei dispatched a three-pronged army of fifty thousand toward Hungary in the south and a smaller, diversionary force of twenty thousand across Poland toward Germany in the north. The Mongol armies swept across some four thousand miles from their home base in Mongolia, on across the plains of eastern Europe, and into Poland and Hungary—right up to the walls of Vienna and the German cities of the Teutonic Knights and the Hanseatic League. In the north, they jumped across Poland like a stone skipping across an icy pond. One city after another fell as the Mongols ripped through the country. Duke Henry II of Silesia assembled an army of thirty thousand, including knights from throughout Germany, France, and Poland; in his panicked conscription of all potential soldiers, he even drafted a contingent of gold miners to fight the invaders. On April 9, 1241, the two armies met at Liegnitz, near the modern German-Polish border. The Mongols chose an open area for the fighting about six miles from the city, and the battlefield became thereafter known in German as Wahlstatt, the Chosen Place.

Duke Henry ordered his cavalry to charge the Mongol ranks. The Mongols repulsed the first wave, but they seemed to yield to the second and then suddenly turned in flight. With cries of victory, the European knights broke ranks and began chasing the Mongols, who retreated slowly, only a short distance beyond the weapons of the knights. Then, precisely when the European horses began to tire under the heavy armor of their riders, thundering explosive noises erupted around them and heavy smoke engulfed them, causing great confusion. As described by chronicler Jan Dlugosz, the Mongols used on the battlefield a device resembling a "great head, from which there suddenly bursts a cloud with a foul smell that envelops the Poles and makes them all but faint, so that they are incapable of fighting." The smoke and noise cut off the European knights from the archers and infantry far behind them. Once again, the Mongols had made their enemies overconfident and then lured them into a fatal trap. Spread out, disorganized, confused, and tiring quickly, the knights and their horses posed easy targets for the Mongols, who turned and began shooting them down.

The Mongols crushed the Germans. European records document the deaths of twenty-five thousand of Duke Henry's thirty thousand men, but Mongols took many of those captive, particularly the miners, an occupation little understood but much appreciated by the Mongols, who constantly sought out people with novel skills and talents. The victors marched thousands of the miners east to begin mining the rich mineral deposits in Dzungaria, the western Mongolian area that was the personal property of Ogodei.

The entire campaign from Kiev to Germany had been merely a Mongol diversion to keep the Europeans from sending soldiers to fend off the real Mongol objective: invading the grassy plains of Hungary. Having succeeded in killing off most of the northern army and in scattering and neutralizing the rest, the Mongol force withdrew from the Polish and German cities; in time, the local people convinced themselves that they actually had won the battle and repulsed the invaders. The fallen Duke Henry II became a martyr as Henry the Devout, and a Benedictine monastery was built with the altar over the exact spot where, according to Christian mythology, his mother, Saint Hedwig, found his headless, naked corpse, identifying it by the six toes on his left foot. Much later, in the nineteenth century, the Prussian government turned the abbey into a military school, where they trained the future German officers with special emphasis on the tactics of the battle that took place there.

Within days, the Mongol tactics used to defeat and massacre the German knights were replayed in Hungary on a larger field with many times more casualties. After Subodei's army of fifty thousand had pillaged much of

Hungary, they began to retreat when King Bela and his army came after them. Subodei retreated for several days until he arrived at the topography best suited to Mongol victory on the Plain of Mohi. There, the Hungarians gathered into a densely packed camp that was fortified with a circle of wagons and heavy iron chains where the king kept them cooped up for several days. For Batu, accustomed to having his men spread out to sleep in small groups, the Hungarian decision to mass in such a tight formation with a chain around them was identical to the circle of rope and felt blankets with which the Mongols engulfed their prey on large group hunts. The Mongols pulled up catapults and began hurling their mysterious assortment of naphtha, gunpowder, flaming oil, and other substances.

Unable to tolerate the smoke and fire, the Hungarians moved out of their camp. They found themselves virtually surrounded by the Mongols, but in one area, it seemed that the Mongols had forgotten to station their horsemen. In what must have seemed a near miracle to the Christian Hungarians, the gap lay precisely in the direction of their capital of Pest, three days flight away. The Hungarians moved out toward home. As the Hungarians fled, their panic grew. They raced on foot and on horseback, broke ranks, spread out, and dropped their equipment in order to flee more quickly. Of course, the Mongols had not left the gap open by accident; they already had stationed horsemen to wait for the fleeing, frightened Hungarians. The Mongols chased many of the men into bogs and marshes to drown them. The chronicler Thomas of Spalato, archdeacon of what is now the city of Split in Croatia, described the Mongols as *de Peste Tartorum*, the Tartar Plague, and he wrote the most vivid account of their slaughter of the Hungarians: "The dead fell to the right and to left; like leaves in winter, the slain bodies of these miserable men were strewn along the whole route; blood flowed like torrents of rain."

Their knights having failed to defeat the Mongols on the battlefield, the clergy now tried to subdue them through supernatural devices. Perhaps in the knowledge that many of the Mongols were Christian, but not knowing how much the Mongols detested and feared exposure to the remains of the dead, Christian priests attempted to keep the Mongols out of Pest by parading the bones and other relics of their saints before the approaching army. The exposure to pieces of dead bodies enraged the Mongols, for whom such acts were ritually contaminating as well as disgusting. The fearful and angry Mongols not only slew the clerics, but burned the relics and the churches as well to purify themselves from the pollution. For Europe, the encounter had proven as much a religious setback as a military loss, for in addition to the soldiers and king killed, Hungary lost a bishop, two archbishops, and many religious knights of the Templars.

The Mongols had destroyed the knighthood of the country and chased King Bela IV south to the Adriatic. Several texts survived to describe the tremendous psychological and emotional impact of the Mongol invasion, including the *Carmen Miserabile super Destructione Regni Hungariae per Tartaros, or Sad Song of the Destruction of Hungary by the Tartars,* by Roger of Torre Maggiore. European knighthood never recovered from the blow of losing nearly one hundred thousand soldiers in Hungary and Poland, what the Europeans mourned as "the flower" of their knighthood and aristocracy. Walled cities and heavily armored knights were finished, and in the smoke and gunpowder of that Easter season of 1241, the Mongol triumph portended the coming total destruction of European feudalism and the Middle Ages.

Later in 1241, only a few months after the Mongol victories, alarm turned to panic when an eclipse blotted out the sun on Sunday, October 6. People across Europe interpreted the solar eclipse on the sacred day as a certain sign of yet more suffering to come at the hands of the Mongols. The panic was fed by the ignorance of the identity of the attackers. In a widely circulated letter filled with erroneous information, a cleric reported to the archbishop of Bordeaux that the Mongols were "cannibals from Hell who eat the dead after a battle and leave only bones, which even the vultures are too noble to peck." According to this detailed and purposefully incendiary account, the Mongols enjoyed eating old women, and they celebrated their victories by gang raping Christian virgins until they died of exhaustion. Then "their breasts were cut off to be kept as dainties for their chiefs, and their bodies furnished a jovial banquet to the savages."

The sequence of consecutive Mongol victories over the Bulgars, the Russians, the Hungarians, the Germans, and the Poles caused widespread alarm and near panic in some quarters. Who were these people and what did they want? As Matthew Paris lamented, no European knew their language: "For never till this time has there been any mode of access to them, nor have they themselves come forth, so as to allow any knowledge of their customs or persons to be gained through common intercourse with other men."

With no other source of helpful information, the Christian clerics looked to the Bible for an answer. The name *Tartar* sounded to them like *Tarshish*, whose king "shall have dominion also from sea to sea, and from the river unto the ends of the earth." The psalm also stated: "They that dwell in the wilderness shall bow before him; and his enemies shall lick the dust. The kings of Tarshish and of the isles shall bring presents."

For the clerics, the mention of bringing presents connected the king of Tarshish with the three kings of the East who brought gifts to the Christ child, and suddenly they saw an explanation to connect these passages with the Mongols. In 1164, German Crusaders returning from foreign campaigns brought home bones that they claimed were from the Three Kings; in 1181, the Germans began construction of an elaborate reliquary of golden enamel to hold the remains in their marvelous new cathedral of Cologne. Consequently, because of this episode and what everyone realized was the theft of sacred relics, the Christians feared that the Tartars were invading Europe in order to reclaim the bones of their ancestors. In that case, the Mongols would likely cut straight through the heart of Europe to reach their goal at Cologne.

When the Mongols veered south from Hungary toward the Balkans and thereby failed to ride on Cologne, the clerics deduced that if the Mongols were not searching for the bones of the Three Kings, perhaps the invaders were exiled Jews who had failed to return home from the Babylonian captivity. They had been shut up and sealed off by a river that ran beyond Persia. Christian chroniclers reported that the year 1241 corresponded to the year 5000 in the Jewish calendar, and that year, many Jews were expecting the coming of the Messiah or a reappearance of King David.

Matthew Paris initially seemed skeptical of this claim since the Mongols did not speak Hebrew and had no law, which clearly contradicted the biblical account of God's giving the law to Moses. With no other better explanation, however, Paris soon found a way to justify the link between the Mongols and the Jews and the parallels between the time of Moses and his own era. These new people could be missing Hebrew tribes since "in the time of the government of Moses their rebellious hearts were perverted to an evil way of thinking, so that they followed after strange gods and unknown customs, so now in a more wonderful manner, owing to the vengeance of God, they were unknown to every other nation, and their heart and language was confused, and their life changed to that of the cruel and irrational wild beast."

Because of "the enormous wickedness of the Jews," the Christians accused them of bringing the wrath of the Mongols on innocent Christians. According to Paris's highly unlikely report, the European Jewish leaders "assembled on a general summons in a secret place." The "wisest and most influential amongst them" spoke, explaining that their "brethren of the tribes of Israel, who were formerly shut up, have gone forth to bring the whole world to subjection to them and to us. And the more severe and the more lasting that our former suffering has been, the greater will be the glory that will ensue to us." The speaker supposedly wanted the other Jews to greet the Mongols "with valuable gifts, and receive them with the highest honour: they are in need of corn, wine, and arms." Accordingly, the Jews collected "all the swords, daggers, and armour, they could find for sale anywhere, and, in order to conceal their treachery, securely, stowed them away in casks." With no better explanation forthcoming, the Christians accepted this story as proof of "the hidden treachery and extraordinary deceit of the Jews." They were therefore at once handed over to the executioners, to be either consigned to perpetual imprisonment, or to be slain with their own swords.

No matter how absurd the details and no matter the lack of evidence, the stories evoked terribly real and disastrous consequences across Europe. Unable to defeat the Mongols, their enemy menacing the boundaries of their civilization, the Europeans could defeat the Jews, their imagined enemies at home. In one city after another from York to Rome, angry Christian crowds attacked the Jewish quarters of their cities. The Christians attempted to punish the Jews with the same treatment that they had heard the Mongols had used in their campaigns. The Christians set fire to Jewish homes and massacred the residents. Those Jews who managed to escape the cities fled from place to place in search of refuge, but in almost all communities, they found more persecution. To clearly identify which refugees were Jewish refugees and to prevent their entering new Christian communities, the church ordered that Jews had to wear distinctive clothes and emblems to mark them for all to see.

With the destruction of the Hungarian army, the route lay open to Vienna, and within weeks, terrified locals saw the Mongol scouting parties prowling around the outlying districts of the city. In a skirmish with one of these advance guards, the Hapsburg troops captured a Mongol officer, who, to the surprise and consternation of the Christians, turned out to be a thirty-year-old literate Englishman who had made his way through the Holy Land, where he seemed to have developed a talent for learning languages and transcribing them. There is some speculation that with his level of education and his flight from England, he may have been involved in the effort to force King John to sign the Magna Carta in 1215. After fleeing England and facing excommunication from the Roman Catholic Church, he ended up in the service of the more tolerant Mongols. The presence of a European, and a former Christian, among the Mongol army made it clear that the Mongols really were humans and not a horde of demons, but the terrified Christians killed the English apostate before they could get a good accounting of the Mongols' mysterious mission outside Vienna.

The capture of the unnamed Englishman coincided with the end of Mongol penetration into Europe. They had followed the grass steppes across central Asia, Russia, Ukraine, Poland, and Hungary; but where the pastures ended, the Mongols stopped. With five horses per warrior, they needed that pasture to function. Their marked advantages of speed, mobility, and surprise were all lost when they had to pick their way through forests, rivers, and plowed fields with crops and ditches, hedges, and wooden fences. The soft furrows of the peasant's field offered an insecure foothold for the horses. The place where fields began also marked the transition from the dry steppe to the humid climate of the coastal zones, where the dampness caused the Mongol bows to lose strength and accuracy.

Despite their probes across the Danube, the full-scale Mongol invasion of western Europe failed to materialize. On December 11, 1241, Ogodei, reportedly in a drunken stupor, died. News of the death reached the Mongol forces in Europe, four thousand miles from Karakorum, within four to six weeks. Chaghatai died at about the same time, and thus in the mere fourteen years since the death of Genghis Khan, all four of his sons had died, and now the princes, Genghis Khan's grandsons, raced home to continue their battles against each other in the quest to become the next Great Khan. The struggle among the lineages would last another ten years—and for at least this decade, the rest of the world would be safe from Mongol invasion.

Over the early months of 1242, the Year of the Tiger, the Mongols withdrew from western Europe back to their stronghold in Russia. The European cities produced little loot, and the armies the Mongols routed had been poorly supplied. The most valuable asset the Mongols took with them were the tents and furnishing of the Hungarian king's camp, which Batu used for his base camp on the Volga River. Despite the lack of goods, the Mongols had found a variety of craftsmen such as the miners from Saxony, scribes and translators, and, from their raids around Belgrade and the Balkans, a contingent of French prisoners that included at least one Parisian goldsmith.

Disappointed with the material reward of their invasion and eager to show some profit, the Mongol officers struck a deal with the Italian merchants stationed in the Crimea. In exchange for large amounts of trade goods, the Mongols allowed the Italians to take many of their European prisoners, especially the young ones, to sell as slaves around the Mediterranean. This began a long and lucrative relationship between the Mongols and the merchants of Venice and Genoa, who set up trading posts in the Black Sea to tap this new market. The Italians supplied the Mongols with manufactured goods in return for the right to sell the Slavs in the Mediterranean markets.

This decision to sell the young people would create a major future problem for the Mongols, because the Italians sold most of their slaves to the sultan of Egypt, who used them in his slave army. In another twenty years, the Mongols were destined to meet this army composed mostly of Slavs and Kipchaks who had plenty of experience fighting the Mongols, and in many cases had even learned the Mongol language before being transported away. That future meeting along the Sea of Galilee in modern Israel would prove to have a far different outcome than the first meeting on the plains of Russia.

7

━━━━⊰○⊱━━━━

Warring Queens

Just as God gave different fingers to the hand so has
He given different ways to men.

M O N G K E   K H A N

W HILE THE MONGOL men stayed busy on the battlefield conquering foreign countries, women managed the empire. Among the herding tribes,
women traditionally managed the affairs at home while men went off to herd,
hunt, or fight, and although the war campaigns now lasted for years rather than
months and the home consisted of not merely a collection of *ger* camps but a
vast empire, women continued to rule. Aside from Russia and eastern Europe,
where the fighting continued the heaviest during Ogodei's reign, women
assumed administration of all remaining parts of the Mongol Empire. Despite
the rivalry with Ogodei Khan, Sorkhokhtani, the widow of Genghis Khan's
youngest son, Tolui, ruled northern China and eastern Mongolia, including the
family homeland where Genghis Khan grew up. Ebuskun, the widow of
Genghis Khan's second son, Chaghatai, ruled Central Asia or Turkestan.

While Ogodei reigned as Great Khan, for long periods of time he was too
drunk to lead the empire, and he gradually conveyed administrative power to
Toregene, the most capable, although not the senior, wife. At his death in 1241,

she became the official regent. For the next ten years, until 1251, she and a small group of other women controlled the largest empire in world history. None of the women had been born a Mongol but had instead been married into the family from a conquered steppe tribe, and most of the women were Christians. Neither their gender nor religion hindered their rise to power nor the struggle against one another as each vied to place the whole of the empire in the hands of her own son.

The struggle for power, no matter how fiercely fought, proved relatively peaceful except when it came to the ultimate treatment of the women themselves, who suffered horrendous fates upon losing a battle. Outside of the court struggles, the era brought a needed decade of peace through the empire, an opportunity to consolidate some of the holdings, and a time to recover from the four decades of the First Mongol World War of 1212–1241 and prepare for the next one.

The oldest surviving record of Toregene's power and prominence in the Mongol court appears in an order to print Taoist texts issued by her as *Yeke Khatun*, Great Empress, under her own name as well as the seal of Ogodei on April 10, 1240. The text shows clearly not only that she was operating the empire but that while the men fought, she pursued an entirely different line of activities, supporting religion and education and working to build buildings and important social structures on an imperial scale.

Having lost his favorite son and other close relatives in the only marginally successful China campaign, Ogodei generally lost interest in political life, but he nominated one of his grandsons to follow him. Toregene, however, wanted to push the candidacy of her quarrelsome and arrogant son Guyuk, who had been so strongly chastised and apparently disliked by his father. Soon after Ogodei's death, Toregene summoned a *khuriltai* to elect Guyuk instead of the grandson nominated by Ogodei, but she could not get a quorum of the Golden Family, which meant that not enough people favored his election. Toregene continued as regent and began five years of meticulous political work to build the support she needed for Guyuk's election. To pursue her goal, she dismissed her late husband's ministers and replaced them with her own, the most important of whom was another woman, Fatima, a Tajik or Persian captive from the Khwarizm campaign who had been brought to work in Karakorum. The chronicler Ata-Malik Juvaini, who disliked her, and seemingly all women involved in politics, wrote that Fatima enjoyed constant access to Toregene's tent, and she "became the sharer of intimate confidences and the depository of hidden secrets." Fatima played a political role while the older "ministers were debarred from executing business, and she was free to issue commands and prohibitions."

By 1246, Toregene had tightened her control of the empire and felt confident that she could orchestrate her son's election. The deliberations and election of Guyuk transpired in private, limited to members of the Golden Family and important functionaries, but Toregene organized his installation as a major affair for foreign dignitaries as well as the Mongol people. Throughout the summer until the ceremony in August, foreign delegates arrived from the distant corners of the empire. Emirs, governors, and grandees jostled along the same roads beside princes and kings. The Seljuk sultan came from Turkey; representatives of the caliph of Baghdad also arrived, as well as two claimants to the throne of Georgia: David, the legitimate son of the late king, and David, the illegitimate son of the same king. The highest-ranking European delegate was Alexander Nevsky's father, Grand Prince Yaroslav II Vsevolodovich of Vladimir and Suzdal, who died suspiciously just after dining with Toregene Khatun.

By happenstance, on July 22, 1246, in the midst of the massive gathering, the first envoy arrived at the Mongol court from western Europe. Friar Giovanni of Plano Carpini, a sixty-five-year-old cleric, who had been one of the disciples of Saint Francis of Assisi, arrived as the agent and spy for Pope Innocent IV, commissioned to find out as much as possible about these strange people who had threatened Europe. After leaving Lyons, France, at Easter of 1245, Carpini required nearly a year to cross Europe to the Mongol lines at Batu's camp in Russia. Once in the Mongol transport system, however, Carpini covered approximately three thousand miles in a mere 106 days—an average of more than twenty-five miles on horseback each day for nearly three and a half months.

Because of the success of their military campaigns in Europe, the Mongols eagerly received Carpini in the mistaken belief that he was bringing the submission of the pope and all the people of western Europe, but his letter carried quite a different message. Pope Innocent IV offered the khan a pedantic synopsis of the life of Jesus and the main tenets of Christianity, all of which was probably well known to the khan through his Christian mother and his frequent attendance of religious services with her. Guyuk was likely a Christian himself; if not, he was certainly well disposed toward Christianity and relied heavily on Christian Mongols in his administration. The pope's letter chastised the Mongols for invading Europe, ordering the khan to "desist entirely from assaults of this kind and especially from the persecution of Christians." He demanded an explanation from the khan "to make fully known to us . . . what moved you to destroy other nations and what your intentions are for the future." The letter informed the khan that God had delegated all earthly power to the pope in Rome, who was the only person authorized by God to speak for Him.

After the Mongol officials found out that Carpini brought no tribute and offered no submission, they mostly ignored him, but in a letter of November 1246 that still survives, Guyuk asked Innocent IV the obvious questions: How do you know whom God absolves and to whom He shows mercy? How do you know that God sanctions the words you speak? Guyuk pointed out that God had given the Mongols, not the pope, control of the world from the rising sun to the setting sun. God intended for the Mongols to spread his commandments and his laws through Genghis Khan's Great Law. He then advised the pope to come to Karakorum with all of his princes in order to pay homage to the Mongol khan.

The first direct diplomatic contact between Europe and the Far East had degenerated into an exchange of comparative theology mixed with religious insults. Despite the extensive spiritual beliefs that the Mongols and Europeans shared in common, the opening relationship had been so negative and misguided that in future years, the entire base of shared religion would eventually erode. The Mongols continued for another generation to foster closer relations with Christian Europe, but in the end, they would have to abandon all such hope, and with it they would, in time, abandon Christianity entirely in favor of Buddhism and Islam.

In the fall of 1246, when Carpini and the other foreign dignitaries departed the royal camp to head home, Guyuk turned attention from public pomp and ceremony to the important political task of solidifying power and making himself the khan in fact, as well as in title. To assert his newly conferred powers, he first attacked Fatima, his mother's trusted adviser. Using an accusation of witchcraft against her as a pretext, he summoned Fatima from his mother's court to his own. His mother refused to let her go: "He sent again several times, and each time she refused him in a different way. As a result his relations with his mother became very bad, and he sent [a] man . . . with instruction to bring Fatima by force if his mother should still delay."

The vague records of what happened next raise more questions than answers. Guyuk won control of Fatima Khatun, and his mother died. Was his mother ill? Killed? Did she die of anger or grief? Most records fall silent. The Persian historian Juzjani wrote that Toregene was sent to join her husband, Ogodei. Since her husband had been dead for six years, the statement appears to be a euphemism for her death, but Juzjani seemed unsure, for he added, "but God knows the truth." All we know is that Guyuk's men seized Fatima Khatun and Toregene Khatun was dead.

Instead of quietly disposing of Fatima, Guyuk submitted her to a gruesome public ordeal. At a time when the Mongols ruled an empire across two continents and still had numerous opportunities to expand it even farther, the court seemed fixated not on the empire but on this one woman, what she had done, and what should be done to her. Guyuk ordered his guards to bring Fatima, stripped naked and tightly bound in ropes, before him in open court. There she was kept publicly, "hungry and thirsty for many days and nights; she was plied with all manner of violence, severity, harshness and intimidation." They beat her and then flogged her with some kind of heated metal rods. Such a public torture may have been appropriate for the treatment of a witch in European society or for a heretic at the hands of the Christian Church, but it violated totally the practices of Genghis Khan, who slew his enemies and ruled with harsh strictness but steadfastly without torture or the infliction of unnecessary pain. It seemed particularly contrary to Mongol tradition since it was directed against a woman; no precedent was known in Mongol history for any comparable spectacle.

The torture of Fatima was perhaps technically legal under the existing code because she was not a Mongol nor married to one, but was instead a war captive of uncertain but unprotected status. When at last the tortured woman confessed to a list of evils, including bewitching Toregene Khatun and other members of the Golden Family, Guyuk imposed on her a punishment of unique cruelty and symbolism. He ordered that all the orifices of her upper and lower body be sewn shut, thereby not permitting any of the essences of her soul to escape from her body, and that she be rolled up inside a felt blanket and drowned in the river. And thus ended the life of Fatima, his mother's adviser, and one of the most powerful women of the thirteenth century.

In keeping with the tone set by the public torture and execution of Fatima, Guyuk's short reign was one of horrible revenge. He unleashed a crude campaign to consolidate power and eliminate rivals. He ordered his soldiers to hunt down and kill everyone connected with Fatima. He began legal proceedings against his uncle Temuge Otchigen, the last surviving full brother of Genghis Khan and thus a legal claimant to the throne, who, shortly before Guyuk's election, had pressed his claim in an abortive attempt to raise an army and invade the lands of Toregene Khatun. Temuge Otchigen had survived his encounter with the shaman Teb Tengeri when he was younger, but he did not survive this confrontation with his grandnephew. In a secret trial closely supervised by Guyuk in a closed *ger,* the male members of the family condemned him to death for attempting to seize the office of Great Khan by military force rather than election.

Guyuk turned attention to the other women in charge of the imperial Mongol lands. He removed the regent widow ruling over the lands of Chaghatai's family, and he ordered an inquiry into the affairs of Tolui's estate, then under the regency of Sorkhokhtani, who had refused to marry Guyuk after her husband's death. During the investigation, he ordered the surrender of all the warriors assigned to her and her sons. With his eastern front thus secured and under his tight control, he assembled his army to move west on what he claimed was to be a massive hunt. In fact, the move was a pretext for a surprise attack on Batu Khan in Russia. He not only wanted revenge against his cousin for prior insults at the victory dinner in Russia, but of all the khans, Guyuk seemed most convinced of the importance of Europe. He wanted to complete that conquest and add Europe to his own personal territory within the Mongol Empire.

Unwilling to defy him publicly in any way, Sorkhokhtani cautiously moved to ensure that he failed in his surprise attack. She secretly dispatched messengers to warn Batu of Guyuk's plan. She quite possibly took direct action against Guyuk himself because once he left his family stronghold in the central Mongolian steppe, the forty-three-year-old, seemingly healthy Guyuk suddenly died of mysterious causes after only eighteen months in office. Someone had probably killed him, but the list of suspects who had cause to do so is too long to analyze. No surviving Mongol document records the details of his death, and the suddenly laconic Persian chronicles report merely that "his predestined hour arrived."

In the continuing political struggles at the center of the empire, the fringes began to unravel. With his great love of metaphors, Juvaini wrote that "the affairs of the world had been diverted from the path of rectitude and the reins of commerce and fair dealing turned aside from the highway of righteousness." He described the land as being in darkness, "and the cup of the world was filled to the brim with the drink of iniquity." The Mongol people and their subjects, "dragged now this way, now that, were at their wits' end, for they had neither the endurance to stay nor did they know of a place to which they might flee."

After the brief respite of Guyuk's rule, the battle of the surviving queens resumed, even more intensely, as Guyuk's widow Oghul Ghaimish stepped forward to take control of the empire just as her mother-in-law Toregene had done when Ogodei died. Oghul Ghaimish lacked the skills of her mother-in-law, and the hour would not belong to her, in great part because her own sons set up rival courts to challenge her right to rule as regent. Sorkhokhtani, with the full support of her four capable sons and a lifetime of preparation and waiting, finally made her move. Rather than wait for Guyuk's widow to call the *khuriltai* at the capital of Karakorum, Batu Khan, at the instigation of his secret ally Sorkhokhtani, called it in 1250 for an area near Lake Issykul in the Tian Shan Mountains, outside of Mongolia and more convenient for him to reach. The *khuriltai* elected Sorkhokhtani's eldest son Mongke, but the Ogodei family boycotted the election on grounds that a legitimate election had to be held in Mongolia proper, in particular in the capital of Karakorum, which their family controlled.

Undaunted, Sorkhokhtani devised a brilliant plan. She lacked access to the imperial capital, but as the widow of Genghis Khan's youngest son, she controlled the ancient family homeland where Genghis Khan had been born, elected, and buried. No one could refuse to attend a *khuriltai* held on this sacred ground. Her ally Batu Khan could not make the long trip from Russia, but he sent her a bodyguard of thirty thousand troops under his brother Berke to protect her and her family through this election and installation process. She organized a second election for this hallowed spot, and on July 1, 1251, the assembled throng proclaimed the forty-three-year-old Mongke Grand Khan of the Mongol Empire. This time, no one could object to the venue.

To celebrate the occasion of his election, Mongke issued an order that for that day each person should rest, and the animals should not be made to work or carry burdens. The earth should not be pierced with tent pegs and water should not be polluted. No one could hunt wild animals, and those animals that were to be killed for feasting should be killed without shedding blood on the sacred earth. After the sacred day, a week of feasting followed. Each day of the festivities, the assembled guests consumed three hundred horses or oxen, three thousand sheep, and two thousand wagons filled with *airak,* the beloved alcoholic drink made from fermented mare's milk.

The celebration marked the culmination of Sorkhokhtani's lifework, and, in one sense, the celebration was more of an honor for her than anyone else. Whereas Genghis Khan himself had produced sons who were relatively weak, prone to drink, and self-centered, she had produced and trained four sons destined to make a major mark in history. Each of her sons was a khan. In the coming years Mongke, Arik Boke, and Khubilai would all carry the title of Great Khan for various lengths of time, and her other son, Hulegu, would become the Il Khan of Persia and the founder of his own dynasty there. Her sons would push the empire to its maximum size by conquering all of Persia, Baghdad, Syria, and Turkey. They would conquer the Chinese Sung dynasty in the south and push into Vietnam, Laos, and Burma. They would destroy the dreaded sect of the Assassins and execute the Muslim caliph.

The family of Ogodei and Guyuk arrived late at the *khuriltai,* after the election itself but in the middle of the celebration. The three important princes of Ogodei's family suddenly strode into the tent to announce that they wished to pay obeisance to the new khan. The new khan had them all arrested and put in chains because his spies already reported that their arrival was a ruse to distract the court while other members of the family gathered nearby to prepare a sneak attack on the celebrating, and therefore inebriated, throng. Mongke easily captured the would-be attackers and began another round of trials. He could not torture or shed the blood of any descendant of Genghis Khan, but he had their advisers, mostly Muslims and Chinese, brought in for a torturous whipping with canes until they confessed against their masters. At the end of the trial, the new khan found his cousins guilty of various crimes. Two of the princes had their mouths stuffed with stones and dirt until they died. Some of the advisers committed suicide. In all, Mongke executed seventy-seven people within or close to Ogodei's lineage.

While Mongke oversaw the trials of the men, his mother tried the women in her court. Sorkhokhtani ordered the arrest of the hapless regent Oghul Ghaimish Khatun, and in an only slightly milder replay of the trial of Fatima, her captors sewed rawhide around her hands and stripped her naked for public ridicule before wrapping her in felt and drowning her and another senior woman from the family. A third woman from their family was wrapped in a blanket and kicked to death.

From his court, Mongke Khan expanded the trials to a grand purge by sending out bands of inquisitors throughout the empire to question, convict, and punish anyone suspected of disloyalty to his branch of the family. The trials took place on a global scale from China and Mongolia in the east to Afghanistan in the south and Persia and Iraq in the west. Even the highest officials, such as the ruler of the Uighurs, were put to death, but the greatest damage was inflicted on the Golden Family itself. Mongke seemed determined to root out all the supporters from the families of his deceased uncles Chaghatai and Ogodei. Mongke seized the city of Karakorum and surrounding territory from Ogodei's descendants. Across the empire, rulers and high officials lucky enough to escape punishment by the ad hoc tribunals still had to travel to Karakorum and present themselves to the new khan, have their record of loyalty examined, and then face the possible threat of punishment. Those officials who survived the test were then reinstated in their old position by the new khan. After the extensive and bloody purge of the Ogodei lineage, Mongke Khan ordered a general amnesty for other types of nonpolitical prisoners and captives.

Power had clearly passed into the lineage of Tolui. Sorkhokhtani had smashed the last obstacles to power for her sons, and she died knowing that her four sons faced no further threat from any branch of the Golden Family. The best description made of her accomplishment came from the writer Bar Hebraeus, who wrote that "if I were to see among the race of women another woman like this, I should say that the race of women was far superior to men." No one in the history of the world had been given so large and rich an empire as Sokhokhtani gave to her sons, but within a few years of her death, her four sons would begin to tear it apart.

Sometime near the Mongol New Year festival in February 1252, either in the final days of the Year of the Pig or the first days of the Year of the Rat, Sorkhokhtani died. With her death, the decade of the ruling women that had begun in 1241 ended. Even as they competed against one another, the women had brought much needed outside talent into the inner circle of Mongol rule, and had given the empire a new foundation with their support of monasteries and schools, the printing of books, and the exchange of ideas and knowledge. After the resumption of the Mongol World War by the men, it would, in the end, be the new institutions begun by these women that would have the greatest impact on the world within and beyond the Mongol Empire. But the full flowering of that would have to await one more round of war.

Mongke's accession to the office of Great Khan of the Mongol Empire in 1251 came nearly a quarter of a century after the death of his grandfather, Genghis Khan, in 1227. In a statement that summarizes his administration and his sober personality as instilled in him by his mother Sorkhokhtani, he said of himself, "I follow the laws of my ancestors; I do not imitate other countries' ways." He was a serious man who showed neither the frivolity of Ogodei nor the recklessness of Guyuk and who, almost alone among members of the Golden Family, avoided the destructive bind of alcoholism.

To increase his legitimacy as the Great Khan of the Mongol Empire and to rewrite history to make it more accommodating to his needs, in 1252 he retroactively awarded his father the title of Great Khan. This was given on the legal claim that as the youngest son, and therefore the *Otchigen,* or Prince of the Hearth, Tolui had been entitled to inherit his deceased father's titles as well as his homeland.

In staking out his territory, Mongke turned attention to his newly claimed capital city of Karakorum, which for twenty years had served as the center and symbol of the power of Ogodei's family. Mongke, however, intended to transform the modest city from the family seat of Ogodei's lineage into an imperial capital of the Mongol Empire. Before Ogodei built Karakorum, the area had belonged to the Kereyid, and in particular to Ong Khan and his family, including Sorkhokhtani, Mongke's mother and the niece of Ong Khan.

He needed to make his own mark on the capital, and since Ogodei had already used Chinese and Persian architects, Mongke turned to the Christian craftsmen captured in his part of the European campaign. Although he showed no appreciation for European architecture, the technical ability of the metalworkers had impressed him. When his army took the city of Belgrade, they had captured Guillaume Boucher, a Parisian goldsmith. Because of his ability to make Christian religious objects, Boucher had been given to Sorkhokhtani, and on her death he passed to Mongke's younger brother Arik Boke. Mongke selected Boucher, together with a team of fifty assistant craftsmen, to add an exotic European flair to the Mongol capital, and he did so in an overwhelming but idiosyncratic style that amazed visitors to his courts.

Envoys to Mongke's court at Karakorum reported the working of an unusual contraption in his palace. A large tree sculpted of silver and other precious metals rose up from the middle of his courtyard and loomed over his palace, with the branches of the tree extending into the building and along the rafters. Silver fruit hung from the limbs, and it had four golden serpents braided around the trunk. At the top of the tree, rose a triumphant angel, also cast in silver, holding a trumpet at his side. An intricate series of pneumatic tubes inside the tree allowed unseen servants to blow into them and manipulate them to produce what seemed to be acts of magic. When the khan wanted to summon drinks for his guests, the mechanical angel raised the trumpet to his lips and sounded the horn, whereupon the mouths of the serpents began to gush out a fountain of alcoholic beverages into large silver basins arranged at the base of the tree. Each pipe discharged a different drink—wine, black *airak,* rice wine, and mead.

The four serpents on the Silver Tree of Karakorum symbolized the four directions in which the Mongol Empire extended, as did the four alcoholic drinks derived from crops of distant and exotic civilizations: grapes, milk, rice, and honey. Trees were rare on the steppe, but they had a more important role in the homeland and origin of the Mongol family of Genghis Khan. In their oral history, the first ancestor to try to unite the Mongol tribes had been made khan under a tree on the Khorkhonag steppe, and it was in this same area that Temujin and Jamuka had taken the oath as *andas* after the Merkid battle. The whole contraption offered a spectacular and pungent reminder of the Mongol origins and of their mission to conquer the entire world in all four directions. Mongke accepted the obligation to bring everything under the rule of the Mongol state that stood like one massive tree at the center of the universe. Mongke Khan took that command as the literal destiny of his nation and as his responsibility to achieve.

As part of his more Western orientation, Christianity temporarily resumed its ascendancy in Mongke's court, a trend reinforced by the large number of Christian wives in the Golden Family and by the steadfast loyalty shown by Christian nations such as Georgia and Armenia. Near the end of 1253, the Year of the Ox, William of Rubruck, a Franciscan monk, came to the Mongol court as an envoy from the French king. From his writings, an intriguing, although not always detailed, description emerged of the rivalries among the Christians and other religions in the Mongol court. Rubruck had the opportunity to see how the Mongol court celebrated Christmas, although he himself had little role to play other than singing "Veni Sancte Spiritus" for them. Mongke Khan and his wife celebrated mass in church, with the two of them seated on a golden couch across from the altar. In keeping with Assyrian Christian tradition, the inside was void of excessive decoration and imagery, but the rafters of the church were draped with silk to give the building the feeling and appearance of a Mongol *ger*. After mass, the khan talked about religion for a short while with the priests. When he left, his wife stayed behind to distribute Christmas presents to everyone. She offered gifts of textiles to Rubruck, but he refused to accept them. Apparently the *khatun* did not notice the intended slight since Rubruck's interpreter accepted the cloth for himself and later sold it back in Cyprus.

After the distribution of gifts, the Christmas celebration began with goblets of red wine, rice ale, and the ubiquitous Mongol *airak*. The French envoys had to sing once again for the *khatun*. Finally, after several more rounds of drinks, the Christmas dinner arrived in the form of large platters of mutton and carp that Rubruck contemptuously noted was served without salt or bread. "I ate a little. In this way they passed the time until evening." The Christmas mass and celebration ended when "the lady, now drunk, got into a cart, while the priests sang and howled, and she went her way."

The Mongol Christians emphasized the association of God with light, particularly the Golden Light that was sacred in their mythology, and they associated Jesus with healing and triumph of life over death. Despite the common religion, Rubruck greatly resented the Assyrian, Armenian, and Orthodox Christians at the Mongol court. Since he considered all non-Catholics to be heretics, he contemptuously designated the Mongol congregants of the Assyrian Church as Nestorians in reference to Nestorius, the fifth-century Patriarch of Constantinople who was condemned as a heretic by the Council of Ephesus in 431. Among the Assyrian beliefs that Rubruck held to be heretical was that the Virgin Mary was the mother of Christ, but not the mother of God. They also differed from the Catholics in their steadfast refusal to portray Christ on the cross as a violation of the Mongol taboos on depicting death or blood. Even when they admitted to being Christians, Mongols did not consider their religion as their primary identification. As one of the Mongol generals who was a follower of Christianity explained, he was no Christian—he was a Mongol.

After making the French envoy wait for many months, Mongke finally received him officially in court on May 24, 1254. Rubruck informed the officials that he knew the word of God and had come to spread it. In front of the assembled representatives of the various religions, the khan asked Rubruck to explain to them the word of God. Rubruck stumbled over a few phrases and stressed the importance to Christians of the commandment to love God, whereupon one of the Muslim clerics asked him incredulously, "Is there any man who does not love God?"

Rubruck responded, "Those who do not keep His commandments, do not love Him."

Another cleric then asked Rubruck, "Have you been in heaven that you know the commandments of God?" He seized upon the implication of what Rubruck was saying to them about God's commandments and challenged him directly: "By this you mean that Mongke Khan does not observe God's commandments?"

The discussion continued for some time, and according to Rubruck's own account, it was obvious that he did not fare well in the sometimes acrimonious arguments. He was unaccustomed to debating with people who did not share his basic assumptions of Catholic Christianity. Evidently, Mongke Khan recognized the problems he was having and suggested that all the scholars present take time to write out their thoughts more clearly and then return for a fuller discussion and debate of the issues.

The Mongols loved competitions of all sorts, and they organized debates among rival religions the same way they organized wrestling matches. It began on a specific date with a panel of judges to oversee it. In this case Mongke Khan ordered them to debate before three judges: a Christian, a Muslim, and a Buddhist. A large audience assembled to watch the affair, which began with great seriousness and formality. An official lay down the strict rules by which Mongke wanted the debate to proceed: on pain of death "no one shall dare to speak words of contention."

Rubruck and the other Christians joined together in one team with the Muslims in an effort to refute the Buddhist doctrines. As these men gathered together in all their robes and regalia in the tents on the dusty plains of Mongolia, they were doing something that no other set of scholars or theologians had ever done in history. It is doubtful that representatives of so many types of Christianity had come to a single meeting, and certainly they had not debated, as equals, with representatives of the various Muslim and Buddhist faiths. The religious scholars had to compete on the basis of their beliefs and ideas, using no weapons or the authority of any ruler or army behind them. They could use only words and logic to test the ability of their ideas to persuade.

In the initial round, Rubruck faced a Buddhist from North China who began by asking how the world was made and what happened to the soul after death. Rubruck countered that the Buddhist monk was asking the wrong questions; the first issue should be about God from whom all things flow. The umpires awarded the first points to Rubruck.

Their debate ranged back and forth over the topics of evil versus good, God's nature, what happens to the souls of animals, the existence of reincarnation, and whether God had created evil. As they debated, the clerics formed shifting coalitions among the various religions according to the topic. Between each round of wrestling, Mongol athletes would drink fermented mare's milk; in keeping with that tradition, after each round of the debate, the learned men paused to drink deeply in preparation for the next match.

No side seemed to convince the other of anything. Finally, as the effects of the alcohol became stronger, the Christians gave up trying to persuade anyone with logical arguments, and resorted to singing. The Muslims, who did not sing, responded by loudly reciting the Koran in an effort to drown out the Christians, and the Buddhists retreated into silent meditation. At the end of the debate, unable to convert or kill one another, they concluded the way most Mongol celebrations concluded, with everyone simply too drunk to continue.

While the clerics debated at Karakorum, their religious brethren were hacking at each other and burning one another alive in other parts of the world outside the Mongol Empire. At almost the same time of Rubruck's debate in Mongolia, his sponsor, King Louis IX, was busy rounding up all Talmudic texts and other books of the Jews. The devout king had the Hebrew manuscripts heaped into great piles and set afire. During Rubruck's absence from France, his fellow countrymen burned some twelve thousand hand-written and illuminated Jewish books. For these and other great services to the furtherance of the Gospel of Jesus Christ, his church canonized him as Saint Louis, thereby making him a figure of veneration that good Christians could emulate and to whom they could pray as an intermediary between humans and God.

During the same time in both the Muslim and Christian kingdoms, the rulers made religious intolerance an official policy of the state. Frustrated in the attempts to conquer the Holy Land or to expand into eastern Europe, the Catholic Church moved into a phase of growing intolerance for religious variation at home. In 1255 the church sanctioned the torturing of people sus-pected of heretical beliefs, and priests, mostly Dominicans, began traveling from city to city to find and torture suspects. Until this time civil authorities used torture to interrogate suspected criminals, traitors, and war prisoners, but priests did not inflict torture for religious purposes.

A few days after the debate at Karakorum, Mongke Khan summoned Rubruck to discharge him and send him back to his home country. He took this occasion to explain to the priest, and through him to the rulers of Europe, that he himself belonged to no single religion, and he lectured Rubruck on Mongol beliefs about tolerance and goodness: "We Mongols believe in one God, by Whom we live and Whom we die and toward Him we have an upright heart." He then explained, "Just as God gave different fingers to the hand so has He given different ways to men. To you God has given the Scriptures and you Christians do not observe them." He cited as evidence that the Christians eagerly placed money ahead of justice. He then explained that instead of the Scriptures, God had given the Mongols holy men, their shamans. In daily life, "we do what they tell us, and live in peace" with one another.

Mongke Khan then sent a letter to the French king Louis IX. It had a sim-ple message: In heaven there is but one Eternal God, and on earth there is but one lord Genghis Khan, the Son of God, and his descendants who ruled the Mongol Empire. Aside from this messianic rhetoric, added after Genghis

Khan's death, the main message remained the same as articulated by the founder of the Mongol Empire in his latter years. Once all people submit to the tolerant rule of the Mongols, then "by the power of the eternal God the whole world from the rising of the sun to going down thereof shall be at one in joy and peace." But Mongke warned the French and all Christians that "if, when you hear and understand the decree of the eternal God, you are unwilling to pay attention and believe it, saying, 'Our country is far away, our mountains are might, our sea is vast', and in this confidence you bring an army against us—we know what we can do."

Despite his theological interrogation of Rubruck, Mongke's interest in him was primarily diplomatic and commercial, not religious. Under Mongke, the entire energy of the state and the Golden Family was redirected toward the original enterprises that Genghis Khan had left unfinished—the conquest of the Sung dynasty and the Arab states of the Middle East. To get the empire back on track, Mongke ordered a series of censuses to record the number of people and animals as well as the orchards and farms and other assets of the empire. Local officials forwarded the information to Karakorum in great registers that supplied Mongke with a detailed demographic and economic portrait of his massive realm. He used this information to plan his policies, organize taxes, and recruit soldiers and laborers. His centralized control of information gave him heightened power over local areas and provided him with more oversight of local officials.

To renew the war campaigns, Mongke needed to stabilize the economy, control government spending, and confront the massive debts accumulated by Guyuk and other administrators over the prior decade. In his short and disastrous reign, Guyuk had purchased vast amounts of goods and paid for them with paper drafts on the promise that the paper could be converted into gold or silver by the merchant when needed. With Guyuk dead, many local officials and advisers no longer wanted to pay off these bills issued by the late khan. Mongke, however, astutely recognized that if he did not meet the financial obligations of Guyuk, it would make merchants and other foreigners reluctant to continue business with the Mongols. Mongke Khan's decision to pay those debts prompted Juvaini to ask, "And from what book of history has it been read or heard . . . that a king paid the debt of another king?"

In a commercial world not yet accustomed to dealing with paper currency,

Mongke grasped the importance of sustaining faith and purity in the monetary system. Genghis Khan had authorized the use of paper money backed by precious metals and silk shortly before his death in 1227. The practice grew erratically in the coming years, but by the time of Mongke Khan's reign, it became necessary to limit the paper money supply in ways that it was not necessary to do with gold and silver coins. Mongke recognized the dangers incurred by earlier administrations that issued paper money and debt on an ad hoc basis, and in 1253 he created a Department of Monetary Affairs to control and standardize the issuance of paper money. The superintendent of the agency centralized control to prevent the overissue of paper money and the erosion of its value through inflation.

The Mongols allowed each nation under its control to continue minting coins in the denominations and weight they had traditionally used, but they established a universal measure based on the *sukhe,* a silver ingot divided into five hundred parts, to which each of the local currencies was tied. This standardization of varied currencies relative to the *sukhe* eased problems in accounting and currency exchange for both merchants and government administrators. Thus, standardization of currency allowed Mongke Khan to monetize taxes, rather then accepting payment in local goods. In turn, the monetization allowed for standardized budgeting procedures for his imperial administration, since instead of accepting taxes in goods, the Mongols increasingly accepted them in money. Rather than relying on government officials to collect and reallocate tribute of grain, arrows, silk, fur, oil, and other commodities, the government increasingly moved money rather than goods. For the first time, a standardized unit of account could be used from China to Persia. So long as the Mongols maintained control of money, they could let merchants assume responsibility for the movement of goods without any loss of government power.

In Karakorum in the spring of 1253, with the finances of the empire on solid footing, Mongke summoned his siblings and close family to a small *khuriltai* to plan their new policies and undertakings. Now that they exercised firm control over the core of the Mongol Empire, what should they do with it? The families of two of Genghis Khan's sons, Ogodei and Chaghatai, had been crushed and deprived of most of their holdings. The third branch, the descendants of Jochi, with whom Sorkhokhtani had made her effective alliance, had been in effect granted their independence to rule over Russia and the European territories as they saw fit. Mongke Khan was ready to resume the expansion of the Mongol Empire, but he sought to do so in a way that primarily benefited himself and his brothers rather than the many cousins, the other grandchildren of Genghis Khan.

Despite his fondness for European contraptions and design, Mongke showed no interest in launching another campaign in that direction. He returned to the dual campaigns of Genghis Khan against the Sung dynasty of South China and the Muslim civilization of the Arabs and Persians. Mongke assigned Hulegu, the brother with the best military training, to take the Army of the Right with the plan to attack the Arab cities of Baghdad, Damascus, and Cairo. Mongke assigned Khubilai, who despite his lack of military experience had a deep knowledge of Chinese culture, to lead the Army of the Left to conquer the Sung dynasty. As Great Khan, Mongke remained at the center in Mongolia, while Arik Boke, their youngest brother and therefore the Prince of the Hearth for their family, stayed behind to assist him in managing the empire. In May 1253, Hulegu and Khubilai headed off to complete the two conquests ordered by their grandfather and now reaffirmed by their eldest brother.

In the customary Mongol preparation for invasion, Hulegu had already dispatched advance troops across central Asia to clear the path of all herds in order to ensure a good supply of pasture when the main army passed through the area. Hulegu allowed his vanguard to probe enemy forces and initiate diplomatic negotiations with potential allies before the threat of his massive army appeared. The main army gathered in the summer to fatten their horses, and in traditional Mongol style would campaign only in winter. Unlike Genghis Khan's warriors, who moved with lightning speed and approached the Muslim cities from several directions at once, Hulegu deliberately advanced more slowly and ostentatiously. Hulegu moved not just with a nomadic army, but with a nomadic empire. Hulegu had a much larger engineering corps of Chinese, and expanded it with European craftsmen to build bridges, catapults, and other machines of war. He also carried a larger medical corps and many more scribes and clerks to administer the larger army. In contrast to his grandfather's warriors, who fed themselves as they crossed the land, Hulegu's caravans included carts laden with wheat, rice, and wine to feed the many different kinds of military men now in his command.

For Hulegu, the ultimate prize was to conquer the Arab cultural and financial capital of Baghdad, but to get there, he had to reassert Mongol authority over several rebellious areas en route. The most difficult of these was to conquer the strongholds of the Nizari Ismailis, a heretical Muslim sect of Shiites more commonly known in the West as the Assassins. They were holed up in perhaps as many as a hundred unconquered mountain fortresses stretching from Afghanistan to Syria, the most important of which was Alamut, the Eagle's Nest, in northern Persia. Members followed without question the orders of their hereditary leader, who was known by many titles, such as Imam, the Grand Master, or Old Man of the Mountain. Because they believed that God chose the Imam, he was therefore infallible; he needed no education since everything he did, no matter how odd it might appear to mortals, was considered divinely inspired. His followers accepted seemingly irrational acts, frequent changes of the law, and even the reversal of the most sacred precepts as evidence of God's plan for humanity.

Despite the lack of a conventional army, the Ismaili sect exercised tremendous political power through a highly sophisticated system of terror and assassination, and the secrecy and success of the group bred many myths, making it, still today, difficult to factor out the truth. The cult apparently had one simple and effective political strategy: kill anyone, particularly leaders or powerful people, who opposed them in any way. The cult recruited young men who were willing to die in their attacks with the assurance that they would achieve instant entry into paradise as martyrs of Islam. The Chinese, Persian, and Arabic sources all relate the same account of how young men were lured by ample quantities of hashish and other earthly delights that awaited them in the special gardens of the cult's castles and fortresses. This was the foretaste of the paradise that awaited them if they died in the Grand Master's service. He then trained them and controlled them with a steady supply of hashish to keep them obedient and make them fearless. Supposedly, because of the importance of narcotics for the Ismailis, the people around them called them *hashshashin*, meaning "the hashish users." Over time, this name became modified into the word *assassin*. Whether the killers had actually used hashish to inspire them or not, the name spread into many languages as the word for the murderer of high officials.

Earlier, in the time of Genghis Khan's first invasion of the region, the Grand Master willingly swore obedience to the Mongols. In the following decades, the Assassins flourished in the power vacuum created by Genghis Khan's defeat of the Turkic sultan of Khwarizm and then the withdrawal of most of the Mongol forces. By the time Mongke Khan ascended the throne, the Assassins feared that the return of a large Mongol army might interfere with their newfound powers. In what may have been only a pretext for Hulegu's attacks, some chroniclers wrote that the Grand Master sent a delegation to Karakorum ostensibly to offer submission to Mongke Khan, but actually trained to kill him. The Mongols had turned them away and prevented the assassination, but because of it Mongke Khan decided to crush the sect permanently and tear down their fortresses.

Before Hulegu's army reached the Assassin strongholds, the drunken and debauched Grand Master was murdered by disgruntled members of his own entourage and replaced by his equally incapable son. Hulegu assessed the difficulty of capturing the heavily fortified castles one by one, and he devised a simple and more direct plan. Because of the sacred role of the Grand Master, Hulegu concentrated on capturing him with a combination of massive military might and the offer of clemency if he should surrender. The Mongols bombarded the Ismaili stronghold, and the Mongol warriors proved capable of scaling the steepest escarpments to surprise the defenders of the fortress. The combination of force, firepower, and the offer of mercy worked, and on November 19, 1256, on the first anniversary of his coming to power, the Imam surrendered to the Mongols.

Once Hulegu had control of the Imam, he paraded him from Ismaili castle to Ismaili castle to order his followers to surrender. To encourage the cooperation of the Imam and keep him happy until the end of the campaign, Hulegu indulged his obsessive interest in watching camels fight and mate, and he supplied him with girls. In the spring of 1257, once the Assassins' castles had been taken, the Imam recognized his loss of usefulness to the Mongols, and he requested permission to travel to Karakorum to meet with the Great Khan Mongke himself, perhaps to work out some plan for his own survival. Hulegu sent him on the long journey to Mongolia, but once the

Imam arrived there, Mongke refused to see him. Instead, the Mongol escort took the Imam and his party out to the mountains near Karakorum and stomped them to death.

With the extermination of the Assassins, Hulegu's army had an open route to Baghdad, the largest and richest city in the Muslim world. Whereas the Ismailis occupied the terrorist fringe of the Muslim world, the grand metropolis of Baghdad on the Tigris River reigned as its center, the Mother of Cities. Mecca, in the middle of Arabia, remained Islam's sacred city, but it was too isolated from the centers of population to function as an important political or commercial center. With the founding of Baghdad in 762, a little more than a century after the foundation of Islam, the Arab world found its metropolitan focus under the Abbasid dynasty of caliphs, who ruled as the titular head of the entire Muslim world. The present Abbasid leader ruled as the Caliph, the thirty-seventh successor to the Prophet Muhammad, and therefore in addition to being the most powerful secular ruler in the Muslim world, he had the position as the symbolic leader of all Muslims. He served as virtually a combination emperor and pope.

Baghdad was the city of Scheherazade, the legendary teller of the tales know as the *Arabian Nights* or the *Thousand and One Nights,* and for five hundred years the wealth of the Muslim world poured into the city where the Caliphs lavished it on palaces, mosques, schools, private gardens, and public fountains. Baghdad was a city of luxurious baths and overflowing bazaars. In addition to meeting the needs of its Muslim majority, the city served as the religious center for many Christians, who erected churches, and a cultural center for Jews, who built numerous synagogues and schools. The metropolis spilled out along both sides of the Tigris River, which were connected by a bridge, while massive walls protected the heart of the city.

In classic Mongol diplomacy, before mounting an attack on the Caliph, Hulegu sent envoys with a list of legal grievances against him. Hulegu accused the Caliph of not sending an army to assist in the suppression of the Ismaili Assassin sect, even though he had once sworn allegiance to Genghis Khan. In Mongol eyes, the Caliph was as much a rebellious vassal as the Imam, and he possibly faced the same fate. If the Caliph did not immediately atone for his misdeeds by surrendering to Mongol rule, Hulegu threatened to conquer his city and capture him. The Caliph seemed as incapable of understanding the danger of the Mongols as the Imam had been, and scoffed at what he felt were the Mongols' preposterous demands. He defiantly announced that the entire Muslim world would rise up to defend the independence of the Caliph and that they would not permit an infidel nation to occupy the Arab capital of Baghdad. He swore that Muslims as far away as the Maghreb along the Atlantic coast of Morocco, would rush to kill the Mongol invaders if they continued in their campaign. Neither God nor the Muslim people, he defiantly claimed, would allow Baghdad to fall into the hands of nonbelievers.

In November 1257, unconvinced of the Caliph's power to speak for either God or the entire Muslim population, Hulegu began to march toward Baghdad. He approached more cautiously than his grandfather would have done, but nevertheless with the same set of proven Mongol strategies and tactics. To supplement his own army, Hulegu summoned the armies of the vassal states of Armenia and Georgia, as well as a variety of Turkic tribes. Thus, while the main army approached in a wide arc from the north and the east, the others approached from the north and west. Although the Tigris and Euphrates Rivers had historically served as natural barriers to foreign attacks on Mesopotamia, the Mongols easily moved back and forth across the rivers with a series of pontoon boats. As the invading armies advanced, they set the local population to flight toward the safety of the fortified city. By the final week of January 1258, the invading armies had encircled the city and occupied the extensive suburbs beyond the city walls, filling the city to its maximum with refugees.

Before commencing the attack, Hulegu sought to exploit political, religious, and ethnic divisions within Baghdad by forging secret ties to the Christians within the city. Because his mother and his two wives were Christians, as well as many of his own men, Hulegu cultivated contacts and nourished respect within the Christian communities across the Middle East, and he had maintained good relations with his Christian vassal kingdoms, Georgia and Armenia. Taking advantage of these connections, Christian envoys secretly slipped back and forth between the city and the Mongol camp, bringing vital reconnaissance to Hulegu and carrying back promises of special treatment to the Christians and other minorities in the city. As a sign of the special favor that the Christians would enjoy under his rule, Hulegu exempted Christian priests from kowtowing at court, since they bowed only to God. Hulegu exploited the fears of the Christians of Baghdad as a small minority in a sea of potentially hostile Muslims. He fed the dreams of Christians and Jews of finally freeing themselves from Muslim domination.

The Caliph also tried to use to his own benefit the close ties of the Mongols and the Christians. He summoned the Catholikos Makikha, the patriarch of the Christian church, and dispatched him and a Muslim minister to negotiate with the Mongols. He offered to make a formal submission, pay enormous tribute, and to read Friday prayers in the mosque in the name of the Great Khan, thereby officially acknowledging his subservience to Mongol rule. Hulegu scoffed at the offer. He knew that he was already too close to victory to settle for such trifles—not when all the wealth of the richest city on earth could easily be his.

The Mongols showed their traditional ability to improvise and use whatever material presented itself as a possible weapon. The largest objects in the vicinity were the tall date palm trees that the Arabs had cultivated and nourished for centuries. The Mongols chopped them down, and turned the trunks into lethal missiles that they fired at the city. Lacking sufficient wood to encircle the large city of Baghdad as the Mongols had done with the cities of Russia, Hulegu nevertheless surrounded the city with a deep ditch and a rampart and began the assault with a terrifying bombardment of the city. The Arabs knew of the use of flamethrowers in combat, but until this point had not encountered the military power of gunpowder.

The Mongols had changed the formula of gunpowder to provide enough oxygen to make it ignite in one rapid blast rather than in the traditional slow burn of the firelance or of rockets. Such instantaneous burning produced an explosion rather than a fire, and the Mongols harnessed these explosions to hurl a variety of projectiles. Craftsmen made some of the tubes small enough that a single man could operate them and thus fire out arrowheads or other metal projectiles. The explosion in these tubes required a stronger material than bamboo; so they were made with iron tubes. The Mongols attached the smaller tubes to a wooden handle for ease of handling, and they mounted the larger ones on wheels for ease of mobility. Larger tubes fired ceramic or metal cases filled with shrapnel or more gunpowder that produced a secondary explosion upon impact. In their assault, the Mongols combined all of these forms of bombardment in an assortment of smoke bombs, proto-grenades, simple forms of mortars, and incendiary rockets. They had developed explosive devices able to hurl projectiles with such force that they may as well have been using real cannons; they managed to concentrate their fire on one area of the city defenses and hammer it down.

The bombardment from such a distance confused and frightened the residents of Baghdad and frustrated its defenders, who had never before been attacked by an enemy too far away to be reached by their weapons. In addition to the gunpowder weapons, Mongol engineers had nearly perfected the use of planted explosives to undermine walls. All of these military innovations complied with the strong Mongol preference to stay as far from the actual fighting and killing as possible. Hulegu destroyed the dams and diverted the Tigris to flood the camp of the Caliph's army and make them take refuge in the city. The wall of water surrounding the city must have had a similar psychological impact on the people of Baghdad as the wooden wall had produced on the people of the Russian cities. On February 5, 1258, the Mongol forces broke through the walls of Baghdad, and after five days, the Caliph capitulated. To prepare the city for looting, Hulegu ordered the people of Baghdad to surrender their weapons, leave all their goods, and march out of the city. Rather than comply with the order, the defending army bolted and tried to escape, but the Mongols gave chase and cut them down.

Hulegu sent his Christian troops into the city to collect the loot, but they found many people had refused the order to evacuate and were still hiding in their homes. For disobeying the order, the invaders killed them. By Mongol order, the churches and Christian property in the city remained secure from plunder, and Hulegu presented one of the Caliph's palaces to the Catholikos Makikha. The Christians inside Baghdad joined their fellow believers to loot the city and slaughter the Muslims, from whom they felt their salvation had finally come. Centuries of hatred and anger spilled out as they defiled and destroyed mosques, and turned many of them into churches. The Christians celebrated joyously throughout the Abbasid lands and beyond. An Armenian chronicler described the exulting joy: "Five hundred and fifteen years have passed since the founding of the city," he wrote. "Throughout its supremacy, like an insatiable leech it [Baghdad] had swallowed up the entire world. Now it restored all that had been taken." Now Baghdad "was punished for the blood it had shed and the evil it had done; the measure of its iniquity was full." The looting lasted seventeen days. During this time, the invaders, accidentally or deliberately, set the city afire.

Hulegu allowed the Christians to destroy the tombs of the long line of

Abbasid Caliphs, and then Hulegu summoned the captive Caliph to his camp outside the city. According to the Armenian chronicler Grigor of Akanc, Hulegu locked up the Caliph for three days without food or water, then brought him out and heaped up his gold and treasure before him. Pointing to the massive piles of wealth looted from the city, Hulegu reportedly ordered the Caliph to eat the gold, and when he could not scolded him for so greedily accumulating wealth instead of building an army to defend himself. He then sentenced the Caliph and his male heirs to death, but as a final gesture of respect for the high status of the condemned, he allowed them the honor of being executed in the Mongol way—without bloodshed. According to the differing but similar accounts, they were either wrapped in carpets or else sewn into sacks and kicked to death by the Mongol warriors or trampled by their horses.

The Mongol army had accomplished in a mere two years what the European Crusaders from the West and the Seljuk Turks from the East had failed to do in two centuries of sustained effort. They had conquered the heart of the Arab world. No other non-Muslim troops would conquer Baghdad or Iraq again until the arrival of the American and British forces in 2003.

While the Mongols defeated the Arabs, the Crusaders, who at this time occupied a series of castles and small cities along the Mediterranean coast, had watched the Mongol approach cautiously. Suddenly, with the fall of Baghdad, they saw an opportunity for themselves to ally with the Mongols and share in their victories. When the Mongols left Baghdad and headed further west toward Damascus, the Crusader knight Bohemond of Antioch came out with his army to attack Damascus from the Mediterranean side, and he brought supplies and food to help the Mongols. Similarly, the Seljuk sultan sent his army from Anatolia to join the Mongol assault.

Damascus surrendered and thereby saved itself from the fate of Baghdad. Soon the Mongol warriors were on the beaches of the Mediterranean Sea for the second time. Eighteen years earlier, in 1241, the Mongols under Batu had reached the Mediterranean via Europe; now, on their second arrival, they approached it via Asia. In the seven years since Hulegu left his brothers at Karakorum, he had conquered or reconquered everything along a distance of some four thousand miles, and he had added millions of Arabs, Turks, Kurds, and Persians to the still-growing empire.

In the six centuries since the birth of Islam, the religion had expanded greatly and lost control of a few border zones, but never had so much of the Muslim world fallen under the rule of pagans. The four decades from Genghis Khan's attack on Bukhara until the fall of Baghdad and Damascus represented the lowest point in Muslim history. While the Crusaders had only managed to take a toehold in a few ports, the Mongols conquered every Muslim kingdom and city from the Indus River to the Mediterranean. They had conquered almost all of the Muslim lands in Asia; only the Arabian Peninsula and North Africa remained beyond their control.

The gleeful gloating of the Christians could hardly have been greater. An account in the Armenian chronicle related an apocryphal story that illustrated more about Christian contempt for and mockery of Muslims than actual Mongol practice. According to the story, after his victory over the Arabs, Hulegu ordered one hundred thousand piglets from Armenia and dispatched two thousand to each Arab city, where he required the Muslim residents to tend the pigs in the middle of their city, feed them almonds and dates daily, and carefully wash them with soap every Saturday. Just as absurdly, the chronicler added that the Mongols demanded that all Arabs eat pork and that they decapitated every Arab who refused.

Although it seemed at the time that the Mongol Empire threatened to swallow all of the Muslim world, the Mongols had, in fact, reached their limit in the West. The empire would not expand any further in that direction. An army of Mamluk slaves, mostly purchased from Italian merchants who brought them from the Kipchak and Slavic people of Russia and sold them to the sultan of Egypt, moved out from Egypt and encountered a Mongol detachment at Ayn al-Jalut, the Springs of Goliath, near the Sea of Galilee in what is today Israel. On the morning of September 3, 1260, a year after Mongke Khan's death, the Mamluks defeated the Mongols. The empire had reached its western border.

Compared with Hulegu's military victories and extensive conquests of land and people across the Middle East, the attempts by his brother Khubilai to similarly overthrow the Sung dynasty and annex its lands in southern China still remained more of a distant dream for the Mongols than a pending reality. Khubilai's apparent lack of military experience stymied fulfillment of his mission. Unlike his brothers who had fought in Europe and the Middle East,

Khubilai had spent most of his life in the Mongol lands south of the Gobi, where he maintained a personal court that was larger and more luxurious than the imperial court at Karakorum in the Mongol heartland. He enjoyed feasting more than fighting. He grew fat and developed gout, which further impaired his ability to be an inspiring military leader on horseback. After receiving the orders from his brother Mongke Khan to move south into China, Khubilai's army found modest success in a series of limited campaigns against border kingdoms to the west of the Sung kingdom. While openly making elaborate preparations for war against the Sung, Khubilai moved very slowly. Not only did he encounter obstacles to extending the Mongol domains, but within his own administrative territory, sectarian violence flared in a struggle for dominance between Taoist and Buddhist monks, further limiting his control over his lands.

Instead of sending news of victories and dispatching caravans of tribute to Karakorum, Khubilai sent frequent excuses for the delays encountered and unexpected conditions. The generous explanation of scholars sympathetic to Khubilai is that he was a mature and thoughtful leader who wanted to proceed with careful organization and not on impulse, and one who combined the best of Chinese and Mongol military strategies and armies. The less generous explanation is that he lacked the Mongol aptitude for war but managed to avoid failure because of the general momentum of the Mongol conquest and the outstanding martial ability of his generals.

An obviously dissatisfied Mongke Khan dispatched a series of investigators to look into the problems with Khubilai. Finding ample evidence of fraud and corruption in Khubilai's administration, they executed many of his important administrators and stripped Khubilai of his financial prerogatives and duties. The investigators proceeded in much the same ominous manner that they had done during the purge of Ogedei's family, and it appeared that not just Khubilai's power was at stake, but possibly his life as well.

Mongke summoned Khubilai to Karakorum, ostensibly to answer for the fiscal irregularities but probably to account for a variety of issues, most important of which was the lack of military success against the Sung. Rather than resist his brother, as some of his advisers recommended, Khubilai traveled to Karakorum as ordered and threw himself on the mercy of his older brother. Following Khubilai's degrading display of regret and fawning loyalty,

Mongke Khan publicly forgave and reconciled with him, but the incident did little to resolve the underlying cause of the tensions between the two men. Nor did it bring the Mongols any closer to the ultimate goal of victory over the Sung. The frustrated Mongke Khan had to devise a new plan.

In the fall of 1257, while Hulegu's troops moved against Baghdad, Mongke Khan summoned a small *khuriltai* to a wooded area of the Khorkhonag Valley on the old family river, the Onon, not far from the sacred mount of Burkhan Khaldun. Here it became clear to him—or at least he made it clear to his court—that he himself would have to lead the campaign against the Sung. Mongke Khan had served extensively in the European campaigns and he had been trained under Subodei, the most accomplished of all Mongol generals, and after the death of his mentor two years earlier, Mongke was probably himself the best general available to lead the campaign against the Sung. For the duration of his absence during the upcoming campaign, Mongke turned over the central administration of the empire at Karakorum, as well as responsibility for his son and heir, to his youngest brother Arik Boke. Mongke Khan ordered Khubilai to return to his territory to end the clerical strife between the warring factions of Taoists and Buddhists, while Mongke took control of the more important military campaign.

Mongke emulated his grandfather's basic military strategy by first attacking the smaller and weaker areas before moving against the larger target. For Mongke, this meant starting the conquest with a campaign against the adjacent lands of Sichuan to the west and Yunnan to the southwest of the Sung, and then slowly capturing the larger prize in the closing Mongol net. If the Mongols could gain control of these areas, they could attack the Sung from all sides at once. In May 1258, only three months after Hulegu's sack of Baghdad, Mongke Khan led his army across the Yellow River. Within a year, they had covered the territory from the cold Onon on the Siberian border to the humid and warm south.

After quickly subduing the outlying kingdoms, Mongke began to move against the Sung dynasty itself during the second year of the campaign, but the weather became extremely hot. The climate differed greatly from anything Mongke, and most of his warriors, had experienced in Mongolia or on their European campaigns. Many of the Mongols suffered from bloody diarrhea, probably dysentery, and then other plagues. Mongke Khan became ill but improved—and then, on August 11, 1259, he suddenly died. Every chronicle lists a different cause of death. The Chinese reported that he died of cholera, the Persians that he died of dysentery, and others claimed he died from a battle arrow. The death of Mongke Khan congealed the empire; advancement ceased.

Rather than racing back home to participate in the selection of a new Great Khan as the Mongol leaders had done after the death of the three previous Great Khans, each faction moved to protect the territory it already held. In the Middle East, the newly triumphant Hulegu occupied the richest lands and cities of the empire; he controlled more wealth than the rest of the Mongol Empire combined. He had already taken some of the prized Azerbaijan pastures of his cousins who ruled Russia. For fear of losing yet more land to him, his cousins held their territory and refused to return to Mongolia for an election. Neither Hulegu in the Middle East nor the Golden Horde, as Jochi's descendants in Russia eventually became known, wanted to risk losing what territory they already controlled in order to haggle over the supreme title of Grand Khan in Mongolia.

The Mongol Empire reached its greatest extent under Mongke Khan, who was the last of Genghis Khan's descendants to be acknowledged and accepted as Great Khan by the whole of the Mongol Empire. Many khans would continue to rule over the various parts of the empire, and of them, many would claim to be the rightful heirs to Genghis Khan and to the title of Great Khan. But no one of them would be recognized by all the other factions and lineages. Mongke Khan began, but never finished, the Second Mongol World War. It ended with neither victory nor defeat; it merely flickered out.

His brothers pursued episodic campaigns, but they concentrated efforts on each other more than on outside enemies. Khubilai suddenly turned his attention away from the Sung to challenge the youngest brother, Arik Boke, who ruled Mongolia from Karakorum. Each of them summoned a separate *khuriltai* in his own territory. The choice between the two contestants, and more importantly between their supporters, seemed sharp and clear. As the better educated, Khubilai had been given lands in the agricultural areas where Chinese culture reigned supreme, and he never inspired the full confidence or approval of other members of the Golden Family. Khubilai preferred buildings and cities. He seemed as comfortable in a palace as in a tent, and he may have even spoken some Chinese. This deviance from the traditional Mongol life contributed to an alien aura that always seemed to engulf him.

In contrast to Khubilai's cosmopolitan persona, Arik Boke lived very much as a man of the steppes, the Mongol who seldom strayed far from his horse. As the youngest son, he was the family *Otchigen,* Prince of the Hearth, like his father, and he could make the same claim of rights over the office of Great Khan that Mongke had made when he posthumously elevated their father to that rank. In addition, Arik Boke inspired confidence from the other members of the Golden Family by posing less of a threat to their control of their own lands, while Khubilai's more imperial style invited suspicion. In keeping with Mongol law, Arik Boke held his *khuriltai* in the homeland of Mongolia. Mongke Khan's widow and sons supported him as the legitimate and best heir, as did most other members of the family aside from his two brothers, Hulegu and Khubilai. In June 1260, representatives of all the family branches proclaimed Arik Boke as the Great Khan at the *khuriltai* in Karakorum.

But Khubilai succeeded in pulling off a coup d'état. Following the advice of his Chinese ministers, Khubilai summoned his *khuriltai* in his own territory. Aside from his followers hardly anyone came, but the small assembly nevertheless proclaimed him Great Khan. In order to win the loyalty of his Chinese subjects, he additionally proclaimed himself emperor in the same year, 1260, and he chose the title of *Zhongtong (Chung-t'ung),* meaning "central rule." This title was a Chinese adaptation of the Mongolian designation of the Great Khan as the Central camp and his armies as the Left and Right.

No matter how untraditional his selection may have been by Mongol standards, Khubilai exercised strong control over the Chinese army as well as his own detachment of Mongols; more important, he controlled the flow of food that Karakorum needed to survive. The population of the Mongol steppe city had swollen too much to survive on the local herds alone, and the land around Karakorum, despite sustained efforts to encourage foreign farmers, proved inhospitable to agriculture. Without substantial and continual food shipments from the farmlands controlled by Khubilai, Karakorum had to be evacuated or face starvation.

Khubilai cut off the food and then sent his army to capture Karakorum. Arik Boke fought hard but withdrew steadily against the overwhelming size of his brother's Chinese army. Karakorum fell quickly to Khubilai, but in 1261 Arik Boke temporarily took it again. The armies of the dueling khans met two more times, but gradually Arik Boke Khan's army weakened and began to atrophy as it faced desertions of allies who saw that the younger khan would never prevail against his older, better-equipped, and probably more intelligent elder brother. Arik Boke also faced the worst threat to the Mongols: *zud*, or animal famine. From 1250 to 1270, Mongolia suffered a lowering of temperatures. In a fragile ecological zone such as Mongolia, a change of only a few degrees in annual temperature severely reduces the small amount of precipitation, restricts the growth of the grass, and thereby weakens or kills the animals. Without strong horses or ample food, the supporters of Arik Boke, already cut off from the agricultural largesse of Khubilai Khan's territory, proved too weak to mount a sustained war. The winter of 1263 proved particularly cruel, and by the following spring, Arik Boke no longer had a viable power base. Unable to feed his followers, Arik Boke proceeded to Shangdu, where he surrendered to Khubilai in 1264.

When the brothers met at the end of the protracted struggle, Khubilai forced Arik Boke to perform a public ceremony of obeisance. Before the assembled court, Khubilai interrogated his brother, demanding to know which of the two sides in the struggle for the office of Great Khan was the correct one. Arik Boke's answer showed the strength of his pride even in the face of defeat. "We were then, and you are today." Other members of the family, including the distant brother, Hulegu, reacted so bitterly to Khubilai's public shaming of his younger brother that they complained to him. Khubilai summoned another *khuriltai* on Mongolian territory to decide the fate of Arik Boke and to ratify himself as the legitimate khan without the taint of his earlier election on Chinese soil. Despite the overwhelming military might of Khubilai's army, the Golden Family refused to attend. They recognized the reality of Khubilai's rule, but none of them proved willing to participate in a criminal trial of Arik Boke, whom they had supported as Great Khan. None of them trusted Khubilai enough to take the chance of leaving their homelands and perhaps never returning. In the absence of a quorum for a *khuriltai*, Khubilai forgave his brother. Khubilai tried and executed many of his brother's supporters, but his only punishment of Arik Boke, at least publicly, was banning him from court. Shortly thereafter, in 1266, mysteriously but conveniently for Khubilai, Arik Boke, still in the prime of life, suddenly sickened and died. He had almost certainly been poisoned.

Khubilai now held the office of Great Khan. He had the world's largest army under his control, and he ruled one of the most populous nations on earth. The victories had come at a steep price; some of the Mongol royal family and their followers refused to recognize his legitimacy, or, at most, they gave symbolic recognition but ignored him and continued to wage intermittent border wars for another generation.

Like the four fountains of the Silver Tree, the Mongol Empire now divided into four primary zones of political administration. Khubilai ruled China, Tibet, Manchuria, Korea, and eastern Mongolia, but he faced constant problems in enforcing his rule over Mongolia and Manchuria. The Golden Horde ruled the Slavic countries of eastern Europe, and they consistently refused to recognize Khubilai as the Great Khan. The lands ruled by Hulegu and his descendants from Afghanistan to Turkey became known as the Ilkhanate, meaning "vassal empire." It was here that Persian culture reemerged from centuries of Arab domination to build the foundation for modern Iran. The most traditional Mongols occupied the central steppes, which became known as Moghulistan and encompassed the modern areas from Kazakhstan and Siberia in the north and across Turkistan in central Asia to Afghanistan in the south. For a while, they had some unity under Ogodei's and Toregene's grandson Khaidu, who ruled from Bukhara and served as a counterpoint to the power of Khubilai Khan, but the area fragmented repeatedly in the centuries ahead.

For a mere three decades, Karakorum had served as capital of the Mongol Empire before the Mongols themselves, under the command of Khubilai, looted and virtually destroyed it. In that short time it had been the center, the pivot of the world. As part of the looting of Karakorum, the Silver Tree was disassembled and carted away.

PART III

The Global Awakening:
1262–1962

Asia is devouring us. Tartar faces in every direction you look.

THOMAS MANN,
The Magic Mountain

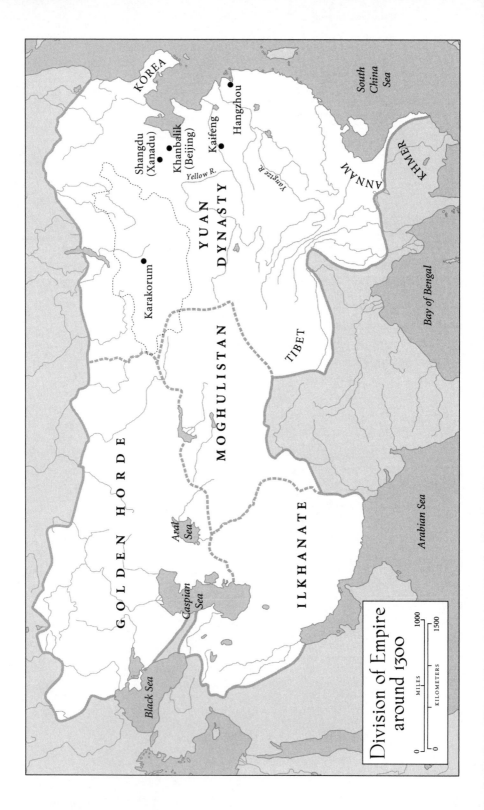

Division of Empire around 1300

8

—————

Khubilai Khan and the
New Mongol Empire

This Great Khan is the mightiest man, whether in
respects of subjects or of territory or of treasure.

MARCO POLO

KHUBILAI KHAN'S GENIUS DERIVED from his recognition that he could not conquer all of China by mere force, no matter how large his army or sophisticated his weapons. Even without the military skills of his grandfather, he had clearly outsmarted everyone in his family. He possessed a keen strategic talent and the ability not merely to have good ideas but to implement them as well; he applied these skills to the management of his territory and, most important, to its expansion toward the south. In the end, he proved able to achieve through public politics what his grandfather had not been able to achieve through brute force—the conquest and unification of all China, the most populous country on earth. He won over the population by skillful manipulation of public opinion, in which martial prowess was an important, but not exclusive, factor. He built a Chinese capital, took Chinese names, created a Chinese dynasty, and set up a Chinese administration. He won control of China by appearing to be more Chinese than the Chinese, or at least more Chinese than the Sung.

For most of its history, China had been a great civilization but not a unified country. While the educated elite shared a written language, classic texts, artistic styles, and other types of high culture, the common people spoke entirely different languages in a constantly changing mosaic of national boundaries and temporary dynasties and ruling families. The educated elite clung to an unfulfilled dream of a united country with all people under a single government. Occasionally a leader or a family temporarily cobbled together several states and then offered, once again, the tantalizing hope of making a unified China a reality. In between these brief periods of unification, the concept of China lingered on as an ideal or a romantic image in the poetry, calligraphy, and essays of the Chinese intelligentsia.

Like no prior leader, Khubilai Khan offered these educated people the enticing opportunity to realize their nationalist desire. Despite his crude origin among steppe barbarians, he proved more capable of fulfilling that ancient dream than the Sung rulers. Everything he did seemed calculated to convince the Chinese people that Heaven had conferred its Mandate unmistakably on him alone, and, in due time, the old dynasty of the Sung would fall since it no longer had the necessary vitality.

Khubilai Khan seemed to recognize that he faced many of the same problems of his grandfather at the time of the original unification of the steppe tribes; namely, how to organize a large number of disparate people into a single cohesive political entity. Although Genghis Khan had faced the problem with a collection of tribes smaller than a hundred thousand each, Khubilai Khan faced the same problem with countries of many millions each. Like Genghis Khan two generations earlier, Khubilai Khan began the arduous process of state building around a core ethnic identity, but for Khubilai that core cultural identity would be Chinese, not Mongol. He had to win the loyal support of the Chinese people, and he had to rebuild or, in many cases, invent institutions to unify disparate people into a viable and strong working whole.

In his struggle for supremacy against his brother Arik Boke in 1260, Khubilai had taken a Chinese title that was a translation of a Mongol one, but in 1264 he modified his reign name to Zhiyuan or Chih-yuan, meaning "complete beginning," and later in 1271, he used this to become the basis of the dynastic name of Da Yuan, meaning "great origins" or "great beginnings," by which the Mongol dynasty became officially known in Chinese history. The new name meant not only a new beginning for his Chinese subjects, but it also signified a new beginning for his Mongol ones as well. Khubilai was no Genghis Khan, but he had embarked upon a venture no less daunting than his grandfather's.

As emperor and founder of a new dynasty, Khubilai sought to sinicize his image and thereby make it not merely acceptable, but alluring, to his Chinese subjects. In 1263, Khubilai ordered the building of an ancestral temple for his family. He commissioned his ministers to conduct traditional Chinese ceremonies honoring the family's ancestors, but, perhaps indicative of the usual Mongol reluctance to avoid anything associated with death, he personally stayed well away from them. By the following year, he erected a series of Chinese-style ancestral tablets to his ancestors. In 1277, after declaring the new Mongol dynasty, he posthumously conferred Chinese names on his ancestors and built a larger temple with eight chambers: one for the founders of the family, Yesugei Baatar and Hoelun, another for Genghis Khan, one for each of Genghis Khan's four sons, and one each for Guyuk Khan and Mongke Khan. In the new official version of the family history, Jochi, whose family had been the most loyal ally to Khubilai's lineage, was fully recognized as a legitimate family member. Just as Mongke had posthumously elevated their father, Tolui, to the office of Great Khan, Khubilai conferred the office of Chinese emperor on him. He ordered portraits made of all of them in Chinese style so that they looked more like Mandarin sages than Mongol warriors.

Khubilai acknowledged the utility of both a strong army and good propaganda, but the third element of his strategy came from good administration and policy. Without necessarily following Confucian principles, that had high appeal to the Chinese upper class but less importance to the common people, he strove to install an orderly system of efficient government that could help him build popular support and de-emphasize the foreign origin of his rule. Toward this goal, he appointed Pacification Commissioners to help restore good relations with Han Chinese in newly conquered territory. The commissioners began by repairing the damage of war and prior neglect to public buildings such as temples, shrines, and structures of deep emotional or symbolic value to the population.

To appear as a powerful Chinese leader, Khubilai needed an impressive court located in a real city, not a peripatetic tent court nor the ad hoc structures erected at Shangdu (Xanadu), in modern Inner Mongolia. The place held special importance for him because he had first been proclaimed Great Khan at the *khuriltai* there, but it had no obvious advantages. Not only was that capital located in a nomadic zone, which the Chinese found quite alien and barbaric, but it had also been the traditional staging area used by his grandfather in the raiding and looting of Chinese cities. Khubilai sought to disassociate himself from the less desirable aspects of that history.

While keeping Shangdu as a summer home and a hunting preserve, he commissioned the building of another city, a real Chinese-style imperial capital, farther south at a place better situated to exploit the agricultural wealth of the lands along the Yellow River. He chose the site of the former Jurched capital of Zhongdu, which had been conquered by Genghis Khan in 1215, the year of Khubilai's birth. In 1272, Khubilai ordered the building of his new capital, and he connected it by canal to the Yellow River. The Mongols called the place Khanbalik, the City of the Khan. His Chinese subjects called it Dadu, the Great Capital, and it grew into the modern capital of Beijing. Khubilai brought in Muslim architects and Central Asian craftsmen to design his city in a new style that offered more of a compromise between the tastes of the nomadic steppe dwellers and the sedentary civilization.

In contrast to the maze of winding alleys in most Chinese cities of the era, Khubilai's capital had broad, straight streets run on a north-south axis with east-west streets perpendicular to them; the guards at one gate could see straight through the city to the guards at the opposite gate. From the imperial palace, they built boulevards, more to accommodate the horses and military maneuvers of the Mongols than the wheelbarrows or handcarts of the Chinese laborers. The boulevards stretched wide enough for nine horsemen to gallop abreast through the city in case the native people rose up against their foreign rulers.

Furthering the Mongol interest in profits from international trade, Khubilai Khan designated sections of the city for Middle Eastern and Mongol populations as well as for people from all over what is today China. The city was host to merchants from as far away as Italy, India, and North Africa. Where so many men lingered, as Marco Polo pointed out in great detail, large numbers of prostitutes gathered in their own districts to serve them. Scholars and doctors came from the Middle East to practice their trades. Roman

Catholic, Nestorian, and Buddhist priests joined their Taoist and Confucian counterparts already practicing in China. Muslim clerics, Indian mystics, and, in some parts of Mongol China, Jewish rabbis added to the mixture of people and ideas that thronged the empire. Far larger than Karakorum, but with many of the same internationalist principles, the city was a true world capital and fit to be capital of the world.

Ultimately, at the heart of the city, however, Khubilai created a Mongol haven where few foreigners, including Chinese, could enter. Behind high walls and guarded by Mongol warriors, the royal family and court continued to live as Mongols. The large open areas for animals in the middle of the city had no precedent in Chinese culture. This Forbidden City constituted a miniature steppe created in the middle of the Mongol capital. During the Mongol era, the whole complex of the Forbidden City was filled with *gers*, where members of the court often preferred to live, eat, and sleep. Pregnant wives of the khan made sure that their children were born in a *ger*, and the children received their school lessons in the *ger* as they grew up. While Khubilai and his successors maintained public lives as Chinese emperors, behind the high walls of their Forbidden City, they continued to live as steppe Mongols.

When the Franciscan friar Odoric of Pordenone visited the Mongol territories in the 1320s, he described the Forbidden City in Khanbalik: "Within the precincts of the said palace imperial, there is a most beautiful mount, set and replenished with trees, for which cause it is called the Green Mount, having a most royal and sumptuous palace standing thereupon, in which, for the most part, the great Can is resident." In a passage that sounds very close to earlier descriptions of Karakorum, he wrote, "Upon the one side of the said mount there is a great lake, whereupon a most stately bridge is built, in which lake is great abundance of geese, ducks, and all kinds of water-fowl; and in the wood growing upon the mount there is a great store of all birds, and wild beasts."

The wooden palace built by Khubilai Khan seemed to have the same basic plan as the one at Karakorum. Khubilai Khan installed mechanical peacocks in his palace; they could spread their tails and cry out in a manner reminiscent of Guillaume Boucher's angel on the Silver Tree in the palace in Karakorum. Khubilai probably brought the magnificent silver tree with him from the Karakorum palace, and he installed at least part of it in Khanbalik. As Marco Polo described it, "in a certain part of the hall near where the Great Kaan holds his table, there is set a large and very beautiful piece of workmanship in the form of a square coffer, or buffet, about three paces each way, exquisitely wrought with figures of animals, finely carved and gilt." The internal operation also resembled that of the Silver Tree: "The middle is hollow, and in it stands a great vessel of pure gold . . . and at each corner of the great vessel is one of similar size, and from the former the wine or beverage flavored with fine and costly spices is drawn off into the latter."

Inside the confines of their Forbidden City, Khubilai and his family continued to act as Mongols in dress, speech, food, sports, and entertainment. This meant that they consumed large amounts of alcohol, loudly slurped their soup, and they cut meat with knives at the table, thereby disgusting the Chinese who confined such acts to the kitchen during preparation. With the emphasis on alcohol and rituals of drinking and drunkenness, the scenes at court must have been somewhat chaotic as the free-roaming, individualistic Mongols tried to imitate the complex and highly orchestrated rituals and ceremonies of the Chinese court. In contrast to the Chinese imperial tradition of courtiers lining up according to rank, the Mongols tended to swarm chaotically, and, perhaps most disturbing to the Chinese, the Mongol women mingled freely among the men on even the most important occasions. The ceremonies in the Mongol court became so disorganized that sometimes the khan's bodyguards had to beat back the crowds of officials and guests with batons.

Like his grandfather, Khubilai recognized the importance of laying down a clear and strong legal code as the center of civil administration. Creating and enforcing new laws was the traditional way that steppe chieftans, as well as Chinese rulers, created legitimacy in the eyes of their subjects. In devising a legal code, Khubilai did not replace Chinese law with Mongol so much as reform it to make it compatible with Genghis Khan's law, and in such a way as to simultaneously win support from both his Mongol and Chinese followers. The law was one more weapon in his struggle for loyalty and support from his subjects, and thus, ultimately, supremacy over the rival Sung dynasty.

Khubilai Khan's administration guaranteed landowners their property rights, reduced taxes, and improved roads and communications. To further garner public support, the Mongols lessened the harsh penal code of the Sung. The Mongols reduced by nearly half the number of capital offenses in

China—from 233 to 135. Khubilai Khan rarely allowed the use of execution even for those offenses that remained. The records of executions survive for all but four of the thirty-four years of his reign. The highest number in a single year was 278 executions in 1283. The lowest was only 7 in 1263, but it is possible that the reason that four of the years are missing from the record is because there were no executions at all in those years. In total, fewer than 2,500 criminals were executed in more than three decades of Khubilai's rule. His annual rate fell considerably short of the number of executions in modern countries such as China or the United States.

Overall, he installed a more consistent system of laws and punishments as well as one that was substantially milder and more humanitarian than the Sung's. Where practical, he substituted fines for physical punishment, and he installed procedures to grant amnesty to criminals who repented of their wrongdoings. In a similar way, Mongol authorities sought to eradicate torture or, at least, to severely curtail its use. Mongol law specified that before torture could be applied to elicit a confession, the officials had to already have substantial evidence, not mere suspicion, that the person had committed a particular crime. The Mongol legal code of 1291 specified that officials must "first use reason to analyze and surmise, and shall not impose abruptly any torture." By comparison, at the same time that the Mongols were moving to limit the use of torture, both church and state in Europe passed laws to expand its usage to an ever greater variety of crimes for which there need be no evidence. Unlike the variety of bloody forms of torture, such as stretching on the rack, being crushed by a great wheel, being impaled on spikes, or various forms of burning, in other countries, Mongols limited it to beating with a cane.

The mildness of Mongol law and the customs of steppe culture showed up in some odd ways. Chinese authorities frequently tattooed a criminal's crimes on his forehead so that he was permanently marked by his crime. Because Mongols considered the forehead the abode of the soul, they maintained that even a criminal's head could not be thus abused. The Mongol authorities allowed the tattooing to continue, where it was already in practice, but specified that the tattoos be placed on the upper arms for the first two offenses and on the neck for the third, but never on the forehead. The Mongols did not allow the punishment to be extended into new areas or to ethnic minorities who did not already have the practice. Rather than writing the crime on the body, Mongol authorities preferred to write the offense on a wall erected in front of a criminal's home so that the entire community could watch him carefully. They also used a system of parole in which freed prisoners had to report twice a month to local officials to have their behavior reviewed. In keeping with the Mongol principle of group culpability and responsibility, the freedom of a prisoner depended, in part, on his willingness to join an auxiliary law enforcement agency in order to apply his knowledge or crime to the apprehension of other prisoners. Criminals, and often their entire families, had to sign documents acknowledging receipt of their sentence and to register their disagreement or complaint with the process. To preserve the record of the event, fingerprints were taken and attached to the document. Whenever practical, Mongol administrators preferred to have as many issues as possible settled at the lowest level without the intervention of officials. Crimes within a family could be settled by the family, or disputes within a group of monks of the same religion could be settled by monks within that religion, and crimes within a profession could be settled by councils of those professionals.

Related to dispute settlement, Mongol authorities encouraged the printing of books on criminology so that individual citizens and these small councils had the benefit of proper guidance. In the area of criminal law, they also set minimum requirements for officials visiting crime scenes to collect, analyze, and report evidence. These included instructions on the handling and examination of a corpse in order to collect as much information from it as practical, the reporting of which had to be made in triplicate, including drawings to depict the location of wounds. The Mongol procedures not only improved the quality of law enforcement, but corresponded with the overarching Mongol policy that all people, not just an educated elite, should know and be able to act through the law. For the Mongols, the law was more a way of handling problems, creating unity, and preserving peace rather than just a tool for deciding guilt or administering punishment.

Instead of educating officials in the classic arts of poetry and calligraphy, Mongols promoted more practical training in a variety of ways. They set minimum standards of knowledge for professions from matchmakers and merchants to doctors and lawyers. On every front, the Mongol policy seemed to be the same. It sought to standardize and raise the level of professions, while at the same time assuring a wide range of individuals access to them and to the benefits and services of the profession.

With so few Mongols ruling over so many people in China, Khubilai Khan seemed forced to accept administration through the traditional mandarins selected through a long process of study and exams, but he refused. Rather than perpetuate the old system, he abolished the exams and turned for administrative assistance to a wide variety of foreigners, particularly Muslims, and, when he could get them, Europeans such as Marco Polo. Like his grandfather, who found the educated Muslim administrators to be skilled in "the laws and customs of cities," Khubilai imported large numbers of such men from his brother's realm in Persia. He repeatedly sent requests to the pope and European kings asking them to send scholars and learned men, but with no response.

Mindful of overdependence on any single nationality or ethnic group and inclined to play one off against another, however, Khubilai constantly mixed Chinese and foreigners in a diverse set of administrators that included Tibetans, Armenians, Khitan, Arabs, Tajiks, Uighurs, Tangut, Turks, Persians, and Europeans. The Mongols staffed each office with an ethnic quota of the three major groups of northern Chinese, southern Chinese, and foreigners so that each official was surrounded by men of a different culture or religion. Just as Genghis Khan promoted men from the lowest levels of society to the highest ranks of leadership based on their skills and achievements rather than birth, Khubilai's administration constantly promoted men from the lowest jobs, such as cooks, gatekeepers, scribes, and translators. Both the promotion of low-ranking men and the movement of them into new areas increased their dependence on and loyalty to their Mongol overlords and lessened their connection to the people ruled.

Without the rigid hierarchy of the ranked mandarins to administer local areas, Khubilai Khan imposed Genghis Khan's system of decisions made through large meetings and councils and constant deliberation. Wherever possible and at whatever level, the Mongols replaced the bureaucracy with councils modeled on the small *khuriltai* of the steppes. The local councils had to meet daily, and any new measure had to come with the seal of approval of at least two officials. The council had to debate the issues and reach a consensus; the decision had to be made by the group, not by a single official. By Chinese standards, this was an extremely inefficient and impractical system that took too much time and energy compared with simply having one official make the decision and the people follow it. The Mongols promoted the use of other small councils, in a variety of ways. Patients displeased with medical service could seek redress from a council composed of representatives of the medical profession and nonmedical officials. Similar groups were formed to settle disputes involving a great variety of professions, from soldiers to musicians.

Whereas the old administrative system relied on unpaid scholarly officials who made a living by extorting money from people who needed their services or stamp of approval, the Mongols hired salaried employees for the lower levels of routine administration. They standardized the salaries throughout Mongol territory with a few regional differentials for the varying cost of living.

The move toward consensual councils and paid civil servants did not take deep root in China, and it failed to outlive the Mongols. As soon as the Ming came to power, they reverted to the traditional institutions of bureaucratic offices and abandoned the council form in favor of rule from above. This experiment in participatory administration was not tried again in Chinese history until the twentieth century, when the founders of the republic and the founders of Communism struggled to reintroduce some of the local councils, debates, salaried administrators, and citizen participation in government.

To further facilitate the speed and safety of commerce through the empire, Khubilai radically expanded the use of paper money. By the time Marco Polo arrived, the system was in full operation. He describes the money as made from mulberry bark in a form that we recognize as paper but which was still largely unknown in Europe. The paper money was cut into rectangles of varying size, marked with its value and stamped with a vermilion seal. The primary advantage of paper money was that it was much easier to handle and ship than the bulky coins then in use. Marco Polo wrote that the money was accepted throughout the empire: "To refuse it would be to incur the death penalty," but most people "are perfectly willing to be paid in paper money since with it they can buy anything including pearls, precious stones, gold, or silver." Mongol authorities in Persia tried but failed to institute the Mongol system of paper money because the concept was alien to the local merchants, and their discontent bordered on revolt at a time when the Mongols could not be certain they had the forces to win. Rather than risk a humiliating loss, the authorities withdrew the paper money.

Where there is paper money, there are increased opportunities for credit and financial disaster. In an important innovation designed to bring consistency to the markets, particularly involving the extension of credit, Mongol law provided for declarations of bankruptcy, but no merchant or customer could declare bankruptcy more than twice as a way to avoid paying debts. On the third time, he faced the possible punishment of execution.

While the Mongols consistently rejected some parts of Chinese culture such as Confucianism and foot binding, the refinement of the monetary system shows their great appreciation for other aspects of Chinese culture. Khubilai proved willing to reach far back into Chinese history for ideas and institutions that showed practical value. Khubilai built schools and revived the Chinese Hanlin Academy, which was composed of the brightest scholars in the country, in order to promote some types of traditional Chinese learning and culture. He founded the Mongolian Language School in 1269, and then the Mongolian National University at Khanbalik in 1271. He added new departments and commissioned scholars to record contemporary events, edit and reprint old texts, and tend the archives.

The Mongol court maintained scribes not only for the Mongol language but also for Arabic, Persian, Uighur, Tangut, Jurched, Tibetan, Chinese, and lesser-known languages; still, they experienced perplexing difficulties with the variety of languages. With only their Mongol-Uighur alphabet, the Mongols found it difficult to record all the administrative information they needed from their vast empire. In everyday administration, clerks had to be able to spell names as diverse as those of Chinese towns, Russian princes, Persian mountains, Hindu sages, Vietnamese generals, Muslim clerics, and Hungarian rivers. Because the subjects of the Mongol Empire used so many different languages, Khubilai Khan attempted one of the most innovative experiments in intellectual and administrative history. He sought to create a single alphabet that could be used to write all the languages of the world. He assigned this task to the Tibetan Buddhist lama Phagspa, who in 1269 presented the khan with a set of forty-one letters derived from the Tibetan alphabet. Khubilai Khan made Phagspa's script the empire's official script, but rather than force the system on anyone, he allowed the Chinese and all other subjects to continue using their own writing system as well in the hope that the new script would eventually replace the old by showing its superiority. Chinese scholars felt too attached to their own ancient language to allow themselves to be cut off from it by a new, and obviously barbarian, system of writing, and most subject people eventually abandoned the Mongol writing system as soon as Mongol power waned.

Peasants traditionally groveled at the bottom of a long line of government officials who commanded the most intimate aspects of their lives. The Mongols upset that ancient hierarchy by organizing the peasants into units of about fifty households called a *she*. These local units exercised broad responsibility and authority over their lives. They oversaw local farming, exercised responsibility for improving the land and managing water and other natural resources, and provided food reserves for time of famine. In general, they functioned as a form of local government, combining elements of Genghis Khan's decimal organization and Chinese peasant tradition.

The *she* also had the task of providing some form of education for peasant children; the Mongols promoted general literacy as a way of improving the quality of life for everyone. Khubilai Khan created public schools to provide universal education to all children, including those of peasants. Until this point, only the rich had the time and income to educate their children and thereby maintain power over the illiterate peasantry for generation after generation. The Mongols recognized that in the winter, peasant children had time to learn, and rather than teaching them in classical Chinese, the teachers used the colloquial language for more practical lessons. The record of the Mongol dynasty lists 20,166 public schools created during Khubilai Khan's reign. Despite possible exaggeration by officials seeking to improve their record, the Mongol achievement is amazing considering that no other country had attempted such an effort for universal education. In the West, it would be another century before writers began to write in the colloquial language, and it would take nearly five hundred more years before governments picked up the responsibility for public education for the children of common people.

In traditional Confucian society, the literary arts had been directed toward the specific kinds of writing used in the national examination system. This meant that literature always fell well within the confines of the bureaucracy and its interests. The Mongols, however, allowed a wider range of literary endeavors, and they encouraged writers to produce material in the colloquial language of the people rather than in the classical style preferred by the scholarly bureaucrats. Mongol tastes coincided more closely with those of the masses than with the refined elite, and they combined folk culture and court culture to create new and more exciting forms of entertainment.

In keeping with the great ceremonies staged at the installation of Genghis Khan in 1206, the Mongols sponsored spectacular ceremonial dramas involving thousands of people for up to weeks at a time. In 1275, they encapsulated Mongol military history in a ceremonial drama performed by the army. It consisted of six parts to symbolize the important phases of the creation of the Mongol Empire from Genghis to Mongke Khan.

With an impresario's ability to manage public spectacle and to capture the popular imagination, Khubilai enthusiastically supported drama, a much-neglected art in traditional Chinese culture, and he frequently had plays staged in the royal compound. The Mongol courtiers enjoyed plays filled with acrobatic action, emotional music, bright makeup, and colorful costumes. Much like the works of William Shakespeare in Europe, the playwrights of the Mongol era sought to be entertaining while seeking to understand issues such as the relation of power to virtue. It is reported, but impossible to verify, that no play was censored during Khubilai's reign. The resulting plays were some of the most enduring in Chinese literature, making the Mongol era rank as the golden age for Chinese drama. Estimates place the total number of new plays performed during the Yuan dynasty at around 500, of which 160 survive.

Traditionally in China, the performing artists such as actors and singers ranked as low in respect and prestige as prostitutes, concubines, and other marginal professions. The Mongol rulers raised their social status as professionals and built theater districts so that the performances would not be confined to marketplaces, brothels, and taverns. The combination of Chinese drama and the Mongolian patronage of music laid the basis for what became the Peking Opera.

In their patronage of popular culture to entertain themselves and the masses, the Mongols adhered to their cultural abhorrence of bloodshed. Although they enjoyed wrestling and archery, they developed no counterpart to the gladiatorial games and public slaughter that fascinated the Romans, nor any of the traditional European sports of pitting animals against each other, as in bear baiting and dogfights, or animals against humans, as in bull-fighting. Mongols did not permit the execution of criminals to become a public sport, as in the beheadings and hangings common in European cities. The Mongols offered no counterpart to the common public entertainment of burning people alive that occurred so frequently in western Europe wherever the Christian church had the power to do so.

Khubilai did not pursue a short-term strategy of winning transitory popular support; rather, he consistently and systematically pursued a nearly two-decades long policy of winning the allegiance of a continental civilization. The Mongols portrayed themselves as the strong leaders favored by heaven to unite the Chinese, in contrast to the effete and detached Sung leaders who wallowed in decadent luxury and valued ostentatious displays of wealth more than martial power. As different as the Mongols were in many respects, the Chinese masses found more common ground with them in their taste and sensibilities than with their own Chinese court officials.

Year by year, soldiers, officials, and peasants deserted the Sung to live under the Mongols or helped the Mongols to take over their local area. More merchants took their trade to the Mongols, more priests and scholars found protection and greater freedom of movement under the Mongols, and eventually Chinese generals and whole regiments of soldiers and sailors deserted to the Mongol lines. The collapse of the Sung dynasty was not a sudden fall or conquest, but a slow erosion as it fell apart.

Throughout this campaign, the Mongols sustained their military pressure on the Sung. Each small victory reinforced the idea that Heaven willed the future to the Mongols and had abandoned the Sung. Khubilai Khan directed the public relations campaign but not the military one, which he left in the hands of his highly competent generals, such as a man named Bayan, who proved nearly as skillful in fighting the Chinese as Subodei had been in his destruction of the European armies from Russia to Hungary. In 1276, the Mongol troops finally overtook the Sung capital at Hangzhou, and over the next few years they wiped up the small pockets of local resistance. Through patient propaganda and shrewd policies, Khubilai Khan had succeeded in doing what Genghis Khan had not been able to do with his mighty army. In keeping with his new image as the personification of Chinese virtues, Khubilai provided excellent care for the dowager empress and allowed most of the royal family to live in a wonderful palace with all the luxuries to which they had been accustomed. To avoid the heir of the deposed Sung becoming a center for rebellion, he sent the young emperor to study in Tibet, where he became a monk in 1296.

For Chinese scholars and literati, the defeated Sung dynasty became a nostalgic memory of a golden era. The poet Xie Ao (Hsieh Ao) captured the nostalgia in a poem titled "On Visiting the Former Imperial Palace at Hangchow."

> *Like an ancient ruin, the grass grows high: gone are the guards and the*
> *   gatekeepers.*
> *Fallen towers and crumbling palaces desolate my soul.*
> *Under the eaves of the long-ago hall fly in and out the swallows*
> *But within: Silence. The chatter of cock and hen parrots is heard no more.*

Khubilai Khan realized what a jewel he had acquired in his conquest of the Sung capital and officials. They represented the height of Chinese civilization, and in the years ahead, he strove to preserve their achievements while reforming and expanding their empire. As the Japanese scholar Hidehiro Okada wrote, "The greatest legacy of the Mongol Empire bequeathed to the Chinese is the Chinese nation itself." The Mongols united not only all of the areas speaking various Chinese dialects, but they combined with it the adjacent kingdoms of the Tibetans, Manchurians, Uighurs, and dozens of smaller kingdoms and tribal nations. The new country under their administration was about five times as large as the civilization where people spoke the Chinese languages. The official Chinese state culture that emerged was certainly not Mongol; not was it Chinese. Khubilai Khan had created a hybrid, and, through his efforts, the culture would have a worldwide impact of unanticipated dimensions and importance.

With his control extended to almost everything reachable by land, Khubilai had to look out to sea to find new lands to conquer. The trading missions of his junks had brought back detailed information on the distant spice islands, Java, Ceylon, and the nearby northern islands of Japan. He wanted to incorporate them into the expanding Mongol Empire. In 1268 he sent an envoy to Japan to demand surrender, but the Japanese refused. Khubilai was still too engaged with the final conquest of the Sung dynasty to launch an attack on Japan, so he continued to send more delegations to persuade them to surrender.

As Khubilai incorporated the defeated Sung navy into his own, he acquired the personnel and skills needed to invade the defiant islands. He revitalized and enlarged the Sung navy, and he tried to transform the navy from mere guardians of the coastal and river districts into a bona fide ocean fleet capable of operating on the high seas in both commercial and military enterprises. He turned the Korean Peninsula into a large shipbuilding facility and a military and naval base from which he attempted to conquer Japan. Although the ships were some of the largest in the world of that era, the speed with which they were built compromised their quality. Archaeological evidence reveals shortcuts such as attaching two large stones together to make an anchor rather than carving a single stone and thereby creating a much more stable anchor. The Mongols loaded the ships with food, armor, and ammunition, including large numbers of melon-sized pottery grenades filled with gunpowder and shrapnel to bombard the Japanese defenders.

Khubilai sent several more envoys to persuade the island nation of Japan to submit to Mongol rule, but the military authorities rejected each one. By 1274, Khubilai had assembled an armada of about nine hundred ships to transport an army of twenty-three thousand Korean and Chinese infantry and an unknown number of Mongol horsemen. In November, they sailed out into the treacherous waters that separated Korea from Japan by 110 miles. The Mongols easily captured Tsushima Island about halfway across the strait and then Ika Island closer to Kyushu. The armada sailed into Hakata Bay and landed its forces and animals.

The samurai warriors rode out against the Mongol forces for individual combat, but the Mongols held their formation. As usual, the Mongols fought as a united force, not as individuals. Instead of coming out for duels, the Mongols bombarded the samurai with exploding missiles and showered them in arrows. The Mongols slaughtered the famed Japanese warriors, and the remaining Japanese withdrew from the coastal zone inland to a fortress. The Mongol forces did not chase the fleeing Japanese into an area about which they lacked reliable intelligence. Instead, they left the battlefield victorious but damaged, and they reloaded the men, horses, and supplies on the ship. The plan of the Mongols remains a mystery. Were they going to return the next day to pursue the Japanese? After winning this battle, did they intend to move farther along the coast and attack at another point? Had they been sent as a test probe to assess Japanese reaction and tactics? Were they more badly damaged in the fight than they appeared and therefore sought to retreat?

That night, with all the invaders on their ships, a terrific fall storm blew in across the ocean. The *Kamikaze,* or Divine Wind, as it was later named by the Japanese, churned up the seas and shattered many of the hurriedly constructed boats against the rocks and shore. In an effort to escape, some thirteen thousand of the invaders died, most by drowning, in the deadly channel that separated them from the safe harbors of Korea. The greatest armada in history had turned into the greatest, but largely bloodless, massacre at sea.

In the mythical explanations that rulers sometimes construct for others but end up believing themselves, Khubilai and his courtiers maintained that the invasion had been a success because the Mongols had defeated the Japanese army in the brief land battle; the subsequent loss of life and destruction of nearly the entire navy seemed less important. So he dispatched envoys back to Japan the following year to demand that the emperor now come in person to the Mongol capital to articulate his submission, after which Khubilai would reinvest him in office as ruler of Japan. The Japanese, equally as convinced that they had won, despite the loss of life on land, rejected the Mongol demands. With new confidence in either themselves or the divine protection of their gods, the Japanese committed the ultimate offense against the Mongols. They executed the envoys by chopping off their heads, spilling their blood, and then displaying the severed heads for public mockery.

Khubilai prepared for another expedition. The Japanese began building a small fleet of ships to fight the invaders on water, and along the shore they erected a stone wall to block the Mongol soldiers and horses from landing.

When more delegates arrived from Khubilai in 1279, the Japanese executed them, and both sides prepared for imminent war. This time the Mongols would invade from two directions, with another Korean fleet of about the same size as the first. Following it would come the main fleet from China with 3,500 ships manned by 60,000 sailors to transport 100,000 soldiers; and this time they were coming in summer, instead of sailing in the fall.

At the end of May 1281 the Korean fleet sailed, and despite heavy Japanese resistance, within a few days, they again conquered the island in the channel. Mongol planning at sea, however, was not as accurate and easily executed as on land. The Chinese ships encountered numerous difficulties and delays. The Korean fleet sailed into Hakata Bay expecting to be backed up by their Chinese counterparts from the south, but they never came. The Japanese wall prevented a successful landing, and the invaders remained cramped in their ships in the sweltering heat of June, quickly becoming ill as small epidemics of unknown diseases broke out. At night, the small Japanese boats came out to attack the large ships under cover of darkness, their intention being to spread panic and confusion more than to inflict decisive military harm. Unable to land and harried by the night attacks, the Korean fleet withdrew on June 30 to return to Takashima Island and await the southern fleet, which finally arrived two weeks later. Disorganized, sick, and already at sea much longer than prepared or supplied to do, the entire armada sailed for Japan in mid-August. Again, a storm churned the seas, capsizing and smashing boats, and perhaps more than one hundred thousand men died. Few ships survived to relate the story of the disaster.

Khubilai's invasions of Japan had failed, but they left a tremendous impact on Japanese social and political life by pushing them toward cultural unification and militaristic government. The Mongols, meanwhile, turned away from Japan, pretending the failures never happened as they looked elsewhere for what they hoped would be easier targets.

The Mongol conquests on land continued. Despite the extreme difficulty of the tropical heat and the unfamiliar landscape, the Mongol army had success in Burma, Annam in northern Vietnam, and Laos. Several of the Southeast Asian kingdoms, including the rulers of Champa in southern Vietnam and Malabar on the coast of India, voluntarily submitted to Mongol rule. In some regard, these acts of submission were more ceremonial than real, and the Mongols lacked the personnel to administer them. The new subjects did, however, send tribute on to the Mongol court, including elephants, rhinoceroses, and a tooth reportedly from the Buddha himself. The exchange of tribute and gifts served as a thin ceremonial disguise for commercial trade that gradually increased in volume and value.

The Mongols not only succeeded in building a unified Chinese state; at the same time, their influence exerted the same pressure on the small states around them. Early on, the Mongols had pushed for the unification of the culturally similar but constantly warring states of the Korean Peninsula into a unified nation. Similarly, in Southeast Asia, which remained beyond direct Mongol administration, the Mongol forces forged together new nations that laid a basis for Vietnam and Thailand. Prior to the Mongol era, the area that today composes the countries of Thailand, Laos, Vietnam, and Cambodia had been decisively Indian in culture and followed the architectural styles, religious practices, and mythology of Hindu India. The Mongols and the Chinese immigrants whom they had brought created a new hybrid culture that thereafter became known as Indo-Chinese.

The Mongols had less success in the islands that are today Indonesia. In 1289, Khubilai dispatched an envoy to Java to request the same submission he had received from the rulers of nearby kingdoms, but the king feared that the Mongols might be planning on taking away Javanese control of the valuable spice trade from the Molucca Islands. The Javanese king defiantly branded the face of the envoy and sent him back to Khubilai, who ordered the preparation of an armada to capture Java and exact revenge on its king, just as he had done in the similar episode in Japan. In 1292, the newly constructed fleet of one thousand ships and boats with twenty thousand soldiers set sail with a year's supply of provisions. When they arrived in 1293, the Mongols met with easy success, soon killed the offending king, and apparently conquered the island with apparent ease. But then they fell into a trap. Believing that they were preparing for a ceremonial submission by the new king, the Mongol leaders were lured into an ambush, where many of the leaders were killed, and the remaining troops retreated in humiliation from the island.

Khubilai had failed to adapt the successful Mongol strategies to the sea. The ancient techniques of the mounted hunter that his grandfather had used as the basis for his campaigns on land, did not translate to campaigns on ships. In contrast to former sea powers such as Rome and Athens, which had operated in small confined areas of the enclosed Mediterranean Sea, the Mongols had made China into an oceanic power. In this regard, the Mongols portended a new type of imperial power based on naval armadas that would rise in Spain, England, and the Netherlands in the coming centuries.

For the time being, however, Khubilai's defeats in Japan and Java had drawn the eastern limit of the Mongol Empire which would never extend across the water, not even to closer islands such as Taiwan or the Philippines. Similarly, the defeat by the Egyptian Mamluks in 1260, at the start of Khubilai's rule, had marked the southwestern border, just as precisely as the voluntary abandonment of Poland and Hungary had marked the northwestern point twenty years earlier. Thus, between 1242 and 1293, the Mongol expansion reached its maximum, and four battles marked the outer borders of the Mongol world—Poland, Egypt, Java, and Japan. The area inside those four points had suffered devastating conquests and radical adjustments to a markedly different kind of rule, but they were about to enjoy an unprecedented century of political peace with a commercial, technological, and intellectual explosion unlike any in prior history.

Every spring when flocks of cranes passed over northern China headed north to breed around the shallow lakes and rivers of Mongolia, Khubilai Khan awaited them in the countryside, stretched out on his silk couch covered with tiger skins in a beautiful gilded pavilion mounted on the backs of four elephants brought to him as part of the plunder from Burma. Too fat to ride a horse and pained by gout, he hunted from the more comfortable confines of this special and elaborately mounted chamber. When he was ready to hunt, the roof of the room rolled back to reveal the white and gray cranes so dense overhead that they appeared as clouds against the crisp blue sky. At the signal from Khubilai, hundreds of falconers lined up on either side of the elephants, removed the leather hoods from their birds, and the gyrfalcons, peregrine falcons, and eagles took flight. They raced after the cranes and, one by one, tore them out of the sky, and brought them back to their handler.

Although his grandfather codified the Mongol preference for hunting only in winter and never in spring, Khubilai did not enjoy hunting in the cold of winter and changed the law. Even with his white ermine coat, sable blankets, and tiger skin rugs on the floor and walls around him, he found the temperature uncomfortable and the wind biting; as a result, he pushed the hunting season into the early spring when the weather proved more agreeable.

In the hunting procession, soldiers rode the horses. Camels transported the goods, and other elephants carried smaller individual pavilions in case the khan wanted to chase the game into more confined areas than his four-elephant mobile palace could fit. The caravan followed the imperial banners of Khubilai and was festooned with brightly colored silks. The procession included hunting tigers riding in mobile cages pulled by powerful oxen, as well as leopards and lynx riding on the hind quarters of horses, alone or seated behind their trainers. When prey appeared, Khubilai dispatched one of his trained predators to bring it down. Dogs sufficed for the bears and smaller game, leopards for the deer, and tigers for the large wild asses or bulls. A phalanx of archers stood ready to shoot at whatever target their master might command if it could not be reached by the hunting animals.

Khubilai's processions across the countryside included a large number of astrologers, diviners, Mongol shamans, and Tibetan monks, whose work, vaguely reminiscent of Genghis Khan's use of shamans before battle, consisted of clearing the path of clouds, rain, and any other form of inclement weather that might hamper the mighty hunter. With the sounds and smells of such a massive caravan, animals had ample warning and opportunity to flee. It was hard for them to be taken by surprise, so Khubilai's caravan moved like the traditional Mongol army. While the emperor, his court and menagerie moved as the center or pivot of the caravan, he kept a *tumen* (nominally of ten thousand men, but in this case perhaps less) spread out to his forward left, and another spread out to the forward right. To show their wing assignment, one side wore scarlet, and the other wore blue. According to Marco Polo, they spread the distance of a whole day's journey in both directions. Accompanied by mastiffs and hunting birds, the retainers drove the animals before them and toward the center so that they would be correctly positioned when the elephants arrived with Khubilai in his portable palace.

In order to cater to the needs of the hunting party after an exhausting day on the backs of the elephants, a vanguard of servants preceded them to erect a camp that resembled a portable city. The largest pavilion held a thousand guests for the rowdy Mongol celebrations. Adjacent tents provided sleeping quarters. A troupe of musicians accompanied the court to perform with singers, acrobats, jugglers, and the contortionists so enjoyed by the court.

At each evening's celebration, everyone wore a *deel* of the same style and assigned color for the day; but lest they appear too egalitarian, rank and power were symbolized in the number and value of the jewels and pearls worked into the costume. They wore golden belts and silver embroidered onto their boots. In the midst of all the celebration, one of the trained tigers entered the pavilion, proceeded slowly among the guests to the khan, bowed, and then took its place seated beside the throne for the evening. The meals were served in dishes of gold and silver. Each servant wore a silk napkin trimmed in gold as a veil across his nose and mouth to prevent his breath, or any other essence, from contaminating the food. The recipes of the dishes served Khubilai Khan still survive. They include a variety of foods but maintain the traditional Mongol emphasis on meat and dairy products. The members of the Mongol court ate such delicacies as strips of mutton tail fat dusted with flour and baked with leeks. Bull testicles fried in hot oil, basted with saffron paste, and sprinkled with coriander. Mutton boiled with cardamom and cinnamon and served with rice and chickpeas. Young eggplant stuffed with chopped mutton, fat, yogurt, orange peel, and basil.

Like true Mongols, they gorged themselves on their favorite drink of fermented mare's milk, but this milk originated from the special imperial herd of pure white mares that had been impregnated by pure white stallions to produce a special milk restricted exclusively for Khubilai and his court. When it came time to retire to his chamber for the night, the khan had his pick of beautiful young women, all of whom had been tested to make sure that they did not snore, have bad breath, or discharge any unpleasant body odors. The next morning, to recover from the excessive drinking, eating, and indulging of every appetite, the khan's mobile unit of doctors and pharmacists served him a tea made from orange peel, kudzu flowers, ginseng, sandalwood, and cardamom. Sipped on an empty stomach, the tea was guaranteed to overcome a hangover and make the khan fit for another day of hunting, eating, and drinking.

Only a few generations earlier, Khubilai's ancestors had used the hunt as the primary means of acquiring food. His great-grandfather Yesugei had been out hunting with his gyrfalcon when he saw the bride Hoelun, whom he seized to make his own wife. Khubilai's grandfather Genghis Khan fed his family by hunting after his father's death, and he had killed his half brother Begter in an argument ostensibly following a hunting quarrel about a bird and a fish. Later in life, Genghis Khan, with the aid of Subodei and other good hunters, adapted the extensive hunting strategies, techniques, and weapons to the task of warfare by treating his enemies as objects of prey to be trapped and stalked, and he thereby conquered his vast empire.

The hunt combined a recreational pastime enjoyed by Khubilai with the imperial needs of ceremonial pomp and wasteful spectacle. Khubilai still participated in some of the traditional features of the Mongol hunt and lifestyle—the emphasis on archery, trained raptors, enjoyment of mare's milk, sleeping in tents, and organization of the Armies of the Left and the Right. But he turned it into a decadent and luxurious recreation that provided costly, if vapid, amusements for the Mongol elite and himself. His great procession was more show than substance. Its meaning came from the public spectacle that it made and the impression it created on his subjects and foreign visitors.

Like the frequent relocation of camp on the Mongol steppe, Khubilai's caravan followed a rider carrying his Spirit Banner before him. The Spirit Banner led him on a frivolous round of entertainments that ultimately meant nothing and ended nowhere. The Mongol Empire would continue on for another century, but already, only three generations after its founding, it had lost its way. It was clear to anyone that the Spirit Banner of Genghis Khan no longer led his descendants and the people who claimed to be his followers.

9

===⧖===

Their Golden Light

*The artists of China and Paris vied with each other
in the service of the great Khan.*

EDWARD GIBBON

DURING MASS ONE DAY in the winter of 1287–1288, King Edward I of
England rose up from his throne to stand in honor of Rabban Bar
Sawma, the newly arrived envoy from the Mongol Emperor Khubilai Khan.
When he reached the court of the English king, Rabban Bar Sawma had
probably traveled farther than any official envoy in history, covering some
seven thousand miles on the circuitous land route from the Mongol capital,
through the major cities of the Middle East, and on to the capitals of Europe.
King Edward stood before the envoy not to offer submission to the Mongol
Khan, but to accept bread from the hand of the Mongol envoy as part of the
Christian sacrament of communion. Since the early European envoys to the
Mongols had been priests, Khubilai Khan had chosen Rabban Bar Sawma
because, although a loyal Mongol, he was also a Christian priest, albeit of the
Assyrian rite.

Rabban Bar Sawma's mission began as a pilgrimage from Khubilai Khan's
capital to Jerusalem, but after reaching Baghdad, his superiors diverted him
to Europe in 1287. In addition to visiting with the Mongol Ilkhan in Persia,
Emperor Andronicus II Palaeologus of Byzantium in Constantinople, the

College of Cardinals in Rome, and King Philip IV of France in Paris, Rabban Bar Sawma made his way to the court of Edward, at the most distant point of his journey. He delivered letters and gifts to each monarch along his route, and he stayed in each court for a few weeks or months before moving on to the next. He used his time sightseeing and meeting with scholars, politicians, and church officials to tell them about the Great Khan of the Mongols, his subordinate the Ilkhan, and their burning desire for peaceful relations with the world. On his way back through Rome, Pope Nicholas IV invited Rabban Bar Sawma to celebrate Mass in his language; and then, on Palm Sunday, 1288, the pope celebrated Mass and personally gave communion to the Mongol envoy.

The crowned heads of Europe received Rabban Bar Sawma openly in their courts, but many prior envoys had been sent, only to be officially ignored by church and state. As early as 1247, during the reign of Guyuk Khan, Matthew Paris reported ambassadors from the Mongols arriving at the French court. Again in the summer of the following year, "two envoys came from the Tartars, sent to the lord pope by their prince." During the earlier visits, however, European officials seemed afraid to let out any information about the Mongols. As Paris wrote, "the cause of their arrival was kept so secret from everyone at the curia that it was unknown to clerks, notaries and others, even those familiar with the pope." Again in 1269, when the Polo brothers, Maffeo and Nicolo, returned from their first trip to Asia, they brought a request from Khubilai Khan to the pope to send the Mongols one hundred priests, that they might share their knowledge with the Mongol court.

With the tremendous emphasis on religious freedom throughout the Mongol Empire, Rabban Bar Sawma was surprised when he arrived in Europe and found that only a single religion was tolerated. He found particularly amazing that the religious leaders had so much political power over nations as well as more mundane powers over the everyday lives of the common people. As a Christian himself, he was delighted with the monopoly that his religion exercised, but it presented a stark contrast to the Mongol Empire where many religions flourished but had the obligation to serve the needs of the empire before their own.

Despite the publicity of his visit and the cordial reception across Europe, Rabban Bar Sawma fared no better in his mission than the other unacknowledged envoys; he failed to secure treaties with a single one of the European monarchs or church officials. His only success was that he managed to get a commitment from the pope to send teachers to the Mongol court as Khubilai had requested several times already. Failing in his diplomatic mission, Rabban Bar Sawma returned to the court of the Ilkhan in Persia, and related the events of his travels that were copied down in Syriac as *The History of the Life and Travels of Rabban Swama, Envoy and Plenipotentiary of the Mongol Khans to the Kings of Europe.* The trip of Rabban Bar Sawma, and particularly his serving communion to the king of England and personally receiving communion from the hands of the pope, illustrates how much the Mongols had changed the world in the fifty years since their army invaded Europe. Civilizations that had once been separate worlds unto themselves and largely unknown to one another, had become part of a single intercontinental system of communication, commerce, technology, and politics.

Instead of sending mounted warriors and fearsome siege engines, the Mongols now dispatched humble priests, scholars, and ambassadors. The time of Mongol conquests had ended, but the era of the Mongol Peace was only beginning. In recognition of the phenomenal changes of expanding peace and prosperity on the international scene, Western scholars later designated the fourteenth century as the Pax Mongolica or Pax Tatarica. The Mongol Khans now sought to bring about through peaceful commerce and diplomacy the commercial and diplomatic connections that they had not been able to create through force of arms. The Mongols continued, by a different means, to pursue their compulsive goal of uniting all people under the Eternal Blue Sky.

The commercial influence of the Mongols spread much farther than their army, and the transition from the Mongol Empire to the Mongol Corporation occurred during the reign of Khubilai Khan. Throughout the thirteenth and early fourteenth centuries, the Mongols maintained trade routes across the empire and stocked shelters with provisions interspersed every twenty to thirty miles. The stations provided transport animals as well as guides to lead the merchants through difficult terrain. Marco Polo, who was at the Mongol court at the same time that Bar Sawma was on his mission to Europe, frequently used the Mongol relay stations in his travels. With perhaps a little more enthusiasm than accuracy, he describes them as not merely "beautiful" and "palatial," but also having "silk sheets and every other luxury suitable for a king." To promote trade along these routes, Mongol authorities distributed an early type of combined passport and credit card. The Mongol *paiza* was a tablet of gold, silver, or wood larger than a man's hand, and it would be worn on a chain around the neck or attached to the clothing. Depending on which metal was used and the symbols such as tigers or gyrfalcons, illiterate people could ascertain the importance of the traveler and thereby render the appropriate level of service. The *paiza* allowed the holder to travel throughout the empire and be assured of protection, accommodations, transportation, and exemption from local taxes or duties.

The expansion and maintenance of the trading routes did not derive from an ideological commitment of the Mongols to commerce and communication in general. Rather, it stemmed from the deeply rooted system of shares, or *khubi,* in the Mongol tribal organization that had been formalized by Genghis Khan. Just as each orphan and widow, as well as each soldier, was entitled to an appropriate measure of all the goods seized in war, each member of the Golden Family was entitled to a share of the wealth of each part of the empire. Instead of the salary paid to non-Mongol administrators, the higher-ranking Mongol officials received shares in goods, a large part of which they sold or traded on the market to get money or other commodities. As ruler of the Ilkhanate in Persia, Hulegu still had twenty-five thousand households of silk workers in China under his brother Khubilai. Hulegu also owned valleys in Tibet, and he had claim on a share of the furs and falcons of the northern steppes, and, of course, he had pastures, horses, and men assigned to him in the homeland of Mongolia itself. Each lineage in the Mongol ruling family demanded its appropriate share of astronomers, doctors, weavers, miners, and acrobats.

Khubilai owned farms in Persia and Iraq, as well as herds of camels, horses, sheep, and goats. An army of clerics traveled throughout the empire checking on the goods in one place and verifying accounts in another. The Mongols in Persia supplied their kinsmen in China with spices, steel, jewels, pearls, and textiles, while the Mongol court in China sent porcelains and medicines to Persia. In return for collecting and shipping the goods, the Mongols in China kept about three-quarters of this output for themselves; nevertheless, they exported a considerable amount to their relatives in other areas. Khubilai

Khan imported Persian translators and doctors as well as some ten thousand Russian soldiers, who were used to colonize land north of the capital. The Russians stayed as permanent residents, and they remained in the official Chinese chronicles until last mentioned in 1339.

Despite political disagreement between contending branches of the family over the office of Great Khan, the economic and commercial system continued to operate with only brief pauses or detours because of sporadic fighting. Sometimes even in the midst of war, the fighting sides allowed the exchange of these shares. Khaidu, the grandson of Ogodei Khan and the ruler of the central steppe, was often in rebellion against his cousin Khubilai. Yet Khaidu also had extensive holdings of craftsmen and farmers around the Chinese city of Nanjing. In between sessions of fighting with Khubilai Khan, Khaidu would claim shipments of his Nanjing goods, and, presumably in exchange, he allowed Khubilai to collect his share of horses and other goods from the steppe tribes. The administrative division of the Mongol Empire into four major parts—China, Moghulistan, Persia, and Russia—did nothing to lessen the need for goods in the other regions. If anything, the political fragmentation increased the need to preserve the older system of shares. If one khan refused to furnish the shares to other members of the family, they would refuse to send him his share in their territories. Mutual financial interests trumped political squabbles.

The constant movement of shares gradually transformed the Mongol war routes into commercial arteries. Through the constantly expanding *ortoo* or *yam*, messages, people, and goods could be sent by horse or camel caravan from Mongolia to Vietnam or from Korea to Persia. As the movement of goods increased, Mongol authorities sought out faster or easier routes than the older traditional ones. Toward this end, Khubilai Khan launched a major expedition in 1281 to discover and map the source of the Yellow River, which the Mongols called the Black River. Scholars used the information to make a detailed map of the river. The expedition opened up a route from China into Tibet, and the Mongols used this as a means of including Tibet and the Himalayan area in the Mongol postal system. The new connections did more to connect Tibet—commercially, religiously, and politically—with the rest of China than anything else during the Mongol era.

During military campaigns, Mongol officials exerted a conscientious effort to locate and appropriate maps, atlases, and other geographic works found in enemy camps or cities. Under Khubilai's rule, scholars synthesized Chinese, Arab, and Greek knowledge of geography to produce the most sophisticated cartography known. Under the influence of the Arab geographers brought in by Khubilai Khan, particularly Jamal al-Din, craftsmen constructed terrestrial globes for Khubilai in 1267, which depicted Europe and Africa as well as Asia and the adjacent Pacific islands.

Despite the initial reliance of commerce on routes created through military conquest, it soon became obvious that whereas armies moved quickest by horse across land, massive quantities of goods moved best by water. Mongols expanded and lengthened the Grand Canal that already connected the Yellow and Yangtze Rivers to transport grain and other agricultural products farther and more efficiently into the northern districts. Adapting Chinese engineering and technology to new environments, they built water projects throughout their territories. In Yunnan, the Mongol governor created a dozen dams and reservoirs with connecting canals that survived until modern times.

The failed invasions of Japan and Java taught the Mongols much about shipbuilding, and when their military efforts failed, they turned that knowledge to peaceful pursuits of commerce. Khubilai Khan made the strategic decision to transport food within his empire primarily by ship because he realized how much cheaper and more efficient water transportation, which was dependent on wind and current, was than the much slower land transport, which was dependent on the labor of humans and animals that required constant feeding. In the first years, the Mongols moved some 3,000 tons by ship, but by 1329 it had grown to 210,000 tons. Marco Polo, who sailed from China to Persia on his return home, described the Mongol ships as large four-masted junks with up to three hundred crewmen and as many as sixty cabins for merchants carrying various wares. According to Ibn Battuta, some of the ships even carried plants growing in wooden tubs in order to supply fresh food for the sailors. Khubilai Khan promoted the building of ever larger seagoing junks to carry heavy loads of cargo and ports to handle them. They improved the use of the compass in navigation and learned to produce more accurate nautical charts. The route from the port of Zaytun in southern China to Hormuz in the Persian Gulf became the main sea link between the

Far East and the Middle East, and was used by both Marco Polo and Ibn Battuta, among others.

En route, the ships also called at the ports of Vietnam, Java, Ceylon, and India, and in each place the Mongol representatives encountered more goods, such as sugar, ivory, cinnamon, and cotton, that were not easily produced in their own lands. From the Persian Gulf, the ships continued outside of the areas under Mongol influence to include regular trade for a still greater variety of goods from Arabia, Egypt, and Somalia. Rulers and merchants in these other areas outside the Mongol system of influence did not operate within the system of shares in the Mongol goods; instead, the Mongol authorities created long-term trading relations with them. Under Mongol protection, their vassals proved as worthy competitors in commerce as the Mongols had been in conquest and they began to dominate trade on the Indian Ocean.

To expand the trade into new areas beyond Mongol political control, they encouraged some of their vassals, particularly the South Chinese, to emigrate and set up trading stations in foreign ports. Throughout the rule of the Mongol dynasty, thousands of Chinese left home and sailed off to settle along the coastal communities of Vietnam, Cambodia, the Malay Peninsula, Borneo, Java, and Sumatra. They worked mostly in shipping and trade and as merchants up and down the rivers leading to the ports, but they gradually expanded into other professions as well.

To reach the markets of Europe more directly, without the lengthy detour through the southern Muslim countries, the Mongols encouraged foreigners to create trading posts on the edges of the empire along the Black Sea. Although the Mongols had initially raided the trading posts, as early as 1226, during the reign of Genghis Khan, they allowed the Genoese to maintain a trading station at the port of Kaffa in the Crimea, and later added another at Tana. To protect these stations on land and sea, the Mongols hunted down pirates and robbers. In the *Pratica della mercatura (Practice of Marketing)*, a commercial handbook published in 1340, the Florentine merchant Francesco Balducci Pegolotti stressed that the routes to Mongol Cathay were "perfectly safe, whether by day or by night."

The opening of new trade routes, combined with the widespread destruction of manufacturing in Persia and Iraq by the Mongol invasions, created new opportunities for Chinese manufacturing. The Mongol conquest of

China had been far less disruptive than the military campaigns in the Middle East, and Khubilai pressed for the expansion of traditional Chinese wares into these markets as well as the widespread transfer of Muslim and Indian technology to China. Through their shares, the members of the Mongol royal family controlled much of the production throughout Eurasia, but they depended on the merchant class to transport and sell these wares. Mongols had turned from warriors into shareholders, but they had no skill or apparent desire to become merchants themselves.

The Mongol elite's intimate involvement with trade represented a marked break with tradition. From China to Europe, traditional aristocrats generally disdained commercial enterprise as undignified, dirty, and, often, immoral; it ranked with the manual trades beneath the interests of either the powerful or the pious. Furthermore, the economic ideal in feudal Europe of this time was not merely that each country should be self-sufficient, but that each manor estate should strive to be as self-supporting as practical. Any goods that left the estate should not be going to trade for other goods for the peasants on the land but to buy jewelry, religious relics, and other luxury goods for the aristocratic family or church. The feudal rulers sought to have their peasants supply all their own needs—to produce their food, grow their timber, make their tools, and weave their cloth—and to trade for as little as possible. In a feudal system, reliance on imported goods represented a failure at home.

The traditional Chinese kingdoms operated under centuries of constraints on commerce. The building of walls on their borders had been a way of limiting such trade and literally keeping the wealth of the nation intact and inside the walls. For such administrators, giving up trade goods was the same as paying tribute to their neighbors, and they sought to avoid it as much as they could. The Mongols directly attacked the Chinese cultural prejudice that ranked merchants as merely a step above robbers by officially elevating their status ahead of all religions and professions, second only to government officials. In a further degradation of Confucian scholars, the Mongols reduced them from the highest level of traditional Chinese society to the ninth level, just below prostitutes but above beggars.

Since the time of Genghis Khan, the Mongols realized that items that were commonplace and taken for granted in one place were exotic and potentially marketable in another. The latter decades of the thirteenth century became a time of nearly frenetic search for new commodities that could be marketed somewhere in the expanding network of Mongol commerce or for old commodities that could be marketed in a new way. It must have seemed that every item, from dyes, paper, and drugs to pistachios, firecrackers, and poison, had a potential buyer, and the Mongol officials seemed determined to find who and where that buyer might be. By responding to the needs of a universal market, the Mongol workshops in China eventually were producing not merely traditional Chinese crafts of porcelains and silks for the world market, but adding entirely new items for specialized markets, including the manufacture of images of the Madonna and the Christ Child carved in ivory and exported to Europe.

The Mongol promotion of trade introduced a variety of new fabrics by taking local products and finding an international market for them. The origins of such textiles can still be seen in the etymology of many of their names. A particularly smooth and glossy type of silk became known in the West as *satin,* taking its name from the Mongol port of Zaytun from which Marco Polo sailed on his return to Europe. A style of highly ornate cloth became known as *damask silk,* derived from the name of Damascus, the city through which most of the trade from the Ilkhanate of Persia passed en route to Europe. Marco Polo mentioned another type of fine, delicate cloth made in Mosul, and it became known as *mouslin* in Old French and then as *muslin* in English.

Even the most trivial items might yield a great profit, as when the new commerce sparked a rapid spread of card playing because merchants and soldiers found the light and easily transported game an entertaining and novel pastime. Compared to the more cumbersome objects needed for chess and other board games, any soldier or camel driver could carry a pack of cards in his gear. This new market stimulated the need to make card production faster and cheaper, and the solution for that process was found in printing them from carved blocks normally used for printing religious scripture. The market for printed cards proved much greater than that for scripture.

Most empires of conquest in history have imposed their own civilization on the conquered. The Romans imposed the Latin language, their gods, and a preference for wine, olive oil, and wheat agriculture even in locales where it did not thrive. Each Roman city from Ephesus in Turkey to Cologne in Germany had the same urban design and architectural style, from markets and baths all the way to the smallest details on the columns or doorways. In other eras, the British erected Tudor buildings in Bombay, the Dutch built windmills in the Caribbean, the Spaniards constructed their own style of cathedrals and plazas from Mexico to Argentina, and Americans erected their distinctive residential compounds from Panama to Saudi Arabia. Merely by studying the physical remains of a place, archaeologists can trace the growth of Hindu, Aztec, Malian, Incan, or Arab empires.

By comparison the Mongols trod lightly on the world they conquered. They brought no distinctive architectural style with them. Nor did they seek to impose their language and religion on the conquered since in most cases they forbade non-Mongols to learn their language. The Mongols did not force cultivation of an alien crop nor impose radical change on their subjects' collective way of life.

Skilled at moving large numbers of people and utilizing new technology for purposes of war, the Mongols continued the same practices during the Mongol Peace and applied itinerant principles of the nomadic society to very conservative areas of life and culture. The Mongol armies rounded up translators, scribes, doctors, astronomers, and mathematicians to be parceled out among the families in the same shares that they parceled out musicians, cooks, goldsmiths, acrobats, and painters. The authorities divided these knowledge workers, together with all the other craftsmen, the animals, and other goods for transportation via a long caravan trek or sea journey to the various parts of the family.

Traditional empires accumulated wealth in a single city. All routes led to the capital city, and the best of everything ended up there. One place so dominated such empires that the name of cities like Rome or Babylon became the names of the empires themselves. The Mongol Empire never had a single major city, and within the empire goods and people constantly traveled from one place to another.

In 1261, Khubilai Khan created the Office for the Stimulation of Agriculture under the authority of eight commissioners who sought ways to improve farmers' lives and their yields. In addition to improving crop cultivation, the office bore responsibility to generally protect and promote the well-being of the peasants. This policy toward farmers constituted a substantial attitudinal shift on the part of a government that preserved the attitudes derived from the Mongols' traditional nomadic lifestyle and had traditionally shown limited concern for the peasantry and for agricultural problems. Prior to the Mongol occupation of China, most farmers within any area cultivated the same set of crops; the crops varied by region, but not within a region. The Mongols encouraged farmers to cultivate those crops that proved most appropriate for the climate, soil type, and drainage pattern. This change in emphasis promoted greater variety within an area and higher productivity. Mongol authorities encouraged the spread of traditional Chinese crops such as tea and rice into new areas, particularly into Persia and the Middle East. The Mongols sought better tools and thus spread the use of an improved, triangular plow introduced into China from Southeast Asia.

As soon as the Mongols assumed control of Persia, they established an office to encourage and improve agriculture there. After thousands of years of cultivation, the soils of the area had been eroded and productivity threatened. The Mongols addressed these problems with extensive importation of seeds from China, and when needed, shoots, branches, and whole trees that they planted in newly created agricultural stations for adaptation to Middle Eastern climate and soil. They brought new varieties of rice and millet, as well as fruit trees and root crops. India, China, and Persia cultivated some variety of citrus fruits before the Mongols, but the Mongols assiduously moved and mixed the varieties so that each region had more types. Near Canton in southern China, the Mongol authorities planted an orchard of eight hundred lemon trees imported from their territories in the Middle East. At Tabriz in Persia, the Mongols similarly planted groves of a different variety of lemon and other citrus trees imported in the opposite direction—from China to the Middle East. The Mongols transplanted an ever-expanding variety of peas, beans, grapes, lentils, nuts, carrots, turnips, melons, and diverse leaf vegetables, and in turn they developed new varieties and hybrids. In addition to food crops for humans and animals, Mongol authorities had a persistent interest in varieties of cotton and other crops for making textiles, as well as various materials for making rope, dyes, oils, ink, paper, and medicine.

Because of the lucrative textile trade and its prominence in generating foreign trade, the Mongol rulers maintained a particular interest in the varieties of wool that they produced from their herds as well as in the silks, cottons, and other fibers produced by farmers. To promote cotton cultivation, they created a Cotton Promotion Bureau in 1289 and dispersed representatives throughout the newly conquered provinces of the southeast coast and along the Yangtze. The bureau devised methods for growing cotton farther north in the wheat areas and promoted better weaving and manufacturing techniques. Although silk maintained higher prestige both within and beyond China, cotton proved to be a valuable new fiber crop. Each innovation in one area brought the likelihood of many other changes. New crops required new styles of plowing, planting, irrigation, pruning, staking, harvesting, cutting, threshing, grinding, transporting, preserving, brewing, distilling, and cooking. The new or slightly altered techniques required the use of new tools and implements, which, in turn, needed new techniques of manufacture.

The Mongols made culture portable. It was not enough to merely exchange goods, because whole systems of knowledge had to also be transported in order to use many of the new products. Drugs, for example, were not profitable items of trade unless there was adequate knowledge of how to use them. Toward this objective, the Mongol court imported Persian and Arab doctors into China, and they exported Chinese doctors to the Middle East. Every form of knowledge carried new possibilities for merchandising. It became apparent that the Chinese operated with a superior knowledge of pharmacology and of unusual forms of treatment such as acupuncture, the insertion of needles at key points in the body, and moxibustion, the application of fire or heat to similar areas. Muslims doctors, however, possessed a much more sophisticated knowledge of surgery, but, based on their dissection of executed criminals, the Chinese had a detailed knowledge of internal organs and the circulatory system. To encourage a fuller exchange of medical knowledge, the Mongols created hospitals and training centers in China using doctors from India and the Middle East as well as Chinese healers. Khubilai Khan founded a department for the study of Western medicine under the direction of a Christian scholar.

The Mongols established a House of Healing near Tabriz to serve as a combination hospital, research center, and training facility in the medical knowledge of both East and West. In Mongol-occupied Persia in 1313, Rashid al-Din published the first known book on Chinese medicine to be published outside of China, including illustrations actually made in China. Chinese acupuncture did not prove popular in the Middle East because it required, according to Muslim values, too much physical contact and manipulation in placing the needles around the body. On the other hand, the Chinese practice of pulse diagnosis proved very popular in the Middle East and India with Muslims because it merely required the physician to touch the patient's wrist before rendering a diagnosis and prescribing treatment. Using this novel method, doctors could treat female patients without violating the honor of her family.

Only a few years after uniting China under his rule, Khubilai created the Academy for Calendrical Studies and a printing office to mass produce a variety of calendars and almanacs. If a ruler had the Mandate of Heaven to rule over his people, then he had to display an ability to mark time, to forecast the phases of the moon, the changing of seasons, and, possibly most important for public prestige and opinion, the timing of lunar and solar eclipses. The Mongol rulers, however, faced a much larger problem with their calendar. In a traditional empire with a single court and capital, a single official calendar sufficed, and it mattered little that other nations kept other calendars. In the multiheaded Mongol Empire, capitals were scattered across great distances, and it became important to coordinate them in order to manage the movement of the large armies and massive amounts of goods. East Asians utilized a twelve-year animal cycle, while Muslims used a moon calendar of progressive years beginning with the foundation of their religion. Persians marked the beginning of the year by the equinox of the sun. Some events were marked by the movement of planets, particularly Mars and Venus, or by the stars. Europeans used a solar calendar, except for religious celebrations such as Lent, Easter, and Epiphany that were calculated on the lunar calendar. Even the Christian sects disagreed on the timing of these events, with the result that despite constant adjustments, their calendars failed to coincide.

As the Mongol empire of conquest expanded into an even larger empire of commerce, it became increasingly important for the Mongols to have a smoothly functioning calendar that operated according to the same principles throughout the empire. With the need to coordinate activities and regulate social life in places with such varied ways of marking time, the Mongols, almost as soon as they conquered an area, created observatories to accurately measure the movement of planets and stars for both practical and religious reasons. They built one immediately near Tabriz, but China needed a series of observatories erected across the land because it was so large. Mongol authorities had specific instructions from the central government to seek out astronomers and astronomical instruments and charts in each newly conquered land. Hulegu sent many of the astronomers captured in the Persian and Arab cities back to his homeland in Mongolia. These included Jamal ad-Din, who was one of the most brilliant astronomers of the era; he brought with him the blueprints for major astronomical devices and new means of scientific measurement unknown in China.

On a scale that surpassed prior civilizations, the Mongols needed to process and record massive amounts of numerical information in the censuses of people, animals, and buildings. Each year they had to settle the accounts for all the goods sent back and forth, as well as for the movement of herds, soldiers, and merchants. The new forms of agriculture, the demands of astronomy, the system of censuses, and myriad other issues of administration taxed the numerical knowledge and ability of the era. They necessitated new approaches to the handling of numbers. To make the needed calculations quickly and efficiently, the clerks working for the Mongols relied on the abacus, which, with the movement of a few beads, allowed them to calculate large sums mechanically with less mental effort than making the calculations mentally or through writing.

Always fastidious about numerical information and with hundreds of millions of people across the vast Mongol Empire, the Mongols searched for simpler methods, shortcuts, and ways of calculating ever-larger quantities and processing them in ever more complex sequences. The larger numbers of calculations required new ways of preserving information through the compilation of complex charts and the coordination of the number systems used in different countries. Mongol administrators found both European and Chinese mathematics too simple and impractical, but they adopted many useful innovations from Arabic and Indian mathematics. The cities of the Khwarizm empire had been a particularly important center for mathematic scholarship; the word *algorithm* was derived from *al Khwarizm*. The Mongols transported knowledge of these innovations throughout their empire. They quickly discerned the advantages of utilizing columns of numbers or place numbers in the style of Arabic numerals, and they introduced the use of zero, negative numbers, and algebra in China.

Not just in numbers and calendars, but on many levels, life itself in various parts of the empire had to be coordinated in a way that prior history had not required. The writing of history proved too important to allow each civilization to proceed in its own manner and according to the conventions developed in their literary traditions. To control the way that they themselves were presented to their subjects, the Mongols had to make the local standards on writing history correlate and articulate with the Mongol story. Written history was much more than a means of recording information; it served as a tool to legitimize the ruling dynasty and spread propaganda about its great conquests and achievements. For the Mongols, written history also became an important tool in learning about other nations in order to conquer and rule them more effectively. Khubilai Khan established the National History Office in the 1260s. In keeping with Chinese practices, he commissioned the compilation of complete histories of the Jurched and Khitan kingdoms, as well as the Sung dynasty. The project was probably the most massive history project ever commissioned and took nearly eighty years, until the 1340s, to complete. In Mongol Persia, the Ilkhan Gazan commissioned the first history of the world from Rashid al-Din, a successor of Juvaini. Rashid al-Din orchestrated a massive undertaking that employed many different scholars and translators in order to create histories of the Chinese, Turks, and Franks, as the Mongols called the Europeans.

The volume of information produced in the Mongol Empire required new forms of dissemination. Scribes could no longer handle the flow by laboriously hand copying everything that needed to be written. They compiled the records, wrote letters, and sent information to those who needed it, but they did not have time to copy agricultural manuals, medical treatises, atlases, and astronomical tables. Information had to be mass produced for mass dissemination, and for this task, the Mongols turned again to technology, to printing.

The Mongols adopted printing technology very early. In addition to the printings sponsored by Toregene during the reign of her husband, beginning in 1236 Ogodei ordered the establishment of a series of regional printing facilities across the Mongol-controlled territory of northern China. Printing with movable letters probably began in China in the middle of the twelfth century, but it was the Mongols who employed it on a massive scale and harnessed its potential power to the needs of state administration. Instead of the printing with thousands of characters, as the Chinese did, the Mongols used an alphabet in which the same letters were used repeatedly. Under the Mongols, printers carved out many copies of each letter that could then be arranged into whatever word was needed. Each time the printer wanted a new page of print, instead of carving the whole text, he needed to merely place the right sequence of already carved letters into position, use them, and then wait until the next printing job, when they would be rearranged and then used again.

General literacy increased during the Mongol dynasty, and the volume of literary material grew proportionately. In 1269, Khubilai Khan established a printing office to make government decisions more widely disseminated throughout the population, and he encouraged widespread printing in general by nongovernmental groups as well. This included religious books and novels in addition to government publications. The number of books in print increased so dramatically that their price fell constantly throughout the era of Mongol rule. Presses throughout the Mongol Empire were soon printing agriculture pamphlets, almanacs, scriptures, laws, histories, medical treatises, new mathematical theories, songs, and poetry in many different languages.

Whether in their policy of religious tolerance, devising a universal alphabet, maintaining relay stations, playing games, or printing almanacs, money, or astronomy charts, the rulers of the Mongol Empire displayed a persistent universalism. Because they had no system of their own to impose upon their subjects, they were willing to adopt and combine systems from everywhere. Without deep cultural preferences in these areas, the Mongols implemented pragmatic rather than ideological solutions. They searched for what worked best; and when they found it, they spread it to other countries. They did not have to worry whether their astronomy agreed with the precepts of the Bible, that their standards of writing followed the classical principles taught by the mandarins of China, or that Muslim imams disapproved of their printing and painting. The Mongols had the power, at least temporarily, to impose new international systems of technology, agriculture, and knowledge that superseded the predilections or prejudices of any single civilization; and in so doing, they broke the monopoly on thought exercised by local elites.

In conquering their empire, not only had the Mongols revolutionized warfare, they also created the nucleus of a universal culture and world system. This new global culture continued to grow long after the demise of the Mongol Empire, and through continued development over the coming centuries, it became the foundation for the modern world system with the original Mongol emphases on free commerce, open communication, shared knowledge, secular politics, religious coexistence, international law, and diplomatic immunity.

Although never ruled by the Mongols, in many ways Europe gained the most from their world system. The Europeans received all the benefits of trade, technology transfer, and the Global Awakening without paying the cost of Mongol conquest. The Mongols had killed off the knights in Hungary and Germany, but they had not destroyed or occupied the cities. The Europeans, who had been cut off from the mainstream of civilization since the fall of Rome, eagerly drank in the new knowledge, put on the new clothes, listened to the new music, ate the new foods, and enjoyed a rapidly escalating standard of living in almost every regard.

The Europeans easily forgot the hysterical commentary of chroniclers such as Matthew Paris and Thomas of Spalato, who wrote about the Mongol invasions back in 1240. Across the intervening century, the Mongols had come to represent sumptuous trade goods and luxurious rarities to the Europeans. The word *Tartar* no longer signified unbridled terror; instead, the Italian writers Dante and Boccaccio and the English writer Chaucer used the phrase *Panni Tartarici*, "Tartar cloth," or "Tartar satin," as terms for the finest cloth in the world. When King Edward III of England ordered 150 garters to be made for his Knights of the Garters, he specified that they be in Tartar blue. Such terms obviously did not apply to textiles or dyes made by the Mongols, but to ones traded by them or originating in their territory.

One technological innovation after another arrived in Europe. The most labor-intensive professions such as mining, milling, and metalwork had depended almost entirely on human and animal labor, but they quickly became more mechanized with the harnessing of water and wind power. The transmission of the technology for improving the blast furnace also arrived in Europe from Asia via the Mongol trade routes, and it allowed metalworkers to achieve higher temperatures and thereby improve the quality of metal, an increasingly important material in this new high-technology era. In Europe, as a result of the Mongol Global Awakening, carpenters used the general adze less and adapted more specialized tools for specific functions to make their work faster and more efficient; builders used new types of cranes and hoists. There was a quick spread of new crops that required less work to produce or less processing after production; carrots, turnips, cress, buckwheat, and parsnips became common parts of the diet. Labor-intensive cooking was improved by mechanizing the meat spit to be turned more easily. The new tools, machines, and mechanical devices helped to build everything, from ships and docks to warehouses and canals, faster and better, just as previously the improved Mongol technology of war helped to tear down and destroy quicker with improved cannons and firepower.

Something as simple as preparing a single page document on vellum or parchment required the labor of a long line of skilled workers. Aside from the herder who raised the sheep, the slaughtering and skinning were so important to make quality writing material that it required a skilled craft of skinners. Over several weeks, the skin had to be cleaned and scraped of hair on the outside and flesh on the inside, soaked in a sequence of chemical baths, stretched on a frequently readjusted frame, sunned, alternately wet and dried in a precise sequence, shaved, and finally cut into pages of the appropriate size. To make the pages into a book, a whole new sequence of trades were drawn on to make the ink, copy the text, illustrate it, color it, and bind it with leather that had already been through its own sequence of workshops.

The replacement of parchment by paper, a Chinese innovation already known but only rarely used in Europe prior to the Mongol era, required more skill in one worker but far fewer steps and thus, in the overall process, less energy and labor. The papermaker cooked down shredded rags and other fibrous materials, dipped a frame into the vat to coat it with a layer of the fibers, treated it with chemicals, and dried it.

The increased demand for paper arose with the spread of printing. One of the most laborious tasks in medieval society had been the copying of manuscripts and documents, all of which had been done by hand in monasteries that functioned as book factories with scribes carefully copying all day in a large scriptorium. Aside from the cost of their meager food and basic upkeep, the labor was free and the money earned from the sale went to other uses within the church. Johannes Gutenberg completed the adaptation with his production of two hundred Bibles in 1455, and started the printing and information revolution in the West. The new technology made the relatively minor trade of book making into one of the most potent forces of public life. It stimulated the revival of Greek classics, the development of written forms of the vernacular languages, the growth of nationalism, the outbreak of the Protestant Reformation, the birth of science, and virtually every aspect of life and learning from agronomy to zoology.

The ideas of the Mongol Empire awakened new possibilities in the European mind. New knowledge from the travel writings of Marco Polo to the detailed star chats of Ulugh Beg proved that much of their received classical knowledge was simply wrong, and at the same time it opened up new paths of intellectual discovery. Because much of the Mongol Empire had been based on novel ideas and ways of organizing public life rather than on mere technology, these ideas provoked new thoughts and experiments in Europe. The common principles of the Mongol Empire—such as paper money, primacy of the state over the church, freedom of religion, diplomatic immunity, and international law—were ideas that gained new importance.

As early as 1620, the English scientist Francis Bacon recognized the impact that changing technology had produced in Europe. He designated printing, gunpowder, and the compass as three technological innovations on which the modern world was built. Although they were "unknown to the ancients . . . these three have changed the appearance and state of the whole world; first in literature, then in warfare, and lastly in navigation." More important than the innovations themselves, from them "innumerable changes have been thence derived." In a clear recognition of their importance he wrote "that no empire, sect, or star, appears to have exercised a greater power and influence on human affairs than these mechanical discoveries." All of them had been spread to the West during the era of the Mongol Empire.

Under the widespread influences from the paper and printing, gunpowder and firearms, and the spread of the navigational compass and other maritime equipment, Europeans experienced a Renaissance, literally a rebirth, but it was not the ancient world of Greece and Rome being reborn: It was the Mongol Empire, picked up, transferred, and adapted by the Europeans to their own needs and culture.

In May 1288, soon after meeting with Rabban Bar Sawma and receiving a letter and gifts from the Mongol court, Pope Nicholas IV issued a papal bull calling for construction of a new mother church at Assisi for his Franciscan order. As the first Franciscan pope, Nicholas IV, together with his fellow Franciscans, seemingly wanted to proclaim the coming of age of their order. For this project, they wanted imagery that not only proclaimed their new status but highlighted the accomplishments of the order. The Franciscans had the closest ties of any Europe group to the Mongol court. Among others, the monks in the delegation of Plano di Carpini, who had served as the first envoy to the Mongols at the time of Guyuk's election as Great Khan, and William of Rubruck, who visited in the time of Mongke Khan's installation, had all been Franciscans. The artists borrowed themes and techniques from the Chinese and Persian art brought in by the Mongols, quite possibly from the gifts brought by Rabban Bar Swama himself.

The paintings shared a common source in the work of Giotto di Bondone and his disciples, and they seem to radiate from a set of paintings in the Franciscan monastery at Assisi. Although the frescoes of the church depicted events from the life of Christ, more than a thousand years before the Mongol Empire, or the life of Saint Francis, only shortly before Mongol contact, the artists depicted many of their subjects as Mongols or used Mongol dress and cloth for them: "In the fresco cycle, Saint Francis's life is literally wrapped in silk—almost every scene depicts painted and figured textiles either defining the stories, or draped below in imaginary swaths." In addition to simple silks, they portray the elaborate brocades that the Mongols liked and sent to the pope and kings as gifts. The artists placed Mongols in a variety of Christian paintings with their distinctive clothing, headgear, and bows. Horses began to appear in the art in the style of Chinese drawings made popular through Mongol commerce. The pictures also showed a strong Asian influence in the depiction of rocky crags and trees. European art, which had been flat and unidimensional throughout the Middle Ages, produced a new hybrid that was neither strictly European nor strictly Asian; it was a style of depth, light, textiles, and horses that became later known as Renaissance art.

By themselves, the images probably represented no more than a new awareness by the artists of the variety of human faces in the world, but in a 1306 illustration of the Robe of Christ in Padua, the robe not only was made in the style and fabric of the Mongols, but the golden trim was painted in Mongol letters from the square Phagspa script commissioned by Khubilai Khan. In the same church, the Vice of Infidelity appeared as a woman wearing the pith helmet style hat favored by Khubilai Khan. Old Testament prophets were depicted holding scrolls open to long, but undecipherable, texts in Mongol script. The direct allusions to the writing and clothing from the court of Khubilai Khan showed an undeniable connection between Italian Renaissance art and the Mongol Empire.

In the same way that Mongol faces and script began to appear in the art of Renaissance Europe, the Mongol ideas also began to show up in the literary and philosophical works of the era. The provocative nature of Mongol ideas and policies appeared decisively in the work of the German cleric Nicolaus of Cusa, whose 1440 essay "On Learned Ignorance" might be considered as the opening of the European Renaissance. He had spent time on church business in Constantinople shortly before its fall to the Ottomans, and, as his subsequent writings revealed, he was well acquainted with the ideas of the Persian, Arab, and Mongol civilizations. In 1453, he wrote a long essay "On the Peace of Faith," in which he presented imaginary dialogues among representatives of seventeen nations and religions concerning the best way to promote global peace and understanding. The author shows some more than superficial awareness of Mongol religious ideology when he quotes the Tatar representative as describing his nation as "a numerous and simple people, who worship the one God above others, are astounded over the variety of rites which others have, who worship one and the same God with them. They deride the custom by which some Christians, all Arabs and Jews are circumcised, that others are marked on their brows with a brand, others are baptized." He also notes the Mongol puzzlement at Christian ritual and theology, in particular that "among these various forms of sacrifice there is the Christian sacrifice, in which they offer bread and wine, and say it is the body and blood of Christ. That they eat and drink this sacrifice after the oblations seems most abominable. They devour what they worship."

The fictional Tatar in the debate echoed precisely the words of Mongke Khan to the French envoy when he denounced the pernicious enmity among the religions of the world: "It is proper to keep the commandments of God. But the Jews say they have received these commandments from Moses, the Arabs say they have them from Muhammad, and the Christians from Jesus. And there are perhaps other nations who honor their prophets, through whose hands they assert they have received the divine precepts. Therefore, how shall we arrive at concord?" The Mongol answer had been that simple religious concord could only be produced by subsuming all religions under the power of the state.

The visit of Mongol envoys such as Rabban Bar Sawma furnished the Europeans with a far different view of the distant and exotic Mongols. No longer feeling a threat from the Mongols, Europeans began to see in Genghis Khan's empire an intriguing alternative to the society in which they lived. Whereas writers used the Muslims to represent everything that the Europeans despised, they saturated the Mongol story with romantic images of a much better world, which in some ways was considered a utopia, the ideal society. The imagery of Mongol greatness received its clearest statement around 1390 by Geoffrey Chaucer, who had traveled widely in France and Italy on diplomatic business and had a far more international perspective than many of the people for whom he wrote. In *The Canterbury Tales,* the first book written in English, the longest story relates a romantic and fanciful tale about the life and adventures of Genghis Khan.

> *This noble king was called Genghis Khan,*
> *Who in his time was of so great renown*
> *That there was nowhere in no region*
> *So excellent a lord in all things.*
> *He lacked nothing that belonged to a king.*
> *As of the sect of which he was born*
> *He kept his law, to which that he was sworn.*

And thereto he was hardy, wise, and rich,
And piteous and just, always liked;
Soothe of his word, benign, and honorable,
Of his courage as any center stable;
Young, fresh, and strong, in arms desirous
As any bachelor of all his house.
A fair person he was and fortunate,
And kept always so well royal estate
That there was nowhere such another man.
This noble king, this Tartar Genghis Khan.

10

─────✦─────

The Empire of Illusion

When Christopher Columbus set sail from Spain in 1492,
he was heading for Cathay, the land of the Great Khan.

DAVID MORGAN

I N 1332, CONFUSION, ALARM, and pain ran amok in the pleasure palaces of
Xanadu, the Mongol summer capital of Shangdu. The royal family
remained there well past the end of summer, and despite efforts to keep the
crisis secret, it became apparent that the Mongol rulers were in a turmoil so
deep that it threatened continuation of the dynasty. The surviving information offers muddled accounts of what was happening, but it appears that the
office of the Great Khan bounced from brother to brother and from father to
son in a flurry of assassinations, disappearances, and inexplicable deaths.
From 1328 to 1332, at least four members of the Golden Family occupied the
throne, and one, the seven-year-old Rinchinbal Khan, had it for only two
months in 1332. Fear gripped everyone. In the household, everyone from the
young to the old, from the lowest servant to the Great Khan, seemed in danger of dying a horrible death.

Nearly as much turmoil and confusion churned outside the capital as
inside, but it was neither foreign invaders nor rebels that threatened the society. The fear arose from something far more sinister and mysterious, but with

quite visible effects everywhere—the plague. A person could appear healthy in the morning, but suddenly break into hot fever that rapidly gave way to chills accompanied by both vomiting and diarrhea. The bodies of individuals who had only a short time earlier appeared active and robust suddenly and inexplicably broke down and began to dissolve before the horrified family observers. Blood began to ooze beneath the skin, which discolored the skin, lumps formed and oozed blood and pus in the groin. The lumps, subsequently called *buboes* from the Greek word for groin, then formed in the armpit and neck, and from them came the medical term for the disease: bubonic plague. When the lumps grew too large, they burst open. The lack of oxygen moving into the body and the dried blood beneath the skin made the person appear to turn black; from this dramatic symptom, the disease became known as the Black Death. After only a few agonizing days of tortured pain, the person usually died. In some victims, the disease attacked the lungs rather than the lymph nodes, and as the air in the lungs turned bloody and frothy, they drowned. As they died, they infected those around them by violent coughing, sneezing, and gasping.

According to the most plausible, but not completely verifiable, accounts, the disease originated in the south of China, and Mongol warriors brought it north with them. The plague bacterium lives in fleas, which traveled on rats transported in shipments of food or other tribute taken from the south. Although the fleas do not normally infect humans and the smell of horses repels them, they can live in sacks of grain, human clothing, and other places in the vicinity of humans while awaiting their chance to jump on them. Once the infected fleas arrived in the Gobi, they easily found hospitable new homes in marmot burrows and the extensive rodent colonies, where they have lived ever since. On the open steppe of Mongolia, the plague remained just as virulent, but it posed less danger in the sparsely inhabited environment. Even today, it kills a handful of victims every year in the summer, but the small population living among so many horses and the lack of fleas in the Mongol dwellings tend to keep the disease from becoming an epidemic. By contrast, in the densely inhabited urban areas of China, and later in other urban areas, the disease found its perfect environment in the rat populations that had lived in close proximity with humans for so long that no one suspected them as sources for the disease.

In 1331, chroniclers recorded that 90 percent of the people of Hopei Province died. By 1351, China had reportedly lost between one-half and two-thirds of its population to the plague. The country had included some 123 million inhabitants at the beginning of the thirteenth century, but by the end of the fourteenth century the population dropped to as low as 65 million.

China functioned as the manufacturing center of the Mongol World System, and as the goods poured out of China, the disease followed, seemingly spreading in all directions at once. Archaeological evidence of graves near trading posts indicates that by 1338 the plague crossed from China over the Tian Shan Mountains and wiped out a Christian trading community near lake Issyk Kul in Kyrgyzstan. The plague was an epidemic of commerce. The same Mongol roads and caravans that knitted together the Eurasian world of the thirteenth and fourteenth centuries moved more than mere silk and spices. The roads and way stations set up by the Mongols for merchants also served as the inadvertent transfer points for the fleas and, thereby, for the disease itself. With the luxurious fabrics, exotic flavors, and opulent jewels, the caravans brought the fleas that spread the plague from one camp to another, one village to another, one city to another, and one continent to another. If plague destroyed only a single, crucial station in a mountain pass or blocked one route through the desert, it potentially isolated a large region within the vast empire.

Plague reached the capital of the Golden Horde at Sarai on the lower Volga in 1345. At this time, Yanibeg, the Kipchak khan, was preparing to lay siege to the Crimean port of Kaffa (modern-day Feodosija in Ukraine), a trading post established by merchants from Genoa primarily for the export of Russian slaves to Egypt. The Mongols had sometimes cooperated with the Italian slave merchants and at other times tried to suppress their trade. The Mongol authorities had closed the trading post and expelled the Genovese on several occasions, but each time they would eventually relent and allow them to return. To protect themselves from further Mongol threats and to safeguard their transit in slaves, the Genoese built a strong protective wall around their city and a second inner wall to protect the heart of the trading post.

When plague broke out in the Mongol army, it forced Yanibeg to lift the siege and retreat, but the disease readily spread from the Mongol camp to the adjacent port. According to a single European report, Yanibeg had the bodies of plague victims catapulted over the walls and into the city, and though the Genovese tried to dispose of the bodies by throwing them in the sea, the disease erupted. Though often repeated, the story was not based on eyewitness accounts; the only known source for it comes from the papers of a lawyer, Gabriele de Mussis, who worked near Genoa in the town of Piacenza. He claimed, in turn, to have heard the story from some sailors. Since the dead bodies could not breathe on their intended targets and spread the disease in the common manner, they would have needed to carry living fleas to infect the city. The story seems doubtful, not because the Mongols were unwilling to spread the disease in that manner, but because it probably would not have been a strategy likely to succeed.

With or without human intention, the disease was already spreading and would continue to do so. When the Genovese and other refugees fled the port by boat, they took the disease with them to Constantinople, from where it easily spread to Cairo in Egypt and to Messina in Sicily. If the city was the ideal home for the plague, the closed environment of the ship was the ideal incubator, a place where humans, rats, and fleas could mix intimately without the noxious presence of horses or fire, the two things that fleas most avoid. Freed from the comparatively slow movement on the trading route, where the disease had to wait for precisely the right cart or cargo of goods, the plague spread with the speed of the wind in the sails. In 1348, it ravaged the cities of Italy, and by June of that year entered England. By the winter of 1350, the plague had crossed the North Atlantic from the Faeroe Islands on through Iceland and reached Greenland. It may have killed 60 percent of the settlers of Iceland, and the plague was probably the single most important factor in the final extinction of the struggling Viking colony in Greenland.

In the sixty years from 1340 until 1400, according to some estimates, the population of Africa declined from 80 million to 68 million inhabitants, and Asia from 238 million to 201 million. The total world population—including the Americas, where the plague did not strike for another two centuries—fell from approximately 450 million to between 350 and 375 million inhabitants, a net loss of at least 75 million, or more than a million people a year for the remainder of the fourteenth century. As more evidence accumulates, scholarly research continues to push the losses higher. The population of Europe declined from around 75 million to 52 million. With a death toll of around 25 million the loss in the European continent alone was roughly the same as the total worldwide toll of AIDS in the twentieth century. For Europe in the fourteenth century, however, the figure represented between a third and one-half of the total population. By comparison, in the tremendous destruction of World War II in Europe, Great Britain lost less than 1 percent of its population, and France, the scene of much fighting, lost 1.5 percent of its population. German losses reached 9.1 percent. Widespread famine pushed the World War II death rates in Poland and Ukraine toward 19 percent, but even these remained well below the rates for the plague in the fourteenth century.

The plague left some areas completely depopulated, while a few cities survived virtually unscathed. One of the few effective measures was taken by the city of Milan. As soon as plague broke out in a house, officials raced to seal up the entire house with everyone—sick and well, friends and servants—sealed inside. Other cities tried less effective means, such as the ringing of bells or the banning of the ringing of bells. Whether it erupted in a particular community or not, the epidemic permanently changed life in every region of the continent. The plague effectively destroyed the social order that had dominated Europe since the fall of Rome, leaving the continent in dangerous disorder. The disease brought down urban dwellers more readily and thereby destroyed the educated class and the skilled craftsmen. Inside and outside the cities, the closed and polluted environments of monasteries and convents provided an ideal opportunity for the disease to kill everyone, a tragedy from which European monasticism in particular, and the Roman Catholic church in general, never recovered. Dense villages faced a similar danger, as did the residents cooped up inside castles and manorial estates.

The social impact of the plague was best recorded in Florence, where it erupted in 1348, in the writings of Giovanni Boccaccio, one of many to lose numerous family members and close friends. In his *Decameron,* ten young noble ladies and ten men flee the plague and find refuge in a country estate, passing the time by telling tales. In the world described by Boccaccio, husband deserted wife, mother abandoned child just to escape the plague. So many died that priests had no time to offer services and diggers could not accommodate the bodies, which were then tossed into group graves or left for dogs and pigs to eat. The "venerable authority of laws, human and divine, was abased and all but totally dissolved." Officials were "unable to execute any office; whereby every man was free to do what was right in his own eyes."

Without understanding the disease's true cause or methods of transmission, people still quickly recognized its close association with commerce and the movement of people in and out of cities. The writings of Boccaccio, Petrarch, and others of the time show the two primary reactions to the disease were to abandon the city, if possible, or at least to close the city to outsiders. Either response immediately halted trade, communication, and transportation. Local authorities throughout Europe enacted plague laws to limit its spread and control popular reaction. In 1348, the small city of Pistoia in Tuscany barred entry of people from infected areas, banned the importation of any type of used textiles, and forbade the sale of fruit or the slaughtering of animals that might cause the smell of death, which they suspected as contributing to the spread of the disease. Similarly, they forbade the tanning trade, and without it the commerce in leather goods ceased. Citizens returning from other places could only bring a small amount of baggage equivalent to about thirty pounds. No one could send a gift to the home of a person who had died of the plague or go there to visit, and no one was allowed to buy new clothing.

Diplomatic delegations and letters ceased to flow. Without the Mongol transportation system, the Catholic church lost touch with its missions in China. Frightened people everywhere blamed foreigners for bringing the disease, further threatening international commerce. In Europe, the Christians once again turned on the Jews, who had a close association with commerce and with the east, from whence the plague came. Some Jews were shut up in their homes and burned; others were taken out and tortured on the rack until they confessed their crimes. Despite a papal bull from Pope Clement VI in July 1348 protecting the Jews and ordering the Christians to stop their persecutions, the campaign against them escalated. On Valentine's Day in 1349, the authorities of Strasbourg herded two thousand Jews to the

Jewish cemetery outside of the city to begin a mass burning. Some Jews were allowed to save themselves by confessing their crimes and converting to Christianity, and some children were forcefully converted. More than a thousand perished over the six days that it took to burn them all, and the city outlawed the presence of any Jew in the city. City after city picked up the practice of publicly burning Jews to thwart the epidemic. According to the boasts of one chronicler, between November 1348 and September 1349, all the Jews between Cologne and Austria had been burned. In the Christian parts of Spain, the people initiated similar persecutions against the resident Muslim minority, driving many of them to seek refuge in Granada and Morocco.

The plague not only isolated Europe, but it also cut off the Mongols in Persia and Russia from China and Mongolia. The Mongol rulers in Persia could no longer procure the goods from the lands and workshops they owned in China. The Golden Family in China could not get its goods from Russia or Persia. With each group cut off from the other, the interlocking system of ownership collapsed. The plague had devastated the country, demoralized the living, and, by cutting off trade and tribute, deprived the Mongol Golden Family of its primary source of support. For nearly a century, the Mongols had exploited their mutual material interests to overcome the political fault lines dividing them. Even while sacrificing political unity, they had maintained a unified cultural and commercial empire. With the onslaught of plague, the center could not hold, and the complex system collapsed. The Mongol Empire depended on the quick and constant movement of people, goods, and information throughout its massive empire. Without those connections, there was no empire.

As foreign conquerors, the Mongols had been tolerated by their subjects, who often outnumbered the Mongols by as much as a thousand to one, because they continued to produce a tremendous flow of trade goods long after the strength of their army had dissipated. In the plague's aftermath, with neither trade nor the likelihood of military reinforcement from other Mongols, each branch of the Golden Family of Genghis Khan had to fend for itself in an increasingly volatile environment that might easily turn hostile. Deprived of their two advantages of military strength and commercial lucre, the Mongols in Russia, central Asia, Persia, and the Middle East searched for new modes of power and legitimacy by intermarrying with their subjects and consciously becoming more like them in language, religion, and culture. Mongol authorities purged the remaining elements of shamanism, Buddhism, and Christianity from their families and strengthened their commitment to Islam, which was the primary religion of their subjects, or, in the case of the Golden Horde in Russia, the religion of the Turkic army that helped keep the family in power.

As the different members of the Mongol royal family aligned themselves with particular religious factions within their subject populations, the rifts between the royal lineages increased. When the Golden Horde in Russia became Muslim, before their cousins in Iraq and Iran converted, they allied themselves with Egypt against the Mongol Ilkhanate. Then, when the Mongol rulers of the Ilkhanate converted to Islam, they moved back and forth between Sunni and Shiite versions as it suited the political moment. During the reign of Oljeitu, the most committed of the Shiites, a severe persecution of minority groups such as Buddhists and Jews was unleashed. The universal principles of Genghis Khan's empire disappeared like ashes in the wind.

By becoming Muslims, the Mongols in the Middle East seemed to have been following the example of Khubilai Khan, who had made himself powerful in China by appearing to be Chinese. Yet Khubilai Khan's successors in China failed to follow, or probably even to understand, the cunning genius of his method. Rather than becoming more Chinese, the Mongol authorities increased repression and isolated themselves. During this chaotic time, some Mongol members of the royal court reported dreams in which Genghis Khan appeared to demand a variety of stringent new measures to further repress the Chinese. Officials in the court decided that they had allotted the Chinese too much freedom and that the Mongols had allowed themselves to become too acculturated to Chinese life. Rather than further integrating into Chinese culture, they intensified their foreign identity and further separated themselves from Chinese language, religion, culture, and intermarriage. In the mounting paranoia, Mongol authorities ordered the confiscation not only of all weapons from the Chinese people, but their iron agricultural tools as well, and limited the use of knives. They forbade the Chinese to use horses, and in fear of secret messages being passed, they stopped performances of Chinese opera and the traditional storytelling and other public and private gatherings. In the face of such extreme measures, the Chinese subjects, in turn, became increasingly discontented and still more mistrustful and fearful of their Mongol rulers. Rumors circulated regarding the mass extermination of Chinese children by the Mongols or of plans to kill everyone bearing specific Chinese family names.

In their new effort to be as un-Chinese as possible, the Mongols dropped the traditional evenhanded approach to diverse religion and granted ever more favor and power to Buddhism, particularly to its Tibetan variation, which contrasted most strongly with the Confucian ideals of the Chinese. Unable to criticize their Mongol rulers directly, the Chinese people turned much of their hatred toward the foreigners who helped the Mongols administer their empire. The Tibetan Buddhist monks in particular became the object of hatred, since local people along the newly opened Mongol route to Tibet carried the obligation not merely of feeding, housing, and transporting the monks, but of carrying their goods for them as well. The monks, often armed, acquired a terrible reputation for abusing people who served them. The Bureau of Buddhist and Tibetan Affairs strongly defended the monks at court and imposed a host of special rights for them. At one point the bureau tried to enforce laws that stipulated that anyone who hit a monk would have his hand cut off, or that anyone who insulted or defamed a monk, if convicted, could have his tongue cut out. The Mongol officials eventually overturned these laws as incompatible with Mongol rule, which forbade the use of body mutilation as a punishment.

Increasingly isolated from their subjects and unable to take effective action against the progress of the plague, the Mongol khans of China took refuge in the spirituality of the Tibetan monks, who encouraged them to turn away from the outside world of illusory problems of society and to perform acts that would help their own individual soul. The monks persuaded the Mongol royal family that each deed of freeing a prisoner would gain them spiritual merit for an improved station in their next life, and monks soon turned the process into a thriving business. In one of the bizarre ceremonies, a monk at the court rode through the palace gates on a yellow ox while wearing the gown of the Mongol Empress, and then he released the prisoners the way one might release a cage of birds.

The Tibetan clergy encouraged new forms of religious practice in their

Tantric rites that proclaimed the path of enlightenment via sexual acts. This movement not only produced a vigorous display of sexual art, but it also encouraged the royal family to engage in elaborate sexual dances and rituals that centered on the eager participation of the Great Khan himself under the watchful eye of the lamas. The rumors of debauchery and the secrecy of the rituals increased paranoia and distrust among the Chinese, who suspected the Tibetan lamas of practicing human sacrifices at court to prolong the life of the khan and to preserve his faltering regime.

While the Mongol rulers of China concentrated on expressing their spirituality and sexuality, the society out beyond the walls of their Forbidden City in the capital collapsed. In perhaps the most telling symptom, Mongol authorities lost control of the monetary system they had so laboriously and meticulously created. The principles by which the economy utilized paper currency had proven more complex and unpredictable than realized by the officials, and the system gradually spiraled out of control. At the least sign of weakness in the Mongol administration, confidence in the paper currency dropped and caused it to fall in value while pushing up the value of copper and silver. Inflation grew so fiercely that by 1356 the paper currency had effectively become worthless.

In Persia and China, the collapse came quickly—in 1335 and 1368, respectively. The Mongols of the Persian Ilkhanate disappeared, either killed or absorbed into the much larger population of their former subjects. In China, the Great Khan Togoon Tumur and some sixty thousand Mongols managed to escape the Ming rebels, but they left behind approximately four hundred thousand who were captured and killed or absorbed by the Chinese. Those that managed to return to Mongolia resumed their nomadic way of pastoralism, almost as if the entire Chinese episode from 1211 until 1368 had been merely an extended stay at their southern summer camp. The Golden Horde of Russia broke into smaller hordes that declined steadily in power through four long centuries. During such an extended interaction, the Mongols and their Turkic allies amalgamated with each other into several different ethnic groups of Turco-Mongols that maintained a separate identity from one another as well as from the larger Slavic society.

After the overthrow of Mongol rule, the triumphant Ming rulers issued edicts forbidding the Chinese from wearing Mongol dress, giving their children Mongol names, and following other foreign habits. In an effort to revitalize the Chinese principles of government and social life, the Ming rulers systematically rejected many of the Mongol policies and institutions. They expelled the Muslim, Christian, and Jewish traders whom the Mongols had encouraged to settle in China, and in a major blow to the commercial system of the Mongols, Ming authorities abolished the failing paper money entirely and returned to metal. They rejected the Tibetan Lamaist Buddhism that the Mongols had sponsored, and replaced it with traditional Taoist and Confucian thought and traditions. After an abortive effort to revitalize the Mongol trade system, the new rulers burned their ocean vessels, banned foreign travel for Chinese, and spent a large portion of the gross national product on building massive new walls to lock foreigners out and the Chinese in. In so doing, the new Chinese authorities stranded thousands of their citizens living in the ports of Southeast Asia.

In the effort to remove themselves from the danger of a new Mongol invasion, the Ming initially moved the capital south to Nanjing, a more Chinese venue, but in the attitudes and actions of the majority of people, the rule of unified China was so closely associated with their northern capital that the Ming had to return their court to the old Mongol capital of Khanbalik. The Ming sought to remake the city, remove the Mongol appearance, and build a new Forbidden City in their own style. With short exceptions, the capital has remained there with changing names, and Beijing still serves as capital for China, which occupies roughly the same national borders that it did under the Mongols.

In one country after another, indigenous rebellions expelled the Mongols and local elites took the reins of government. While Korea, Russia, and China returned to the hands of native dynasties, the Muslim territories experienced a more complex transition from Mongol rule. Instead of returning to the control of Arabs who had been the traders, the intermediaries, the bankers, the shippers, and the caravan drivers who connected Asia and Europe, a new cultural hybrid emerged that combined a Turco-Mongol military system with the legal institutions of Islam and the ancient cultural traditions of Persia. The eastern part of the Muslim world had found a new cultural freedom in which they could still be Muslims but without the domination of Arabs, whom they never allowed to regain power. New dynasties, such as the Ottoman of Turkey, the Safavid of Persia, and the Moghul of India, sometimes called Gunpowder Empires, relied primarily on the vast innovations in Mongol weaponry, a military organization based on both a cavalry and an armed infantry, and the use of firearms, to fight foreign enemies and, perhaps more important, to maintain domestic power over their ethnically varied subjects.

Despite the plague and collapse of the commercial system, revolts, and the subsequent dismemberment of the Mongol Empire, even the rebels seemed reluctant to let the old empire go completely. The new rulers hung on to the trappings and illusions of the old system to legitimize their own new rule. The facade of the Mongol Empire continued standing long after the internal structure had collapsed and the Mongols were all gone.

Following their purge of Mongol influence in public life, the Ming rulers went to great effort searching for the official seal of the Mongols, and they preserved the use of the Mongol language in diplomacy as a way of maintaining continuity with the past. As late as the Ottoman conquest of Constantinople in 1453, the Chinese court sent its letters in the Mongol language. In turn, the Manchu, who overthrew the Ming in 1644, strategically intermarried with the descendants of Genghis Khan so that they could claim legitimacy as his heirs in blood as well as in spirit.

At the heart of central Asia, the descendants of Genghis Khan continued in power in the area known as Moghulistan, the Persian name for the Mongol territory. By the end of the fourteenth century, the Mongol holdings in central Asia had fallen under the control of Timur, also known as Timur the Lame or Tamerlane, a Turkic warrior who claimed, with flimsy evidence, descent from Genghis Khan. He sought to revive the Mongol Empire, and he conquered much of its former territory from India to the Mediterranean. In an effort to closely associate himself with Genghis Khan, Timur sponsored a variety of books that linked them. To ensure that his lineage would acquire the blood of Genghis Khan and the Mongols, his family intermarried with some of Genghis Khan's true descendants. Despite all that Emir Timur sought to do in restoring the Mongol Empire, he did not follow the ways of Genghis Khan. He slaughtered without reason and seemed to find a perverse but persistent pleasure in torturing and humiliating his prisoners. When he seized the sultan of the Seljuk kingdom of Turkey, he forced him to watch as his wives and daughters served Timur naked at dinner and, in some reports, satisfied his sexual demands. It was said that Timur harnessed the sultan like an animal and made him pull the royal chariot, and then exhibited him in a cage.

Because Timur claimed to be a Mongol, and was legitimately a son-in-law to the dynasty of Genghis Khan, his deeds became inextricably intertwined with those of the original Mongols in the minds of the people who had been conquered by both. One Mongol was hard to distinguish from another. When Timur delighted in public torture or piled up pyramids of heads outside his conquered cities, it was assumed that he was carrying on the traditions of his Mongol people. The practices of Timur were anachronistically assigned back to Genghis Khan.

The descendants of Timur became known in history as the Moghuls of India. Babur, the founder of the new dynasty in 1519, was thirteen generations descended from Genghis Khan's second son, Chaghatai. The Moghul Empire reached its zenith under Babur's grandson Akbar, who ruled from 1556 until 1608. He had Genghis Khan's genius for administration as well as his appreciation of trade. He abolished the hated *jizya* tax, the tax on non-Muslims. Akbar organized his cavalry along the traditional Mongol units of ten (up to five thousand) and instituted a civil service based on merit. Just as the Mongols made China into the most productive manufacturing and trading center of their era, the Moghuls made India into the world's greatest manufacturing and trading nation and—contrary to both Muslim and Hindu traditions—raised the status of women. He continued the universalist attitude toward religion and tried to amalgamate all religion into one Divine Faith, Din-i-Illah, with one God in Heaven and one emperor on earth.

With so many empires striving to maintain the illusion of the Mongol Empire in everything from politics to art, public opinion seemed obstinately unwilling to believe that it no longer existed. Nowhere was the belief in the empire longer lasting or more important than in Europe, where, in 1492, more than a century after the last khan ruled over China, Christopher

Columbus convinced the monarchs Isabella and Ferdinand that he could reestablish sea contact and revive the lost commerce with the Mongol court of the Great Khan. With the breakup of the Mongol communication system, the Europeans had not heard about the fall of the empire and the overthrow of the Great Khan. Columbus, therefore, insisted that although the Muslims barred the land route from Europe to the Mongol court, he could sail west from Europe across the World Ocean and arrive in the land described by Marco Polo.

Columbus embarked on his voyage to find the Mongols while carrying with him a printed copy of Marco Polo's travels, into which he had jotted copious notes and observations for his planned arrival at their court. For Columbus, Marco Polo was not merely an inspiration but also a practical guide. When he reached Cuba after visiting several smaller islands, Columbus believed that he was on the edge of the Great Khan's realm and would soon find the Mongol kingdom of Cathay. Columbus remained convinced that the lands of the khan lay only a little farther to the north within what we today recognize as the mainland of the United States. Since he had not found the land of the Great Khan of the Mongols, he decided that the people he met must be the southern neighbors of the Mongols in India, and thus Columbus called the native people of the Americas *Indians,* the name by which they have been known ever since.

Whereas the Renaissance writers and explorers treated Genghis Khan and the Mongols with open adulation, the eighteenth-century Enlightenment in Europe produced a growing anti-Asian spirit that often focused on the Mongols, in particular, as the symbol of everything evil or defective in that massive continent. As early as 1748, the French philosopher Montesquieu set the tone in his treatise *The Spirit of the Laws,* holding the Asians in haughty contempt and blaming much of their detestable qualities on the Mongols, whom he labeled "the most singular people on earth." He described them as both servile slaves and cruel masters. He attributed to them all the major attacks on civilization from ancient Greece to Persia: "They have destroyed Asia, from India even to the Mediterranean; and all the country which forms the east of Persia they have rendered a desert." Montesquieu glorified the tribal origins of Europeans as the harbingers of democracy while he condemned the tribal people of Asia: "The Tartars who destroyed the Grecian Empire established in the conquered countries slavery and despotic power: the Goths, after subduing the Roman Empire, founded monarchy and liberty." Based on this history, he summarily dismissed all of Asian civilization: "There reigns in Asia a servile spirit, which they have never been able to shake off, and it is impossible to find in all the histories of that country a single passage which discovers a freedom of spirit; we shall never see anything there but the excess of slavery."

Genghis Khan became the central figure of attack. Voltaire adapted a Mongol dynasty play, *The Orphan of Chao,* by Chi Chün-hsiang, to fit his personal political and social agenda by portraying Genghis Khan, whom Voltaire used as a substitute for the French king, as an ignorant and cruel villain. *The Orphan of China,* as he renamed it, debuted on the Paris stage in 1755 while Voltaire enjoyed a safe exile in Switzerland. "I have confined my plan to the grand epoch of Genghis Khan," he explained. "I have endeavored to describe the manners of the Tartars and Chinese: the most interesting events are nothing when they do not paint the manners; and this painting, which is one of the greatest secrets of the art, is no more than an idle amusement, when it does not tend to inspire notions of honor and virtue." Voltaire described Genghis Khan as "The king of kings, the fiery Genghis Khan/Who lays the fertile fields of Asia waste." He called him "a wild Scythian soldier bred to arms/And practiced in the trade of blood." In Voltaire's revisionist history, the Mongol warriors were no more than the "wild sons of rapine, who live in tents, in chariots, and in fields." They "detest our arts, our customs, and our laws; and therefore mean to change them all; to make this splendid seat of empire one vast desert, like their own."

Genghis Khan's only redeeming quality, in Voltaire's play, was that he reluctantly recognized the moral superiority of the better educated. "The more I see," Voltaire quoted Genghis Khan as saying, "the more I must admire this wondrous people, great in arts and arms, in learning and in manners great; their kings on wisdom's basis founded all their power." Genghis Khan ended the play with a question: ". . . what have I gained by all my victories, by all my guilty laurels stained with blood?" To which Voltaire answered: ". . . the tears, the sighs, the curses of mankind." With these words, Voltaire himself began the modern cursing of the Mongols.

Despite all the negative images of Genghis Khan, Voltaire's real target was the French king, whom he was too afraid to criticize directly. Instead, he projected his France, with the Mongols representing all that was wicked. Other writers quickly copied the method of holding up the Mongols as symbols for world evils, and the Mongols became the victims of an extended literary and scientific assault. The new critique appeared obliquely in the work of Italian poet and playwright Giovanni Casti, who spent much time in the Hapsburg court and later in the court of Catherine the Great of Russia. Unwilling to openly criticize the monarchs who supported him, he used the image of the Mongols as his foil in *Poema Tartaro* and in the 1778 opera *Kublai, the Great Khan of the Tartars,* for which Antonio Salieri, the rival of Wolfgang Mozart at the Hapsburg court, composed the music. Recognizing the potentially dangerous ideas in the play, the Holy Roman Emperor suppressed the opera in fear that it might encourage revolutionaries.

The most pernicious rationale for Asian inferiority did not emerge from the philosophers and artists in Europe, however, as much as from the scientists, the new breed of intellectuals spawned by the Enlightenment. In the mid-eighteenth century, the French naturalist, the Compte de Buffon, compiled the first encyclopedia of natural history in which he offered a scientific description of the main human groups, of which the Mongol ranked as the most important in Asia. His descriptions seemed like a return to the hysterical writings of Matthew Paris and Thomas of Spalato, more than five hundred years earlier. "The *lips* are large and thick, with transverse fissures," Buffon wrote. "The *tongue* is long, thick, and is much roughened. The *nose* is small. The *skin* has a slight dirty-yellow tinge, and is deficient in elasticity, giving the appearance of being too large for the body." He proclaimed the Tartar women "as deformed as the men." Their culture seemed as ugly to him as their faces: "The majority of these tribes are alike strangers to religion, morality, and decency. They are robbers by profession." Translated from French into all the major European languages, his work became one of the classic sources of information during the eighteenth and nineteenth centuries.

European scientists sought to classify everything from the breeds of dogs and horses to the types of roses and dandelions. German zoologist Johann Friedrich Blumenbach, a professor of medicine at Göttingen University from 1776 until 1835, created zoological classifications for human beings based on comparative anatomy, particularly on skin pigmentation, hair and eye color, skull type, and facial features such as size and form of the nose, cheeks, and lips. According to his study, humans divided naturally into three primary races corresponding to Africa, Asia, and Europe, and to two less important subcategories of American and Malay. On the theory that Asians originated in Mongolia, he classified all of them under the rubric *Mongols.* European scientists rapidly accepted his theory, making it scientific gospel.

The categories, of course, also implied an evolutionary ranking of the different races as articulated by Scottish scientist Robert Chambers in his best-selling book of 1844, *Vestiges of the Natural History of Creation.* "The leading characters," he explained, "of the various races of mankind, are simply representatives of particular stages in the development of the highest or Caucasian type." By comparison to the white race, the "Mongolian is an arrested infant newly born."

Soon it became clear to these theorists that the Mongoloid race exhibited a close relationship to the orangutan, the Asian ape. The similarity showed not only in facial traits but in postures. Asians, like orangutans, sat with folded legs in the "Mongolian" or "Buddha" position. The category of Mongoloid expanded steadily to include all American Indians and Eskimos, as well as "the northern Chinese, the southern Chinese, the Tibetans, the tribal peoples of southern China, the Mongols, some of the Turks, and the Tungus, Koreans, Japanese, and Paleo-Asiatic peoples."

Once in place and widely accepted in Western science, the system of Mongoloid classification inspired new applications. Based on the physical description of some retarded children as marked by Asian facial features, it became apparent to the scientists of the era that they must also belong to the Mongoloid race. The first recorded link between retarded children and the "Mongoloid race" occurred in the 1844 study by Robert Chambers, who associated the malady with incest: "Parents too nearly related tend to produce offspring of the Mongolian type—that is, persons who in maturity still are a kind of children." In 1867, Dr. John Langdon Haydon Down, Medical Superintendent of the Earlswood Asylum for Idiots in Surrey, England, formalized the new system of categories in "Observations on the Ethnic Classification of Idiots" in the British *Journal of Mental Science.* In addition to incest and other forms of deviant behavior posited as the cause of the Mongoloid condition, medical doctors also suggested dietary deficiencies, maternal anxiety, excessive use of perfume, paternal alcoholism, and two-headed sperm.

In the search for a more directly historical explanation for why these children bore Asian physical characteristics, scientists found a precise biological connection by looking back at the Mongol invasions of Europe in the thirteenth century. According to their new explanation, through the ages, marauding tribes of Huns, Avars, and Mongols had left their genetic impact on Europe when they supposedly raped the white women. The descendants of these genes occasionally erupted in the modern era, when apparently "normal" European women gave birth to a child that was a throwback to the Mongols. Dr. Down's son refined his father's theory by revealing that in his research as a medical doctor, he found that these imbeciles derived from an earlier form of the Mongol stock and should be considered more "pre-human, rather than human."

In a popular 1924 book, *The Mongol in Our Midst,* British physician Francis G. Crookshank easily moved back and forth between Mongoloids as a race and as a mental category in what he delineated as the "Mongolian stigmata," including small earlobes, protruding anuses, and small genitals among both males and females. The obvious conclusion of this linking of retarded children with another race was that these children do not belong in the communities, or even the families, into which they were born. As Crookshank explained, these individuals "are a race apart. For better or for worse, they are not *quite* as are other men and women around them. They are indeed 'Mongol expatriates.' " Because these children belonged to a different race from the parents, so doctors and officials reasoned, they should be removed. The retarded child was only the extreme example of a wider occurring phenomenon of "Atavistic Mongolism (or Orangism)." According to this theory, the Occidental Mongols bore responsibility not merely for retardation but for much of the crime and feeblemindedness found in the West. According to this theory, Jews, in particular, sustained much of the Mongol influence because they had interbred with Khazars and other steppe tribes, and then brought that degraded genetic influence with them throughout Europe.

In evolutionary theories of race and retardation, the scientific community supplied hard and supposedly dispassionate evidence of what political demagogues and newspaper editors of the nineteenth and early twentieth centuries called the Yellow Peril. Because many East Asian nations proved reluctant to accept Western colonization, the colonial Europeans heaped increasing invectives on them. Although the fear of the Yellow Peril applied to any group such as Filipinos and Koreans, it focused on the two major dangers of China and Japan. As Japan industrialized and built a large army, and as China continued to rebuff colonization or coerced conversion to Christianity, the Asians became enemies in the public perceptions of the West.

Throughout the nineteenth century, fear of Asians mounted in Europe; it can be clearly seen in a poem that Russian symbolist poet Vladimir Sergeevich Soloviev wrote in 1894, entitled simply "Pan Mongolism." The threat of China and Japan to the values of modern civilization were, in his eyes comparable to the era of Genghis Khan when "from the East an unknown and alien people" attacked and destroyed civilization. The same thing was happening again today: "A swarm of waking tribes prepares for new attacks. From the Altai to Malaysian shores/the leaders of Eastern isles/have gathered a host of regiments/by China's defeated walls./Countless as locusts/and as ravenous,/shielded by an unearthly power/the tribes move north." Soon "your tattered banners" will be "passed like toys among yellow children," he warns his readers. "Pan Mongolism! The name is monstrous."

In the intervening years since the Renaissance and the Mongol Empire, Genghis Khan had been degraded to the lowest level of human history. In its newfound colonial power and its self-imposed mission to rule the world, modern Europe had no room for Asian conquerors. Christian colonialists and Communist commissars alike sought to rescue the Asians from the horrible legacy of barbarian dictatorship and bloodthirsty savagery imposed upon them by Genghis Khan and his Mongol hordes. The focus on the Mongols as the source of Asian problems, and therefore the rationale for European conquest of them from Japan to India, developed as an integral theme in the ideology of European conquest and colonization. The supposed horrors of Genghis Khan and the Mongols became part of the excuse for rule by the more civilized English, Russian, and French colonialists.

In direct opposition to the European scientists and politicians, the victims of this ideology, Asian intellectuals and activists, found a new hero in Genghis Khan. Across Asia, from India to Japan, the new generation of twentieth-century Asians, wishing to free themselves from European domination, found inspiration in Genghis Khan and the Mongols as the greatest Asian conquerors in history and a vivid counter to the doctrines of European superiority. In part because the Europeans, including the Russians, had so vehemently attacked and thoroughly discredited the memory of Genghis Khan and his role in world history, an increasingly large cadre of Asian political activists turned to his memory for guidance and as a way to rebuke the powers and values of the West.

One of the first to reevaluate Genghis Khan was an unlikely candidate: peace advocate Jawaharlal Nehru, the father of Indian independence. As he sat isolated in a prison cell on New Year's Day, 1931, he received word that British colonial authorities had just arrested his wife and incarcerated her in another prison, and that according to the newspapers, she had been mistreated. Knowing that their thirteen-year-old daughter Indira, who would herself grow up to become the prime minister of India, would be quite afraid and depressed, particularly since she could see her parents only once in two weeks, Nehru began writing a series of long letters to explain history to her as an antidote to what she had learned in colonial schools. Over the next three years, he wrote these letters of four or five pages almost daily; in them, he attempted, despite his Western education, to understand the place of his country of India and his continent of Asia in world history. It was his way to "dream of the past, and find our way to make the future greater than the past." As he wrote to her in the first letter, "It would be foolish not to recognize the greatness of Europe. But it would be equally foolish to forget the greatness of Asia."

One of his intellectual tasks as an Asian man and scholar was struggling to understand the historical role of Genghis Khan, whom the West had used in building its harsh images of Asia. By contrast, Nehru depicted Genghis Khan as a part of an ancient struggle of Asian people against European domination. In reference to the sudden appearance of the Mongols on the world scene, he wrote that "one can well imagine what the amazement of the Eurasian world must have been at this volcanic eruption. It almost seemed like a great natural calamity, like an earthquake, before which man can do little. Strong men and women they were, these nomads from Mongolia, used to hardship and living in tents on the wide steppes of northern Asia. But their strength and hard training might not have availed them much if they had not produced a chief who was a most remarkable man." Nehru then described Genghis Khan as "a cautious and careful middle-aged man, and every big thing he did was preceded by thought and preparation."

Nehru realized that although the Mongols did not live in cities, they nevertheless had created a remarkable civilization. "They did not know, of course, many of the city arts, but they had developed a way of life suitable to their world, and they created an intricate organization." Nehru recognized that though they were small in numbers they "won great victories on the field of battle" because "of their discipline and organization. And above all it was due to the brilliant captainship of Chengiz." Echoing the description of Chaucer, Nehru concluded that "Chengiz is, without doubt, the greatest military genius and leader in history." In direct comparison with the greatest European conquerors, he wrote, "Alexander and Caesar seem petty before him." Yet despite all the military prowess, he wanted friendly relations with the world: "His idea was to combine civilization with nomadic life. But this was not, and is not, possible." The Mongol Khan believed in "the *unchangeable law* for ever and ever, and no one could disobey it. Even the emperor was subject to it." Nehru then offered a personal insight: "I have given you more details and information about Chengiz Khan than was perhaps necessary. But the man fascinates me."

As the West's fear of the Yellow Peril grew, Asians increasingly examined the concept of Pan Mongolism as a viable path to creating a common identity for themselves. If they could all unite the way the Mongol Empire had once been, then together they could much better fight off the growing power of the Western nations. The theory offered a way for the Asians to transcend nationalist loyalties and work together in their shared quest. In Inner Mongolia, the new spirit led to the temporary creation of a calendar based on the year 1206, when Genghis Khan created the Mongol nation, as

Year 1. Under the new Mongol calendar, 1937 became the Genghis Khan Year 731.

Particularly in Japan, which increasingly saw itself as the leader of Asia in the first half of the twentieth century but also needed to distinguish itself from Europe, Pan Mongolism exerted an increasing allure. In the scramble to become the leader of the new Asia, the image of Genghis Khan became a valuable prize. Whoever could claim control of his body, his shrine, or his homeland had a stronger claim for control over his heritage and therefore over the lands he had once ruled. Some Japanese scholars circulated the story that Genghis Khan had actually been a samurai warrior who had fled his homeland after a power struggle and found refuge among the steppe nomads, whom he then led on a conquest of the world.

In the years leading up to World War II, Genghis Khan ironically took on a new importance as a topic not only of propaganda and ideology, but also of practical military application. The Soviets, the Japanese, and the Germans all pushed to decipher, translate, and interpret the newly available *Secret History* in the hope that it might provide a useful key to unlocking the Mongol military tactics that allowed them to prevail over China and Russia.

The twentieth-century development of the tank allowed cavalry and artillery to again be combined in one military unit in a way that had not been practical since the Mongol mounted archers. The military minds of all countries looked to these earlier Mongol models for clues of how to fight in the modern era of tank warfare. The Germans found the most effective application in their strategy of the blitzkrieg, which followed the Mongol's sudden appearance with a highly mobile army that raced across the landscape and kept the enemy surprised and disoriented. In their effort to more precisely understand the Mongol tactics, they began a translation of the *Secret History* into German. Erich Haenisch, professor of sociology at the Friedrich Wilhelm University in Berlin, prepared a German translation. Haenisch traveled to Mongolia to search for an original Mongol-language version of the *Secret History*, but he failed to find it. From the Chinese-Mongol text, he managed to make his translation and dictionary. War shortages in Germany delayed the printing until 1941, when a small edition was printed; but even then, difficulties in transportation delayed distribution.

The boxes of books remained in Leipzig until 1943, when they went up in flames during an Allied bombing raid. The secrets of the history remained secret from the Nazis.

While the German military pursued its studies of the Mongols, the Soviets had been doing the same. In Stalin's obsession to understand the two Asian conquerors, Genghis Khan and Timur, he had the body of Timur exhumed, and he sent several unsuccessful military expeditions to the area of Burkhan Khaldun to find the body of Genghis Khan as well. Other scholars busied themselves with translations and some highly eccentric interpretations of Mongol history, such as the angle and power of the sun striking the earth in Mongolia being different than in other parts of the world. From the mixture of the absurd and the serious, the Soviets followed their own version of Mongol strategy in World War II. In a large-scale adaptation of the tactics Subodei used to defeat the Russians at the Kalka River in 1223, the Soviets lured the Germans ever deeper into Russia until they were hopelessly spread out over a large area, and then the Russians began to counterattack and pick them off one by one.

Virtually unnoticed in 1944 during the final bellowing paroxysms of World War II, Sayid Alim Khan, the former emir of Bukhara and the last reigning descendant of Genghis Khan, died in Kabul, Afghanistan, after nearly a quarter of a century in exile from the city he had ruled as a young man. The emir, who claimed descent through Jochi and the Golden Horde, had outlasted other branches of the family. In 1857, the British army removed the last Moghul emperor of India, Bahadur Shah II, and in the following year sent him off to exile in Burma in order that they might bestow his title on Queen Victoria, who became Empress of India in 1877.

When Alim Khan of the Manghit dynasty assumed power as emir of Bukhara in 1910, the Russians had already controlled his homeland for two generations, and he ruled more as a pampered puppet than did his ancestors of earlier centuries. Seven hundred thirty-one years after the first tribal *khuriltai* met on the shores of the Blue Lake by Back-Heart-Shaped Mountain in 1189, a much different group, also calling itself a *khuriltai* but consisting of the delegates of the Bukhara Communist Party, met to depose his last descendant.

In the final week of August, he fled Bukhara, and after a brief attempt to mount a resistance from Tajikistan, he found refuge under British protection in Afghanistan, where he lived for the remainder of his life. As the emir departed, Bolshevik forces under Mikhail Vasilyevich Frunze attacked the citadel in Bukhara, the same fortress where, precisely seven centuries earlier, the Spirit Banner of Genghis Khan had led the Mongols to their first victory in central Asia. On September 2, 1920, Frunze reported to Lenin that "the fortress of old Bukhara was taken today following a powerful attack by Red and Bukharian units." With a dramatic flourish, he added that "tyranny and coercion have been vanquished, the red flag of revolution is floating over the Registan."

Throughout most of the twentieth century, Russia and China maintained an accord dividing the homeland of Genghis Khan between them, with China occupying Inner Mongolia, the part south of the Gobi, and the Soviet Union occupying the other half, Outer Mongolia, north of the Gobi. The Soviets turned Mongolia into a buffer zone that they kept largely empty between themselves and the Chinese. Just as the British executed the sons and grandson of the last Moghul emperor of India in the nineteenth century, the Soviets purged the known descendants of Genghis Khan remaining in Mongolia in the twentieth century, marching whole families into the woods to be shot and buried in unmarked pits, exiling them into the gulag of Soviet camps across Siberia where they were worked to death, or simply causing their mysterious disappearance into the night of history.

In April 1964, the official Soviet newspaper *Pravda* issued a stern warning against attempting "to place the bloodthirsty barbarian Genghis Khan on a pedestal as a historically progressive personage." The Chinese Communists countered the Soviet attack by charging that the Russians should be more appreciative of the Mongols since their invasion of Russia gave the Russians the opportunity "to get acquainted with a higher culture." No matter how offended the Mongols may have been by the Soviet attacks on their hero, they remained fiercely loyal to the Russians.

The ensuing persecutions in Mongolia destroyed a whole generation of linguists, historians, archaeologists, and other scholars who specialized in topics tangentially connected to Genghis or the Mongol Empire. Somewhere in the 1960s, eight centuries after the birth of Genghis Khan, his *sulde,* the

Spirit Banner that he had carried across Eurasia, disappeared from where the Communist authorities had kept it. From the time of this purge, the *sulde* of Genghis Khan has not been seen or accounted for. Many scholars assume that the authorities destroyed it in a final act of malice toward his soul. Still others hope that just perhaps the *sulde* lies forgotten in some dusty basement or bricked-up room from which it will, one day, be brought out to lead and inspire the Mongols once again.

Epilogue

The Eternal Spirit of Genghis Khan

---⊰⊱---

Is it our fault we have forgotten our history?
D .   J A R G A L S A I K H A N

GENGHIS KHAN'S WAS THE last great tribal empire of world history. He was the heir of ten thousand years of war between the nomadic tribes and the civilized world, the ancient struggle of the hunter and herder against the farmer. It was a history as old as the story of the Bedouin tribes that followed Muhammad to smash the pagan idolatry of the city, of the Roman campaigns against the Huns, of the Greeks against the wandering Scythians, of the city dwellers of Egypt and Persia who preyed on the wandering tribes of Hebrew herders, and, ultimately, of Cain, the tiller, who slew his brother Abel, the herder.

The clash between the nomadic and urban cultures did not end with Genghis Khan, but it would never again reach the level to which he brought it. Civilization pushed the tribal people toward the ever more distant edges of the world. Chiefs such as Sitting Bull and Crazy Horse of the Lakota Sioux, Red Eagle of the Muskogee, Tecumseh of the Shawnee, and Shaka Zulu of South Africa valiantly but vainly continued the quest of Genghis Khan over the coming centuries. Without knowing anything about the Mongols or Genghis Khan, these other chiefs faced the same struggles and fought the same battles across Africa and throughout the Americas, but history had moved beyond them. In the end, sedentary civilization won the long world war; the future belonged to the civilized children of Cain, who eternally encroached upon the open lands of the tribes.

Although he arose out of the ancient tribal past, Genghis Khan shaped the modern world of commerce, communication, and large secular states more than any other individual. He was the thoroughly modern man in his mobilized and professional warfare and in his commitment to global commerce and the rule of international secular law. What began as a war of extinction between the nomad and the farmer ended as a Mongol amalgamation of cultures. His vision matured as he aged and as he experienced different ways of life. He worked to create something new and better for his people. The Mongol armies destroyed the uniqueness of the civilizations around them by shattering the protective walls that isolated one civilization from another and by knotting the cultures together.

The great actors of history cannot be neatly tucked between the covers of a book and filed away like so many pressed botanical specimens. Their actions cannot be explained according to a specific timetable like the coming and going of so many trains. Although scholars may designate the beginning and ending of an era with exact precision, great historical events, particularly those that erupt suddenly and violently, build up slowly, and, once having begun, never end. Their effects linger long after the action faded from view. Like the tingling vibrations of a bell that we can still sense well after it has stopped ringing, Genghis Khan has long passed from the scene, but his influence continues to reverberate through our time.

In April 2000, I followed the trail that Temujin and his family probably took eight centuries earlier when they fled from the attacking Merkid who had come to kidnap Borte. After locating the likely spot of the attack on Temujin's camp, the direction from which the Merkid came, and the path by which the group fled, we set off to follow the chase from the steppe to the mountains. The local herding boys were themselves about the same age as the ones whose trail we were now retracing. They were just as skilled with horses as their ancient predecessors, and they wore the traditional Mongol *deel* with a tightly wrapped sash of bright gold silk just below the waist. Except for the occasional baseball cap, sunglasses, or jeans worn under the *deel*, their clothes were still the same heavy layers of wool, fleece, and felt garments worn by their ancestors.

Our nine horses, like those of Hoelun's fleeing family, were geldings, and the descriptions of the horses in the *Secret History* are so precise that we could have matched them up by age, color, shape, and other characteristics. Instead, we simply rode with the horses that an old and slightly drunk herder had designated as most appropriate for our task. We did not need to search for the route so much as merely follow the guidance and intuition of the nomads. They knew precisely how a horse and rider would get from here to there. They knew where the ice was too thin to cross the river, where the snow was too deep in the small depressions, and where a cluster of marmot burrows might trip one of the racing horses.

The wind made the new snow dance around the horse's hooves as we slowly climbed the rocky slope of Burkhan Khaldun, the most sacred mountain in Mongolia. The horse nervously snorted moist puffs of steam into the crisp air. His head jerked. Under the strain of a long, hard climb in such a thin altitude, his heart pounded so loudly that I heard it above the rushing wind, and I felt it throbbing up through my legs to my heart. When we paused in the bright crystal clear light, we saw all the way to the horizon in all directions—across the mountain peaks, boulder fields, winding rivers, and frozen lakes.

When he had finished his work, Genghis Khan returned here, as he always had after each victory, for rest, recovery, and renewal. He had changed the world but had allowed nothing to change in the land of his birth. Today, hawks soar overhead in spring, and the insects still sing in summer just as they did in his day. Nomads move to the hills in autumn, and wolves prowl in winter. When I close my eyes, I can still hear the distant thunder of his horse's hooves as they gallop off to China, Europe, and India.

Leaving the forested mountains and riding back to find our Jeeps, we decided to return to where the story and our expedition began, the place where the Merkid kidnapped Borte from Temujin. The steppe stretched to the horizon in every direction, barren of trees and unmarred by buildings, roads, fences, electric lines, or other scars of the modern world. During my repeated visits, I had learned to mark the land as the Mongols do, by color of season. The brief green summer lured the mating birds; the yellow fall enticed the horses to race and goats to gnaw at the drying plants. The white winter would find camels wandering slowly up and down the frozen river searching for patches of dried grass, and the brown spring provided only a time of waiting for new grass by the animals and the humans who live off them. Isolated, remote, and unchanged by the centuries, this locale marks the place where Temujin became a man and changed the Mongols from a tribe into a nation.

Upon our return to the windy place where we thought the abduction had occurred, our group grew quiet in the bitter wind that whipped around us. We had fulfilled the mission, and we returned to the spot with a new sense of amazement at what had happened here. The outline of many old campsites were clearly marked by large stones that once were used to tie down the *ger* in the fierce winds. The Mongol camps now lay cold and empty. Yet it seemed that if I only kicked the dust, I would feel the warmth of the smoldering ashes rising from his last campfire. If I brushed away the snow, I would see the prints of his horses in the frozen mud. The stones seem to have been left quite casually, as though at any time now the owner might return, dust them off, and once again erect either a winter camp for his yaks and sheep or an imperial capital of the world—whichever is most needed at the moment.

We stood in a silent cluster in the whistling wind, tightened our jackets, pulled down our hats, and stared at the ground. One by one, members of the group walked away to gather a few stones and piled them on the spot, in the way that nomadic people have marked important places for thousands of years. The senior horseman, a local headman, gathered some of the dried horse dung, piled it in front of the stones, and, as others blocked the wind by spreading open their flowing *deels*, lit the dung in much the same way that a mother kindles the fire before the family erects their *ger* around it.

Once the dung ignited, Professor. O. Sukhbaatar sprinkled some incense of finely ground cedar into the fire. The smell generated a soothing effect that softened the excitement of the long search, and at the same time focused our attention on the fire itself. The smoke wafting from the incense and dung signaled the success and conclusion of this phase in our quest. All the men shuffled a little and gradually pulled themselves up more erectly. Every culture has its proper way to dress and appear respectful. For the Mongols, the three breast buttons had to be securely fastened, their collars pulled straight, and the sleeves of the *deels* pulled down to cover their wrists and part of the upper hand. Each man tightened the wide gold sash and then bloused out the upper part of the *deel* to make it loose and full.

When we had identified the place on our earlier passage through here, the herders had asked Professor Sukhbaatar to mark a stone on this place so that everyone would know what had happened. A lady who lived nearby explained that because such knowledge was forbidden for so long, they wanted their children to know it now. For them, the way to remember it was to have it carved in stone. All of the herders respected the elderly professor. They knew him from the years after the purge of scholars, when alone and at great risk to his life, he set out on his journey of more than a million kilometers tracing the route of Genghis Khan and relying on the hospitality of the herders to protect, house, and feed him in his quest.

Now, after completing our journey, Professor Sukhbaatar consented to their request to erect a stone to commemorate the kidnapping of Borte from Temujin. It was quickly decided that he would write the text, Professor T. Jamyansuren would design the calligraphy of the Old Mongol script, and the students would find a stone and engrave it. After sending a student to fetch his well-worn almanac, Professor Sukhbaatar squinted through his smudged glasses to follow a long series of charts and diagrams. He made notes with a stubby pencil on a small slip of paper, performed some quick calculations, and looked up more charts in the almanac. He then announced the most propitious day on which the students should return to this spot to erect the stone.

This piece of business behind us, Professor Lkhagvasuren pulled a bottle of vodka out from the hidden recess of his *deel,* sprinkled it on the stones, threw some into the air, and touched it to his forehead. In some intimate way or other, each person connected directly back to the story we were researching. Lkhagvasuren had traveled this area many times with his teacher and mentor, the archaeologist Perlee, and when the authorities put Perlee in prison, they also arrested Lkhagvasuren's father for being too much of a nationalist. They sent his stepmother into internal exile far out in the country, and as the children of political prisoners Lkhagvasuren and his younger siblings were turned out into the streets of Ulaanbaatar. In the months before the authorities came to take him away to the Children's Prison, he managed to heap enough dirt over a small shed outside of town to serve as a home for his siblings through the winter while they would be alone. After spending his teen years in prison and in forced service on a distant border, he resumed the archaeological work of his mentor.

For each person—whether herder or scholar—the history around us was neither abstract nor distant; their Mongol history cut through their lives as sharply as if the events had happened only last week. For me, the quest across Mongolia and back through time had begun in nearly childlike curiosity that had developed into an intellectual and scholarly quest, but for my Mongol colleagues each step in our search grew much more personal and much more deeply emotional. Each day, as we understood better the hardships and heroism of their ancestors, we slipped farther back into time. Where we stood was not just another historical place; on this spot, the mother of the Mongol nation had been attacked, kidnapped, and ravished. When she was taken from him, the boy Temujin risked all, including his young life, to get her back. He rescued her, and for the rest of his life he fought to keep his own people safe from outside attack, even though that meant that he would spend his life attacking outsiders. In the process, he changed the world, and he created a nation.

They knelt before the small pile of smoking dung, sniffling and with tears pooling in the corners of their eyes. In the golden but dimming light of dusk, eight centuries melted away, and the pain of that dawn of terror so long ago floated in the smoke around us. As the incense burned on the small mound of stones, each person stepped forward individually to honor this place. He took off his hat, knelt before the stones, touched his head to the frozen earth of this sacred spot, and then got up and walked slowly three times around the stones while tossing vodka into the air.

Each person pulled out something as a small personal gift to leave on the stones—the stub of a sugar cube, a few matches, a candy wrapped in crinkling paper, a sprinkle of tea leaves. It was almost as though they wanted to reach back through the centuries to offer these small gifts of nourishment and warmth to the fleeing and frightened Borte as her kidnappers slung her on a horse and galloped away with her to an unknown future. It was as though the members of our muted group wanted to tell her, their mother, that everything would be all right, that she and they, her children, would survive it all for eight more centuries. After all, they are still the children of the Golden Light, the offspring of a wolf and a doe, and in the wispy clouds of the Eternal Blue Sky of Mongolia, the Spirit Banner of Genghis Khan still waves in the wind.

Notes

===✦===

These notes are to help the reader find information from a variety of sources. Works are cited in languages other than English only if no English translation could be identified.

Introduction: The Missing Conqueror

xv *"Genghis Khan was a doer"*: Joel Aschenbacher, "The Era of His Ways: In Which We Chose the Most Important Man of the Last Thousand Years," *Washington Post,* December 31, 1989, p. F01.

xxiii *unprecedented rise in cultural communication:* For more information on the cultural exchange, see Thomas T. Allsen, *Culture and Conquest in Mongol Eurasia* (Cambridge, U.K.: Cambridge University Press, 2001).

xxiv *Roger Bacon observed:* The quotes are from Bacon's *Opus Majus,* trans. Robert Belle Burke (Philadelphia: University of Pennsylvania Press, 1928), vol. 1, p. 416; vol. 2. p. 792.

xxiv *"we imagined your appearance"*: From "Chinggis Khaan," composed by D. Jargalsaikhan and performed by the musical group Chinggis Khaan.

xxv *Rashid al-Din described:* The quotes are from Allsen, *Culture and Conquest in Mongol Eurasia,* p. 88.

xxvi *Arab politicians:* Quoted in Eric L. Jones, *Growth Recurring: Economic Change in World History* (Oxford, U.K.: Clarendon Press, 1988), p. 113.

xxviii *"tendencies directed at idealizing the role of Genghis Khan"*: Almaz Khan, "Chinggis Khan: From Imperial Ancestor to Ethnic Hero," in *Cultural Encounters on China's Ethnic Frontiers,* ed. Stevan Harrell (Seattle: University of Washington Press, 1995), pp. 261–262.

xxix *anti-party elements, Chinese spies, saboteurs, or pests:* Tom Ginsburg, "Nationalism, Elites, and Mongolia's Rapid Transformation," in *Mongolia in the Twentieth Century: Landlocked Cosmopolitan,* ed. Stephen Kotkin and Bruce A. Elleman (Armonk, N.Y.: M. E. Sharpe, 1999), p. 247.

xxxi *I worked closely with:* Most Mongolians today use a single name such as Lkhagvasuren or Sukhbaatar, but when necessary to distinguish among those with the same name, they identify themselves by the initial (or first two letters in the case of sh, ch, kh or ts) of a parent.

I. The Reign of Terror on the Steppe: 1162–1206

1 *"Nations! What are nations?"*: Henry David Thoreau, *Journal* (Princeton, N.J.: Princeton University Press, 1981), entry for May 1, 1851.

1. The Blood Clot

3 *"There is fire in his eyes": Secret History,* § 62.
5 *"choked with horsemen":* Ata-Malik Juvaini, *Genghis Khan: The History of the World Conqueror,* trans. J. A. Boyle (Seattle: University of Washington Press, 1997), p. 98.
5 *"whoever yields":* Ibid., p. 15.
6 *"a man of tall stature":* Minhaj al-Siraj Juzjani, *Tabakat-I-Nasiri: A General History of the Muhammadan Dynasties of Asia,* trans. Major H. G. Raverty (Bengal: Asiatic Society of Bengal, 1881; reprint, New Dehli: Oriental Books, 1970), p. 1077.
7 *"it is the great ones, among you":* Ibid. p. 105.
8 *"like a red-hot furnace":* Juvaini, p. 106.
12 *"If you but live": Secret History,* § 56.
17 *Targutai boasted: Secret History,* § 149.
18 *early age of nine:* The early events in Temujin's life prove difficult to date precisely with confidence. The Mongols counted each new year as beginning at the end of winter when spring came. Each greening of the steppe counted as one new year, and age was counted according to the number of greenings a child had been through. Thus, the birth of Temujin at the start of spring gave him an immediate age of one, and each successive greening made him one year older. For purposes of this book, however, ages are calculated in the traditional Western way.
19 *Yesugei's sons by his other wife:* Regarding the marriage of a widow to a stepson, in one known case of an aristocratic Mongol family in the seventeenth century, after a woman's husband died, she married one of his sons; after that husband died, she then married his son. Finally, when this husband also died, she married his son. Thus, in her lifetime she was married to four men from the same family: her first husband, his son, his grandson, and his great-grandson. See J. Holmgren, "Observations on Marriage and Inheritance Practices in Early Mongol and Yüan Society, with Particular Reference to the Levirate," *Journal of Asian History* 20 (1986), p. 158.
20 *"of the skins of dogs and mice":* Juvaini, *Genghis Khan,* p. 21.
22 *"food that could not be digested": Secret History,* § 201.
23 *the eldest son assumed that role:* The Mongol language reflects the importance of older siblings by having distinct words for older brother *(akh)* and older sister *(egch),* whereas younger siblings, both male and female, are lumped together in one term *(düü).* The *akh,* "Elder Brother," had such importance that his title eventually became synonymous with the leader of a family cluster or other small group. In the case of full siblings, the ranking is obvious: by birth order. But for half siblings, the ranking order of the children depends on many factors, including, most particularly, the relative ranking of their mothers.
24 *"Destroyer! Destroyer!": Secret History,* § 78.
27 *ten years in slavery:* "Meng-Ta Peu-Lu Ausführliche Aufzeichnungen über die Mongolischen Tatan von Chao Hung, 1221," In Peter Olbricht and Elisabeth Pinks, *Meng-Ta Pei-Lu und Hei-Ta Shih-Lüeh: Chinesische Gesandtenberichte über die frühen Mongolen 1221 und 1237* (Weisbaden: Otto Harrassowitz, 1980), p. 12.

2. Tale of Three Rivers

31 *"The banner of Chingiz-Khan's fortune":* Ata-Malik Juvaini, *Genghis Khan: The History of the World Conqueror,* trans. J. A. Boyle (Seattle: University of Washington Press, 1997), p. 22.
33 *supernatural power:* The etymology of many Mongol and Turkic words show a constant intertwining of physical and political prowess with supernatural strength. Khan, Mongolian for chief, is almost identical to the Turkic term for shaman, kham. The Mongolian female shaman was called an idu-khan, while the term for male shaman originated in the same word for wrestler or athlete.

36 *"We have made their breasts to become empty:"* Francis Woodman Cleaves, trans., *The Secret History of the Mongols* (Cambridge, Mass.: Harvard University Press, 1982), par. 113, pp. 47–48.

36 *"let us love one another":* Urgunge Onon, trans., *The History and the Life of Chinggis Khan (The Secret History of the Mongols),* (Leiden: E. J. Brill, 1990), § 117.

38 *Jamuka and Temujin rode together:* For a contrasting interpretation of the class relations between the two men, see Boris Y. Vladimirtsov, *The Life of Chingis-Khan,* trans. Prince D. S. Mirsky (New York: Benjamin Blom, 1930).

45 *"Barren Island":* Rachewiltz's translation of *The Secret History,* § 136, 1972.

49 *never forgot how Jelme saved him:* Temujin's wound closely paralleled the nearly simultaneous battle wound suffered by King Richard the Lionhearted of England. In April 1199, while combating one of his rebel vassals, an arrow pierced his left shoulder. Richard tried to pull out the arrow, but its iron barb held and the shaft broke. For the next agonizing days, doctors treated him but without being able to combat the growing infection and fever. Finally, on the eleventh day, he died. His body was embalmed but disassembled to be buried with great ostentation in different places of sentimental importance to him. His brain was removed and sent for burial in an abbey in Poitiers. His heart went to the cathedral in Rouen, and his body to the Abbey Fonteurault. In marked contract, by sucking the blood from Temujin's wound, Jelme prevented him from following the painful and untimely fate of King Richard.

52 *He organized his warriors:* For more information on troop estimates, see Bat-Ochir Bold, *Mongolian Nomadic Society: A Reconstruction of the "Medieval" History of Mongolia* (New York: St. Martin's Press, 2001), p. 85.

53 *"Let no one set up camp": Secret History,* § 179.

54 *People of the Felt Walls:* This phrase is still used in Mongolia, "Esgii Tuurgatan."

3. War of the Khans

55 *"All the tribes were of one color":* Ata-Malik Juvaini, *Genghis Khan: The History of the World Conqueror,* trans. J. A. Boyle (Seattle: University of Washington Press), p. 38.

56 *"Is not Genghis Khan ashamed":* Marco Polo, *The Travels of Marco Polo,* trans. Ronald Latham (London: Penguin Books, 1958), p. 94.

57 *Lake Baljuna:* Baljuna is called a lake in the text, but it may have been a river or a small lake connected to the Balj River, a tributary of the Onon. The exact timing of the event is in great debate. Some scholars believe that it occurred at another point in the long civil wars and not as part of the betrayal by Ong Khan. A few scholars discount the story entirely, but based particularly on heavy Chinese documentation, most scholars accept it. For a full discussion of the event and the various versions of it, see Francis Woodman Cleaves, "The Historicity of the Baljuna Covenant," *Harvard Journal of Asiatic Studies* 18, nos. 3–4 (December 1955), pp. 357–421.

61 *"more fires than the stars in the sky": Secret History,* § 194.

62 *"If he sends me into fire":* "Hei-Ta Shih-Lüeh Kurzer Bericht über die schwarzen Tatan von P'eng Ta-Ya und Sü T'ing, 1237," in Peter Olbricht and Elisabeth Pinks, *Meng-Ta Pei-Lu und Hei-Ta Shih-Lüeh: Chinesische Gesandtenberichte über die frühen Mongolen 1221 und 1237* (Welisbaden: Otto Harrassowitz, 1980), p. 161.

62 *"rotten logs": Secret History,* § 96.

63 *"Let us be companions":* Urgunge Onon, trans., *The History and the Life of Chinggis Khan (The Secret History of the Mongols)* (Leiden: E. J. Brill, 1990), § 200.

65 *the headwaters of the Onon River:* Regarding the location of the *khuriltai* of 1206, the *Secret History* describes the place as simply the headwaters of the Onon, but the seventeenth-century *Erdeni-yin Tobchi* places it more precisely on the island of Kherlen River. Paul Kahn, *The Secret History of the Mongols: The Origins of Chingis Khan,* exp. ed. (Boston: Cheng & Tsui, 1998), p. 189.

66 *"placed him upon a black Felt Carpet"*: François Pétis de la Croix, *The History of Genghizcan the Great: First Emperor of the Ancient Moguls and Tartars* (London: Printed for J. Darby, etc., 1722), pp. 62–63.

67 *"obstinate and has a petty, narrow mind"*: *Secret History,* § 243.

67 *The Great Law of Genghis Khan:* For more information on the law of Genghis Khan, see Valentin A. Riasanovsky, *Fundamental Principles of Mongol Law,* Uralic and Altaic Series, vol. 43 (Bloomington: Indiana University Publications, 1965), p. 33.

68 *haggling over the value of a wife:* For more information on marriage, see Paul Ratchnevsky, *Genghis Khan: His Life and Legacy,* trans. Thomas Nivison Haining. Oxford, U.K.: Blackwell, 1991), pp. 191.

69 *Theft of animals:* For more information, see ibid., p. 155.

69 *hunting rights for wild animals:* See *Secret History,* § 199.

69 *tax exemptions:* For more information on Genghis Khan's tax law, see Riasanovsky, *Fundamental Principles of Mongol Law,* p. 83.

70 *the supremacy of the rule of law:* For more information on the application of law to the royal family, See Boris Y. Vladimirtsov, *The Life of Chingis-Khan,* trans. Prince D. S. Mirsky (New York: Benjamin Blom, 1930), p. 74.

71 *"punish the thieves":* Onon, *Secret History,* § 203.

72 *a system of fast riders:* For a discussion of postal stations, see Bat-Ochir Bold, *Mongolian Nomadic Society: A Reconstruction of the "Medieval" History of Mongolia* (New York: St. Martin's Press, 2001), p. 168.

73 *Genghis Khan's shaman:* Teb Tengeri's name was Kokochu. In the *Secret History,* four men had this name, and the text is not always clear on which is meant as the trustee of Hoelun's estate. Two Kokochus were already dead before this episode. In addition to the shaman, Kokochu was the name of the Tayichiud boy adopted by Mother Hoelun, and who later became the leader of a unit of one thousand. Many scholars assume that the adopted Kokochu was placed in charge of Mother Hoelun's people, but a case can be made that since Kokochu Teb Tengeri took over Mother Hoelun's people after her death, he was the Kokochu named as an administrator. While the issue of precise identity is perplexing, it is probably not particularly important.

74 *"Have you seen these?":* *Secret History,* § 244.

76 *the Uighur khan:* In the *Secret History* (§ 238), the Uighur leader is referred to as the Idu'ut, which means something like king, prince, or khan.

II. The Mongol World War: 1211–1261

79 *"By the arms of Zingis":* Edward Gibbon, *Decline and Fall of the Roman Empire* (London, J. M. Dent, 1910), vol. 5, p. 76.

4. Spitting on the Golden Khan

81 *"The hooves of our Mongol horses":* Quoted by a Sung representative in "Meng-Ta Peu-Lu Ausführliche Aufzeichnungen über die Mongolischen Tatan von Chao Hung, 1221," in Peter Olbricht and Elisabeth Pinks, *Meng-Ta Pei-Lu und Hei-Ta Shih-Lüeh: Chinesische Gesandtenberichte über die frühen Mongolen 1221 und 1237* (Weisbaden: Otto Harrassowitz, 1980), p. 210.

81 *their capital city of Zhongdu:* The same place had many names at different times. Under the Jurched, it was Zhongdu. When Khubilai Khan created his capital here it became known as Khanbalik (the khan's city) to Mongolians and other foreigners; the Chinese called it Dadu (or Ta-tu). Later, it was named Peking, and now Beijing.

82 *"reverently upon the ground"*: Peking Gazette, June 30, 1878, quoted in C. W. Campbell's *Travels in Mongolia: 1902* (reprint, London: Stationery Office, 2000), p. 74.

83 *the full commitment of every warrior*: see Sechen Jagchid and Paul Hyer, *Mongolia's Culture and Society* (Boulder: Westview, 1979), p. 370.

84 *"Our empire is like the sea"*: "Meng-Ta Peu-Lu Ausführliche Aufzeichnungen über die Mongolischen Tatan von Chao Hung, 1221," in Peter Olbricht and Elisabeth Pinks, *Meng-Ta Pei-Lu und Hei-Ta Shih-Lüeh*, p. 61.

86 *Mongol military*: Thomas J. Barfield, *The Perilous Frontier: Nomadic Empires and China, 221 B.C. to A.D. 1757* (Cambridge, Mass.: Blackwell, 1992).

87 *Mongol warriors could travel ten days*: Marco Polo, *The Travels of Marco Polo*, trans. Teresa Waugh (New York: Facts on File, 1984), p. 57.

87 *needed no fires to cook*: See "Meng-Ta Peu-Lu Ausführliche Aufzeichnungen über die Mongolischen Tatan von Chao Hung, 1221," in Peter Olbricht and Elisabeth Pinks, *Meng-Ta Pei-Lu und Hei-Ta Shih-Lüeh*, p. 58.

87 *the central camp for each unit*: See "Hei-Ta Shih-Lüeh Kurzer Bericht über die schwarzen Tatan von P'eng Ta-Ya und Sü T'ing, 1237," in Peter Olbricht and Elisabeth Pinks, *Meng-Ta Pei-Lu und Hei-Ta Shih-Lüeh: Chinesische Gesandtenberichte über die frühen Mongolen 1221 und 1237* (Weisbaden: Otto Harrassowitz, 1980), p. 187.

88 *communications became more important*: Walther Heissig, *A Lost Civilization: The Mongols Rediscovered*, trans. D. J. S. Thompson (London: Thames & Hudson, 1966), p. 35.

92 *The Mongols referred to these grass-eating people*: For more on the Mongol terminology for settled people, see Uradyn E. Bulag, *Nationality and Hybridity in Mongolia* (Oxford, U.K.: Clarendon Press, 1998), p. 213.

94 *"they come as though the sky were falling"*: See "Hei-Ta Shih-Lüeh Kurzer Bericht über die schwarzen Tatan von P'eng Ta-Ya und Sü T'ing, 1237," in Peter Olbricht and Elisabeth Pinks, *Meng-Ta Pei-Lu und Hei-Ta Shih-Lüeh*, p. 187.

102 *In 1219, the Year of the Hare:* There is debate about whether some of these events occurred in 1207 or 1219, since both were the Year of the Hare.

103 *"red bull"*: Secret History, § 240.

103 *Kashgar, a trading city:* Regarding the events in Kashgar, the *Secret History* placed this invasion in the Year of the Ox, 1205, but almost all other sources show that it occurred in the Year of the Ox, 1217.

104 *Jebe's army defeated the army of Guchlug:* For more information on the Mongol campaign against Guchlug, see René Grousset, *The Empire of the Steppes: A History of Central Asia*, trans. Naomi Walford (New Brunswick, N. J.: Rutgers University Press, 1970), p. 234.

104 *"to be one of the mercies of the Lord"*: Ata-Malik Juvaini, *Genghis Khan: The History of the World Conqueror*, trans. J. A. Boyle (Seattle: University of Washington Press, 1997), p. 67.

104 *"Jebe pursued Guchlug"*: Secret History, § 237.

105 *"He had brought about complete peace and quiet"*: Juvaini, *Genghis Khan*, p. 77.

105 *"this Emperor having nothing more to fear"*: François Pétis de la Croix, *The History of Genghizcan the Great: First Emperor of the Ancient Moguls and Tartars* (London: Printed for J. Darby, etc. 1722), pp. 119–120.

106 *"I have the greatest desire to live in peace"*: Quoted in René Grousset, *Conqueror of the World*, trans. Marian McKellar and Denis Sinor (New York: Orion Press, 1966), p. 209.

106 *"henceforth the abscess of evil"*: Juvaini, *Genghis Khan*, pp. 79–81.

106 *"laid waste a whole world"*: Ibid., p. 80.

106 *"the whirlwind of anger"*: Ibid., p. 80.

107 *he uncovered "his head"*: Ibid., p. 80.

5. Sultan Versus Khan

108 *"War for the nomadic people"*: Sechen Jagchid, *Essays in Mongolian Studies* (Provo: Brigham Young University Press, 1988), p. 12.

110 *the story of the tattooed messenger:* François Pétis de la Croix, *The History of Genghizcan the Great: First Emperor of the Ancient Moguls and Tartars* (London: Printed for J. Darby, etc., 1722), p. 136

111 *"Commanders, elders, and commonality"*: Henry H. Howorth, *History of the Mongols,* pt. 1, *The Mongols Proper and the Kalmuks* (London: Longmans, Green, 1876), p. 81.

111 *"it is the will of God"*: Robert P. Blake, and Richard N. Frye, "History of the Nation of the Archers (the Mongols) by Grigor of Akanc," *Harvard Journal of Asiatic Studies* 12 (December 1949), p. 301.

113 *"effaced from off the earth"*: Yaqut al-Hamawi quoted in Edward G. Browne, *The Literary History of Persia,* vol. 2 (Bethesda, Md.: Iranbooks, 1997), p. 431.

113 *"the greatest joy a man can know"*: Michael Prawdin, *The Mongol Empire: Its Rise and Legacy,* trans. Eden Paul and Cedar Paul (London: George Allen & Unwin, 1940), p. 143.

114 *"Stories have been related to me"*: Quoted in Browne, Literary History of Persia, p. 430.

115 *All the Mongol prisoners:* The murder of the Mongol warriors is related by Luc Kwanten, *Imperial Nomads: A History of Central Asia, 500–1500* (Philadelphia: University of Pennsylvania Press, 1979), p. 131.

115 *nails into their heads:* Stuart Legg, *The Barbarians of Asia: The Peoples of the Steppes from 1600 B.C.* (New York: Dorset, 1970), p. 274.

117 *Those cities that surrendered:* For a fuller account of these campaigns, see David Morgan, *The Mongols* (Cambridge, Mass.: Blackwell, 1986), pp. 60–61.

118 *the numbers given by historians:* For more on the supposedly high number of people killed, see Legg, *Barbarians of Asia,* p. 277.

120 *"if all my sons"*: Paul Ratchnevsky, *Genghis Khan: His Life and Legacy,* trans. Thomas Nivison Haining (Oxford, U.K.: Blackwell, 1991), p. 140.

121 *"When you tell Jochi to speak"*: Paul Kahn, *The Secret History of the Mongols: The Origins of Chinggis Khan* (Boston: Cheng & Tsui, 1998), p. 153.

121 *"She didn't run away from home"*: Ibid., § 254.

121 *"from a single hot womb"*: Ibid., § 254.

122 *"game killed by mouth"*: Ibid., § 255.

122 *"Mother Earth is broad"*: Ibid., § 255.

123 *"laid the knee of courtesy"*: Ata-Malik Juvaini, *Genghis Khan: The History of the World Conqueror,* trans. J. A. Boyle (Seattle: University of Washington Press, 1997), pp. 182–183.

123 *"because of————"*: Rashid al-Din, *The Successors of Genghis Khan,* trans. John Andrew Boyle (New York: Columbia University Press, 1971), p. 98.

125 *"the vision should never stray"*: Colonel Kh. Shagdar, "Ikh Khaadin surgaal gereeslel," *Chingis Khaan Sydlal,* vol. 4 (2002), pp. 3–35; translated from the Mongolian.

125 *"People conquered on different sides"*: Ibid., pp. 3–35.

126 *his men cordoned off:* For a fuller description of the group hunting procedures, see "Hei-Ta Shih-Lüeh Kurzer Bericht über die schwarzen Tatan von P'eng Ta-Ya und Sü T'ing, 1237," in Peter Olbricht and Elisabeth Pinks, *Meng-Ta Pei-Lu und Hei-Ta Shih-Lüeh: Chinesische Gesandtenberichte über die frühen Mongolen 1221 und 1237* (Weisbaden: Otto Harrassowitz, 1980), p. 117.

128 *Yesui prepared the body:* For more information on Mongol funeral practices, see V. V. Barthold, "The Burial Rites of the Turks and the Mongols," trans. J. M. Rogers, *Central Asiatic Journal* 14 (1970), pp. 195–227.

129 *"A mighty name"*: The cleric's comments come from Minhaj al-Siraj Juzjani, *Tabakat-I-Nasiri: A General History of the Muhammadan Dynasties of Asia,* trans. Major H. G. Raverty (Bengal: Asiatic Society of Bengal, 1881; reprint, New Dehli: Oriental Books, 1970), pp. 1041–1042.

129 *the text of a letter:* The English text of the letter of Genghis Khan can be found in E. Bretschneider, *Mediæval Researches from Eastern Asiatic Sources,* vol. I (New York: Barnes & Noble, 1967), pp. 37–39.

131 *"died in the fullness of years and glory":* Edward Gibbon, *Decline and Fall of the Roman Empire* (London: J. M. Dent, 1910), vol. 6, p. 280.

6. The Discovery and Conquest of Europe

132 *"For our sins":* The Chronicle of Novgorod: 1016–1491; trans. Robert Michel and Novill Forbes, Camden 3rd Series, vol. 25 (London: Offices of the Society, 1914), p. 64.

133 *"was ever spreading the carpet of merrymaking":* Ata-Malik Juvaini, *Genghis Khan: The History of the World Conqueror,* trans. J. A. Boyle (Seattle: University of Washington Press, 1997), p. 202.

134 *"exceedingly tall in structure":* Rashid al-Din, *The Successors of Genghis Khan,* trans. John Andrew Boyle (New York: Columbia University Press, 1971), pp. 61–62.

135 *newly recruited clerks:* For more information on the growing administration, see Thomas T. Allsen, "The Rise of the Mongolian Empire and Mongolian Rule in North China," in *The Cambridge History of China,* vol. 6, *Alien Regimes and Border States, 907–1368,* ed. Herbert Franke and Denis Twitchett (Cambridge, U.K.: Cambridge University Press, 1994), p. 397.

135 *"a castle with doors":* Juvaini, *Genghis Khan,* pp. 236–237.

136 *"would sit, every day":* al-Din, *Successors of Genghis Khan,* pp. 84–85.

136 *a 10 percent bonus:* For more information on the bonus, see Larry Moses and Stephen A. Halkovic Jr. *Introduction to Mongolian History and Culture* (Bloomington, Ind.: Research Institute for Inner Asian Studies, 1985), p. 71.

136 *In an effort to improve trade:* See Thomas J. Barfield, *The Perilous Frontier: Nomadic Empires and China, 221 B.C. to A.D. 1757* (Cambridge, Mass.: Blackwell, 1992), p. 206.

136 *weights and measures:* See Henry H. Howorth, *History of the Mongols,* pt. 1, *The Mongols Proper and the Kalmuks* (London: Longmans, Green, 1876), p. 156.

136–137 *"that wherever profit":* Juvaini, *Genghis Khan,* p. 77.

142 *"every tenth returned to his home":* The Chronicle of Novgorod: 1016–1471, trans. Robert Michel and Nevill Forbes, Camden 3rd Series, vol. 25 (London: Offices of the Society, 1914), p. 66.

142 *"the Tartars turned back":* Ibid., p. 66.

146 *"Tartars came in countless numbers":* Ibid., p. 81.

146 *"They have hard and robust breasts:* The quotes in this paragraph are from Matthew Paris, *Matthew Paris's English History from the Year 1235 to 1273,* trans. J. A. Giles, 1852. (London: Henry G. Bohn; reprint, New York: AMS Press, 1968), vol. 1, p. 469.

148 *"no eye remained open to cry for the dead":* J. J. Saunders, *The History of the Mongol Conquests* (Philadelphia: University of Pennsylvania Press, 2001), p. 82.

148 *"an immense horde of that detestable race of Satan":* Paris, *Matthew Paris's English History,* vol. 1, p. 314.

148 *"ravaged the eastern countries":* Ibid., p. 314.

149 *"They clothe themselves":* Ibid., p. 314.

149 *"They have no human laws":* Ibid., p. 314.

150 *"clouds of Tatars":* Saunders, *History of the Mongol Conquests,* p. 83.

150 *"To thee, Tsar, I bow":* Chronicle of Novgorod, pp. 87–90.

151 *"headstrong and brave":* al-Din, *Successors of Genghis Khan,* p. 138.

151 *"You broke the spirit of every man":* Secret History, § 277.

152 *the two armies met:* For information on the battle, see Erik Hildinger, "Mongol Invasion of Europe," *Military History* (June 1997).

153 *"great head":* Jan Dlugosz, *The Annals of Jan Dlugosz,* trans. Maurice Michael, commentary by Paul Smith, Chichester, United Kingdom: IM Publications, (1997), entry for the year 1241.

154 *"The dead fell":* James Ross Sweeney, "Thomas of Spalato and the Mongols," *Florilegium: Archives of Canadian Society of Medievalists* 12 (1980).

155 *"cannibals from Hell":* Paris, *Matthew Paris's English History,* vol. 1, pp. 469–472.

155–156 *Christian clerics looked to the Bible:* Information on the hypothetical biblical connections to the Mongols can be found in Axel Klopprogge, *Ursprung und Auspraegung des abdendlaendischen Mongolenbildes im 13. Jahrhundert: Eine Versuch zur Ideengeschichte des Mitterlaters* (Wiesbaden: Harrassowitz Verlag, 1993).

156 *"in the time of the government":* Paris, *Matthew Paris's English History,* vol. 1, p. 314.

157 *"the enormous wickedness of the Jews":* The quotes in this paragraph are from ibid., pp. 357–358.

158 *a thirty-year-old literate Englishman:* For an interesting novel on the identity of the English knight, see Gabriel Ronay, *The Tartar Khan's Englishman* (London: Cassell, 1978).

7. Warring Queens

160 *"Just as God":* Christopher Dawson, ed. *The Mongol Mission: Narratives and Letters of the Franciscan Missionaries in Mongolia and China in the Thirteenth and Fourteenth Centuries* (New York: Sheed & Ward, 1955), p. 195.

161 *record of Torogene's power:* For a fuller discussion of Toregene's edict, see Igor de Rachewiltz, "Töregene's Edict of 1240," *Papers on Far Eastern History* 23 (March, 1981), pp. 38–63.

162 *"became the sharer":* Ata-Malik, Juvaini, *Genghis Khan: The History of the World Conqueror,* trans. J. A. Boyle (Seattle: University of Washington Press, 1997), pp. 245–246.

163 *"desist entirely":* Christopher Dawson, ed., *The Mongol Mission: Narratives and Letters of the Franciscan Missionaries in Mongolia and China in the Thirteenth and Fourteenth Centuries* (New York: Sheed & Ward, 1955), pp. 73–76.

164 *"He sent again":* Juvaini, *Genghis Khan,* p. 245.

164 *"but God knows the truth":* Minhaj al-Siraj Juzjani, *Tabakat-I-Nasiri: A General History of the Muhammadan Dynasties of Asia,* trans. Major H. G. Raverty (Bengal: Asiatic Society of Bengal, 1881; reprint, New Delhi: Oriental Books, 1970), p. 1144.

164 *"hungry and thirsty":* Juvaini, p. 245.

166 *"his predestined hour arrived":* Juvaini, *Genghis Khan,* p. 185.

166 *"the affairs of the world":* Ibid., p. 556.

168 *Mongke Khan expanded the trials:* For more on the purge, see Thomas T. Allsen, "The Rise of the Mongolian Empire and Mongolian Rule in North China," in *The Cambridge History of China,* vol. 6, *Alien Regimes and Border States, 907–1368,* ed. Herbert Franke and Denis Twitchett (Cambridge, U.K.: Cambridge University Press, 1994), p. 394.

168 *"if I were to see among the race of women":* Morris Rossabi, "The Reign of Khubilai Khan," in *The Cambridge History of China,* vol. 6, *Alien Regimes and Border States, 907–1368,* ed. Herbert Franke and Denis Twitchett ed. (Cambridge, U.K.: Cambridge University Press, 1994), p. 414.

169 *"I follow the laws of my ancestors":* Thomas T. Allsen, *Mongol Imperialism: The Politics of the Grand Qan Mongke in China, Russia, and the Islamic Lands, 1251–1259* (Berkeley: University of California Press, 1987), p. 36.

170 *Guillaume Boucher:* For more information on the goldsmith, see Leonardo Olschki, *Guillaume Boucher: A French Artist at the Court of the Khans* (New York: Greenwood, 1946), p. 5.

171 *"I ate a little":* William of Rubruck, "The Journey of William of Rubruck," in *The Mongol Mission: Narratives and Letters of the Franciscan Missionaries in Mongolia and China in the Thirteenth and Fourteenth Centuries,* ed. Christopher Dawson (New York: Sheed & Ward, 1955), p. 163.

172 *"Is there any man":* Ibid., p. 189.

173 *"no one shall dare to speak"*: Ibid., p. 191.

174 *"We Mongols believe in one God"*: Ibid., p. 195.

175 *by the power of the eternal God"*: Ibid.

175 *"And from what book"*: Juvaini, *Genghis Khan*, p. 604.

175 *a commercial world not yet accustomed*: For more on the Mongol monetary system, see Allsen, *Mongol Imperialism*, pp. 171–188, and Allsen, "Rise of the Mongolian Empire," p. 402.

178 *the word assassin*: Dante became one of the earliest European writers to use the word in print. It appeared in Book XIX of *The Divine Comedy*, and his usage made it apparent that he expected the reader to know its meaning full well: "Io stava come il frate che confessa Lo perfido assassin . . ." ("like a friar who is confessing the wicked assassin . . .").

183 *"Five hundred and fifteen years"*: René Grousset, *The Empire of the Steppes: A History of Central Asia*, trans. Naomi Walford (New Brunswick, N.J.: Rutgers University Press, 1970), p. 357.

184 *The Armenian chronicler Grigor of Akanc*: in "History of the Nation of the Archers (the Mongols) by Grigor of Akanc," trans. Robert P. Blake and Richard N. Frye. *Harvard Journal of Asiatic Studies* 12 (December 1949).

184 *had conquered the heart of the Muslim World*: For more on the Mongol conquests, see David Morgan, *The Mongols* (Cambridge, Mass.: Blackwell), 1986, pp. 154–155.

185 *Hulegu ordered one hundred thousand piglets*: See Blake and Frye, "History," p. 343.

189 *Khubilai's cosmopolitan persona*: On all issues related to Khubilai khan, the most authoritative source is Morris Rossabi, *Khubilai Khan: His Life and Times* (Berkeley: University of California Press, 1988).

189 *"Central Rule"*: Herbert Franke, *From Tribal Chieftain to Universal Emperor and God: The Legitimation of the Yüan Dynasty* (München: Verlag der Bayerischen Akademie der Wissenschaften, Sitzungsberichete, vol. 2, 1978), page 27.

190 *a lowering of temperatures*: For information on weather and climate in the Mongol imperial era, see William Atwell, "Volcanism and Short-Term Climatic Change in East Asia and World History, c. 1200–1699," *Journal of World History* 12, no. 1 (Spring 2001), p. 50.

190 *"We were then, and you are today"*: Rashid al-Din, *The Successors of Genghis Khan*, trans. John Andrew Boyle (New York: Columbia University Press, 1971), p. 261.

III. The Global Awakening: 1262–1962

193 *"Asia is devouring us"*: Thomas Mann, *The Magic Mountain*, trans. John E. Woods (New York: Alfred A. Knopf, 1995), p. 238.

8. Khubilai Khan and the New Mongol Empire

195 *"This Great Khan"*: Marco Polo, *The Travels of Marco Polo*, trans. Ronald E. Latham (London: Penguin, 1958), p. 113.

199 *"Within the precincts"*: Sir John Mandeville, *The Travels of Sir John Mandeville, the Voyage of Johannes de Plano Carpini, the Journal of Friar William de Rubruquis, the Journal of Friar Odoric* (New York: Dover, 1964), p. 348.

199 *"in a certain part of the hall"*: Marco Polo, *The Travels of Marco Polo: The Complete Yule-Cordier Edition* (New York: Dover, 1993), vol. 1, p. 382.

200 *the number of capital offenses*: Figures on executions are taken from Paul Heng-chao Ch'en, *Chinese Legal Tradition Under the Mongols: The Code of 1291 as Reconstructed* (Princeton, N.J.: Princeton University Press, 1979), pp. 44–45.

201 *"first use reason to analyze"*: Ibid., p. 154.

203 *"the laws and customs of cities"*: Secret History, § 263. For a fuller description of Mongol law, see Valentin A. Riasanovsky, *Fundamental Principles of Mongol Law*, Uralic and Altaic Series, vol. 43 (Bloomington: Indiana University Publications, 1965), p. 83.

203 *Khubilai's administration:* For an extensive assessment of the Mongol administration, see Elizabeth Endicott-West, *Mongolian Rule in China: Local Administration in the Yuan Dynasty* (Cambridge, Mass.: Harvard University Press, 1989).

204 *"To refuse it would be to incur the death penalty:"* Marco Polo, *The Travels of Marco Polo,* trans. Teresa Waugh (New York: Facts on File, 1984), p. 88.

205 *rejected some parts of Chinese Culture:* For more on Mongol cultural influences, see Adam T. Kessler, *Empires Beyond the Great Wall: The Heritage of Genghis Khan* (Los Angeles: Natural History Museum, 1993).

206 *promoted general literacy:* For more on Mongol education in China, see Morris Rossabi, "The Reign of Khubilai Khan," in *The Cambridge History of China,* vol. 6, *Alien Regimes and Border States, 907–1368,* ed. Herbert Franke and Denis Twitchett (Cambridge, U.K.: Cambridge University Press, 1994), p. 447.

207 *consisted of six parts:* The parts commemorated and reenacted the conquests of the Kereyid and Ong Khan; the Tangut; the Chin-Chin; the West and Honan (south of the Yellow River); Sichuan and the Thai state of Nanchao; and Korea and Vietnam. Sechen Jagchid and Paul Hyer, *Mongolia's Culture and Society* (Boulder: Westview, 1979), p. 241.

207 *performing artists such as actors and singers:* For more information on Mongol support of the arts, see Morris Rossabi, *Khubilai Khan: His Life and Times* (Berkeley: University of California Press, 1988), p. 161.

209 *"Like an ancient ruin":* Quoted in Jacques Gernet, *Daily Life in China on the Eve of the Mongol Invasion, 1250–1276,* trans. H. M. Wright (New York: Macmillan, 1962), p. 237.

209 *"The greatest legacy of the Mongol Empire":* Hidehiro Okada, "China as a Successor State to the Mongol Empire," in *The Mongol Empire and Its Legacy,* ed. Reuven Amitai-Preiss and David O. Morgan (Leiden: Koninklijke Brill NV, 1999), p. 260.

210 *revitalized and enlarged the Sung navy:* For information on the Mongol fleet and the invasions of Japan, see James P. Delgado, "Relics of the Kamikaze," *Archaeology* (January 2003), pp. 36–41, and Theodore F. Cook Jr., "Mongol Invasion," *Quarterly Journal of Military History* (Winter 1999), pp. 8–19.

215 *In the hunting procession:* Marco Polo, *The Travels of Marco Polo,* trans. Ronald Latham (London: Penguin, 1958), pp. 141–145.

216 *the traditional Mongol emphasis on meat and dairy products:* For more information on Mongol food in China, see Paul D. Buell, *Historical Dictionary of the Mongol World Empire* (Lanham, Md.: Scarecrow, 2003), pp. 309–312, and Paul D. Buell and Eugene N. Anderson, *A Soup for the Qan: Chinese Dietary Medicine of the Mongol Era as Seen in Hu Szu-Hui's* Yin-Shan Cheng-Yao (London: Kegan Paul, 2000).

9. Their Golden Light

218 *"The artists of China":* Edward Gibbon, *Decline and Fall of the Roman Empire* (London, J. M. Dent, 1910) vol. 6, p. 287.

219 *"two envoys came from the Tartars":* Matthew Paris, *Matthew Paris's English History from the Year 1235 to 1273,* trans. J. A. Giles, 1852 (London: Henry G. Bohn; reprint, New York: AMS Press, 1968), p. 155.

220 *related the events of his travels:* For the complete text of Rabban Bar Sawma's account, see E. A. Wallis Budge, *The Monks of Kublai Khan, Emperor of China; or, The History of the Life and Travels of Rabban Swama, Envoy and Plenipotentiary of the Mongol Khans to the Kings of Europe, and Markos Who as Mar Yahbhallaha III Became Patriarch of the Nestorian Church in Asia* (London: Religious Tract Society, 1928).

221 *"silk sheets and every other luxury":* Marco Polo, *The Travels of Marco Polo,* trans. Teresa Waugh (New York: Facts on File Publications, 1984), p. 89.

221 *Mongols in Persia supplied their kinsmen:* For a thorough account of the exchange between China and the Ilkhanate, see Thomas T. Allsen, *Culture and Conquest in Mongol Eurasia* (Cambridge, U.K.: Cambridge University Press, 2001).

223 *the most sophisticated cartography known:* For more information on science in China under the Mongols, see Joseph Needham, *Science and Civilization,* vols. 4 and 6 (Cambridge U.K.: Cambridge University Press, 1971, 1986).

223 *moved some 3,000 tons by ship:* For information on the Mongol navy, see Louise Levathes, *When China Ruled the Seas* (New York: Simon & Schuster, 1994).

224 *"perfectly safe":* Ronald Latham, introduction to *The Travels of Marco Polo,* by Marco Polo, trans. Ronald Latham (London: Penguin, 1958), p. 15.

225 *attacked the Chinese cultural prejudice:* For more information on the Mongol's cultural attitudes toward their subjects, see Erich Haenisch, *Die Kulturpolitik des Mongolishchen Welstreichs* (Berlin: Preussische Akademie der Wissenschaften, Heft 17, 1943), or Larry Moses and Stephen A. Halkovic Jr. *Introduction to Mongolian History and Culture,* (Bloomington, Ind.: Research Institute for Inner Asian Studies, 1985).

231 *massive amounts of numerical information:* For more information on number systems and mathematics, see Joseph Needham, *Science and Civilization,* vol. 3 (Cambridge, U.K.: Cambridge University Press, 1970).

236 *"unknown to the ancients:"* Francis Bacon, *Novum Organum,* vol. 3, *The Works of Francis Bacon,* ed. and trans. Basil Montague (1620; reprint, Philadelphia: Parry & MacMillan, 1854), p. 370.

237 *"In the fresco cycle":* Lauren Arnold, *Princely Gifts and Papal Treasures: The Franciscan Mission to China and Its Influence on the Art of the West, 1250–1350* (San Francisco: Desiderata Press, 1999), p. 39.

238 *"a numerous and simple people":* Nicolaus of Cusa, *Toward a New Council of Florence: "On the Peace of Faith" and Other Works by Nicolaus of Cusa,* ed. William F. Wertz Jr. (Washington, D.C.: Schiller Institute, 1993), pp. 264.

239 *"among these various forms of sacrifice":* Ibid., p. 264.

239 *"It is proper to keep the commandments":* Ibid., pp. 266–267.

239 *imagery of Mongol greatness:* For more on "The Squire's Tale" and the Mongols, see Vincent J. DiMarco, "The Historical Basis of Chaucer's Squire's Tale," *Edebiyat,* vol. 1, no. 2 (1989), pp. 1–22, and Kathryn L. Lynch, "East Meets West in Chaucer's Squire's and Franklin's Tales," *Speculum* 70 (1995), pp. 530–551.

239 *"This noble king":* The original text by Chaucer reads as follows:

Heere Bigynneth the Squieres Tale

At Sarray, in the land of Tartarye,
Ther dwelte a kyng that werreyed Russye,
Thurgh which ther dyde many a doughty man.
This noble kyng was cleped Cambyuskan,
Which in his tyme was of so greet renoun
That ther was nowher in no regioun
So excellent a lord in alle thyng.
Hym lakked noght that longeth to a kyng.
As of the secte of which that he was born
He kept his lay, to which that he was sworn;
And therto he was hardy, wys, and riche,
And pitous and just, alwey yliche;
Sooth of his word, benigne, and honourable,
Of his corage as any centre stable;
Yong, fressh, and strong, in armes desirous

As any bacheler of al his hous.
A fair persone he was and fortunat,
And kepte alwey so wel roial estat
That ther was nowher swich another man.
This noble kyng this Tartre Cambyuskan.

10. The Empire of Illusion

241 *"When Christopher Columbus"*: David Morgan, *The Mongols* (Cambridge, Mass.: Blackwell, 1986), p. 198.

241–42 For information on the plague in Mongol territories, see Michael W. Dols, *The Black Death in the Middle East* (Princeton, N.J.: Princeton University Press, 1977).

241–46 For more information on the plague in general, see Robert S. Gottfried, *The Black Death* (New York: Free Press, 1983), and David Herlihy, *The Black Death and the Transformation of the West* (Cambridge, Mass.: Harvard University Press, 1997).

244 *bodies of plague victims catapulted over the walls*: Belief that the Mongols deliberately spread the plague remained strong enough to inspire imitation of it through the years, but without success. Russian troops reportedly used the tactic against Sweden in 1710, and in World War II, Japan tried it by dropping infected fleas from airplanes onto Chinese villages. The fleas had been exposed to a particularly virulent form of plague and did infect some villagers, but they did not create an epidemic.

244 *the population of Africa declined*: For population estimates, see Massimo Livi-Bacci, *A Concise History of World Population*, 2nd ed., trans. Carl Ipsen (Malden, Mass.: Blackwell, 1997), p. 31, and Jean-Noel Biraben, "An Essay Concerning Mankind's Evolution," *Population* (December 1980).

245 *the epidemic permanently changed life*: For a fuller discussion of the impact of the plague and similar diseases, see William H. McNeill, *Plagues and People* (Garden City, N.Y.: Doubleday, 1976), pp. 132–175.

246 *"venerable authority of laws"*: Boccaccio, *The Decameron*, trans. M. Rigg (London: David Campbell, 1921), vol. 1, pp. 5–11.

246 *Christians once again turned on the Jews*: For information on the Jews being blamed for the plague, see Rosemary Horrox, *The Black Death* (Manchester, U.K.: Manchester University Press, 1994), pp. 209–226.

248 *the Mongol authorities increased repression*: Regarding anti-Chinese policies on the Mongols, see John W. Dardess, *Conquerors and Confucians: Aspects of Political Change in Late Yüan China* (New York: Columbia University Press, 1973).

249 *granted ever more favor and power to Buddhism*: Regarding Tibetan Buddhism under the Mongols, see Hok-lam Chan and William Theodore de Bary, eds., *Yüan Thought: Chinese Thought and Religion Under the Mongols* (New York: Columbia University Press, 1982), p.484.

250 *the collapse came quickly*: For an account of the end of Mongol rule in China, see Udo Barkmann, "Some Comments on the Consequences of the Decline of the Mongol Empire on the Social Development of the Mongols," in *The Mongol Empire and Its Legacy*, ed. Reuven Amitai-Preiss and David O. Morgan (Leiden: Koninklijke Brill NV, 1999).

251 *expelled the Muslim, Christian, and Jewish traders*: For more on the impact of trade, see Andre Gunder Frank, *ReORIENT: Global Economy in the Asian Age* (Berkeley: University of California Press, 1998), p. 112.

254 *Columbus embarked on his voyage*: For more on Christopher Columbus and the Mongol influence, see John Larner, *Marco Polo and the Discovery of the World* (New Haven: Yale University Press, 1999).

254 *"the most singular people on earth"*: The quotes in this paragraph are from the Baron de

Montesquieu, *The Spirit of the Laws,* Trans. Thomas Nugent (New York: Hafner, 1949), pp. 268–280.

255 *"I have confined my plan":* The quotes in this paragraph are from Voltaire, *The Orphan of China, in The Works of Voltaire,* vol. 15, trans. William F. Fleming (Paris: E. R. DuMont, 1901), p. 180.

255 *"The more I see":* Ibid., p. 216.

255 *"what have I gained":* Ibid., p. 216.

256 *"The lips are large":* The quotes in this paragraph are from George Louis Leclerc Buffon, *Buffon's Natural History of the Globe and Man* (London: T. Tegg, 1831), p. 122, quoted in Kevin Stuart, *Mongols in Western/American Consciousness* (Lampeter, U.K.: Edwin Mellen, 1997), pp. 61–79.

257 *"The leading characters:"* Robert Chambers, *Vestiges of the Natural History of Creation* (London: John Churchill, 1844; reprint, Chicago: University of Chicago Press, 1994), p. 307.

257 *"the northern Chinese":* Carleton Coon, *The Living Races of Man* (New York: Knopf, 1965), p. 148.

257 *"Mongoloid race":* John Langdon Haydon Down, "Observations on the Ethnic Classification of Idiots," *Journal of Mental Science* 13 (1867), pp. 120–121, Quoted in Stuart, *Mongols in Western/American Consciousness.*

257 *"Parents too nearly related":* Chambers, Vestiges, p. 309.

258 *"pre-human, rather than human":* quoted in Francis G. Crookshank. *The Mongol in Our Midst: A Study of Man and His Three Faces* (New York: Dutton, 1924), p. 21.

258 *"Mongolian stigmata":* Ibid., pp. 72–73.

258 *"Mongol expatriates":* Ibid., p. 13.

258 *"Atavistic Mongolism":* Ibid., p. 92.

259 *"from the East":* Vladimir Sergeevich Soloviev, *Pan Mongolism,* in *From the Ends to the Beginning: A Bilingual Anthology of Russian Verse,* available at http://max.mmic.northwestern.edu/~mdenner/Demo/index.html.

260 *"dream of the past":* Jawaharlal Nehru, *Glimpses of World History* (New York: John Day, 1942), p. 5.

261 *calendar based on the year 1206:* For Information on the Genghis Khan calendar, see Sechen Jagchid and Paul Hyer, *Mongolia's Culture and Society.* Boulder: Westview, 1979), p. 115.

262 *translation of the* Secret History: During World War I, the Russian and Chinese Revolutions prevented much study of the *Secret History.* In the 1920s, the French sinologist Paul Pelliot prepared a French translation, but it failed to be published until after World War II. The German publisher Bruno Schindler of Verlag Asia Maior prepared the German text for publication in Leipzig, but because of growing Nazi persecutions, Schindler had to flee to England. He left the manuscript behind, where it was eventually taken over by another publishing house, Verlag Otto Harrassowitz, which managed to set it in type in 1940. In France, Pelliot's translation was finally published in 1949. A complete Russian translation was made public about the same time, and the German edition appeared in 1981. Except for the few eccentric international scholars who worked on the manuscript, the world took little notice. Over the subsequent decades, these dedicated scholars from several countries labored to reconstruct and translate the history first into proper Mongolian and Chinese, then into Russian and French, and still now many debates still rage over particular passages. Some excerpts from Russian, German, and French translations did make their way into English, but overall the English-speaking world seemed to show a profound lack of interest in the Mongols in general, including this so-called *Secret History.*

264 *"the fortress of old Bukhara":* Helene Carrere D'Encausse, *Islam and the Russian Revolution: Reform and Revolution in Central Asia,* trans. Quintin Hjoare (Berkeley: University of California Press, 1988), pp. 164–165.

264 *"to place the bloodthirsty barbarian Genghis Khan"*: Larry Moses and Stephen A. Halkovic Jr., *Introduction to Mongolian History and Culture* (Bloomington, Ind.: Research Institute for Inner Asian Studies, 1985), p. 168.

Epilogue

266 *"Is it our fault"*: From "Chinggis Khaan," composed by D. Jargalsaikhan and performed by the musical group Chinggis Khaan.

A Note on Transliteration

——⟨⟩——

Transliteration

There are at least a dozen systems for transliterating classical and modern Mongolian names and words into Latin letters, but no single system has been agreed upon. In the belief that scholars can easily understand all the spellings, I opted to use the renderings that are easiest for the English speaker to read, understand, and pronounce, and in so doing I adhere to the following principles.

1. If a common form already exists in English, I use it. Thus, I use the Persian name *Genghis*, simply because that spelling is more recognized than *Chinggis, Jenghiz, Djingis*, or the many other renditions of the name. Similarly, for the old capital I use the widely known Turkic form *Karakorum*, rather than the modern Mongolian name *Kharkhorin* or the more scholarly name *Qaraqorum*.

2. For toponyms, I prefer modern Mongolian names whenever possible— such as *Kherlen* River, rather than *Herlen, Kerulen,* or *Qerelen*. I use the Mongolian version of the modern capital *Ulaanbaatar* rather than the Russian form of *Ulan Bator*.

3. I use *khan* for tribal leader or Mongol king, but I use *Great Khan* for the highest office. To follow modern Mongol usage of *khan* for king and *khaan* for the Great Khan would be too confusing for the English reader.

4. One of the most common consonants in Mongol is the Mongol *kh*—similar to *ch* in German *ich* or Scottish *loch*. It is sometimes written as *q, h,* or an apostrophe.

5. Whenever possible, I avoid umlauts or diacritical marks. In Mongolian, as in the other Altaic languages, the differences between front vowels and back vowels is of critical importance. Anyone who speaks the Mongolian language will know whether the names are pronounced in the front or the back of the mouth, and for most other readers, the marks are probably not relevant.

Glossary

=≡=≡=

airak   Fermented mare's milk.

anda   Sworn brothers. Temujin and Jamuka were *andas*. Yesugei (Temujin's father) was the *anda* of Torghil Khan, known as Ong Khan of the Kereyid.

Arik Boke   Youngest son of Tolui, defeated by his brother Khubilai in the quest to become Great Khan. Born about 1217; died in 1264.

Avarga   First capital of the Mongol Empire at the base camp of Genghis Khan after he seized the territory from the Jurkin; located at the confluence of the Kherlen and Tsenker Rivers.

Baljuna, Lake   Place where the Baljuna Oath or Covenant was made between Genghis Khan and a handful of his most faithful followers. It may actually have been a river.

Batu   Son of Jochi, khan over Russia from 1227 until his death in 1255.

Begter   Half brother of Temujin, who killed him. Son of Yesugei and Sochigel.

Belgutei   Half brother of Temujin, to whom he remained loyal throughout his long life of more than a hundred years. Died in 1255.

Berke   Son of Jochi; after his brother Batu Khan, he became the khan over Russia from 1257 to 1267. He fought with his cousins in the Ilkhanate and refused to recognize Khubilai as Great Khan.

Boorchu   Early companion of Temujin, later a major general in the Mongol army.

Borijin   Genghis Khan's clan name.

Borte   First and primary wife of Temujin. Born around 1160; died around 1222.

Burkhan Khaldun   "God Mountain," located in the Khentii range.

busgui   Male; literally, "beltless."

Cathay   Early European spelling for the Khitan, relatives of the Mongols and rulers of northern China during the period 907–1125, called the Liao dynasty by the Chinese.

Chaghatai   Second son of Genghis Khan and Borte (1183–1242); his descendents ruled most of central Asia and eventually became the Moghul dynasty of India.

Chiledu   Merkid tribesman, first husband of Hoelun before her kidnapping by Yesugei.

deel   traditional Mongolian robe worn by men and women.

Genghis Khan   Title given to Temujin in 1206, although he may have also used it as early as 1189, when he first became khan.

ger   Portable home made of felt over a latticework frame, called a *yurt* by outsiders.

Guchlug   Son of Tayang Khan of the Naiman, later ruler of the Black Khitan Kingdom.

Gur-khan   Ancient title meaning supreme khan.

Guyuk   Great Khan of the Mongol Empire (1246–1248); son of Ogodei.

Hoelun   Mother of Genghis Khan. Around the year 1161, she was kidnapped from Chiledu of the Merkid by Yesugei, with whom she had four sons and a daughter.

Hulegu   Conqueror of Baghdad, and founder of the Ilkhanate over Persia. Died in 1265.

Ikh Khorig   The Great Taboo, name applied to the area around Genghis Khan's burial site.

Jadaran clan   Descended from the first son born after Bodonchar the Fool kidnapped a pregnant wife. (The Borijin clan descended from the last son born to her.)

Glossary

Jamuka *Anda* of Genghis Khan, and for a brief time Gur-khan of the Mongols until executed by Genghis Khan.

Jochi Eldest son of Genghis Khan and Borte, but his legitimacy was not acknowledged by his brothers. He died in 1227, the same year as his father; his descendants became the Golden Horde of Russia.

Jurched Manchurian tribes that ruled in northern China. Also known as the Jin (Chin) dynasty, 1115–1234; ruled by the Golden Khan.

Jurkin Lineage closely related to Genghis Khan.

Karakorum Also known as Kharkhorin; second capital of the Mongol Empire (from 1235 until 1260). It was built by Ogodei on the Orkhon River in central Mongolia in the land that had once belonged to Ong Khan of the Kereyid.

Kereyid Tribe or collection of tribes of central Mongolia, along rich pasturelands of the Orkhon and Tuul Rivers; ruled by Torghil, the Ong Khan.

Khaidu Grandson of Toregene and Ogodei (1236–1301); khan over much of central Asia and rival to his cousin Khubilai Khan.

Khan Chief or king. Steppe titles can be very confusing. In addition to khan, the most common designation for the emperor in the dynasty of Genghis Khan was the title that is written in modern Mongolian as *khaan* or is transliterated from classical Mongolian as *kha'an, khagan, qahan, qaghan,* or *qa'an.* To avoid confusion between the Mongolian titles of khan and khaan in this book, only khan is used with names, as in Khubilai Khan or Batu Khan, and Great Khan is used instead of emperor or khaan. For example, "Genghis Khan's son Ogodei was elected Great Khan in 1229."

Khanbalik Mongol capital built by Khubilai and now the city of Beijing. In the Mongol era, it was also known as Da-Du or Ta-Tu to the Chinese; previously, it had been Zhongdu when it served as the Jurched capital.

Khasar Brother next in age to Genghis Khan; he was both a strongman and a marksman.

khatun Mongol queen.

Kherlen River One of the three rivers that flows from Burkhan Khaldun. Temujin lived on this river when Borte was taken by the Merkid, and he later made his base camp farther downstream at Avarga.

Khitan Tribe closely related to Mongols. They ruled northern China as the Liao dynasty (907–1125), but were defeated and replaced by the Jurched. The Mongols used this name for all of northern China, and Marco Polo picked it up with the word *Cathay.*

Khodoe Aral Name used for the area around Avarga, near the confluence of the Kherlen and Tsenker Rivers.

khubi Share of booty, hunt, or loot.

Khubilai Khan Grandson of Genghis Khan (1215–1294); claimed the title of Great Khan and established the Yuan dynasty over China.

khuriltai An official council or meeting, usually summoned to confirm elections or make major decisions such as whether to go to war.

Kipchak Turkic tribe in southern Russia.

Merkid Tribe along the Selenge River, modern border of Mongolia and Siberia.

Mongke Khan Eldest son of Tolui, Great Khan from 1251 to 1259.

morin huur Horsehead fiddle.

naadam Celebration involving wrestling, archery, and horse racing.

Naiman Tribe of western Mongolia, ruled by Tayang Khan until defeated by Genghis Khan in 1205.

nerge Line used to enclose the animals at the start of a group hunt.

Oghul Ghaimish Wife of Guyuk; as his widow, she tried to rule as regent of the Mongol Empire but was defeated by Sorkhokhtani and her sons.

Ogodei Third son of Genghis Khan and Borte, Great Khan of the Mongol Empire from 1229 to 1241.

Ong Khan Ruler of the Kereyid tribe. Also known by his name Torghil as well as by Wang

Khan or Van Khan, variations of his title. Because his tribe was Christian, he was often assumed by Europeans to have been the fabled Prester John.

Onon River One of the three rivers that flows from Burkhan Khaldun; the river on which Genghis Khan was born and spent his childhood.

ordu or *horde* The court of the khan. The word came into English as *horde*. It was also used in Turkish, *ordu*, and became the word *Urdu*, the camp or army language that became the official language of Pakistan.

ortoo Mongolian postal system; also called *yam*.

Otchigen Youngest son of the family; Prince of the Hearth, or Prince of the Fire.

Shankh Monastery Buddhist monastery founded by Zanabazar and the resting place of the black *sulde* of Genghis Khan.

Shigi-Khutukhu Tatar boy raised by Hoelun, born around 1180 and died about 1262. Supreme judge of the Mongol Empire and the likely author of *The Secret History of the Mongols*.

Sochigel Mother of Begter and Belgutei, who were fathered by Yesugei, to whom she may or may not have been married. Her name is not mentioned in the *Secret History*.

Sorkhokhtani Wife of Tolui, mother of Mongke, Khubilai, Hulegu, and Arik Boke. By defeating the ruling family of Ogodei in 1251, she gave control of the Mongol Empire to her sons, but she died shortly thereafter.

Sulde Banner; soul; spirit.

Tangut Tribal dynasty over kingdom of Xia-Xia (Hsia-Hsia) along upper Yellow River, including Ordos, ruled by Burkhan Khan, who was killed by the Mongols in 1227 when his kingdom was incorporated into the Mongol Empire.

Tayang Khan Ruler of the Naiman of western Mongolia.

Tayichiud Close relatives of Temujin's family, but they deserted his family when his father died.

Teb Tengeri The shaman who created discord in Genghis Khan's family and was killed by Temuge, the youngest brother of Genghis Khan.

Temuge Youngest brother (Prince of the Hearth or Fire) of Genghis Khan.

Temujin Birth name of Genghis Khan.

Temujin Uge Tatar warrior killed by Yesugei, who subsequently gave his son that name.

Temulun Youngest sibling and only sister of Temujin.

Tolui Youngest son of Genghis Khan (1193–1233). Married to Sorkhokhtani, who managed to seize control of the empire for their four sons, with power eventually falling to their son Khubilai.

Toregene Wife of Ogodei Khan, regent of the Mongol Empire during the period (1241–1246).

tumen Military unit of ten thousand.

Uighur Turkic people now living in western China; first foreign nation to seek admission to the Mongol Empire of Genghis Khan.

Ulaanbaatar Modern capital of Mongolia; name means Red Hero.

Xanadu Western name for Khublai's capital of Shangdu in inner Mongolia. After he built Khanbalik as the permanent capital, Shangdu became the summer capital.

Yeke Khatun Great Empress.

Yeke Mongol Ulus Great Mongol Nation.

Yesugen and Yesui Tatar sisters who married Genghis Khan.

Zanabazar Buddhist lama, descendant of Genghis Khan and founder of the Shankh Monastery.

For a complete listing of names, terms, and alternate spellings, see Paul D. Buell, *Historical Dictionary of the Mongol World Empire* (Lanham, Md.: Scarecrow Press, 2003).

Selected Bibliography

Abu-Lughod, Janet L. *Before European Hegemony: The World System* A.D. *1250–1350*. New York: Oxford University Press, 1989.

Achenbacher, Joel. "The Era of His Ways: In Which We Chose the Most Important Man of the Last Thousand Years." *Washington Post*, December 31, 1989.

al-Din, Rashid. *The Successors of Genghis Khan*. Trans. John Andrew Boyle. New York: Columbia University Press, 1971.

Allsen, Thomas T. *Mongol Imperialism: The Politics of the Grand Qan Mongke in China, Russia, and the Islamic Lands, 1251–1259*. Berkeley: University of California Press, 1987.

———. *Commodity and Exchange in the Mongol Empire: A Cultural History of Islamic Textiles*. Cambridge, U.K.: Cambridge University Press, 1997.

———. *Culture and Conquest in Mongol Eurasia*. Cambridge, U.K.: Cambridge University Press, 2001.

Amitai-Preiss, Reuven. *Mongols and Mamluks*, Cambridge, U.K.: Cambridge University Press, 1995.

Amitai-Preiss, Reuven, and David O. Morgan, eds. *The Mongol Empire and Its Legacy*. Leiden: Koninklijke Brill NV, 1999.

Arnold, Lauren. *Princely Gifts and Papal Treasures: The Franciscan Mission to China and Its Influence on the Art of the West, 1250–1350*. San Francisco: Desiderata Press, 1999.

Atwell, William. "Volcanism and Short-Term Climatic Change in East Asia and World History, c. 1200–1699." *Journal of World History* 12, no. 1 (Spring, 2001).

Bacon, Francis. *Novum Organum*. Vol. 3, *The Works of Francis Bacon*. Ed. and trans. Basil Montague. 1620. Reprint, Philadelphia: Parry & MacMillan, 1854.

Bacon, Roger. *Opus Majus*. 2 vols. Trans. Robert Belle Burke. Philadelphia: University of Pennsylvania Press, 1928.

Barfield, Thomas J. *The Perilous Frontier: Nomadic Empires and China, 221* B.C. *to* A.D. *1757*. Cambridge, Mass.: Blackwell, 1992.

———. *The Nomadic Alternative*. Englewood Cliffs, N. J.: Prentice-Hall, 1993.

Barthold. V. V. "The Burial Rites of the Turks and the Mongols." Trans. J. M. Rogers. *Central Asiatic Journal* 14 (1970).

Bawden, Charles R. *The Mongol Chronicle Altan Tobchi*. Weisbaden: Göttinger Asiatische Forschungen, 1955.

Bazargür, D., and D. Enkhbayar. *Chinggis Khaan Historic-Geographic Atlas*. Ulaanbaatar: TTS, 1997.

Becker, Jasper. *The Lost Country: Mongolia Revealed*. London: Hodder & Stoughton, 1992.

Beckingham, Charles F., and Bernard Hamilton, eds. *Prester John, the Mongols, and the Ten Lost Tribes*. Aldershot, U.K.: Variorium, 1996.

Berger, Patricia, and Terese Tse Bartholomew. *Mongolia: The Legacy of Genghis Khan*. London: Thames & Hudson, 1995.

Selected Bibliography

Biran, Michal. *Qaidu and the Rise of the Independent Mongol State in Central Asia.* Richmond, U.K.: Curzon, 1997.

Blake, Robert P., and Richard N. Frye. "History of the Nation of the Archers (the Mongols) by Grigor of Akanc." *Harvard Journal of Asiatic Studies* 12 (December 1949).

Boinheshig, *Mongolian Folk Design.* Beijing: Inner Mongolian Cultural Publishing House, 1991.

Bold, Bat-Ochir. *Mongolian Nomadic Society: A Reconstruction of the "Medieval" History of Mongolia* New York: St. Martin's Press, 2001.

Boldbaatar, J. *Chinggis Khaan.* Ulaanbaatar: Khaadin san, 1999.

Bretschneider, E. *Mediæval Researches from Eastern Asiatic Sources.* Vol. 1. New York: Barnes & Noble, 1967.

Browne, Edward. G. *The Literary History of Persia.* Vol. 2. Bethesda, Md.: Iranbooks, 1997.

Budge, E. A. Wallis. *The Monks of Kublai Khan, Emperor of China; or, The History of the Life and Travels of Rabban Swama, Envoy and Plenipotentiary of the Mongol Khans to the Kings of Europe, and Markos Who as Mar Yahbhallaha III Became Patriarch of the Nestorian Church in Asia.* London: *Religious Tract Society, 1928.*

———. *The Commentary of Gregory Abu'l Faraj, Commonly Known as Bar Hebraeus.* London: Oxford University Press, 1932.

Buell, Paul D. *Historical Dictionary of the Mongol World Empire.* Lanham, Md.: Scarecrow, 2003.

Buell, Paul D., and Eugene N. Anderson. *A Soup for the Qan: Chinese Dietary Medicine of the Mongol Era as Seen in Hu Szu-Hui's Yin-Shan Chang-Yao.* London: Kegan Paul, 2000.

Buffon, George Louis Leclerc. *Buffon's Natural History.* Vol. 1. London: Bishop Watson, J. Johson, et al., 1792.

Bulag, Uradyn E. *Nationality and Hybridity in Mongolia.* Oxford, U.K.: Clarendon Press, 1998.

———. *The Mongols at China's Edge.* Lanham, Md.: Rowman & Littlefield, 2002.

Carpini, Friar Giovanni DiPlano. *The Story of the Mongols Whom We Call the Tartars.* Trans. Erik Hildinger. Boston: Branding Publishing, 1996.

Chambers, James. *Genghis Khan.* London: Sutton Publishing, 1999.

Chan, Hok-Lam. *China and the Mongols.* Aldershot, U.K.: Ashgate, 1999.

Chan, Hok-Lam, and William Theodore de Bary, eds. *Yüan Thought: Chinese Thought and Religion Under the Mongols.* New York: Columbia University Press, 1982.

Ch'en, Paul Heng-chao. *Chinese Legal Tradition Under the Mongols: The Code of 1291 as Reconstructed.* Princeton. N.J.: Princeton University Press, 1979.

Christian, David. "Silk Roads or Steppe Roads?" *Journal of World History* 11, no. 1, (Spring 2000).

———. *A History of Russia, Central Asia, and Mongolia.* Vol. 1, *Inner Eurasia from Prehistory to the Mongol Empire.* Malden, Mass.: Blackwell, 1998.

The Chronicle of Novgorod: 1016–1471. Trans. Robert Michel and Nevill Forbes. Camden 3rd Series, vol. 25. London: Offices of the Society, 1914.

Cleaves, Francis Woodman. "The Historicity of the Baljuna Covenant." *Harvard Journal of Asiatic Studies* 18, nos. 3–4 (December 1955).

———. trans. *The Secret History of the Mongols.* Cambridge, Mass.: Harvard University Press, 1982.

Conermann, Stephan, and Jan Kusber. *Die Mongolen in Asien und Europa.* Frankfurt: Peter Land GmbH, 1997.

Cook, Theodore F., Jr. "Mongol Invasion." *Quarterly Journal of Military History* (Winter 1999).

Crookshank, Francis G. *The Mongol in Our Midst: A Study of Man and His Three Faces.* New York: Dutton, 1924.

Curtin, Jeremiah. *The Mongols: A History.* Westport, Conn.: Greenwood Press, 1907.

Dardess, John W. *Conquerors and Confucians: Aspects of Political Change in Late Yüan China.* New York: Columbia University Press, 1973.

———. "Shun-ti and the End of Yüan rule in China." In *The Cambridge History of China,* vol.

6, *Alien Regimes and Border States, 907–1368,* ed. Herbert Franke and Denis Twitchett. Cambridge, U.K.: Cambridge University Press, 1994.

Dawson, Christopher, ed. *The Mongol Mission: Narratives and Letters of the Franciscan Missionaries in Mongolia and China in the Thirteenth and Fourteenth Centuries.* New York: Sheed & Ward, 1955.

DeFrancis, John. *In the Footsteps of Genghis Khan.* Honolulu: University of Hawaii Press, 1993.

de Hartog, Leo. *Russia and the Mongol Yoke.* London: British Academic Press, 1996.

———. *Genghis Khan: Conqueror of the World.* New York: Barnes & Noble, 1999.

Delgado, James P. "Relics of the Kamikaze." *Archaeology* (January 2003).

D'Encausse, Helene Carrere. *Islam and the Russian Revolution: Reform and Revolution in Central Asia.* Trans. Quintin Hjoare. Berkeley: University of California Press, 1988.

Di Cosmo, Nicola. "State Formation and Periodization in Inner Asian History." *Journal of World History* 10, no. 1 (Spring, 1999).

DiMarco, Vincent J. "The Historical Basis of Chaucer's Squire's Tale." *Edebiyat,* vol. 1, no. 2 (1989), pp. 1–22.

Dlugosz, Jan. *The Annals of Jan Dlugosz.* Trans. Maurice Michael, Chichester, U.K.: IM Publications, 1997.

Dols, Michael W. *The Black Death in the Middle East.* Princeton, N.J.: Princeton University Press, 1977.

Dunn, Ross E. *The Adventures of Ibn Battuta.* Berkeley: University of California Press, 1989.

Elias, N., and E. Denison Ross. *A History of the Moghuls of Central Asia: Being the Tarikhi-I-Rashidi of Mirza Muhammad Haidar, Dughlát.* London: Curzon Press, 1895.

Elverskog, Johan. "Superscribing the Hegemonic Image of Chinggis Khan in the *Erdeni Tunumal Sudur.*" In *Return to the Silk Routes,* ed. Mirja Juntunen and Birgit N. Schlyter. London: Kegan Paul, 1999.

Endicott-West, Elizabeth. "Imperial Governance in Yüan Times." *Harvard Journal of Asiatic Studies* 46 (1986).

———. *Mongolian Rule in China: Local Administration in the Yuan Dynasty.* Cambridge, Mass.: Harvard University Press, 1989.

Fernandez-Gimenez, Maria E. "Sustaining the Steppes." *Geographic Review* 89, no. 3 (July 1999).

Fletcher, Joseph F. "The Mongols: Ecological and Social Perspectives." *Harvard Journal of Asiatic Studies* 461 (June 1986).

Frank, Andre Gunder. *The Centrality of Central Asia.* Amsterdam: VU University Press, 1992.

———. *ReORIENT: Global Economy in the Asian Age.* Berkeley: of University of California Press, 1998.

Franke, Herbert. "Sino-Western Contacts Under the Mongol Empire." *Journal of the Royal Asiatic Society* (Hong Kong Branch) 6 (1966).

———. *From Tribal Chieftain to Universal Emperor and God: The Legitimization of the Yüan Dynasty.* München: Verlag der Bayerischen Akademie der Wissenschaften, Vol. 2, 1978.

———. *China Under Mongol Rule.* Brookfield, V.: Ashgate, 1984.

———. "The Exploration of the Yellow River Sources Under Emperor Qubilai in 1281." In *Orientalia Iosephi Tucci memoriae dicata,* ed. G. Gnoli and L. Lanciotti. Rome: Instituto italiano per il medio ed estermo oriente, 1985.

Franke, Herbert, and Denis Twitchett, eds. *The Cambridge History of China.* Vol. 6, *Alien Regimes and Border States, 907–1368.* Cambridge, U.K.: Cambridge University Press, 1994.

Gibbon, Edward. *Decline and Fall of the Roman Empire* Vol 5. London: J. M. Dent, 1910.

Ginsburg, Tom. "Nationalism, Elites, and Mongolia's Rapid Transformation," *Mongolia in the Twentieth Century: Landlocked Cosmopolitan.* Ed. Stephen Kotkin and Bruce A. Elleman. Armonk, N.Y.: M. E. Sharpe, 1999.

Gluschenko, Nick. "Coinage of Medieval Rus." *World Coin News* (June 1998).

Gottfried, Robert S. *The Black Death.* New York: Free Press, 1983.

Grousset, René. *Conqueror of the World*. Trans. Marian McKellar and Denis Sinor. New York: Orion Press, 1966.

———. *The Empire of the Steppes: A History of Central Asia*. Trans. Naomi Walford. New Brunswick, N.J.: Rutgers University Press, 1970.

Haenisch, Erich. *Die Kulturpolitik des Mongolishchen Welstreichs*. Berlin: Preussische Akademie der Wissenschaften, 1943.

Halperin, Charles J. *Russia and the Golden Horde*. Bloomington: Indiana University Press, 1985.

———. *The Tatar Yoke*. Columbus, Ohio: Slavica Publishers, 1985.

Heissig, Walther. *A Lost Civilization: The Mongols Rediscovered*. Trans. D. J. S. Thompson. London: Thames & Hudson, 1966.

———, ed. *Die Geheime Geschichte der Mongolen*. Düsseldorf: Eugen Diederichs Verlag, 1981.

Herlihy, David. *The Black Death and the Transformation of the West*. Cambridge, Mass.: Harvard University Press, 1997.

Hildinger, Erik. "Mongol Invasion of Europe." *Military History* (June 1997).

———. *Warriors of the Steppe*. Cambridge, Mass.: Da Capo, 1997.

Hoang, Michel. *Genghis Khan*. Trans. Ingrid Canfield. London: Saqi Books, 2000.

Holmgren, J. "Observations on Marriage and Inheritance Practices in Early Mongol and Yüan Society, with Particular Reference to the Levirate." *Journal of Asian History* 20 (1986).

Howorth, Henry H. *History of the Mongols*. pt. I, *The Mongols Proper and the Kalmuks*. London: Longmans, Green, 1876.

Hsiao Ch'i-ch'ing. "Mid-Yüan Politics." In *The Cambridge History of China*, vol. 6, *Alien Regimes and Border States, 907–1368*, ed. Herbert Franke and Denis Twitchett. Cambridge, U.K.: Cambridge University Press, 1994

Humphrey, Caroline. *Shamans and Elders*. New York: Oxford University Press, 1996.

Hyer, Paul. "The Re-Evaluation of Chinggis Khan." *Asian Survey* 6 (1966).

Jackson, Peter. "The State of Research: The Mongol Empire, 1986–1999," *Journal of Medieval History*. 26–2. (June 2000).

Jagchid, Sechen. *Essays in Mongolian Studies*. Provo: Brigham Young University Press, 1988.

Jagchid, Sechen, and Paul Hyer. *Mongolia's Culture and Society*. Boulder: Westview, 1979.

Jagchid, Sechen, and Van Jay Symons. *Peace, War, and Trade Along the Great Wall*. Bloomington: Indiana University Press, 1989.

Jones, Eric L. *Growth Recurring: Economic Change in World History*. Oxford, U.K.: Clarendon Press, 1988.

Juvaini, Ata-Malik. *Genghis Khan: The History of the World Conqueror*. Trans. J. A. Boyle. Seattle: University of Washington Press, 1997.

Kahn, Paul. *The Secret History of the Mongols: The Origins of Chingis Khan*. Boston: Cheng & Tsui, 1998.

Kaplonski, Christopher. "The Role of the Mongols in Eurasian History: A Reassessment." In *The Role of Migration in the History of the Eurasian Steppe*, ed. Andrew Bell. New York: St. Martin's Press, 2000.

Keegan, John. *A History of Warfare*. New York: Knopf, 1993.

Kessler, Adam T. *Empires Beyond the Great Wall: The Heritage of Genghis Khan*. Los Angeles: Natural History Museum, 1993.

Khan, Almaz. "Chinggis Khan: From Imperial Ancestor to Ethnic Hero." In *Cultural Encounters on China's Ethnic Frontiers*, ed. Stevan Harrell. Seattle: University of Washington Press, 1995.

Khazanov, Anatoly M. *Nomads and the Outside World*. Madison: University of Wisconsin Press, 1994.

Khoroldamba, D. *Under the Eternal Sky*. Ulaanbaatar: Ancient Kharakhorum Association, 2000.

Klopprogge, Axel. *Ursprung und Auspraegung des abdendlaendischen Mongolenbildes im 13. Jahrhundert: Eine Versuch zur Ideengeschichte des Mitterlaters*. Wiesbaden: Harrassowitz Verlag, 1993.

Komaroff, Linda, and Stefan Carboni, eds. *The Legacy of Genghis Khan: Courtly Art and Culture in Western Asia, 1256–1353.* New York: Metropolitan Museum of Art, 2002.

Komroff, Manuel, ed. *Contemporaries of Marco Polo,* New York: Liveright, 1928.

Kotkin, Stephen, and Bruce A. Elleman, eds. *Mongolia in the Twentieth Century: Landlocked Cosmopolitan* Armonk, N.Y.: M. E. Sharpe, 1999.

Kwanten, Luc. *Imperial Nomads: A History of Central Asia, 500–1500.* Philadelphia: University of Pennsylvania Press, 1979.

Lamb, Harold. *Genghis Khan.* New York: Garden City Publishing, 1927.

Lane, George. *Early Mongol Rule in Thirteenth-Century Iran: A Persian Renaissance.* London: RoutledgeCurzon, 2003.

Larner, John. *Marco Polo and the Discovery of the World.* New Haven: Yale University Press, 1999.

Latham, Ronald. Introduction to *The Travels of Marco Polo,* by Marco Polo, trans. Ronald Latham. London: Penguin, 1958.

Lattimore, Owen. *Studies in Frontier History.* New York: Oxford University Press, 1962.

———. "Chingis Khan and the Mongol Conquests." *Scientific American* 209, no. 2 (August 1963).

Legg, Stuart. *The Barbarians of Asia: The Peoples of the Steppes from 1600 B.C.* New York: Dorset, 1970.

Levathes, Louise. *When China Ruled the Seas.* New York: Simon & Schuster, 1994.

Lhagvasuren, Ch. *Ancient Karakorum.* Ulaanbaatar: Han Bayan, 1995.

———. *Bilge Khaan.* Ulaanbaatar: Khaadin san, 2000.

Liu, Jung-en, ed. *Six Yüan Plays.* Middlesex, U.K.: Penguin, 1972.

Livi-Bacci, Massimo. *A Concise History of World Population.* 2nd ed., Trans. Carl Ipsen. Malden, Mass.: Blackwell, 1997.

Lynch, Kathryn L. "East Meets West in Chaucer's Squire's and Franklin's Tales." *Speculum* 70 (1995).

McNeill, William H. *Plagues and People.* Garden City, N.Y.: Doubleday, 1976.

———. *The Pursuit of Power.* Chicago: University of Chicago Press, 1982.

Man, John. *Gobi: Tracking the Desert.* New Haven: Yale University Press, 1999.

Mandeville, Sir John, *The Travels of Sir John Mandeville, the Voyage of Johannes de Plano Carpini, the Journal of Friar William de Rubruquis, the Journal of Friar Odoric.* New York: Dover, 1964.

Marshall, Robert. *Storm from the East.* Berkeley: University of California Press, 1993.

Montesquieu, Baron de. *The Spirit of the Laws.* Trans. Thomas Nugent. New York: Hafner, 1949.

Morgan, David. *The Mongols.* Cambridge, Mass: Blackwell, 1986.

Moses, Larry, and Stephen A. Halkovic Jr. *Introduction to Mongolian History and Culture.* Bloomington, Ind.: Research Institute for Inner Asian Studies 1985.

Needham, Joseph. *Science and Civilization in China.* vol. 3, 4, 6. Cambridge: U.K. Cambridge University Press, 1954–1998.

Nehru, Jawaharlal. *Glimpses of World History.* New York: John Day, 1942.

Nicolaus of Cusa. *Toward a New Council of Florence: "On the Peace of Faith" and Other Works by Nicolaus of Cusa.* Ed. William F. Wertz Jr. Washington, D.C.: Schiller Institute, 1993.

Olbricht, Peter, and Elisabeth Pinks. *Meng-Ta Pei-Lu and Hei-Ta Shih-Lüeh: Chinesische Gesandtenberichte über die frühen Mongolen 1221 und 1237.* Weisbaden: Otto Harrassowitz, 1980.

Olschki, Leonardo. *Marco Polo's Precursors.* Baltimore: Johns Hopkins University Press, 1943.

———. *Guillaume Boucher: A French Artist at the Court of the Khans.* New York: Greenwood, 1946.

Onon, Urgunge, trans. *The History and the Life of Chinggis Khan (The Secret History of the Mongols).* Leiden: E. J. Brill, 1990.

———. *The Secret History of the Mongols: The Life and Times of Chinggis Khan.* Richmond, U.K.: Curzon Press, 2001.

Ostrowski, Donald. *Muscovy and the Mongols.* Cambridge, U.K.: Cambridge University Press, 1998.

Paris, Matthew. *Matthew Paris's English History from the Year 1235 to 1273.* Trans. J. A. Giles, 1852. London: Henry G. Bohn. Reprint, New York: AMS Press, Vol. 1, 1968.

Pegg, Carole. *Mongolian Music, Dance, and Oral Narrative.* Seattle: University of Washington Press, 2001.

Pétis de la Croix, François. *The History of Genghizcan the Great: First Emperor of the Ancient Moguls and Tartars.* London: Printed for J. Darby, etc., 1722.

Polo, Marco. *The Travels of Marco Polo.* Trans. Ronald Latham. London: Penguin, 1958.

————. *The Travels of Marco Polo: The Complete Yule-Cordier Edition.* 2 vols. New York: Dover, 1993.

Prawdin, Michael. *The Mongol Empire: Its Rise and Legacy.* Trans. Eden Paul and Cedar Paul. London: George Allen & Unwin, 1940.

Purev, Otgony. *The Religion of Mongolian Shamanism,* trans. Narantsetseg Pureviin and Elaine Cheng. Ulaanbaatar, Mongolia: Genco University College, 2002.

Rachewiltz, Igor de. *Papal Envoys to the Great Khans.* Standford, Calif.: Stanford University Press, 1971.

————. "The Secret History of the Mongols: Introduction, Chapters One and Two." *Papers on Far Eastern History* pp. 115–163. (Canberra: Department of Far Eastern History, Australian National University) no. 4 (1971).

————. "The Secret History of the Mongols: Chapter Three." *Papers on Far Eastern History* (Canberra: Department of Far Eastern History, Australian National University) no. 5 (1972), pp. 149–175.

————. "Some Remarks on the Ideological Foundations of Chingis Khan's Empire." *Papers on Far Eastern History* (Canberra: Department of Far Eastern History, Australian National University) no. 7 (1973), pp. 21–36.

————. "The Secret History of the Mongols: Chapter Four." *Papers on Far Eastern History* (Canberra: Department of Far Eastern History, Australian National University) no. 10 (1974), pp. 55–82.

————. "The Secret History of the Mongols: Chapter Five." *Papers on Far Eastern History* (Canberra: Department of Far Eastern History, Australian National University) no. 13 (1976), pp. 41–75.

————. "The Secret History of the Mongols: Chapter Six." *Papers on Far Eastern History* (Canberra: Department of Far Eastern History, Australian National University), no. 16 (1977), pp. 27–65.

————. "The Secret History of the Mongols: Chapter Seven." *Papers on Far Eastern History* (Canberra: Department of Far Eastern History, Australian National University), no. 18 (1978), pp. 43–80.

————. "The Secret History of the Mongols: Chapter Eight." *Papers on Far Eastern History* (Canberra: Department of Far Eastern History, Australian National University), no. 21 (1980), pp. 17–57.

————. "The Secret History of the Mongols: Chapter Nine." *Papers on Far Eastern History* (Canberra: Department of Far Eastern History, Australian National University), no. 23 (1981), pp. 111–146.

————. "Töregene's Edict of 1240." *Papers on Far Eastern History* 23 (March 1981), pp. 39–63.

————. "The Secret History of the Mongols: Chapter Ten." *Papers on Far Eastern History* (Canberra: Department of Far Eastern History, Australian National University), no. 26 (1982), pp. 39–84.

————. "The Secret History of the Mongols: Chapter Eleven." *Papers on Far Eastern History* (Canberra: Department of Far Eastern History, Australian National University), no. 30 (1984), pp. 81–160.

————. "The Secret History of the Mongols: Chapter Twelve." *Papers on Far Eastern History*

(Canberra: Department of Far Eastern History, Australian National University), no. 31 (1985), pp. 21–93.

————. "The Secret History of the Mongols: Additions and Corrections." *Papers on Far Eastern History* (Canberra: Department of Far Eastern History, Australian National University), no. 33 (1986), pp. 129–138.

Rashid al-Din. *The Successors of Genghis Khan.* Trans. John Andrew Boyle. New York: Columbia University Press, 1971.

Ratchnevsky, Paul. *Genghis Khan: His Life and Legacy.* Trans. Thomas Nivison Haining. Oxford, U.K.: Blackwell, 1991.

Reid, Robert W. *A Brief Political and Military Chronology of the Mediaeval Mongols, from the Birth of Chinggis Qan to the Death of Qubilai Qaghan.* Bloomington, Ind.: Publications of the Mongolia Society, 2002.

Riasanovsky, Valentin A. *Fundamental Principles of Mongol Law.* Uralic and Altaic Series, vol. 43. Bloomington: Indiana University Publications, 1965.

Ronay, Gabriel. *The Tartar Khan's Englishman.* London: Cassell, 1978.

Roosevelt, Theodore. Forward to *The Mongols,* by Jeremiah Curtin. Westport, Conn.: Greenwood, 1907.

Rossabi, Morris. *Khubilai Khan: His Life and Times.* Berkeley: University of California Press, 1988.

————. "The Reign of Khubilai Khan." In *The Cambridge History of China,* vol. 6, *Alien Regimes and Border States, 907–1368,* ed. Herbert Franke and Danis Twitchett. Cambridge, U.K.: Cambridge University Press, 1994.

Roux, Jean-Paul. *Genghis Khan and the Mongol Empire.* Trans. Toula Ballas. New York: Harry N. Abrams, 2003.

Sabloff, Paula L. W., ed. *Modern Mongolia: Reclaiming Genghis Khan.* Philadelphia: University of Pennsylvania Museum of Archaeology and Anthropology, 2001.

Saunders, J. J. *The History of the Mongol Conquests.* Philadelphia: University of Pennsylvania Press, 2001.

Schmieder, Felicitas. *Europa und die Fremden.* Sigmaringen: Thorbecke, 1994.

Shen, Fuwei. *Cultural Flow Between China and the Outside World Throughout History.* Beijing: Foreign Languages Press, 1996.

Sinor, Denis, ed. *The Cambridge History of Early Inner Asia.* Cambridge, U.K.: Cambridge University Press, 1990.

————. *Studies in Medieval Inner Asia.* Brookfield, Vt.: Ashgate Publishing, 1997.

Skelton, R. A., Thomas E. Marston, and George D. Painter. *The Vinland Map and the Tartar Relation.* New Haven: Yale University Press, 1965.

Soloviev, Sergei M. *Russia Under the Tatar Yoke, 1228–1389.* Vol. 4 of *History of Russia.* Trans. Helen Y. Prochazka. Gulf Breeze, Fla.: Academic International Press, 2000.

Spence, Jonathan D. *The Chan's Great Continent.* New York: W. W. Norton, 1998.

Spuler, Bertold. *The Mongols in History,* Trans. Geoffrey Wheeler. New York: Praeger, 1971.

————. *History of the Mongols Based on Eastern and Western Accounts of the Thirteenth and Fourteenth Centuries. Trans. Helga and Stuart Drummond. Berkeley: University of California Press, 1972.*

Stuart, Kevin. *Mongols in Western/American Consciousness.* Lampeter, U.K.: Edwin Mellen, 1997.

Sweeney, James Ross. "Thomas of Spalato and the Mongols." *Florilegium: Archives of Canadian Society of Medievalists* 12 (1980).

Tanaka, Hedemichi. "Giotto and the Influence of the Mongols and Chinese on His Art." *Art History* (Tohoku University) vol. 6 (1984).

————. "Oriental Scripts in the Paintings of Giotto's Period." *Gazette des Beaux-arts* Vol. 113 (January–June 1989).

Togan, Isenbike. *Flexibility and Limitation in Steppe Formations.* New York: Brill, 1998.

Trubetzkoy, Nikolai S. *The Legacy of Genghis Khan.* Trans. Anatoly Liberman. Ann Arbor: Michigan Slavic Publications, 1991.

Vaughan, Richard. *Chronicles of Matthew Paris.* New York: St. Martin's Press, 1984.

Vladimirtsov, Boris Y. *The Life of Chingis-Khan.* Trans. Prince D. S. Mirsky. New York: Benjamin Blom, 1930.

Voltaire. *The Orphan of China.* In *The Works of Voltaire,* vol. 15, trans. William F. Fleming. Paris: E. R. DuMont, 1901.

Waldron, Arthur N. *The Great Wall of China.* Cambridge, U.K.: Cambridge University Press, 1992.

Waley, Arthur. *The Travels of an Alchemist.* London: Routledge & Kegan Paul, 1931.

———. *The Secret History of the Mongols and Other Pieces.* New York: Barnes & Noble, 1963.

Wang, Edward. "History, Space, and Ethnicity: The Chinese Worldview." *Journal of World History* 10, no. 2 (1999).

Acknowledgments

⟩⟨

The Mongolian nation founded by Genghis Khan in 1206 survives today, and my first thanks go to the state officials who made my research possible, particularly to President N. Bagabandi, to Minister A. Tsanjid of the Ministry of Science, Technology, Education, and Culture, and to Parliament Member A. Shagdarsuren of the Ikh Hural.

I appreciate the spontaneous gestures of support from teachers and herders all over Mongolia. Because of the respect the people had for my companions, Professors Kh. Lkhagvasuren and O. Sukhbaatar, wherever we went, people sought us out to help in our study. As an unknown foreigner, I was the constant beneficiary of the honor given to them.

It is hard to describe the dedication with which people came out to help me. Even when camped in what seemed to be the most remote place we could find, it was never long before a girl appeared on the horizon leading her yak cart filled with water or with dried dung for our fire. One warm day someone might give a small canister made from tightly sewn birch bark and filled with wild berries and dried yogurt, and another day a young hunter would bring a freshly prepared marmot or a bowl of milk. Herders not only offered me shelter and food along the way, but they also brought horses and sheep to make a personal contribution to the study of their ancestors. More than once a whole family dropped what they were doing and, leaving a boy in charge of their herd, set out to accompany us and discuss our work. On one of the most grueling days, while the older men rode horses, four armed young men voluntarily accompanied us on foot, usually running, for more than thirty miles to protect us in a wolf-infested area.

Sometimes people brought gifts of overwhelming generosity—shimmering pelts or highly polished animal horns. Others brought small wooden fig-

301

ures carved in the form of a horse, a sheep, or a goat. Shamans offered prayers for the success of our research, and monks donated incense for us to burn on the holy places we encountered. Some people with little else to offer simply gave me small stones that I might remember the place where they lived. Such debts can never be repaid.

While I alone bear responsibility for the shortcomings of this work, credit for any achievements must be shared among many people. I appreciate the guidance of Professor J. Boldbaatar of the Faculty of Social Science of the National University of Mongolia. I was consistently helped by the staff, faculty, and students of Chinggis Khaan College in Ulaanbaatar. When I published the original edition of this book and a series of related articles in Mongolian, they kindly critiqued my work and helped to improve it. For this great service, I thank Professors O. Purev, Kh. Shagdar, D. Bold-Erdene, and G. Baatartsooj. I gratefully acknowledge the valuable assistance of T. Jamyansuren, A. Mungunzul, Ts. Khishigbayar, and D. Chimedlkham in matters of translation, and to the students O. Hashbat and D. Ochirdorj for their help in the field. The drawings for this book were made by Dr. S. Badral, and I thank him deeply.

For assistance in making travel arrangements and procuring equipment and supplies, I am indebted to T. Bold, Sh. Munhtsag, D. Tsetsegjargal, Sh. Batsugar, and T. Battulga. For additional travel from the United States, I appreciate the help of Douglas Grimes, Annie Lucas, and Angela Halonen-Webb.

Although no government grant or foundation fellowship was used for any part of this research, I was greatly assisted by Macalester College throughout the research. I particularly appreciate the librarians and staff in the DeWitt Wallace Library for finding texts from around the world. I gratefully acknowledge the many contributions of my colleagues: Daniel Balik, Mary Lou Byrne, Kay Crawford, Jimm Crowder, John Davis, Juanita Garciagodoy, Martin Gunderson, Arjun Guneratne, Gitta Hammarberg, Daniel Hornbach, David Itzkowitz, Manazh Kousha, David Lanegran, David McCurdy, Michael McPherson, Karen Nakamura, Kathleen Parson, Sonia Patten, Ahmed Samatar, Khaldun Samman, Dianna Shandy, Paul Solon, Anne Sutherland, and Peter Weisensel. Above all, I thank my students, who so good-heartedly tolerated my obsessions and who generously sought to help me in my work.

For additional help in various stages of the work, I appreciate the advice, assistance, and encouragement of Raydean Acevedo, Christopher Atwood, Brian Baumann, Naran Bilik, Daniel Buettner, Leah and Rodney Camper, Harm DeBlij, John Dinger, D. Enkhchuluun, Kevin Fagan, James Fisher, Ray Gatchalian, Zaida Giraldo, Tjalling Halbertsma, Ts. Jargalsaikhan, Walt Jenkins, Christopher Kaplonski, D. Khoroldamba, Philip Kohl, David McCullough, Navid Mohseni, Axel Odelberg, B. Otgonbayar, Lee Owens, Qi Yi, Marc Swartz, and Don Walsh.

I always appreciate the diligent efforts of my agent, Lois Wallace, who has worked with me for twenty-five years, and the help of James O. Wade, with whom I worked for as many years. For guidance in the long editorial process, I owe an immeasurable debt to the clear vision of my editors, Emily Loose and Christopher Jackson, as well as to Mary Vincent Franco and Lynn Olson.

Of all the gifts from the Mongols throughout the years of this project, none was more precious than the gift of song. When I was exhausted and struggling to catch up with other riders, someone would sing to give me strength. At the end of a long day, when we found refuge with a herding family, a young girl would stand before me and, although trembling in fear at the sight of such a foreign person and afraid to look me in the face, open her mouth widely to sing with such beauty and emotion that it seemed surely time itself would stand still.

Gradually, I realized that the songs were more than entertainment or diversions; they contained a wealth of valuable information and offered deep insights into Mongolian culture and history. Because of their life of constant movement, nomads such as the Mongols must carry their books and pictures with them in the form of song. Mongolian music records and maps the landscape of their land, not merely in words, but in the rising and falling of notes corresponding to the flow of the land itself. The *morin huur,* or horsehead fiddle, usually played by a man, can make the sound of birds and animals, and the long-song singer, usually a woman, can call up the landscape of distant places with the special skill of her voice. Examples of many of these were compiled through numerous years of research by Carole Pegg and made available on a compact disc as part of her scholarly study, *Mongolian Music, Dance, and Oral Narrative.*

Even when I was away from Mongolia, people sent me videos and recordings of Mongolian music to inspire my work. Since the gifts often came anonymously, I now wish to thank all of them here. I appreciate the *morin huur* recordings of Ts. Purevkhuu and D. Ariunaa and the incredible singing of N. Norovbansad, the greatest Mongol singer of the twentieth century. In addition to the inspiration found in the music of D. Jargalsaikhan and the group Chinggis Khaan, my work also benefited from the talents of Altai-Hangai, Black Horse, Black Rose, Khonkh, Tenger Ayalguu, and Tumen Ekh. More than all the words in any book, the music of N. Jantsannorov, one of the world's greatest composers, paints the beauty of the Mongolian landscape and portrays the passions of its history.

My son, Roy Maybank, assisted me on one of my trips to Mongolia and China, and, throughout the research, I greatly benefited from the encouragement and help of my daughter, Walker Buxton. My greatest debt is to my wife, Walker Pearce, who not only helped me in the field in Russia, China, and Mongolia but was a source of constant inspiration and humor throughout the six years of the project. I look forward to the day when she and I will ride with our grandchildren across the steppes of Genghis Khan.

Index

Abacus, 231
Abbasid dynasty, 180, 183, 184
Acupuncture, 229, 230
Adultery, 68–69
Afghanistan, 9, 105, 109, 117–118, 126, 191, 263, 264
Agriculture, 227–229, 235
AIDS (acquired immune deficiency syndrome), 245
Akbar, 253
Alamut (Eagle's Nest), 178
Alan the Beautiful, 23–24
Altaic languages, 14
Altai Mountains, 14, 64, 72
Altan Khan, 28
Amu Darya, 4
Anatolia, 109, 184
Andronicus II Palaeologus of Byzantium, 218
Animal rustling, 69
Annam, 212
Arabian Peninsula, 185
Aral Sea, 124
Arik Boke, 167, 170, 177, 187–190, 196
Armenia, 142, 171, 181
Army of the Left, 87, 177
Army of the Right, 87, 177
Arrow messengers, 72
Assassins, 167, 178–180
Assyrian Church of the East, 28, 171
Astronomy, 230, 231, 236
Avarga, 45–46, 53, 104, 123, 132
Avarga Stream, 101
Ayn al-Jalut (Springs of Goliath), 185
Azerbaijan, 140, 188

Babur, 253
Babylonian captivity, 156

Bacon, Francis, 236
Baghdad, 137, 167, 177, 178, 180–185, 187
Bahadur Shah II, 263
Balasagun, 104
Baljuna Covenant, 58
Ballista, 94
Bamiyan valley, 117–118
Bar Hebraeus, 168
Basil, Emperor, 116
Battering ram, 147, 148
Batu Khan, 143–145, 150–151, 154, 159, 165, 166, 184
Bayan, 208
Beg, Ulugh, 236
Begter, 18, 23–25, 64, 74, 217
Beijing, 81, 96–99, 111, 198, 251
Bela IV, King of Hungary, 154, 155
Belgrade, 170
Belgutei, 23, 24, 27, 29, 32, 41, 43, 45
Berke, 166
Black-boned lineages, 37–38, 41, 53
Black Death, 242–247, 252
Black Forest, 28
Black Khitan (Kara Khitan), 62, 85, 103–105, 112
Black River, 222
Black Sea, 105, 139, 142, 224
Black Tatars, 14
Blitzkrieg, 152, 262
Blue Lake, 39, 263
Blue Turks, 14
Blumenbach, Johann Friedrich, 256–257
Boccaccio, Giovanni, 234, 245–246
Bodonchar the Fool, 37
Bohemond of Antioch, 184
Boorchu, 29, 32, 40, 89
Borijin clan, 13

Index

About the Author

JACK WEATHERFORD is the Dewitt Wallace Professor of Anthropology at Macalester College in St. Paul, Minnesota. He earned his Ph.D. at the University of California, San Diego, and he received an honorary Doctorate of Humanities from Chinggis Khaan College in Mongolia. Other books include *Indian Givers, Savages and Civilization,* and *The History of Money.*

About the Author

JACK WEATHERFORD is the Dewitt Wallace Professor of Anthropology at Macalester College in St. Paul, Minnesota. He earned his Ph.D. at the University of California, San Diego, and he received an honorary Doctorate of Humanities from Chinggis Khaan College in Mongolia. Other books include *Indian Givers, Savages and Civilization,* and *The History of Money.*